SUPERVISION
Human Perspectives

SUPERVISION
Human Perspectives

Third Edition

Thomas J. Sergiovanni
University of Illinois
Urbana-Champaign

Robert J. Starratt
Fordham University

McGraw-Hill Book Company
New York   St. Louis   San Francisco   Auckland   Bogotá   Hamburg
Johannesburg   London   Madrid   Mexico   Montreal   New Delhi
Panama   Paris   São Paulo   Singapore   Sydney   Tokyo   Toronto

SUPERVISION: HUMAN PERSPECTIVES

1234567890   DOCDOC   89876543

ISBN 0-07-056312-8

This book was set in Quorum Book by Black Dot, Inc. (ECU).
The editor was Marian D. Provenzano;
the designer was Charles A. Carson;
the production supervisor was Charles Hess.
Project supervision was done by The Total Book.
The cover illustration was done by Charles A. Carson.
R. R. Donnelley & Sons Company was printer and binder.

Library of Congress Cataloging in Publication Data

Sergiovanni, Thomas J.
    Supervision: human perspectives.

    Includes bibliographical references and index.
    1. School supervision.   2. School management and organization.   I. Starratt, Robert J.   II. Title.
LB2805.S52   1983   371.2'013   82-10084
ISBN 0-07-056312-8

CONTENTS

FOREWORD

It is exciting to work in the field of (educational) supervision these days. Supervisory work, both for the purpose of helping and for the purpose of judging or evaluating, is becoming more and more recognized as a crucial and legitimate function within the education profession. The literature of supervision is burgeoning, and its quality is notably on the rise. The once-small cadre of professors and research workers whose special scholarly focus is on supervision has become a much larger and stronger group; and the attention being paid to improvement of their technical supervisory skills by school principals and other administrative/supervisory personnel has increased dramatically.

This book is ample testimony of the progress that is being made. When the first edition appeared in 1971, the textbooks with which it competed were relatively few in number and, however meritorious at that moment in time, relatively unsophisticated by our current (1982–1983) standards. Its focus on humanistic aspirations and its solid, scholarly treatment of the human dimensions in supervision helped to raise the level of discourse and also to link educational supervision more directly with the rich literatures that undergird the helping as well as the managerial professions outside of education itself.

As the authors remind us in their Preface, the second edition, 8 years later, made a careful distinction between *human relations* and *human resources* supervision; and by emphasizing the latter it further expanded the concept of supervision as a staff-development activity geared to a formative approach. In that edition I welcomed the authors' appreciation of collaborative supervision as a promising development, and of the need for understanding and taking operational account of the total context within which supervisory activities take place. Their recognition of the aesthetic and artistic dimensions of supervision was another highlight of that volume.

A distinct advantage of writing the Foreword to a book is that one sees the volume long before it reaches the marketplace. Other readers, or potential readers who are consulting the front pages before deciding to buy, might be heartened by the fact that I will refuse to return the galley pages to the authors until I am able to have the actual book in hand. There is too much good stuff in those pages to let them get away from me. My own scholarship in the field has already been enhanced and further perusal especially of the extensive new material will serve me well.

I like the way the material is arranged in this edition. The opening section (Part One, comprising nine chapters) helps the reader to a comprehensive understanding of human resources supervision in relationship to organizational leadership. Of special interest is the new second chapter, which contrasts normative and descriptive views of supervision and, while acknowledging the realistic usefulness of descriptive approaches, suggests that normative approaches provide necessary standards of excellence and goals for future direction. Part Two is a special section on theory, which pulls together and synthesizes the social science and management theories that were presented in Part One, and then examines the normative, qualitative, and uplifting aspects of leadership.

My guess is that of the creative ideas in the volume, future authors will most frequently be quoting the "10-P Model of Quality Leadership" that is introduced in Chapter 11. Sergiovanni evidently spent a lot of time with his dictionary, in order to find a "p" word for each of the 10 constructs, which "bring together instrumental and substantive issues to form the basis for human resources supervision."

One of the problems with many texts nominally (i.e., in their titles) devoted to supervision is that they neglect the functions of direct assistance and overplay curriculum development and related nonsupervisory matters. In Part Three, which examines the human curriculum, these authors avoid that tendency by dealing much less with curriculum theory and a more general concern with educational programs, and much more with classrooms, instruction, and teaching. I was particularly impressed with the operational usefulness of materials in Chapter 15 on evaluation, and Chapter 16 on teacher effectiveness.

In the final chapters of the book, Part Four, the evaluation materials from the second edition have been strengthened and updated (in Chapter 17), and there is an outstanding new chapter (19) on theory which, I believe, breaks new ground. In recent years it has become all the more apparent that without a strong connection to theoretical frameworks, improvements that are made in technical skills and in practical designs for supervision and evaluation of teaching can be superficial rather than powerful.

Although the second edition remains one of the two or three most useful books in the field, so much has happened in the relatively short space of time (3 or 4 years) since its appearance that a new and updated work makes good sense. Apparently the authors have kept in close touch with professors and graduate students who used the previous edition(s), and they have tried to rearrange and expand the material in ways that will facilitate reader understanding. I believe they have succeeded. The restructuring, and the additions, to which their Preface refers make the third edition a distinctly fresh statement, rather than a rehashing and a cosmetic transformation. It is clear that the authors have put more effort into this edition than is usually invested in revisions of well-established works. I assess this not only as a reflection of the authors' high professionalism, but also as proof of the dynamic state-of-the-art. Our growth in knowledge, and perhaps also in wisdom, about supervision has become virtually exponential. Tom Sergiovanni and Jerry Starrat, in whose careers I have long had an admiring interest, have managed to harness that knowledge and to reflect that wisdom in ways that will benefit us all.

Robert H. Anderson
Professor and Dean
College of Education
Texas Tech University

PREFACE

We are now in the third edition of this book and are heartened by its reception. Particularly encouraging is that its theme, "human resources supervision," is gaining wider acceptance in practice. The third edition has many new features and includes some restructuring of parts as well as the addition of some important new chapters.

Humanistic aspirations characterized the first edition of this book. Such aspirations were to be fulfilled by linking more carefully educational program and instructional matters with compatible organizational and supervisory arrangements. Quoting from the preface of the first edition, "We believe that humanizing education, with its focus on self-actualization of youngsters, can be achieved only in a humanizing organization which focuses on self-actualization of teachers and other educational professionals." The second edition unfolded similarly, giving attention to the supervisor's role in organizational leadership, in educational leadership, and in instructional leadership.

In the second edition, a distinction was made between *human relations* and *human resources* supervision. Human relations, often mistaken for being humanistic, lacks the potency, involvement, maturity, and emphasis on intrinsic satisfaction found in human resources supervision. True, both are concerned with people and their needs, but unlike human relations, which seems concerned only with security and social needs, human resources supervision views people as having the desire and potential for motivation, responsibility, and success at work.

Human resources supervision requires a more open and active partnership between and among students, teachers, and supervisors. Older patterns of supervision, with their stress on authority, compliance, and control, and with their identification of wisdom with hierarchical position, put teachers in a position of passively accepting the directives of the principal, supervisor, or department chairperson. In turn, teachers have tended to view their students as being in the same passive position in relation to them. The human resources tradition articulated in the first and second editions continues to be developed in the third edition.

Restructuring of the book's contents is considerable in this edition as we attempt to respond to new issues, new pressures, and advances in knowledge. Throughout the first two editions many users have commented that the theory chapter (old Chapter 2) appears too early in the book. Originally intended as a road map of what was to follow, this chapter now provides a summary and integration of the array of social science concepts, management theories, and leadership skills discussed in Part One. In revised form the original theory chapter now appears as Chapter 10, "An Instrumental Theory of Supervisory Leadership." Chapter 11, "A Substantive Theory of Supervisory

Leadership," is a companion chapter emphasizing more qualitative aspects of leadership. It includes the 10-P Model of Quality Leadership as its integrating framework. Together, these chapters comprise a new Part Two entitled "Developing a Relevant Theory of Supervisory Practice." Parts Two and Three of the second edition now become Three and Four in the third edition.

Three other chapters are new to this edition. Chapter 2 now concerns itself with contrasting normative and descriptive views of supervision. Normative views are concerned with what ought to be done, help to set standards of excellence, and prescribe solutions to problems. Descriptive views, by contrast, are concerned with the real world and work of supervision. The gap between the normative and descriptive in supervision is considerable as suggested in Chapter 2. Nevertheless, both perspectives are necessary if we seek a fuller understanding of our art and a sense of direction for improvement.

Chapter 16 is new to Part Four and is themed to supervising for classroom effectiveness. This chapter provides an integrated view of teacher effectiveness research and insights as well into what these findings do and do not mean and how they might be sensibly put into practice. The perspective in this chapter is that of contingency theory rather than of ideological debates.

Chapter 19 points the way toward developing a unique theory of supervisory practice which relies on, but is not the same as, measurement and evaluation theory. This chapter seeks to bring together scientific and artistic ways of knowing by emphasizing the integration of descriptive, normative, and intepretive sciences in supervisory practice.

Significant revisions of existing chapters include the introduction of an experiential approach designed to directly involve readers. This approach is particularly noticeable in Chapter 4 dealing with organizational climate, Chapters 5 and 6 dealing with leadership, Chapter 8 dealing with motivation, and Chapter 9 dealing with group supervision.

The chapters throughout Part Three of the third edition have been revised to bring about a somewhat better balance between curriculum and educational program matters and those of teaching in the classroom. Chapter 17 in Part Four, dealing with clinical supervision, now contains a section on summative teacher evaluation. Nearly all the remaining chapters have been revised and updated.

Despite the substantial revisions, many features of the first two editions remain. From a supervisory point of view the school is still seen as encompassing three interdependent subsystems—organizational, educational, and instructional. The supervisor's unique role is portrayed as that of linking pin for all three subsystems. The book continues to rely heavily on theoretical foundations, sacrificing perhaps discussions of some job-entry competencies needed by supervisors in favor of building long-term perspectives of what supervision is and can be. Our interest, therefore, is less in the immediate intricacies of the job and more building a career long view of supervision.

Readers are encouraged to begin their journey through the book by first reading the introductions to each of the four parts. Part One, "Human Resources Supervision and Organizational Leadership," sets the stage for supervision. Whatever curricular and instructional goals supervisors have are achieved through and with others in an organizational setting. Part Two, "Developing a Relevant Theory of Supervisory Practice," brings together the array of scientific findings scattered throughout the first nine chapters into an integrated framework and adds to this instrumental view requirements for developing quality in supervisory leadership. Part Three, "Human Resources and Educational Leadership," provides supervisors with the compass settings and the sense of direction they need to be able to navigate with purpose. Refining the reader's educational platform is the intent here. Part Four, "A Human Resources Approach to Staff Development, Clinical Supervision, and Teacher Evaluation," focuses on the three important task areas traditionally associated with the supervisor's instructional leadership responsibilities.

The book as a whole could not have been written without the long hours of discussion and encouragement which the authors were privileged to share with each other. The list of creditors to this book is long. Colleagues and students have contributed generously of their ideas and to them we are grateful. Special recognition must go to Professor Charles M. Galloway of Ohio State University and Professor Donald J. McCarty of the University of Wisconsin for the painstaking care with which they critiqued the manuscript in various stages and the generosity with which they offered suggestions. We are grateful as well to the supervision community for its support in the development of these ideas and in helping us to understand better what human resources supervision is and can be.

Thomas J. Sergiovanni
Robert J. Starratt

PART ONE

HUMAN RESOURCES SUPERVISION AND ORGANIZATIONAL LEADERSHIP

INTRODUCTION: THE NATURE OF SUPERVISION

Supervision has been a relatively dormant activity in schools, and those designated specifically as supervisors have typically been seen as minor functionaries. Supervisory staffs have become progressively smaller as the demands for economy have increased, and many supervisory activities have been assigned, at least in a titular sense, to others with more administrative responsibilities. As could be expected, overburdened administrators typically give only cursory attention to new responsibilities.

Signs exist, however, which suggest that supervision may be experiencing a mild renaissance. At the national level the Association for Supervision and Curriculum Development is placing stronger emphasis on supervision. The literature in the field is expanding and improving in quality. With respect to general supervision, for example, less emphasis is given to delineating job descriptions and task areas for supervisors and more emphasis is given to developing concepts basic to supervision and articulating supervisory processes. With respect to classroom supervision, clinical strategies and aesthetic strategies are beginning to compete successfully with the more traditional approaches to teacher evaluation.

Publications focusing on problems and issues in supervision are among the most popular offered by the Association for Supervision and Curriculum Development. Supervisory topics are appearing more frequently on the programs of this organization's national conference and series of National Curriculum Study Institutes. The founding of the Conference of Professors of Instructional Supervision in 1976 is evidence that scholars interested in problems in supervision are increasing in numbers, interested in identifying themselves, establishing better communications networks, and developing more systematic approaches to research and development.

Local school districts throughout the country are showing unprecedented interest in teacher evaluation, supervision, and staff development. Educational program design and instructional strategy development are also receiving top priority.

THE CHANGING SCENE

What are the reasons for this renewed interest in supervision? As is so often the case, "necessity is the mother of invention." One such necessity for school districts has been adjusting to declining enrollments. In Illinois, for example, enrollments increased approximately 113 percent during the 25-year period 1946–1971. Enrollments have since steadily declined and are expected to continue to decline until a leveling point is reached in the mid- to late eighties. This situation in Illinois parallels similar national trends. School districts are faced with the necessity of rethinking present strategies for improving the quality of educational services as a result of declining enrollments and related problems such as smaller budgets, demands for accountability, closing and combining schools, teacher surpluses, and teacher entrenchment as manifested by low mobility and turnover rates. As growth-oriented organizations in an expanding economy, schools had in the past been able to obtain increases in quality of education by adding new programs, increasing staff size, and providing new services. In periods of modest growth, zero growth, or decline, however, changes in quality depend more heavily on changes in present staff and present programs. Program evaluation, teacher evaluation, staff development, curriculum development, and other activities typically associated with supervision have become critical leverage points in improving educational quality under present growth conditions. Since improvements must be made within existing human, material, and financial resources, the supervisory function increases in importance. But the situation is more complex than it first appears.

Changing present conditions provide a new set of leadership demands on the school in both an educational and an organizational sense. Not only do good educational decisions need to be made but teachers need to have strong identity with, and commitment to, these decisions. The leadership burden in obtaining this commitment increasingly falls to supervisors who are closest in competence and affinity to teachers and their work.

Consider, for example, the problem of staff stability. Good teaching jobs are difficult to find, and teachers are less likely to leave once they are employed. Low teacher turnover is often viewed initially as a blessing, particularly to those who just a few years ago experienced difficulty in finding and keeping teachers. But in reality low turnover poses a serious problem for schools. Dissatisfied teachers are now less likely to leave. The reasons for staying on the job are too important. But if reasons for staying are limited to job security and other bread-and-butter concerns, we may well have large numbers of teachers who remain on the job for the wrong reasons. As a result, instructional quality is endangered. In the absence of easy turnover, the maintenance and development of job satisfaction, motivation, and commitment in teachers becomes more important. Again the burden increasingly falls on supervisors who are closest to teachers and their work.

Consider the problem of change as another example. In an expanding district one can impose structural changes on existing staff and by the process of staff attrition and careful replacement, transfers, and creative new assignments obtain internalized changes.[1] But under current conditions of stability, structural changes must be

---

[1]Structural changes refer to changes in design. Team teaching, open classroom, and Individually Guided Education (IGE) are examples of structural changes. Internalized changes refer to changes in assumption, beliefs, and behavior of teachers. Internalized changes support structural changes, and both are necessary.

accompanied by internalized changes in the *present* teaching staff. Teachers need to accept, believe in, and be committed to new practices. This sort of change creates strong leadership challenges for the school. Again the burden falls on supervisors who are closest to teachers and their work.

As a final example consider the problem of staff development as it relates to staff stability. Many schools are faced with the prospect of a relatively young teaching staff who are likely to grow old together over the next 2 decades. Age in itself has the potential to provide natural benefits that accrue from experience and maturity. But this potential can be lost unless marked by a commitment to continuous personal and professional development. Staff development of the quality and quantity needed in the decades ahead makes strong demands on school leadership—a burden again likely to fall increasingly on supervisors.

The increased importance attributed to supervisors is attractive, if not euphoric, for those interested in this field. But whether this new emphasis will develop into promises fulfilled or promises broken will depend, we believe, on the form that supervision takes.

THREE FORMER IMAGES OF SUPERVISION

Present supervisory practices in schools are based on one, or a combination, of three general supervisory theories—traditional scientific management, human relations, and neoscientific management.[2] Traditional scientific management represents the classical autocratic philosophy of supervision in which teachers are viewed as appendages of management and as such are hired to carry out prespecified duties in accordance with the wishes of management. Control, accountability, and efficiency are emphasized in an atmosphere of clear-cut boss-subordinate relationships. Vestiges of this brand of supervision can still be found in schools, though by and large traditional scientific management is not currently in favor.

Human relations supervision has its origins in the democratic administration movement advocated in the thirties and is still widely preached and practiced. Human relations supervision was a successful challenger to traditional scientific management. Teachers were to be viewed as "whole people" in their own right rather than as packages of needed energy, skills, and aptitudes to be used by administrators and supervisors. Supervisors worked to create a feeling of satisfaction among teachers by showing interest in them as people. It was assumed that a satisfied staff would work harder and would be easier to work with, to lead, and to control. Participation was to be an important method, and its objective was to make teachers *feel* that they are useful and important to the school. "Personal feelings" and "comfortable relationships" were the watchwords of human relations.

Human relations supervision is still widely advocated and practiced today, though its support has diminished. Human relations promised much but delivered little. Its problems rest partly with misunderstandings as to how the approach should work and partly with faulty theoretical notions inherent in the approach itself. The movement

[2]This section follows closely T. J. Sergiovanni, "Beyond Human Relations," in T. J. Sergiovanni (ed.), *Professional Supervision for Professional Teachers*, Washington, D.C.: Association for Supervision and Curriculum Development, 1975, pp. 1–4.

actually resulted in widespread neglect of teachers. Participatory supervision became permissive supervision, which in practice was laissez-faire supervision. Further, the focus of human relations supervision was and still is an emphasis on "winning friends" in an attempt to influence people. To many, "winning friends" was a slick tactic that made the movement seem manipulative and inauthentic, even dishonest.

In 1967 the Association for Supervision and Curriculum Development's Commission on Supervision Theory concluded its 4 years of study with a report entitled *Supervision: Perspectives and Propositions.*[3] In this report William Lucio discussed scientific-management and human relations views of supervision and spoke of a third view—that of the revisionists—which sought to combine features of both scientific management and human relations. Standard-bearers of the revisionists were Douglas McGregor, Warren Bennis, Chris Argyris, and Rensis Likert.[4]

If ever a misunderstanding existed between theorists and practitioners, the revisionist movement would be a prominent example. This was largely a paper movement that in practice rarely amounted to much more than a more sophisticated form of human relations. What the revisionist writers intended was never really understood by many or properly implemented on a wide scale. Whereas the earlier human relations movement put the emphasis on the teachers' social-interaction needs and physical comfort, the revisionist view was articulated as a superficial attempt to make teachers *feel* a part of the school primarily through relatively controlled or safe participation practices. To old human relations add one part participation and stir well. Nothing important seemed really changed. The ideas of the revisionists are still important, we think, and if properly understood and implemented, they can lead us away from our present inadequacies in supervisory practice.

Neoscientific management, the most recent image of supervision, is in large part a reaction against human relations supervision, particularly its neglect of the teacher in the classroom. Neoscientific management shares with traditional scientific management an interest in control, accountability, and efficiency. The code words of this movement are "teacher competencies," "performance objectives," and "cost-benefit analysis." The task dimension, concern for job, and concern for highly specified performance objectives, all so lacking in human relations supervision, are strongly emphasized in neoscientific management, though often at the expense of the human dimension. Neoscientific management relies heavily on externally imposed authority and as a result often lacks acceptance from teachers.

The three images of supervision share a lack of faith and trust in the teacher's ability and willingness to display as much interest in the welfare of the school and its educational programs as that presumed by administrators, supervisors, and the public. In traditional scientific management, teachers are heavily supervised in an effort to ensure for administrators, supervisors, and the public that good teaching will take place. In human relations supervision, teachers are nurtured and involved in efforts to

---

[3]William Lucio (ed.), *Supervision: Perspectives and Propositions,* Washington, D.C.: Association for Supervision and Curriculum Development, 1967.
[4]Douglas McGregor, *The Human Side of Enterprise,* New York: McGraw-Hill, 1960; Warren Bennis, "Revisionist Theory of Leadership," *Harvard Business Review,* vol. 39, no. 2, pp. 26–38, 1961; Chris Argyris, *Personality and Organization,* New York: Harper, 1957; and Rensis Likert, *New Patterns of Management,* New York: McGraw-Hill, 1961.

increase their job satisfaction so that they might be more pliable in the hands of administrators and supervisors, thus ensuring that good teaching will take place. In neoscientific management, impersonal, technical, or rational control mechanisms substitute for face-to-face close supervision. Here it is assumed that if visible standards of performance, objectives, or competencies can be identified, then the work of teachers can be controlled by holding them accountable to these standards, thus ensuring, for administrators and supervisors and the public, better teaching.

HUMAN RESOURCES SUPERVISION

In the first edition of this book we referred to emerging patterns of supervision that showed promise for moving schools away from scientific-management images of supervision. The emerging patterns were clearly a part of the revisionist movement and were described as enlightened supervision. Many scholars and practitioners have confused enlightened supervision with human relations supervision. Because of this confusion and because of our better understanding of concepts and practices associated with enlightened patterns, we have chosen to refer to them as human resources supervision. The distinction between human relations supervision and human resources supervision is critical.[5] Whereas human relations and human resources supervision are, for example, both concerned with teacher satisfaction, human relations views satisfaction as a means to a smoother and more effective school. The human relations supervisor might adopt shared decision making because it would increase teacher satisfaction. Satisfied teachers, it is assumed, would in turn be easier to work with, and indeed to lead, and therefore effectiveness would be increased.

The Human Relations Supervisor

The rationale behind this strategy is that teachers want to *feel* important and involved. This feeling in turn promotes in teachers a better attitude toward the school, and therefore they become easier to manage.

The human resources supervisor, by contrast, views satisfaction as a desirable end toward which teachers will work. Satisfaction, according to this view, results from the successful accomplishment of important and meaningful work, and this sort of accomplishment is the key component of school effectiveness. The human resources supervisor would adopt shared decision-making practices because of their potential to increase school effectiveness. He or she assumes that better decisions will be made,

[5]This distinction was first made by Raymond Miles, "Human Relations or Human Resources?" *Harvard Business Review,* vol. 43, no. 4, pp. 148–163, 1965; and by Mason Haire, Edwin Ghiselli, and Lyman Porter, *Managerial Thinking: An International Study,* New York: Wiley, 1966. See Chapter 8 for further elaboration of this distinction.

teacher ownership and commitment to these decisions will be increased, and the likelihood of success at work, an antecedent to school effectiveness, will increase.

The Human Resources Supervisor

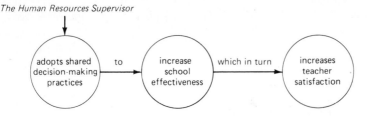

Much of the success of the now-popular neoscientific-management images of supervision—those that rely on impersonal quality-control mechanisms, such as performance contracts, accountability to predetermined objectives, and competency standards—results from the confusion that exists between human relations and human resources supervision. Indeed, many of the forces contributing to a revival of interest in supervision articulated earlier in this introduction require that we abandon human relations notions in favor of more job-centered and task-oriented approaches. But the problems we see in adapting neoscientific approaches are that, while they provide a needed emphasis on the work of the school, they assume a rationality and perspective that neglect the human dimension in organization, educational programs, and instruction. Neoscientific management, for example, often assumes a list of competencies, performance criteria, and other specifications that apply to all teachers, to all teaching situations, to all students, at all times—assumptions both unrealistic and undesirable. The human resources view, as we shall argue, provides the needed integration between person and organization, and personality and accomplishment, as applied to teachers and schools, as well as to students and classrooms.

SUMMARY

In this introduction important trends influencing supervisory practice were discussed. It was noted that such factors as declining enrollments, staff stability, and limited resources have contributed to a renewed interest in supervision. Three former images of supervision (scientific management, human relations, and neoscientific management) were discussed and judged inadequate as models to meet present conditions. A fourth image, human resources supervision, was proposed.

CHAPTER 1

PERSPECTIVES FOR SUPERVISION

Many of the issues associated with supervision over the years remain intact at this writing. Confusion in role definition still plagues the field, and uncertainty exists in determining who are supervisors, what are the key components of their jobs, how much authority they should have, and what their relationship to administrators and teachers should be. Further at issue is whether supervision should be viewed as a special role or as a process component of several roles. Recently, scholars have given attention to what the real word of supervision is like and the match between this reality and views that prescribe what ought to be.

VIEWPOINTS OF SELECTED AUTHORS

In this section selected statements from key authors in the field of supervision are provided as a means to suggest what each views as the essential components of supervision. The statements are provided without editorial comment. Readers may wish to compare points of view among the authors, and between them and the points of view expressed in this book. What do these views share with human resources supervision and how are they different?

Ben Harris defines *supervision* as:[1]

> What school personnel do with *adults* and *things* to maintain or change the school operation in ways that directly influence the teaching processes employed to promote pupil learning. Supervision is highly instruction-related but not highly pupil-related. Supervision is a major function of the school operation, not a task or a specific job or a set of techniques. Supervision of instruction is directed toward both maintaining and improving the teaching-learning processes of the school.

Kimball Wiles views supervision as those activities that are designed to improve instruction at all levels of the school enterprise. He describes supervisors as follows:[2]

> They are the expediters. They help establish communication. They help people hear each other. They serve as liaison to get persons into contact with others who have similar

[1]Ben N. Harris, *Supervisory Behavior in Education,* 2d ed., Englewood Cliffs, N.J.: Prentice-Hall, 1975, pp. 10–11.
[2]Kimball Wiles, *Supervision for Better Schools,* 3d ed., Englewood Cliffs, N.J.: Prentice-Hall, 1967.

problems or with resource people who can help. They stimulate staff members to look at the extent to which ideas and resources are being shared, and the degree to which persons are encouraged and supported as they try new things. They make it easier to carry out the agreements that emerge from evaluation sessions. They listen to individuals discuss their problems and recommend other resources that may help in the search for solutions. They bring to individual teachers, whose confidence they possess, appropriate suggestions and materials. They sense, as far as they are able, the feelings that teachers have about the system and its policies, and they recommend that the administration examine irritations among staff members. They provide expertness in group operation, and provide the type of meeting place and structure that facilitate communication. They are, above all, concerned with helping people to accept each other, because they know that when individuals value each other, they will grow through their interaction together and will provide a better emotional climate for pupil growth. The supervisor's role has become *supporting, assisting,* and *sharing,* rather than directing. The authority of the supervisor's position has not decreased, but it is used in another way. It is used to promote growth through assuming responsibility and creativity rather than through dependency and conformity.

William Burton and Leo Brueckner, two pioneers in the area of supervision whose classic 1955 book, *Supervision: A Social Process,*[3] seems remarkably contemporary, identify certain principles which govern the operation of supervision as follows:

PRINCIPLES GOVERNING THE OPERATION OF SUPERVISION

1. Administration is *ordinarily* concerned with providing material facilities and with operation in general.
2. Supervision is *ordinarily* concerned with improving the setting for learning in particular.
3. Administration and supervision considered *functionally* cannot be separated or set off from each other. The two are co-ordinate, correlative, complementary, mutually shared functions in the operation of educational systems. The provision of any and all conditions favorable to learning is the common purpose of both.
4. Good supervision is based on philosophy and science.
   a. Supervision will be sensitive to ultimate aims and values, to policies, with special reference to their adequacy.
   b. Supervision will be sensitive to "factness" and to law, with special reference to their accuracy.
   c. Supervision will be sensitive to the emergent, evolutionary nature of the universe and of democratic society in particular, hence should be permeated with the experimental attitude, and engage constantly in re-evaluation of aims and values, of policies, of materials and methods.
5. Good supervision is (in the United States) based upon the democratic philosophy.
   a. Supervision will respect personality and individual differences between personalities, will seek to provide opportunities for the best expression of each unique personality.
   b. Supervision will be based upon the assumption that educational workers are capable of growth. It will accept idiosyncrasies, reluctance to cooperate, and antagonism as human characteristics, just as it accepts reasonableness, co-operation, and energetic activity. The former are challenges; the latter, assets.
   c. Supervision will endeavor to develop in all a democratic conscience, that is, recognition that democracy includes important obligations as well as rights.

[3]William H. Burton and Leo J. Brueckner, *Supervision: A Social Process,* 3d ed., New York: Appleton-Century-Crofts, 1955, pp. 85, 88. Reprinted by permission of Appleton-Century-Crofts, Division of Meredith Corporation.

    d. Supervision will provide full opportunity for the cooperative formulation of policies and plans, will welcome and utilize free expression and contributions from all.

    e. Supervision will stimulate initiative, self-reliance and individual responsibility on the part of all persons in the discharge of their duties.

    f. Supervision will substitute leadership for authority. Authority will be recognized as the authority of the situation and of the facts within the situation. Personal authority if necessary will be derived from group planning.

    g. Supervision will work toward co-operatively determined functional groupings of the staff, with flexible regrouping as necessary; will invite specialists when advisable.

6. Good supervision will employ scientific methods and attitudes in so far as those methods and attitudes are applicable to the dynamic social processes of education; will utilize and adapt to specific situations scientific findings concerning the learner, his learning processes, the nature and development of personality; will co-operate occasionally in pure research.

7. Good supervision, in situations where the precise controlled methods of science are not applicable, will employ processes of dynamic problem-solving in studying, improving, and evaluating its products and processes. Supervision either by scientific methods or through orderly thought processes will constantly derive and use data and conclusions which are more objective, more precise, more sufficient, more impartial, more expertly secured, and more systematically organized than are the data and conclusions of uncontrolled opinion.

8. Good supervision will be creative and not prescriptive.

    a. Supervision will determine procedures in the light of the needs of each supervisory teaching-learning situation.

    b. Supervision will provide opportunity for the exercise of originality and for the development of unique contributions, of creative self-expression; will seek latent talent.

    c. Supervision will deliberately shape and manipulate the environment.

9. Good supervision proceeds by means of an orderly, co-operatively planned and executed series of activities.

10. Good supervision will be judged by the results it secures.

11. Good supervision is becoming professional. That is, it is increasingly seeking to evaluate its personnel, procedures, and results; it is moving toward standards and toward self-supervision.

PRINCIPLES GOVERNING THE PURPOSES OF SUPERVISION[4]

1. The ultimate purpose of supervision is the promotion of pupil growth and hence eventually the improvement of society.

2. A second general purpose of supervision is to supply leadership in securing continuity and constant readaptation in the educational program over a period of years; from level to level within the system; and from one area of learning experience and content to another.

3. The immediate purpose of supervision is co-operatively to develop favorable settings for teaching and learning.

    a. Supervision, through all means available, will seek improved methods of teaching and learning.

    b. Supervision will create a physical, social, and psychological climate or environment favorable to learning.

    c. Supervision will co-ordinate and integrate all educational efforts and materials, will supply continuity.

[4]Ibid.

d. Supervision will enlist the co-operation of all staff members in serving their own needs and those of the situation; will provide ample, natural opportunities for growth by all concerned in the correction and prevention of teaching difficulties, and for growth in the assumption of new responsibilities.

e. Supervision will aid, inspire, lead, and develop that security which liberates the creative spirit.

More recently John Lovell, in revising Kimball Wiles's book, views supervision as an instructional behavior system.[5]

Instructional supervisory behavior is assumed to be an additional behavior system formally provided by the organization for the purpose of interacting with the teaching behavior system in such a way as to maintain, change, and improve the provision and actualization of learning opportunities for students. The instructional supervisor, operating from his own unique conceptual base, works to achieve certain tasks through various operations and activities. From this frame of reference, instructional supervisory behavior can be a dimension of many roles in the educational organization. A superintendent of schools, with special competence in the teaching of reading, working with a group of primary teachers to evaluate a proposed "reading program," would be participating in instructional supervisory behavior. A teacher appointed by the administration to chair a curriculum planning committee would be participating in instructional supervisory behavior to achieve the task. The critical factor is not the title of the role but the nature of the behavior.

Following Lovell, Robert Alfonso, Gerald Firth, and Richard Neville also view supervision as an instructional behavior system that interacts with the school's counseling, teaching, administrative, and student behavior system. In their view:[6]

Instructional supervision is herein defined as: *Behavior officially designated by the organization that directly affects teacher behavior in such a way as to facilitate pupil learning and achieve the goals of the organization.*

There are three key elements in this definition. First, the behavor exhibited is "officially designated." It is not random, casually determined activity, but it bears the stamp of organizational request and formal authority. Secondly, it "directly influences teacher behavior." This rules out the multitude of tasks performed by supervisors that, while they may be important to the organization, are *not* supervision. It provides a test as to whether one is really engaging in supervisory behavior—does it clearly affect the teachers?—the teacher behavior subsystem. Thirdly, it specifies an ultimate outcome tied directly to the reason for the existence of the school: the facilitation of student learning. This element also provides focus for influencing teacher behavior—not willy-nilly, but purposeful change in teacher behavior in order to improve learning.

Oliva's view of supervision is admirably characterized by both simplicity and grace. To him,

. . . supervision is conceived as a service to teachers, both as individuals and in groups. Supervision is a means of offering to teachers specialized help in improving instruction. The words "service" and "help" should be underscored. . . .[7]

---

[5]Kimball Wiles and John T. Lovell, *Supervision for Better Schools*, 4th ed., Englewood Cliffs, N.J.: Prentice-Hall, 1975, pp. 6, 8.

[6]Robert J. Alfonso, Gerald R. Firth, and Richard F. Neville, *Instructional Supervision: A Behavioral System*, Boston: Allyn and Bacon, 1975, pp. 35–36.

[7]Peter F. Oliva, *Supervision for Today's Schools*, New York: Thomas Y. Crowell, 1976, p. 7.

The authors agree that supervision is a set of activities and role specifications specifically designed to influence instruction. Harris's statement best summarizes this view. Wiles, and to a lesser extent Burton and Brueckner, provide a human relations portrait of supervision immersed in the principles of democracy and equality as a means to influence instruction. More recent works, as represented by Lovell and by Alfonso, Firth, and Neville, view supervision as a special kind of behavior that is distinguished from other behavior by its deliberate focus on the school's teaching behavior system. These authors rely heavily of a broad social science base characterized by scientific rationality and objectivity in prescribing research-based principles of supervisory behavior.

Human resources supervision shares many of the features of the points of view discussed. It, too, focuses on the improvement of instruction, though it views the links between organization, leadership, educational program, and instruction as being far more deliberate and interdependent. An assumption basic to human resources supervision, for example, is that humane classrooms and humane curriculum designs can only be accomplished in humanistic organizations.

Human resources supervision builds upon many of the ideas of Wiles, though in human resources, more emphasis is given to integrating individual needs with school objectives and tasks. One way that this is done is by emphasizing the importance of meaningful work to teachers and by viewing teacher satisfaction, *derived from accomplishment,* as a critical key to building motivation and commitment and therefore improving instruction. In many ways human resources is a refinement and extension of Burton and Brueckner's views.

Human resources supervision shares an interest in the social sciences with the views of Lovell and of Alfonso, Firth, and Neville, though in a much more *subjective* fashion. In the view of human resources supervision values, too, play an important part and social science concepts need to be evaluated for appropriateness to educational settings before they can be put into practice. In this sense, educational administration and supervision are applied sciences drawing upon both science (research and theory) and art (experience and intuition) for concepts and ideas that are evaluated for consistency with *educational values* before they are adapted to practice.[8]

Confusion often exists in our field between supervisory roles and supervisory processes. In the sections that follow, various images of supervision with implications for practice are discussed and an attempt is made to differentiate supervisory processes from those considered administrative.

THE ROLE-PROCESS DILEMMA

Supervision is often viewed on the one hand as a process component of a variety of roles and on the other hand as a useful label to categorize a group of school roles whose primary function is the improvement of instruction. Essentially, incumbents of roles whose primary function is the improvement of instruction also engage in supervisory processes. Chairpersons, curriculum directors, subject-matter supervisors, and many

[8]See, for example, T. J. Sergiovanni and F. D. Carver, *The New School Executive: A Theory of Administration,* 2d ed., New York: Harper & Row, 1980, esp. Chap. 2, "Applied Science and the Role of Value Judgments," and Chap. 3, "A Belief Pattern for Decision-Making."

elementary school principals are examples of people whose roles are considered supervisory. They engage in such supervisory processes as staff development, motivation, and shared decision making but typically within the context of instructional improvement. Superintendents, however, engage in similar processes as they "supervise" central office staff. In short, many of the characteristics of supervision are shared by a number of roles, though typically those labeled supervisors engage in these activities more deliberately within the context of instructional improvement.

It seems useful to us to distinguish between modes of behavior that can be described as supervisory and others that cannot. Deciding on what constitutes supervisory behavior helps us to realize the scope and breadth of supervision. Below are several statements that help to clarify our view of the concept of supervision. In each case the distinctions we make are conceptual and are designed to increase our understanding. In operation the distinctions are less clear.

1. Viewing supervision as a process is in some respects more meaningful than viewing supervision as a role or the supervisor as a particular role incumbent.

When supervision is viewed as a process, then all personnel who practice supervision in schools (superintendents, principals, librarians, staff personnel, department or division chairpersons, classroom teachers, and others, including nonprofessional personnel) are supervisors at one time or another.

Farwell   ⚹ **2.** Supervision is a process used by those in schools who have responsibility for one or another aspect of the school's goals and who *depend directly upon others* to help them achieve these goals.

A crucial aspect that differentiates supervisory behavior from other forms of organizational behavior is *action to achieve goals through other people.* A principal who works to improve the effectiveness of the educational program for students by helping teachers become more effective in the classroom is behaving in a supervisory way. A critical aspect of this relationship is that the principal is dependent upon the teacher in attempting to increase program effectiveness.

3. Since behavior is a significant part of the supervisory process, for understanding the process as a whole it is often useful as an analytical method to focus on this aspect of supervision.

The supervisory process requires attention to the social, cultural, attitudinal, and behavioral ethos of the total supervisory environment, but it is often analytically easier to discuss the process in terms of behavior. Thus supervisory behavior is an important construct in this book and, as such, forms the basis for analyzing other aspects of the supervisory process and their relationship to supervisory effectiveness.

Farwell   ⚹ **4.** Behavior of administrators and others in school organizations that is characterized by action toward achievement of school goals but is *not* dependent upon others for success is described as administrative rather than supervisory.

When administrators and supervisors work with things and ideas rather than with people in pursuing school goals, they tend to be operating in an administrative way rather than in a supervisory way. Work on the budget, the master schedule, or the program for a summer workshop and preparation of a memo for the superintendent may all be related to achieving or facilitating school purposes, but the principal is often justified in carrying out these activities and responsibilities in a way that does not require dependence upon others for success.

5. Depending upon the circumstances, one may choose to behave in an administrative way—directly—or in a supervisory way—through people—to achieve school goals.

Certain aspects of school goals are more effectively (and in some cases exclusively) accomplished through administrative behavior, while other aspects are more effectively accomplished through behavior described as supervisory. Nevertheless, as schools mature and develop as professional organizations, the supervisory way of behaving becomes the dominant pattern.

CHARACTERISTICS OF SUPERVISORY ROLES

Supervisors work primarily in the area of instructional improvement. Organizational demands require most personnel in schools to be involved in some aspects of administrative behavior, but for those who work in the area of instructional improvement, supervisory behavior will tend to predominate. Supervisory roles can be further differentiated from the more administrative roles by such characteristics as (1) heavy reliance on expertness as an educational program leader and instructional leader, (2) the necessity of living in two worlds and of speaking two languages, and (3) limits imposed on their authority.

Supervisors in education, as in other fields ranging from medicine to industry, are expected to be experts in the production system of their organizations. A high school principal who functions primarily as an administrator-manager can get along quite well with only a conversational acquaintance with classroom organizational patterns, problems, and prospects, but a high school principal or a department chairperson who functions as a supervisor needs a more detailed perspective to be successful. Supervisors are expected to be experts in educational and instructional matters. As educational and instructional leaders, their work exhibits a high concern for:

Curriculum and teaching objectives

Educational program content, coordination, and scope

Alternatives and options

Curriculum and teaching innovations

Structured knowledge

Grouping and scheduling patterns

Lesson and unit planning

Evaluating and selecting learning materials

Patterns of teacher and student classroom influence

Developing and evaluating educational encounters

Teaching styles, methods, and procedures

Classroom learning climates

Teacher, student, and program evaluation[9]

A second characteristic differentiating supervisory from other roles is the necessity of living in two worlds and of speaking two languages—the language of teachers and the language of administrators. Teachers and administrators operate from different perspectives, each of which often makes one unintelligible to the other. True, most administrators have been teachers previously, but having been cast into a different arena and subjected to different pressures, they often have difficulty in understanding the problems teachers face. Teachers, on the other hand, view the school from a limited, often unrealistic, perspective. Their perspective is frequently accompanied by an unsympathetic view of the administrator and his or her role. Supervisors are forced to live in both worlds and to mediate difficulties in communication and perspective between the two worlds without alienating either—no small order!

A third characteristic, cited earlier, involves limitations placed on the supervisor's authority. Supervisors are often considered "staff" rather than "line" officers, though admittedly the difference between the two is more muddled than neat. As such, supervisors and line administrators with supervisory responsibility rely heavily on functional authority conferred by their knowledge as educational and instructional leaders and on personal leadership characteristics as sources of authority to influence both teachers and administrators. We will discuss supervisory authority more fully in Chapter 7.

THE SUPERVISOR IN THE HIERARCHY

Contrast supervision in a midwestern state with approximately 1,100 independent school districts complete with superintendents and school boards with supervision in one of our southeastern states that contains only 40 independent school districts. Since the school districts in this midwestern state are generally small, specialized supervisors are rarely employed. Instead, responsibility for the direct supervision of educational programs and teaching and for such supervisory areas as staff development is assumed by building principals and (particularly where principals are not employed) by the superintendent. In the southeastern state, by contrast, governance is more centralized, and though principals and superintendents still maintain supervisory responsibilities, specialists in supervision are employed. Some of these specialists may have responsibility for working with teachers on matters of curriculum and instructional organization. Others may have responsibility for classroom observations and the evaluation of teaching, and still others for staff development. In many districts supervisors have a broader responsibility for one or more of these areas—a desirable feature in our

[9]See, for example, Thomas J. Sergiovanni, *Handbook for Effective Department Leadership,* Boston: Allyn and Bacon, 1977, p. 4. Parts Three and Five of this book give attention to building a conceptual base for understanding and enriching the supervisor's potential for educational and instructional leadership.

opinion. This book applies to those for whom supervisory responsibility is but one dimension of their total job as well as to supervisory specialists. When one gets down to the basics of supervision, the problems are similar for both groups.

Just what is the supervisor's place in the hierarchy of the school? Keith Davis identifies five different views of the supervisor's role, which range from affording the supervisor a critical place in the hierarchy to affording the supervisor a marginal place.[10] The viewpoints are illustrated in Figure 1-1.

The *person-in-the-middle* view of the supervisor is characterized by a process of mediating between the two opposing worlds of teachers and administrators. Here administrators are seen as emphasizing task-oriented leadership and a variety of quality-control mechanisms in efforts to push teacher and school closer to achieving

[10]Keith Davis, *Human Behavior at Work: Human Relations and Organizational Behavior,* 4th ed., New York: McGraw-Hill, 1972, pp. 120–123.

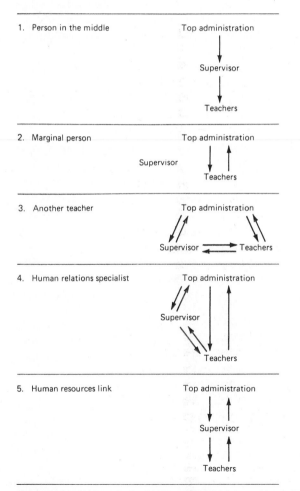

Figure 1-1 Viewpoints on the supervisor's role. *(From Keith Davis,* Human Behavior at Work: Human Relations and Organizational Behavior, *4th ed., New York: McGraw-Hill, 1972.)*

objectives and increasing production. Teachers as human beings, however, are seeking a more relaxed, trusting, and congenial atmosphere within which to work—one that is secure from tension and responsive to their needs. Supervisors are caught in the middle, struggling valiantly to reconcile what may well be impossible differences. In this sense, supervisors are seen as buffers, or persons in the middle.

As a *marginal person,* the supervisor is also in the middle but is excluded from or on the margin of important decisions affecting the school. Here the supervisor is not accepted by either group and is ignored for the most part by both groups. As a result the marginal-person supervisor often spends more time as a curriculum administrator, as a materials procurer, or engaged in some other impersonal activity associated with desk work.

The *another-teacher* view of supervision is characterized by affording supervisors low authority and status and by permitting them only minimum discretion. Supervisors, in this view, are often considered liaison persons upon whom administrators rely to get the word down to teachers. Housekeeping chores and maintenance activities, rather than leadership responsibilities, occupy the attention of this type of supervisor. Many secondary school chairpersons, for example, can be characterized as supervisors of this sort.

As a *human relations specialist* the supervisor is considered a staff specialist charged with the caring for, and maintaining of, the human side of the school enterprise. The need for such a specialist is based on the assumption that in any organization job demands and human demands are in conflict. Teachers have needs and feelings and are subject to frustration, disappointment, and other maladies that can endanger morale. According to this view, poor morale is not good for the school and should be avoided. The supervisor's job as human relations specialist is to get along with teachers, be sympathetic to their problems, and otherwise tend to their idiosyncrasies in an attempt to gain their cooperation and compliance to administrative directives.

As a *human resources link,* the supervisor is not viewed as an administrative tool or organizational buffer but as a key member of the school's leadership team. Here the supervisor is a critical link between the school's organizational and management subsystem and its educational-instructional subsystem. This is indeed an in-the-middle view, but here the supervisor serves an integrating rather than a buffering role. It is assumed that though educational programs and instruction exist within an organized setting, organization and management exist to serve educational programs and instruction. That being the case, the integrating role of the supervisor is considered critical in the administrative hierarchy, and he or she assumes a key role in school district decision making. The reasons why the school exists constitute the supervisor's primary area of responsibility.

The supervisor should be viewed as a human resources link in the administrative hierarchy and as such should assume a critical role in district decision making. This is a normative view of supervisors that prevails in the literature, is believed by many including top administration, and fits a growing number, but still a minority, of schools.[11] A descriptive view represents a more realistic appraisal, which reveals that

---

[11]As noted in the introduction to Part One, more emphasis is presently being given to supervision as a key role in building school effectiveness not only by professional organizations and journals but by changes in practice in school districts throughout the country.

most supervisors are viewed either as marginal members of the school hierarchy or as persons in the middle. A large number are viewed as human relations specialists, and this may well be a first step toward upgrading supervisory roles in a fashion that approximates the human resources viewpoint. The other-teacher image of supervision is fading as collective bargaining becomes widespread.

SUMMARY

This chapter presented perspectives on supervision. Viewpoints of selected authors were provided and contrasted. Supervision can be viewed, on the one hand, as a process component of a variety of administrative and supervisory roles and, on the other hand, as a label to categorize roles the primary responsibility of which is the improvement of instruction. The dependency relationship that exists between leader and individual or group distinguishes administrative behavior from supervisory behavior. Supervisory behavior was prescribed, for instance, when the leader needed to obtain individual or group commitment to goals and tasks in order to be effective.

Supervisory roles were characterized by three distinguishing features: (1) heavy reliance on expertness as an educational program and instructional leader, (2) the necessity to live in two worlds and to speak two languages, and (3) limits imposed on their authority. Five viewpoints of supervisory roles within the administrative hierarchy were then described. They included the person in the middle, marginal person, another teacher, human relations specialist, and human resources link. The human resources link perspective was then proposed as the most effective model for supervision.

STUDY GUIDE

Recall the concepts, ideas, and meanings associated with each of the following phrases and terms included in this chapter. Can you discuss each of them with a colleague and apply them to the supervisory context of your school? If you cannot, review them in the text and record the page number for future reference.

1. Buffering role _____
2. Dependency relationship _____
3. Descriptive view of supervision _____
4. Distinguishing characteristics of supervisory roles _____
5. Educational-leadership concerns _____
6. Human relations specialist _____
7. Human resources link _____
8. Instructional supervisory behavior _____
9. Integrating role _____
10. Marginal person _____
11. Normative view of supervision _____
12. Person in the middle _____
13. Purposes of supervision _____
14. Role-process dilemma _____
15. Supervision as instruction-related _____
16. Supervisors as expediters _____
17. Supervisory authority _____
18. Teacher behavior subsystem _____
19. Worlds and languages of supervisors _____

EXERCISES

1. Who are the persons in your school or district that are considered primarily as supervisors? How is their work distinguished from those considered primarily as administrators?

2. Review persons in your school or district in both supervisory and administrative roles. Develop a chart listing the role, the type of supervisory activities demonstrated in the role, and the percentage of time spent on each supervisory activity in a typical week. Base your estimates of percentage on the total time spent in all activities (administrative and supervisory) for each role.

3. Using Figure 1-1 as a guide, classify each person in your school or district whom you have identified primarily as a supervisor.

4. Describe the "ideal" supervisor as seen by the average teacher in your school or district. How does this description measure up to your analysis of supervisory roles in 2 and 3 above? How does this description measure up to your view of the "ideal" supervisor?

CHAPTER 2

NORMATIVE AND DESCRIPTIVE VIEWS OF SUPERVISION

Up to this point we have been discussing normative views of supervision. Normative views are concerned with what ought to be done, with prescribing actions designed to produce the best solutions. This perspective will continue throughout the book despite the fact that care will be taken to support other views with appropriate research. When one writes a book on the topic of supervision, invariably the intent is to improve the field. Authors want to make things better, and professional books usually prescribe best ways of operating or propose a series of propositions hopefully designed to improve matters.

A NORMATIVE VIEW

A normative view of supervision is depicted in Figure 2-1.[1] Here it is assumed that choices are made by supervisors to maximize certain desirable values and objectives. The supervisor, being faithful to certain value statements and committed to certain objectives, uses the resources available to him or her to achieve goals in accordance with a maximum cost/benefit exchange. To this end, the supervisor performs certain processes such as planning, organizing, leading, helping, supporting, developing, and evaluating.

Normative theories have a number of advantages. They specify what should be done. They challenge individuals who are involved with the school to place highest priority on moral rather than instrumentive values; on what is most effective rather than on some lesser condition. They help to set goals, to reach agreement on future directions, and to develop plans for future action. And they set the standard for improving present levels of supervision. Despite these important advantages, normative theories fail to capture the world and work of supervision as it really is. By contrast, descriptive theories are concerned with what is, with accurately describing the activities and events they represent.

---

[1] This discussion follows T. J. Sergiovanni, M. Burlingame, F. S. Coombs, and P. W. Thurston, "The Work of Educational Administration: A Descriptive View," Chap. 12, *Educational Governance and Administration*, Englewood Cliffs, N.J.: Prentice-Hall, 1980, pp. 314–333.

Following the decision-rule "Choices are made to maximize values and objectives," a supervisor <u>should</u> behave as follows:

Figure 2-1 A normative view of supervision. *(Adapted from T. J. Sergiovanni, M. Burlingame, F. S. Coombs, and P. W. Thurston, Educational Governance and Administration, p. 315. © 1980. Adapted by permission of Prentice-Hall, Englewood Cliffs, N.J.)*

A DESCRIPTIVE VIEW

A key difference between normative and descriptive theories is that in the latter it is assumed that choices are made to satisfy constraints rather than to maximize objectives. As is depicted in Figure 2-2, the supervisor is conscious of and interested in value statements and goals important to his or her school and desires to perform supervisory processes in an ideal way, but this desire is mediated by such realities of organizational life as politics, the pressure for conflict resolution, the constraints of bureaucracy, limits on rationality, and the distribution of power and authority. Satisfactory goal achievement and self-serving behavior tend to be more accurate descriptions of outcomes as supervisors seek to satisfy these constraints.

Following the decision-rule, "Choices are made to satisfy constraints, " a supervisor behaves as follows:

Figure 2-2 A descriptive view of supervision. *(From T. J. Sergiovanni, M. Burlingame, F. S. Coombs, and P. W. Thurston, Educational Governance and Administration, p. 317. © 1980. Adapted by permission of Prentice-Hall, Englewood Cliffs, N.J.)*

Accounts of gaps between normative and descriptive views of supervision are not necessarily cause for alarm. Presently, abundance and richness characterize the normative literature but not the descriptive literature. The need exists, therefore, for researchers to focus more talent and attention on mapping and describing the real world and work of supervision.[2]

Recently, a number of studies have been conducted that attempt to develop accurate descriptions of supervisory reality. One such study was commissioned by the Association for Supervision and Curriculum Development and conducted by the ASCD Working Group on Roles and Responsibilities of Supervisors chaired by A. W. Sturges.[3] The report of this group covers a number of topics but focuses its attention on discrepancies between the real and ideal in supervision. One study summarized was concerned with the amount of supervision actually experienced by teachers in Tennessee. The researchers, Lovell and Phelps,[4] note that 83 percent of the teachers in Tennessee reported no observations of their teaching by a supervisor during the 1974–75 academic year. When observations were held, more than two-thirds of the teachers reported that they were not scheduled in advance, were not preceded by a conference, or were not requested. Further, one-half of this group reported that no follow-up conference took place. Contrast these findings with views presented in this book and in other books on the topic of supervision that prescribe what supervisors should be doing.

In summing the report of the working group Sturges notes the following inconsistencies between normative and descriptive views of supervision:

NATURE AND OBJECTIVES OF THE INSTRUCTIONAL SUPERVISOR

Intended: The instructional supervisor should assist in the improvement of instruction. This includes (1) direct psychological and technical support, service and help to teachers; (2) curriculum development, coordination and evaluation of instruction; (3) development and evaluation of educational goals; (4) professional development of personnel; (5) evaluation of personnel performance; and (6) the evaluation of educational outcomes. The maintenance and continuing support of ongoing programs and people are included, as well as the teachers' desire for supportive and non-threatening services that are directly related to the improvement of teachers' classroom performance.

Actual: Teachers perceive some instructional supervisors as primarily concerned with administrative responsibilities. Some individuals with primary administrative or management responsibilities (e.g., principals, assistant superintendents for curriculum and/or instruction) employ their supervisory responsibilities to assist them in accomplishing tasks that may be indirectly related to the improvement of instruction at the classroom level.

Conflict: Teachers want direct assistance to improve instruction; some educators with

[2]Blumberg's book gives more attention than most to the descriptive world of supervision. See Arthur Blumberg, *Supervisors and Teachers: A Private Cold War*, Berkeley, Calif.: McCutchan, 1974.

[3]A. W. Sturges, R. J. Krajewski, J. T. Lovell, E. McNeill, and M. G. Ness, "The Roles and Responsibilities of Instructional Supervisors," *Report of the ASCD Working Group on the Roles and Responsibilities of Supervisors*, Alexandria, Va.: Association for Curriculum and Development, October 1978.

[4]John T. Lovell and Margaret S. Phelps, "Supervision in Tennessee: A Study of Perceptions of Teachers, Principals and Supervisors," Tennessee Association for Supervision and Curriculum Development, July 1976, reported in Sturges et al., op. cit., p. 35. See also *Educational Leadership*, vol. 35, pp. 226–228, 1977, for a summary of this study.

supervisory responsibilities combine both administrative and supervisory responsibilities to meet more global goals than at the specific classroom levels.

THE ACTIVITIES OF THE INSTRUCTIONAL SUPERVISOR

Intended: The instructional supervisor should provide direct assistance to the classroom teacher for the improvement of instruction and the improved learning by children. This assistance can include instructional materials, demonstration teaching, and the acquisition of appropriate facilities and equipment. Evaluation of teaching performance is to provide specific assistance toward the improvement of teaching.

Actual: Some teachers do not perceive the instructional supervisor as devoting enough time to the improvement of instruction in the individual classrooms. Administrative responsibilities that require the instructional supervisor to spend time at the central office rather than with specific teachers are perceived as restricting direct assistance by the instructional supervisor. The conflict resulting from the line versus staff responsibilities of instructional supervisors is illustrated by criticisms by some teachers of the lack of classroom visits and the limited direct assistance by the instructional supervisor.

Conflict: Teachers want assistance at the classroom level. Those educators with mixed assignments of instructional supervision and administration/management do not provide the type of assistance desired by teachers.

THE ORGANIZATIONAL STRUCTURE FOR INSTRUCTIONAL SUPERVISION

Intended: The instructional supervisor should be as close as possible to the teachers being assisted. This can include the housing of a supervisor in the building where the teachers are to be assisted.

Actual: Instructional supervisors are frequently assigned to work with teachers in several buildings; instructional supervisors often have offices at a central location in the school district.

Conflict: Teachers want more direct and immediate access to assistance from instructional supervisors that are familiar with the environment of specific classrooms. Other types of instructional supervisors (e.g., principals) have a role conflict of administrator versus the direct and extensive instructional assistance desired by teachers.

THE PREPARATION OF INSTRUCTIONAL SUPERVISORS

Intended: To meet the aspirations that teachers hold for instructional supervisors, appropriate preparation would include coursework, practical and field experiences to help supervisors accurately analyze existing classroom conditions and make appropriate recommendations for improving the learning environment of children.

Actual: Less than half the states offer certification for instructional supervisors; very few specify a minimum number of hours in supervision, and few require an internship. Among those states requiring certification, there is a wide range between the lowest and highest number of hours in supervision that are required.

Conflict: There seems to be little agreement between what teachers want instructional supervisors to do, and the ways in which they are being prepared by universities. [5]

[5]Sturges et al., op. cit., pp. 67–70.

THE NATURE OF SUPERVISORY WORK

The publication in 1973 of Henry Mintzberg's book, *The Nature of Managerial Work*,[6] has sparked a great deal of interest in descriptive studies of administration and supervision. Instead of attributing roles to administrators, Mintzberg sought to infer real roles based on what administrators actually did. This is an inductive approach that relies on continued, detailed, and systematic study of administrative actions. Using diaries and engaging in direct observation over an extended period, Mintzberg studied five executives, including a school superintendent. Mintzberg was able to identify 10 administrative roles that reflected the actual activities observed. The roles were then grouped into three major categories as follows:

INTERPERSONAL	
Figurehead	Symbolic head; obliged to perform a number of routine duties of a legal or social nature.
Leader	Responsible for the motivation and actions of subordinates; responsible for staffing, training, and associated duties.
Liaison	Maintains self-developed network of contacts and informers who provide favors and information.
INFORMATIONAL	
Monitor	Seeks and receives wide variety of special information (much of it current) to develop thorough understanding of organization and environment, emerges as nerve center of internal and external information of the organization.
Disseminator	Transmits information received from outsiders or from other subordinates to members of the organization; some information factual, some involving interpretation and integration of diverse value positions of organizational influences.
Spokesperson	Transmits information to outsiders on organization's plans, policies, actions, results, etc.; serves as expert on organization's industry.
DECISIONAL	
Entrepreneur	Searches organization and its environment for opportunities and initiates "improvement projects" to bring about change; supervises design of certain projects as well.
Disturbance handler	Responsible for corrective action when organization faces important, unexpected disturbances.
Resource allocator	Responsible for the allocation of organizational resources of all kinds—in effect the making or approving of all significant organizational decisions.
Negotiator	Responsible for representing the organization at major negotiations.*

*Mintzberg, The Nature of Managerial Work, Table 2 (pp. 92–93). Copyright © 1973 by Henry Mintzberg. Reprinted by permission of Harper & Row, Publisher.

[6]Henry Mintzberg, *The Nature of Managerial Work*, New York: Harper & Row, 1973.

Replication of Mintzberg's work in other areas, including education, has shown that the 10 roles and three categories are stable.[7] That is, they seem to categorize the nature of managerial work in a variety of fields. Recently, Sullivan tested the Mintzberg framework with supervisors.[8] She limited her study to "system level supervisors" in a metropolitan area. Following Mintzberg's methods, she recorded 14,753 minutes of actual supervisory behavior and used this as a basis for her analysis. Are Mintzberg's categories stable when applied to supervisors in education? Sullivan was able to classify 98 percent of all of the supervisory activity actually recorded into this framework; thus the answer, based on her study, is yes.

In sorting out the activities of supervisors across the 10 roles Sullivan found that 30 percent of the activities could be classified as resource allocator, 19 percent as monitor, and 16 percent as disseminator. By contrast, the three interpersonal roles of figurehead, liaison, and leader accounted for only 10, 9, and 8 percent, respectively. On the basis of this distribution, she concluded that the supervisors in her study were primarily insiders concerned with internal operations.

Normative views of supervision tend to elevate the interpersonal roles over others, with the greatest emphasis given to leadership. It is assumed that these roles have the most to do with quality in supervision. Informational roles are often emphasized and the supervisor is seen as a key communications link between teachers and administrators, among teachers, and between teachers and developments that occur outside of the school. Less important in the literature are the decisional roles. Typically these roles are associated with more administrative positions. Sullivan found almost the opposite configuration when she categorized supervisory activities into the role categories. Informational roles, for example, accounted for 30 percent of the activities, decision-making roles for 33 percent, and interpersonal roles for only 27 percent.

One problem with the Mintzberg approach is the tendency to treat all activities equally—to disregard their proportionate impact on quality and effectiveness. The leadership act and other interpersonal encounters, for example, get the same weight as reading a memo or filing a report. If one were to weight role activities according to the categories with the assumption that some role categories are more important than others, then a more qualitative assessment could be made of what supervisors do.

Let us assume, for example, that role activity in the interpersonal categories is twice as important to supervisory quality as informational roles and that decision-making roles lie somewhere between the two in importance. To reflect this judgment, let us give informational roles a weight of 5, decision-making roles a weight of 7.5, and interpersonal roles a weight of 10. By multiplying the percentage of role activity found in a given category by its weight, we are able to get a more qualitative estimate of how supervisors in Sullivan's study spend time. Consider the following calculations:

---

[7]For a discussion of the roles within the context of educational administration, see Sergiovanni, Burlingame, Coombs, and Thurston, op. cit., pp. 320–326.

[8]Cheryl Granade Sullivan, "The Work of the Instructional Supervisor: A Functional Analysis," Ph.D. dissertation, Atlanta, Ga.: Emory University, Division of Educational Studies, 1980.

Role category	Percent of role activity recorded	Quality weight	Weighted score	Sum of weighted scores	"Quality percent"
Inter-personal	27	× 10	= 270	÷ 707	= 38
Decision making	33	7.5	247	707	35
Informa-tional	38	5	190	707	27

When weighted in this fashion, we find that interpersonal roles, though accounting for less of the actual supervisory activity, make the largest "contribution" to quality supervision. Of course, some may disagree with our weights, but the point is that the Mintzberg avenue of inquiry can be misleading by treating all actions as the same.[9] Sullivan's study examined the types of activities engaged in by supervisors within roles as well. She found, for example, that 61 percent of supervisory time was spent in verbal contact, 18 percent in desk work, 7 percent in travel, 7 percent in technical work, and the remaining in an array of miscellaneous categories. Her observation that most of this 61 percent of verbal communications was directed at others in lateral positions is disconcerting. Only 9 percent was directed at superiors and *only 14 percent was with teachers*. The finding that only 7 percent of supervisory time is spent in technical work such as classroom supervision and in-service education is further cause for alarm. These findings stand in stark contrast to what most authorities say supervisors should be doing.

ACCOMMODATING DISCREPANCIES

No wonder supervisors become cynical when they read the literature on supervision with its typical normative bias. After all, some conclude, if you want to survive out there you have to accommodate yourself to the real world. We recognize that there exists a temptation to abandon standards and ideals and to play the game as it is. On the other hand, one wonders if games without meaning and purpose are worth playing at all. Obviously, our position is that the normative side of the enterprise cannot be ignored. But still, we recognize that there is no hope of improving things if we remain naive

[9]Since much of this discussion relies on Sullivan's work, it is important to point out that while we find her study to be significant and useful, we do not agree with all of her interpretations of what the findings mean. She notes, for example, that since she was able to account for 98 percent of supervisory activity in terms of Mintzberg's "managerial" categories, supervisors are really managers or administrators rather than educators or educational supervisors. She asks, "What about their involvement in clinical supervision or in helping teachers with materials?" She may be right in her assessment on this account that supervisors are not spending the time that they should in these areas, but the process of clinical supervision and of helping teachers with educational materials can also be explained in terms of required supervisory behaviors. The Mintzberg categories fit very nicely here. Clinical supervision, for example, involves leading, monitoring, disseminating, entrepreneuring, and probably other roles as well. The same could be said for such supervisory functions as in-service education, evaluating instruction, and so on.

about existing practices and conditions in supervision. The two go hand in hand. Descriptive views provide us with accurate images of the world of supervision and normative views with standards toward which we strive. One task of this book is to help to bring the views closer together with a minimum of sacrifice to the normative view.

SUMMARY

Normative and descriptive views of supervision were discussed in this chapter. Normative views specify what should be done and describe a more ideal world of supervision. They are, therefore, useful in setting standards and for helping to select targets and goals toward which supervisors might strive. Descriptive views, by contrast, focus specifically on the real world of supervision and provide descriptions of actual behavior and events. A number of descriptive studies of supervision were presented in this chapter and contrasted with more normative views. It was pointed out that differences exist between the two views. Readers were cautioned that though descriptive views are useful in helping to understand events as they are, leadership requires that supervisors work to improve events, and so normative theories are important too.

STUDY GUIDE

Recall the concepts, ideas, and meanings associated with each of the following phrases and terms included in this chapter. Can you discuss each of them with a colleague and apply them to the supervisory context of your school? If you cannot, review them in the text and record the page number for future reference.

1. Decisional roles _____
2. Descriptive theory _____
3. Discrepancies _____
4. Informational roles _____
5. Interpersonal roles _____
6. Normative theory _____

EXERCISES

1. Identify a supervisor with whom you work. Take a recent 2-week period and review how this person seemed to use his or her time. Write a brief job description for this supervisor based on what he or she actually does. As part of this description identify primary job objectives and major responsibilities and tasks.
2. Review official documents and job descriptions for supervisors in your school. Contrast these with what your supervisor is actually doing.

CHAPTER 3

THE ORGANIZATIONAL ENVIRONMENT FOR SUPERVISION

Our concern in this chapter is with those actions initiated by the supervisor that are concerned with the more organizational aspects of the school. Ultimately the purpose of supervision is to enhance educational programs and instructional effectiveness in the school. These educational concerns are very much influenced by broader characteristics that make up the school's organizational subsystem. Humanism in educational programs' design and implementation, for example, depends upon humanism in organizational design and school structure. This chapter deals selectively with the application of analytical concepts from organizational theory. The language of organizational theory will be foreign to many but worth deciphering, for the ideas are important to understanding the context of modern supervision.

THE SCHOOL AS A COMPLEX ORGANIZATION

We live in an organized world and the world is full of organizations. To quote from a recent book on organization: "Children are born into the physical confines of large medical organizations—hospitals—spend much of their growing years in even larger organizations—schools—and graduate, most of them, into the employ of even larger businesses or government organizations. Many of our large high schools are as populous as small towns, universities are veritable cities, and multinational corporations are virtual nation states."[1]

Romantic vestiges of the little red schoolhouse still exist in America, but most schools, like most organizations, have experienced phenomenal growth in size, areas serviced, and professional complexity. The emergence and spread of the large high school, for example, has accelerated to the point where this unit dominates American secondary education. The operation of the large high school is usually characterized by an emphasis on conserving resources through sophisticated management techniques,

---

[1]H. Randolf Bobbitt, Jr., Robert Breinholt, Robert Doktor, and James McNaul, *Organizational Behavior: Understanding and Predicting*, Englewood Cliffs, N.J.: Prentice-Hall, 1974, p. 1.

scientific staff utilization, computerized scheduling, diverse program offerings, and a variety of student services. Elementary schools share many of these features, though on a smaller scale.

Modern organizations are characterized by a high degree of specialization as well as by size. Schools are not unlike other organizations in this regard in that they have their share of experts who claim monopolies over certain aspects of the management system (directors, vice-principals, division heads for instructional units, student personnel administrators, finance experts, and so on) as well as over certain aspects of the technical system (subject-matter specialists, hardware experts, early childhood-disadvantaged-compensatory education specialists, and sociopsychological practitioners, for example).[2] The numerous new positions and functional roles that have appeared in the last 2 decades in American education have made schools, as organizations, more complex.

In larger communities, the diversity of the schools' goals, combined with the large number of employees, often makes them comparable in complexity with other organizations. Size in itself, however, is not a sufficient criterion for identifying complexity. Schools are complex primarily because of the sophistication of their technology, the diversification of their goals, the varied nature of their tasks, and their patterns of structure.

BUREAUCRATIC ELEMENTS AND TENDENCIES IN SCHOOLS

What does the word "bureaucracy" mean to you? Chances are, this word conjures up negative feelings and reactions from most Americans. The antibureaucracy bias, unfortunately, limits and inhibits rational discussion of the positive and negative bureaucratic characteristics of schools. We perhaps contribute to this bias by designating schools as either bureaucratically oriented or professionally oriented. For the purposes of this discussion, the bureaucratic designation for schools is used in a negative sense, in that human resources supervision will tend not to thrive there. The professional designation for schools is used in a positive sense to indicate an ideal environment for supervision. Yet underlying these perspectives, the authors recognize that schools are actually on a continuum extending from more bureaucratic to less bureaucratic. We also concede that except for large high schools and for large school districts, schools, when compared with many other community institutions, seem considerably less bureaucratic.

The person responsible for introducing the concept of bureaucracy, with its accompanying characteristics, to the political and social science literature was Max Weber. He believed that "the decisive reason for the advance of bureaucratic organization has always been its purely technical superiority over other forms of organization."[3] Weber's ideal bureaucracy is characterized as follows: (1) the division of

---

[2]The terms "management systems" and "technical systems" are used, after Parsons, to differentiate between the administrative sphere and the educotechnical sphere. See Talcott Parsons, "Some Ingredients of a General Theory of Organization," in Andrew W. Halpin (ed.), *Administrative Theory in Education,* Chicago: University of Chicago, Midwest Administration Center, 1958.

[3]Max Weber, "Bureaucracy," in Hans Gerth and C. Wright Mills (eds.), *From Max Weber,* New York: Oxford, 1946, p. 214.

labor and the specific allocation of responsibility; (2) reliance on fairly exact hierarchical levels of graded authority; (3) administrative thought and action based on written policies, rules, and regulations; (4) an impersonal, universalistic bureaucratic environment for all inhabitants; and (5) the development and longevity of administrative careers.[4]

The extent to which schools follow the bureaucratic model varies, of course, from school to school. Yet all schools exhibit some bureaucratic tendencies.[5] A comparison of general bureaucratic characteristics and bureaucratic tendencies of schools follows:

Weber

Characteristics of Bureaucracy	*Applied to Schools*
1. Organization tasks are distributed among the various positions as official duties. Implied is a clear-cut division of labor among positions, which makes possible a high degree of specialization. Specialization, in turn, promotes expertness among the staff both directly and by enabling the organization to hire employees on the basis of their technical qualifications.	1. The school organization has clearly been influenced by the need for specialization and the division of tasks. The division of the school into elementary and secondary units; the establishment of science, mathematics, music, and other departments within a school; the introduction of guidance programs and psychological services; and, indeed, the separation of the administrative function from the teaching function all represent responses to this need.
2. The positions or offices are organized into a hierarchial authority structure. In the usual case this hierarchy takes on the shape of a pyramid, wherein each official is responsible for his subordinates' decisions and actions as well as his own to the superior above him in the pyramid, and wherein each official has authority over the officials under him. The scope of authority of superiors over subordinates is clearly circumscribed.	2. The school organization has developed a clearly defined and rigid hierarchy of authority. Although the term "hierarchy" is seldom used in the lexicon of the educational administrator, the practices to which it refers are prevalent. The typical organization chart is intended specifically to clarify lines of authority and channels of communication. Even in the absence of such a chart, school employees have a clear conception of the nature of the hierarchy in their school systems. In fact, rigid adherence to hierarchical principles has been stressed to the point that failure to adhere to recognized lines of authority is viewed as the epitome of immoral organizational behavior.
3. A formally established system of rules and regulations governs official decisions and actions. In principle the operations in such administrative organizations involve the application of these general regulations to particular cases. The regulations ensure the uniformity of operations and, together with the authority structure, make possible the coordination of various activities. They also provide for continuity in operations regardless of changes of personnel, thus promoting a stability lacking . . . in charismatic movements.	3. The school organization has leaned heavily upon the use of general rules to control the behavior of members of the organization and to develop standards which would assure reasonable uniformity in the performance of tasks. Whether they have taken the form of

---

[4]Max Weber, *Theory of Social and Economic Organization,* A. M. Henderson and T. Parsons (trans.), New York: Oxford, 1947, pp. 333–336.
[5]Any list of items that characterize or describe bureaucracy in reference to "ideal type" is limited in that no one organization fits the description exactly.

4. Officials are expected to assume an impersonal orientation in their contacts with clients and with other officials. Clients are to be treated as cases, the officials being expected to disregard all personal considerations and to maintain complete emotional detachment, and subordinates are to be treated in a similar impersonal fashion. The social distance between hierarchical levels and that between officials and their clients is intended to foster such formality. Impersonal detachment is designed to prevent the personal feelings of officials from distorting their rational judgment in carrying out their duties.

5. Employment within the organization constitutes a career for officials. Typically an official is a full-time employee and looks forward to a lifelong career in the agency. Employment is based on the technical qualifications of the candidate rather than on political, family, or other connections. Usually such qualifications are tested by examination or are verified by certificates that demonstrate the candidate's educational attainment—college degrees, for example. Such educational qualifications create a certain amount of class homogeneity among officials, since relatively few persons of working-class origin have college degrees, although their number is increasing. Officials are appointed to positions, not elected, and thus are dependent on superiors in the organization rather than on a body of constituents. After a trial period officials gain tenure of position and are protected against arbitrary dismissal. Remuneration is in the form of a salary, and pensions are provided after retirement. Career advancements are "according to seniority or to achievement or both."[6]

policy manuals, rules and regulations, staff handbooks, or some other type of document, general rules have been used extensively to provide for the orderly induction of new employees into the organization and to eliminate capricious behavior on the part of all school personnel, including administrators and members of boards of education.

4. Despite frequent proclamations regarding togetherness and democracy, the school organization has made extensive application of Weber's principle of impersonality in organizational relationships. Authority has been established on the basis of rational considerations rather than on the basis of charismatic qualities or traditional imperatives; interpersonal interactions have tended to be functionally specific rather than functionally diffuse; and official relationships have been governed largely by universalistic, as contrasted with particularistic, considerations. Thus, by operating in a spirit of "formalistic impersonality," the typical school system has succeeded, in part, in separating organizational rights and obligations from the private lives of individual employees.

5. Employment in the educational organizations has been based upon technical competence and has constituted for most members a professional career. Promotions have been determined by seniority and by achievement; tenure has been provided; and fixed compensation and retirement benefits have been assured.[7]

[6]Peter M. Blau and W. Richard Scott, *Formal Organizations: A Comparative Approach,* San Francisco: Chandler, 1962, pp. 32–33. Copyright ©1962 by Chandler Publishing Company.
[7]Max G. Abbott, "Hierarchical Impediments to Innovation in Educational Organizations," in M. G. Abbott and John Lovell (eds.), *Change Perspectives in Educational Administration,* Auburn, Ala.: Auburn University School of Education, 1965, pp. 44–45.

BUREAUCRATIC DYSFUNCTION

The modern organization is seen by some people as a marvel of accomplishment and efficiency, and by others as a beast that dehumanizes the spirit, cripples creativity, and warps the personality. Supervisors should not be advocates or enemies of organizations but rather should accept the reality that most schools are fairly complex organizations and as such have benefits and costs. Certain goals, objectives, and educational activities can be successfully pursued only in an organized setting, but others suffer somewhat because of this organized setting. Are the benefits worth the cost? Can the costs be lived with? Are the benefits of long-term value? Are some costs so high that benefits need to be forsaken? These are important questions for supervisors.

Bureaucracy provides us with costs and benefits. Its benefits are in the orderliness and efficiency that it brings to the schools. Its costs are in its deterministic and programming characteristics, which often result in rigid and impersonal organizational structures. The basic dimensions of bureaucracy seem less offensive than the excessive application of its underlying assumptions of rationality by many administrators and supervisors. Cyert and March,[8] March and Simon,[9] and Thompson,[10] for example, suggest that a basic fallacy behind early attempts to study organizations has been our tendency to view them as rational structures. In this context, we have assumed that problem-solving activity in schools included carefully delineating *all* the alternative solutions to a given problem, anticipating the effects of these solutions to a given problem, and weighing each of the alternatives systematically. The alternative with the highest score is then chosen as the best solution. This process represents a most formidable task, quite beyond the capabilities of all but superhumans and superorganizations. Indeed, one needs to exercise caution when viewing schools as maximizing organizations. People tend to seek not the best needle in a haystack, but rather one that satisfies the reason for their search. Schools tend to seek not maximizing solutions to their problems, but rather solutions that they can accept as satisfying current needs. *Organizations are notoriously "satisficing" as they follow their own impulses,* and in this sense the bureaucratic image of rational organization seems not to approximate reality.

It should be pointed out, however, that though schools may be better characterized as "satisficing" than as maximizing organizations, this does not preclude their ability to value and strive for that which is good, just, and excellent. Indeed, basic to the human resources view is the acceptance of the human capacity to set goals, to believe, and to strive, even though it seems afflicted somewhat by this "satisficing" tendency.[11] Weber's concept of bureaucracy provides a framework for prescribing action, but much of what is intended by administrators and supervisors may result in unanticipated reactions from the human organization and dysfunctional consequences for the school.

[8]Richard M. Cyert and James G. March, *A Behavioral Theory of the Firm,* Englewood Cliffs, N.J.: Prentice-Hall, 1963.
[9]James G. March and Herbert A. Simon, *Organizations,* New York: Wiley, 1958.
[10]James Thompson, *Organizations in Action,* New York: McGraw-Hill, 1968.
[11]See, for example, Thomas J. Sergiovanni, "The Odyssey of Organizational Theory in Education: Implications for Humanizing Education," in Richard H. Weller (ed.), *Humanistic Education: Visions and Realities,* Berkeley, Calif.: McCutchan, 1977, pp. 197–232.

It is difficult to conceive of any supervisor consciously intending school dysfunction. The actions of supervisors are undoubtedly well intended when such dysfunction does occur, but working under the norms of rationality typically associated with the bureaucratic view, they may be unaware of the possibility of unanticipated results.

We discuss in detail in the last section of this chapter the nature of dysfunction that contributes to teacher militancy, student militancy, and other symptoms of general disengagement between and among teachers, administrators, and students. Here, our discussion will be limited to only one aspect of the problem—what we intend to accomplish and do not intend to accomplish as we work to increase control over the achievement of school goals through an emphasis on *reliability, delegation of authority*, and the use of *universal impersonal rules*.[12] Each of these variables is a crucial component of the ideal bureaucracy.

EMPHASIS ON RELIABILITY

As administrators and supervisors attempt to increase control over achievement of the school's goals, they frequently work to increase reliability in decision-making processes and in behavior of teachers and students. This is often accomplished by instituting and implementing policies, standard operating procedures, rules, and regulations to guide behavior within the human organization. Uniformity of behavior is seen as a powerful means to move large numbers of people toward goals, with a minimum amount of confusion and conflict.

Organizational and client reactions to an emphasis on reliability of behavior through the development of rules is illustrated in Figure 3-1.[13] The intended result of reliability through rules is uniform and programmed decision making. This in turn decreases the search for alternatives to problems and results in more programmed behavior on the part of supervisors. The entire system also provides supervisors with a mechanism that permits them to escape personal accountability for their actions. If teachers do not like rules enforced by supervisors, they blame the rules structure or the system. With reference to classroom rules, it is presumed that students will vent hostility on the rules, the system, or the establishment, rather than on the teacher when he or she enforces dress codes, gum-chewing regulations, marking policies, and other policies characteristic of a "tyranny of rules." Supervisors optimistically work under the same assumption in applying the rules to teachers.[14] (tyranny of rules)

The unanticipated consequences of an emphasis on reliability are described by Merton as (1) increases in the visibility of power and authority that supervisors have by virtue of position; (2) increases in levels of dissatisfaction and frustration of clients; (3) resistance, complaints, militancy, and conspiracy among clients as a result of this

---

[12]This discussion relies heavily on James G. March and Herbert A. Simon's discussion of the Merton, Selznick, and Gouldner formulations, which appears in *Organizations*, New York: Wiley, 1958, pp. 36–47.
[13]This model and the three that follow are adapted from March and Simon, op. cit., pp. 36–47.
[14]We do not suggest that unanticipated consequences always occur. Such consequences may or may not occur, depending upon a number of contingency variables. In this case, where egalitarian values are strong, clients will resent increases in visible power by superordinates. Where egalitarian values are not strong, the unanticipated consequences are less likely to occur. The same caution applies as well to the Selznick and Gouldner formulations that follow.

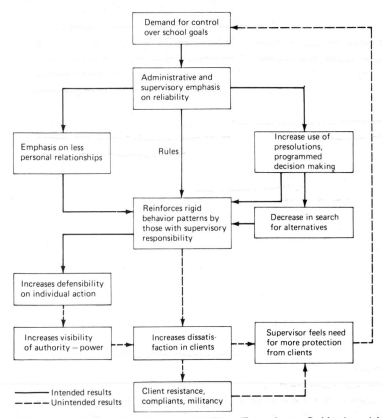

Figure 3-1 Merton: Emphasis on reliability. *(From James G. March and Herbert A. Simon,* Organizations, *New York: Wiley, 1958.)*

dissatisfaction and frustration; (4) a need felt by supervisors for more protection from client hostility, which (5) results in an increase in control; and so the cycle continues. This is an example of a school getting better and getting worse at the same time.

EMPHASIS ON DELEGATION OF AUTHORITY

Schools have been formally characterized by a division of labor since the introduction of the graded system. As professional and technical skill expands, the division of tasks becomes eclipsed by personal and professional specialization. Both represent a form of delegation of authority in that division carries with it some autonomy and responsibility for action. The rationale for delegation is that the competency of the specialist will be utilized in order to increase his or her performance and thus close the gap between performance and school goals. In the large high school the typical form of delegation is found in departmentalization. Selznick describes organizational and client reaction to delegation of authority and division of labor in Figure 3-2.

The danger of departmentalization, delegation, and division is the emergence of

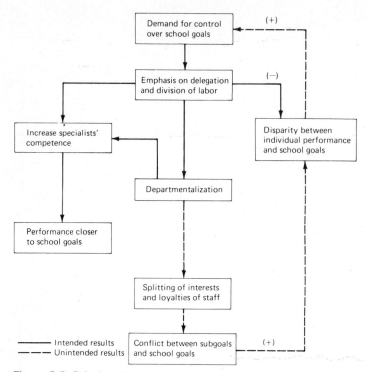

Figure 3-2 Selznick: Emphasis on delegation. *(From James G. March and Herbert A. Simon,* Organizations, *New York: Wiley, 1958.)*

Tendency is for each dept to assy be concerned with itself, it warred redaenes around Sci dept.

subgoals for the newly formed subgroups. As these subgoals become internalized, they tend to assume priority over the total school mission. Some of this is natural, of course, particularly at budget time, but over the long run such goal conflict actually lowers the performance of the total school goals. A number of variables tend to increase or decrease the possibility of unanticipated consequences of delegation as described by Selznick. If total school goals, for example, are remote or are beyond realizing, teachers tend to focus on their own department or grade-level goals as they seek guides to their professional performance.

High school departments, grade levels in elementary schools, bureaus in the central office, special teacher groups, the new academic and vocational division units (divisions of humanities, social science, physical science, vocational education, and so on) appearing as substitutes for departments in many high schools, schools within the school, teaching teams, and the like, all run the risk of negative consequences as described by Selznick.

EMPHASIS ON GENERAL AND IMPERSONAL RULES

The literature is nearly unanimous in suggesting to administrators and others that the legitimacy of their supervisory role as perceived by subordinates is largely a function of low visibility of power (nonauthoritarianism) and low levels of interpersonal tension. As a result of this, those in authority tend to rely on the use of general and impersonal rules in order to regulate or modify the behavior of subordinates. This phenomenon and its interesting potential consequences are described by Gouldner in Figure 3-3.

Gouldner's model portrays the inherent dangers in relying on general-impersonal rules. It suggests that when supervisors attempt to decrease power visibility and interpersonal tension in order to obtain satisfaction and compliance in teachers through the use of general rules, they obtain results opposite to those intended. When one wishes to regulate the behavior of a few through the use of rules that apply to all, one announces and legitimizes *minimum* organizational expectations for everyone. This in turn may lead to teachers focusing on or meeting minimum requirements exclusively, which often results in reduced performance. Any reduction in performance is likely to receive an organizational response in the form of close supervision. Close supervision tends to increase power visibility and interpersonal tension. This tends to decrease the legitimacy of supervision, particularly in egalitarian cultures such as ours, and decreases teacher satisfaction. The model works remarkably well when applied to classroom management, with students as clients.

The likelihood of the Gouldner reaction is considerably reduced if members have high commitment and loyalty to the school and have largely internalized the goals of the school. One of the dangers of discussing examples of unanticipated consequences is that the simple examples we use might be viewed as fixed relationships. There are numerous variables—many still undiscovered—that have an effect as to whether one or another of the models presented will come out as we have described. Perhaps in summary it is

Intended results
Unintended results

Figure 3-3 Gouldner: Emphasis on general and impersonal rules. *(From James G. March and Herbert A. Simon,* Organizations, *New York: Wiley, 1958.)*

sufficient to caution that seemingly simple administrative-supervisory acts, however well intended, have complex and often negative ramifications in the human organization of the school and in the school itself. Such ramifications can be reduced by viewing the school more realistically as an organization that possesses some bureaucratic characteristics but that in reality is far less rational in organization, structure, and functioning than is typically assumed.

PROFESSIONAL ELEMENTS AND TENDENCIES IN SCHOOLS

Although the school contains many bureaucratic characteristics, it possesses some distinguishing characteristics common to professional organizations as well.

Professional organizations, or more appropriately those that are professionally oriented, tend to differ from other organizations primarily in the nature of their authority and power systems. This type of organization is characterized by the development and application of a pluralistic power structure that is (1) dispersed throughout the organization on the basis of ability and competence; (2) dynamic, in the sense that it shifts from person to person and from time to time on the basis of task; (3) interdependent, in that usually coalitions of individuals are needed to marshal sufficient competence to command authority at a given time; and (4) functional, in that it tends not to keep well in storage but needs to be constantly examined for "goodness of fit" in terms of competence and task. The professionally oriented organization tends to rely on task-oriented rather than people-oriented power bases.[15]

Professionally oriented people can be characterized as having (1) considerable advanced formal preparation; (2) skills not readily available in others, including other professionals; (3) a commitment to their profession, discipline, or area that often assumes priority over a commitment to their place of employment; and (4) an interest in a reward system that emphasizes growth and development, achievement, and responsibility but does not ignore bread-and-butter items such as security and salary.

Not all teachers can be described as professionals, but many can. Teachers in some schools have outdistanced them in moving toward professionalization. Where this is the case, we are confronted with a large number of professionally oriented employees who are expected to operate and grow in schools that are by and large bureaucratically oriented.

AN AXIOMATIC THEORY OF ORGANIZATIONS

At this point we have established that most schools and school districts can be described as fairly complex organizations that contain both bureaucratic and professional characteristics. But schools vary in the extent to which one or another of these characteristics is emphasized. In this section an *axiomatic theory of organization* is

[15]Like any "rule" or "truism," this one has exceptions. As competency becomes established in people—that is, as their professional reputation increases—their authority base may shift to themselves as people (who they are rather than what they can contribute) or may include themselves as people (who they are and what they can contribute). At the group level, if one pessimistically applies "Michel's iron law of oligarchy" to this process, one is led to conclude that what starts as ability authority soon turns into status authority.

presented as a useful framework for describing the professionally oriented school, contrasting it with the bureaucratically oriented school, and describing an organizational system of interaction that helps to map the sociological environment of schools for supervision.

THE STRUCTURAL-FUNCTIONAL SYSTEM

Organizations have structures and functions. Emphasizing some structures contributes more to certain functions than others. Further, when some structures are emphasized others are de-emphasized. Knowing the relationships between and among organizational structures and functions can provide supervisors with powerful understandings and tools for action.

Gerald Hage has proposed a theory of organizations that maps out these relationships very effectively.[16] His theory identifies, describes, and charts patterns of interaction between eight key components found in schools and other organizations. Four of these components are *structural* and constitute the means by which schools organize to achieve ends. Structurally, schools, departments, and units are concerned with degrees of centralization, formalization, stratification, and complexity as means to achieve ends. Four other components are *functional* and constitute categories within which school ends might be sorted. Functionally, schools, departments, and units are concerned with the emphasis given to production, efficiency, adoption, and satisfaction goals. The structural and functional characteristics of organization are described as follows:

THE SCHOOL'S STRUCTURAL-FUNCTIONAL SYSTEM

Structure-Organizational Means

Complexity This refers to how specialized the school is organizationally and administratively as well as to the degree of professional and technical specialization which exists in the teaching staff. Complexity is concerned with *specialization in people*, not in jobs or tasks. The heart surgeon is a person specialist, the assembly line worker is a task specialist. Normally, the teacher who is an expert on constitutional government is a person specialist, but normally the teacher who teaches nothing but sophomore American history is a task specialist. The more professional the staff, the more complex the organization. The more complex the organization, the more influence professionals have in decisions relating to their work.

Centralization The extent to which levels of decision making correspond to predetermined hierarchical arrangements or organizational charts determines the school's centralization tendencies. When responsibility and authority for important decision making is dispersed throughout the school we have low centralization. When important decision making is primarily the prerogative of the central office or principal, we have high centralization. Schools can be characterized by low centralization with regard to adults (teachers heavily involved) but high centralization with regard to students (students not involved).

Formalization This refers to the extent a school relies on standardized rules and

[16]This discussion is based primarily on Gerald Hage, "An Axiomatic Theory of Organizations," *Administrative Science Quarterly*, vol. 10, no. 3, pp. 289–320, December 1965.

regulations or standard operating procedures in order to increase uniformity in decision making and similarity in behavior. High formalization is related to high centralization because it programs the decision making of teachers, students, and often administrators, and funnels upward any situations which are varied and cannot be accounted for by the rules or by standard operating procedures.

Stratification This refers to the amount of status differences which exist between and among hierarchical levels in the school. As status differences increase, that is, as rights and privileges of people at one level increase over those at other levels, stratification increases.

Function-Organizational Ends

Production This refers to school output which can be counted and easily measured. The number of students graduated, the number of courses offered, the number of Carnegie units accumulated, the number of pages read or problems completed are examples of production. *Production does not refer to quality.* When schools are more concerned with the quality of services they render to students, and work to improve this quality as opposed to increasing the *number* of services rendered or the *number* of clients served, they are de-emphasizing production.

Efficiency This refers to costs per unit of output. Costs include not only money, but utilization of staff, time, materials, and space as well. A teacher-student ratio of 35 to 1 is more efficient than one of 25 to 1.

Adaptiveness This refers to the school's ability to respond and its emphasis on responding to changing professional and societal environments. An adaptive school is one which utilizes the most advanced professional and technical knowledge and know-how and whose educational program adjusts to changing student needs.

Satisfaction This refers to the extent the school focuses on the worth of its human organization as a manifest school goal. Need fulfillment and professional and personal growth and development of teaching staff are considered legitimate and important goals which are ranked with student learning, growth, and development.

The eight structural-functional characteristics of schools are related in fairly predictable ways. For example, as a school department or unit increases its emphasis on *centralized* control and decision making, it is likely to become more *formalized* and its *stratification* system is likely to become more pronounced. At the same time, its emphasis on *complexity,* or person autonomy and specialization, will decrease. Higher centralization, formalization, and stratification and lower complexity are very likely to increase the school's *production* and *efficiency* levels, but the school will become less responsive and *adaptive* and people will become less *satisfied.*

The basic propositions of the theory as proposed by Hage are as follows:

The higher the centralization, the higher the production.
The higher the formalization, the higher the efficiency.
The higher the centralization, the higher the formalization.
The higher the stratification, the lower the job satisfaction.
The higher the stratification, the higher the production.
The higher the stratification, the lower the adaptiveness.
The higher the complexity, the lower the centralization.[17]

[17]Ibid., pp. 297–299.

Perhaps the easiest way to understand the relationship between and among the eight organizational dimensions is to view them as being in two groups—one more characteristic of bureaucratically oriented schools and the other, of professionally oriented schools. The group associated with bureaucratically oriented schools is composed of centralization, formalization, stratification, production, and efficiency. The professional group is composed of complexity, adaptability, and satisfaction. When one dimension in the bureaucratic group increases, each of the others with the same sign also increases. Those with the opposite sign decrease. The same relationships hold for dimensions in the professional group—changes in one produce similar changes in each of the others. *Further, any change in the bureaucratic group produces opposite changes in the professional group and vice versa.* All the groups are shown below (L =lower; H =higher):

Bureaucratically Oriented Schools

L	complexity	L	adaptiveness
H	centralization	H	production
H	formalization	H	efficiency
H	stratification	L	job satisfaction

Professionally Oriented Schools

H	complexity	H	adaptiveness
L	centralization	L	production
L	formalization	L	efficiency
L	stratification	H	job satisfaction

THE IDEAL SCHOOL TYPES SUMMARIZED

Bureaucratically oriented schools tend to be precise in defining roles, obligations, and rights and relations (high formalization and high stratification); are detailed in prescribing rules and regulations in seeking to program decision making for teachers and students (high formalization); seek to funnel decision making that is varied and unpredictable to the top while standardizing decision making at lower levels (high centralization); and are concerned with processing the largest number of students at the least cost in terms of personnel, money, equipment, space, and the like (high production and high efficiency). Since all the structural features of schools are interdependent, a change in one variable results in changes in other variables. Thus, bureaucratically oriented schools, while increasing in formalization, centralization, and the like, display a low tolerance for innovativeness and change (low adaptiveness); an unwillingness to permit power to be diffused to lower organizational levels and thus an unwillingness to encourage authority based on ability rather than simply position (low complexity); and thereby encourage a reluctance to provide teachers with meaningful reward systems that will permit them to function as respected, autonomous, and responsible professionals (low job satisfaction).

The ideal professional type of school stresses adaptiveness rather than production and is characterized by its complexity and the level of job satisfaction available to its members. The emergence and spread of professionally oriented organizations in education are a reflection of four closely related trends in teaching as an occupation: (1) the increased specialization of semiprofessional and professional workers; (2) the quality and sophistication of their academic and professional training; (3) the knowledge explosion that has occurred in virtually all curriculum areas, teaching fields, and educational technologies; and (4) the belief (real or imagined) that schools as they are currently functioning do not meet their commitment to provide all students with an intellectual, social, and emotional experience appropriate for growth in society as we know it today or in the years ahead. These trends are compounded by a prevalent desire for autonomy that seems to permeate every aspect of our society.

The professionally oriented large school, for example, is one that seeks to accommodate the need for expression that professional workers require. It is complex (in terms of its administrative diversification as well as the degree of personal specialization that exists in the staff) and highly innovative, and provides teachers, students, and other members with opportunities for their personal as well as professional fulfillment. This type of school tends also to be wasteful and expensive;[18] it ignores or circumscribes hierarchically defined status and authority systems; and it tolerates no more than a minimum use of rules and other forms of programmed decision making. Advocates of the professional model argue that the production emphasis of the bureaucratic model is incompatible with providing high-quality education for youth and is in fact damaging and demoralizing to teachers and students. Schools seem to be shifting from orientations we describe as bureaucratic to orientations we describe as professional. That professionalization is being realized at different rates for different schools, school systems, and communities should not be allowed to mask the long-term trend.

A CONTINGENCY APPROACH TO ORGANIZATIONAL STRUCTURE

A popular organizational principle to which we subscribe is that *form should follow function.* Form follows function when the school is organized and operated in a way that facilitates the goals, objectives, and activities of people. Function follows form when the work of people is modified to fit the structure and operating style of the organization. In reality, however, the relationship between form and function is less direct. Indeed, the two interact constantly, with each making demands on the other. At any given moment function may be determined by the demands of form, but over the long haul supervisors need to work at keeping the balance in favor of form following

[18]When the same standards are applied to professionally oriented and bureaucratically oriented schools, the former are found lacking in the efficiency category. In terms of quality of output, however, the professionally oriented school seems immeasurably more able.

function. Organizational structure is the central nervous system of the school, and when it is functioning properly, it permits the organization to perform a variety of related motions and activities—often simultaneously. But like any nervous system, it has limits. Some motions and activities are modified or prohibited because they make excessive demands on the school's nervous system—its organizational structure. Take the principles of individualized instruction and teacher autonomy, for example. The school can be and should be much more responsive to, and flexible in, providing teachers with discretion and autonomy. But we cannot individualize to the point at which a separate school would be created for each student or each teacher. To do so would, in essence, destroy the school as an organized institution.

The overall purposes and functions of the school seem better served by organizational and structural forms described as professionally oriented. These structures seem best able to accommodate the unique characteristics of the technology of educational organizations. "Technology" refers to methods and characteristics associated with the school's professional and instructional subsystem. Adjusting the structure of an organization to fit unique aspects or demands of that organization's technology is a concept associated with sociotechnical theories of organization.[19]

James Thompson, in the tradition of sociotechnical thinking, identifies three major categories of technology: long-linked, mediating, and intensive.

An organization with a long-linked technology is characterized by fixed demands in product, certainty in goals, and programmed activities or, in Thompson's words, "serial interdependence in the sense that act Z can be performed only after successful completion of act Y, which in turn rests on X, and so on".[20] Scientific management in one or another of its forms seems compatible with organizations of this type.

An organization with a mediating technology has as its primary function the linking of clients or customers who are interdependent. Banks, post offices, insurance companies, and telephone utilities are examples of organizations with mediating technologies. In each case the organization is faced with the challenge of handling diverse inputs in standard ways. Borrowers' needs may vary, but standard rules govern the loan. Organizations of this type find needed comfort within the bureaucratic model.

Organizations with intensive technologies bring to bear a variety of resources in order to bring about a change in a particular object. The selection, combination, and order of application of these resources, however, are determined on the basis of interaction with this object. When the object in question is human, according to Thompson, the intensive technology is regarded as therapeutic, as is the case in a general hospital. In Thompson's words, "the intensive technology is a custom technology. Its successful employment rests in part on the availability of all the capacities potentially needed, but equally on the appropriate custom combination of selected capacities as required by the individual case or project."[21] The professionally

[19]See, for example, Paul Lawrence and Jay Lorsch, "Differentiation and Integration in Complex Organizations," *Administrative Science Quarterly*, vol. 12, no. 1, 1967; Joan Woodward, *Industrial Organization: Theory and Practice*, London: Oxford, 1965; and F. E. Emery and E. L. Trist, "The Causal Texture of Organizational Environments," *Human Relations*, vol. 18, no. 3, 1963. This discussion of sociotechnical theory follows that which appears in T. J. Sergiovanni, op. cit.
[20]James D. Thompson, *Organizations in Action*, New York: McGraw-Hill, 1967, p. 16.
[21]Ibid., p. 18.

oriented view of organizations, particularly as articulated by human resources theorists, seems most suited to intensive technologies.

SOCIOTECHNICAL THEORY AND THE SCHOOL

The sociotechnical and other contingency theorists differ from the classical-management and behavioral theorists in that they deny that there is a universal image of effective supervision and organization. Indeed, in their view, the effectiveness question is dependent upon institutional-level demands for adaptiveness and perform-ance on the one hand and unique properties of the organization's professional subsystem (technology) on the other. The sociotechnical view elevates the importance of a school's technology, or professional subsystem, and accords it the positions of key determiner of organizational structure and equal partner in the mediation between the organization and its institutional level. Indeed, this view emphasizes the principle that form follows function.

What are the patterns of institutional-level demands for the school, and what technical properties do they possess? Schools are complex organizations in that they pursue a variety of goals and are subjected to multiple expectations. Variability exists between schools with regard to which expectations are emphasized, but all schools feel some pressure to perform and adapt. Performance-oriented expectations are, for example, concerned with the achievement of predetermined objectives[22] and with the learning of culturally defined meanings.[23] Schools and communities vary in the extent to which they define and standardize the core of knowledge that they believe is worth knowing, but some core exists nevertheless. Adaptive-oriented expectations are more concerned, for example, with intrinsic objectives, or learning for its own value, and with the students' personal meanings. Again variability exists in the extent to which adaptive expectations are emphasized, but recognition is nonetheless always given to the notion that students vary greatly in ability, motivation, values, and interests.

An imbalance currently exists in most schools in favor of emphasis on performance expectations. Here the professional subsystem of the school is likely to approximate the long-linked technology, and scientific-management principles are likely to be appropri-ate. Or in some quarters the adaptive qualities of youngsters are seen as a problem to be dealt with and somehow weakened. Here the school works to take this varied input in student dispositions and mediate it in standardized ways. The professional subsystem of the school is likely to take on mediating technology characteristics, and bureaucratic principles are seen as appropriate.

But schools that take on long-linked, or mediating, qualities in the organization of their professional subsystems still need to deal with the human factor. Waller describes this dilemma as the plight of the teacher who must work in an impersonal, bureaucratic structure but who needs the cooperation of students in order to be effective.[24] Work

[22]Abraham Maslow, "Some Basic Propositions of a Growth and Self Actualizing Psychology," in Arthur Combs (ed.), *Perceiving, Behaving, Becoming,* Washington, D.C.: Association for Supervision and Curriculum Development, 1962.
[23]James MacDonald, "An Image of Man: The Learner Himself," in Ronald Doll (ed.), *Individualized Instruction,* Washington, D.C.: Association for Supervision and Curriculum Development, 1964.
[24]Willard Waller, *The Sociology of Teaching,* New York: Wiley, 1932.

concerns are therefore separated from human concerns and are dealt with sequentially rather than simultaneously, to avoid conflict. Counseling is institutionalized as a special function. Homeroom is the time scheduled for personal concerns. Personal interests are pursued through extracurricular activities or during free time. Recess is the time for fun, and school is the time for work, and so on. These are human relations devices intended to appease social needs so that people will be more accepting of controls with regard to the work of the organization.

Not so common but seen as desirable by many humanists is a school characterized by a clear imbalance in favor of adaptive goals and expectations. Given this imbalance, the school would take on the characteristics of a *simple*-intensive technology, which would be characterized by client feedback and custom tailoring of client services. Clearly this would be a client-centered organization whose survival would depend upon client assurance that his or her specifications, preferences, and needs would be met. Further, since client preferences and needs can be expected to vary, the school would engage in craftlike or tailor-made activities to ensure particularistic products. Some combination of human relations and human resources supervision, perhaps with human relations dominating, might be appropriate for this simple-intensive technology.

But none of these is desirable as the exclusive image of a school. We prefer to view the school as a *complex*-intensive organization characterized by a moderately open system, one with a fairly steady-state flow of input in the form of community expectations, clients, and financial resources, but one that is able to effectively interact with and influence this input. The degree of the school's impact will depend upon the strength of its professional subsystem and upon its having administrators and supervisors who are capable of arguing convincingly on behalf of certain educational-program values and intents.

Since the demands for both performance and adaptability seem reasonable if balanced, an important function of this professional subsystem is to define the balance. If both performance and adaptability are to be honored, then an organizational structure capable of integrating the two must be sought. Such a structure should possess the capacity to shift its form and focus in accordance with a variety of technical-level demands. A school or classroom, for example, would have the capacity to function either simultaneously or sequentially in a long-linked fashion for certain kinds of activities and in a custom-tailored fashion for others.

Consider, for example, one important property of the school's professional subsystem—the nature of goals and objectives. To the extent that it is appropriate for objectives to be predetermined and stated precisely, the instructional system, together with its organizational features, should take on long-linked characteristics in accordance with scientific-management principles. In instances where it is desirable to leave the discovery of objectives entirely to students, a more laissez faire instruction system more in tune with human relations principles might be suitable. And where it is desirable for teachers and students to interact together to establish or discover objectives, human resources concepts would likely be suitable.

Much value exists in viewing the school under the rubrics of sociotechnical thinking as an intensive-complex organization that adjusts its organizational form and educational-program structure according to technical demands. Such an organization would be considered professional in character because of its adaptive capacities.

Further, such adjustments require a distribution of authority and talent throughout the organization, which precludes relying as a matter of policy on standardization, formalization, stratification, centralization, and other traditional bureaucratic characteristics.

An additional professional subsystem property particularly important to human organizations such as schools is the question of values. Schools are normative organizations. People involved in normative organizations are concerned with questions of appropriateness as well as efficiency and efficacy. Indeed, it is not uncommon for the former concern to take precedence over the latter two.

In this sense, then, organization and supervision in education constitute a normative science concerned with the consequences of choice in terms of preferred values.[25] Each of the views of supervision and organization discussed in this chapter has much to contribute to good practice in education, though only human resources theory possesses, in our opinion, the value richness to serve as the overall framework for supervision in the school. Therefore, the extent to which sociotechnical thinking can be applied humanistically in education will depend upon the extent to which its principles are articulated within a broad commitment to the values of human resources theory.

THE SUPERVISOR'S ORGANIZATIONAL RESPONSIBILITIES

The focus of this chapter has been in an area not typically of concern to those with supervisory responsibilities. Yet supervisors are invariably charged with some aspect of change and are required to work for it in constant interaction with the structural-functional system of the school. To be sure, the focuses of supervision are people and program. Supervisors work with other professionals through an educational program to effect positive change in students. Success largely depends upon the realization that this work does not take place in a vacuum. Realism requires that the supervisor not ignore the organizational context of schools. Human resources supervision is dependent upon a realistic appraisal and understanding of the school as an organization.

The sociotechnical view of organizations with its accompanying principle that form follows function requires that the supervisor assume a more active role in organizational matters. The supervisor is in a position to best understand critical aspects of the school's technology and professional subsystem and therefore is in a position to help administrators develop supporting and accommodating organizational structures and to evaluate existing structures to determine how well they fit with the school's educational-program intents and activities.

SUPERVISORY CONFLICT

Supervisors will often find themselves face to face with the stresses and strains that accompany life in formal organizations. Particularly common are strains associated with

---

[25]See, for example, T. J. Sergiovanni and Fred D. Carver, *The New School Executive: A Theory of Administration,* 2d ed., New York: Harper & Row, 1980.

three organizational dilemmas related to professional and bureaucratic roles, ability and authority, and autonomy and coordination.

1. _Professional and bureaucratic role dilemma._ Some evidence seems to exist that contemporary organizations in American society are undergoing a process of simultaneous professionalization and bureaucratization.[26] Corwin[27] suggests that this is indeed the case for schools. He observes that administrators hold primarily bureaucratic expectations for behavior in schools, while teachers hold primarily professional expectations. This comparison is presented in Table 3-1.

[26]Litwak, for example, proposes several models of bureaucracy, one of which is the professional model that combines Weberian concepts with those of the human relations movement. He maintains that this model is most effective where jobs deal with both uniform and nonuniform events or with social skills as well as the traditional knowledge area. Eugene W. Litwak, "Models of Bureaucracy Which Permit Conflict," _The American Journal of Sociology_, vol. 67, no. 3, pp. 177–184, September 1961.

[27]Ronald Corwin, "Professional Persons in Public Organizations," _Educational Administration Quarterly_, vol. 1, no. 3, pp. 1–23, Autumn 1965.

TABLE 3-1
CONTRASTS IN THE BUREAUCRATIC- AND PROFESSIONAL-EMPLOYEE PRINCIPLES OF ORGANIZATION

Organizational characteristics	Bureaucratic-employee expectations	Professional-employee expectations
Standardization		
Routine of work	Stress on uniformity of clients' problems	Stress on uniqueness of clients' problems
Continuity of procedure	Stress on records and files	Stress on research and change
Specificity of rules	Rules stated as universals; and specific	Rules stated as alternatives; and diffuse
Specialization		
Basis of division of labor	Stress on efficiency of techniques; task orientation	Stress on achievement of goals; client orientation
Basis of skill	Skill based primarily on practice	Skill based primarily on monopoly of knowledge
Authority		
Responsibility for decision making	Decisions concerning application of rules to routine problems	Decisions concerning policy in professional matters and unique problems
Basis of authority	Rules sanctioned by the public	Rules sanctioned by legally sanctioned professions
	Loyalty to the organization and to superiors	Loyalty to professional associations and clients
	Authority from office (position)	Authority from personal competence

From Ronald Corwin, "Professional Persons in Public Organizations," _Educational Administration Quarterly_, vol. 1, no. 3, p. 7, Autumn 1965.

In an analysis of school conflict identified through research based on this comparison, Corwin makes the following observation:

> Approximately forty-five percent of all the incidents involved teachers in opposition to members of the administration; about one-fifth of these disputes were "open" discussions involving direct confrontations of parties in an argument or "heated" discussions (as judged by content analysis), or "major incidents" including a third party in addition to those teachers and administrators initially involved; this is a larger number of open conflicts than reported among teachers themselves. About one-half of all incidents involved *groups* of teachers (teachers' organizations in seven percent of the cases).
>
> Twenty-four percent of all conflict incidents fell in the categories of classroom control, curriculum management, and authority in the school; these incidents embraced such issues as the use of proper teaching techniques and procedures, changing the curriculum and selection of textbooks. About half of these involved administrators. Of the 159 incidents that were in the open, about one-fourth were with the administration over these issues of authority.[28]

The higher the professional orientation of teachers, according to Corwin's findings, the higher the rates of conflict. He concludes, "The weight of evidence from this very limited sample suggests that there is a consistent pattern of conflict between teachers and administrators over the control of work, and that professionalization is a militant process."[29] The dilemma for the supervisor is, of course, reconciling for himself or herself and for the human curriculum and its beneficiaries the increasing bureaucratization and professionalism that Corwin and others see as two simultaneous but conflicting thrusts for schools.

2. *The ability-authority dilemma.* This dilemma is a result of a distinction being emphasized in schools between the right to decide and the power and expertise to do. Teachers have, on the basis of authority derived from ability, successfully co-opted many functions previously reserved for administrators. Administrative reaction to increased teacher authority is generally mixed with pessimism and often with fear. Most of what administrators have yielded deals with curriculum and teaching matters, although no administrative responsibility is immune from co-optation on the basis of ability authority.

The dilemma, of course, is how those who administer and supervise as part of their legal responsibility are to maintain control over school developments. Human resources supervision offers clues to solving the dilemma in that it advocates the development and extension of ability monopolies for administrators. These ability monopolies will lie not so much in instructional and curriculum areas but rather in the management, growth, and development of the human organization of the school. The distinction that Parsons makes between the management system and the technical system in organizations seems useful here.[30] Administrators and to some extent

[28] Ibid., p. 12.
[29] Ibid., p. 15.
[30] The terms "management systems" and "technical systems" are used here, after Parsons, to differentiate between the administrative sphere and the educotechnical sphere in schools. See Talcott Parsons, "Some Ingredients of a General Theory of Organization," in Andrew W. Halpin (ed.), *Administrative Theory in Education,* Chicago: University of Chicago, Midwest Administration Center, 1958.

supervisors, on the basis of ability authority, contribute to school goals through the management system. Teachers and to some extent supervisors, on the basis of ability authority, contribute to school goals through the technical system. Human resources supervision recognizes and respects the legitimacy of a number of sources of authority, but it focuses primarily on ability authority.

3. _The autonomy-coordination dilemma._ As teachers become more sophisticated and specialized in terms of professional and academic training, interests, and perform-ance, and as their personal specialization and ability bases expand, teachers increase their demands for autonomy from administrators. Yet as the personal specialization phenomenon increases, teachers become more interdependent in order to achieve school goals. The typical organizational reaction to interdependence among specialists is one of coordination.[31] However, coordination of professional specialists imposes limits on the autonomy of each and is a threat to their ability monopolies. The supervisory dilemma can be reduced to this: How is it possible to cope with a situation in which teachers are becoming more autonomous in their specialization as they become less autonomous in the larger sphere of accomplishing schoolwide goals?

Pusic portrays the drama of professional specialization versus coordination as follows:

> Professional specialization leaves the specialist in possession of the necessary knowledge and skill to perform complex and meaningful activities. He is much less in danger of being separated from the meaning of his work and, therefore, much more independent. He knows his work and does not need to wait for others to assign tasks to him. Still the work of the individual specialist has to be co-ordinated and integrated into larger contexts. An individual physician in a hospital, a social worker in an agency, a scientist in a laboratory, a teacher in a school, an administrator in an office can make their full contribution only as their work is brought into rational relationships with the work of others. The very independence of their individual activities, however, makes co-ordination both more necessary and more difficult. The classical school of administrative science early became aware that the span of control—the number of people to be co-ordinated by one superior—was in inverse proportion to the professional level of the work co-ordinated.[32]

Recognizing the importance of coordination to administrators and to the organiza-tion, Pusic nevertheless sees dangers in overemphasis. Addressing himself to welfare agencies, he makes the following comments:

> The methods of co-ordination practiced within the traditional structure of organization seem to be ill adapted to the task of tying together the work of professional specialists. The work of individuals is co-ordinated within an organization by a hierarchy of superiors who are responsible for the allocation of work tasks to those below them as well as for the control and necessary correction of their work performances. With the increasing complexity of organizations and of the work done by their individual members the hierarchical method of co-ordination and of reports up the line becomes more abundant.

---

[31]The phenomenal growth of directors, staff assistants, and other coordinators in schools seems to substantiate this trend.

[32]Eugen Pusic, "The Political Community and Future of Welfare," in John Morgan (ed.), _Welfare and Wisdom,_ Toronto: University of Toronto Press, 1967, p. 67.

> More time is spent in meetings and other forms of face-to-face contact. More writing and reading for purposes of co-ordination have to be done at all levels. Administrative procedures become more involved, formalities more numerous as the organizational system tries to counteract the centrifugal tendencies of specialization. This increase of co-ordinating activities, however, has to find its place within the fixed time-budget at the disposal of the organization. Co-ordination can ultimately expand only at the expense of the main activity, which is the initial social reason for the existence of the system. More co-ordination means less health work, less social welfare services, less education, less research by the respective organizations. The point of diminishing returns can be clearly seen: it is the moment when the balance between co-ordination and basic activity becomes so unfavorable that organization will no longer be the socially most economical method of human co-operation.[33]

Additional supervisory dilemmas in the organizational context of schools can be identified and discussed. Of particular interest to supervision are the relationships that exist between the demands and needs of organization and those of their human inhabitants. The interface is discussed in the next section, where the school is considered as a social system.

THE SCHOOL AS A SOCIAL SYSTEM

The most widely recognized and perhaps the most useful framework for studying and understanding administrative and supervisory behavior is the social systems analysis developed for educators by Jacob Getzels and Egon Guba.[34] This formulation is reviewed and modified for supervision below.

The social systems theorists[35] view administration and supervision as a social process that occurs within a social system. Process and context can be examined, according to this view, from structural, functional, and operational perspectives. Structurally, administration and supervision are considered to be a series of superordinate-subordinate relationships within a social system. Functionally, this hierarchy of relationships (principal to teacher, teacher to student, and so on) is the basis for allocating and integrating roles, personnel, and facilities to accomplish school goals. Operationally, the process occurs in person-to-person interaction.

The term *social system* is used by Getzels and Guba in a conceptual rather than a descriptive way. They conceive of this system as containing two interdependent but interacting dimensions. The first dimension consists of the *institution,* which is defined in terms of its *roles,* which are in turn defined in terms of *role expectations,* all of which are carefully designed to fulfill the goals of the institution.

---

[33]Ibid., p. 68.

[34]The following discussion is based on a number of sources. Documentation is loose in view of the general familiarity and acceptance of the Getzels and Guba social systems model. See, for example, J. W. Getzels, "A Psycho-sociological Framework for the Study of Educational Administration," *Harvard Educational Review,* vol. 22, pp. 235–246, Fall 1952; J. W. Getzels and E. G. Guba, "Social Behavior and the Administrative Process," *The School Review,* vol. 65, pp. 423–441, 1957; J. W. Getzels, "Administration as a Social Process," in Andrew W. Halpin (ed.), *Administrative Theory in Education,* Chicago: University of Chicago, Midwest Administration Center, 1958; and more recently J. W. Getzels et al., *Educational Administration as a Social Process: Theory, Research, Practice,* New York: Harper & Row, 1968, Especially basic to this discussion is the Getzels and Guba 1957 article.

[35]Cf. Talcott Parsons, *The Social System,* New York: Free Press, 1951.

Institution ⟶ Roles ⟶ Role expectations ⟶ Institutional goal achievement

All institutions have certain characteristics and imperative functions in common:

1. *Institutions have purposes.* They are established to perform certain functions and are legitimized by client groups and societal groups on the basis of these functions. Purposes for schools are generally of two kinds: those that are manifest—the educational and custodial functions that win community and societal support—and those that are latent—the power gratification and growth rewards that members (teachers and administrators) seek.

2. *Institutions are structural.* Institutional goals are achieved through task diversification. Therefore roles are established with appropriate role descriptions. Each role is assigned certain responsibilities and resources, including authority for implementing given tasks. The ideas are conceived and responsibilities allocated in terms of actors, as defined below, rather than of personalities.[36]

3. *Institutions are normative.* Roles serve as norms for the behavior of those who occupy the roles. Each actor or role incumbent is expected to behave in certain predetermined ways in order to retain a legitimate position in the school. Teachers, for example, who adopt modes of behavior typical of the student culture have difficulty in maintaining their legitimate position in the eyes of other teachers, administrators, and perhaps even of students.

4. *Institutions are sanction bearing.* Institutions have at their disposal appropriate positive and negative sanctions for ensuring compliance with established norms. Teachers who are rate-busters in the eyes of other teachers, for example, may be subject to a silent treatment or to a whisper campaign. Those who appear to be deviants to the principal wait longer for school supplies, are given undesirable class assignments, and are swamped with classroom visitations.

The operation of institutions is defined and analyzed in terms of the subunit role. Roles represent the various positions, offices, and status prerogatives that exist within the institution and are themselves defined in terms of role expectations. Roles are generally institutional givens and, therefore, are not formulated to fit one or another personality. Behaviors associated with a given role are arranged on a conceptual continuum extending from those required to those prohibited. Certain behaviors are considered absolutely mandatory (that the teacher at least show up for school), and others are absolutely forbidden (that the teacher not become romantically involved with students). Between these extremes are other behavior patterns—some recommended, others disapproved, but all to varying degrees permissible. Roles are best understood when examined in relation to other roles. The student role helps us to understand the teacher role, and so on.

In the absence of individuals with complex and unique personalities, the organizational dimension described above provides for maximum organizational predictability.

---

[36]A survey of a typical first-grade class on the first day of school will reveal reliable, even though stereotyped, descriptions of the role of principal as compared with the role of teacher.

This aspect of the social system is called the nomothetic dimension. The second aspect, the ideographic dimension, adds the human element to the social system formulation.[37] As the institutional dimension was analyzed in terms of role and expectation, so the individual dimension is similarly analyzed and defined operationally in terms of personality and need disposition.

The ideographic dimension is similar in format (but not in substance) to the nomothetic dimension in that individuals, like institutions, have goals that they express through their personalities and pursue according to their unique need dispositions.

The two dimensions of the social system are assumed to be in constant interaction. In its nomothetic dimension the organization strives to socialize the individual to its own image and ends, while in its ideographic dimension the individual strives to socialize the organization to his or her own image and ends.[38] Behavior, then, in any social system is a function of the interaction between unique personalities and preestablished roles. Conformity to the institution, its roles, and its expectations leads to organizational effectiveness, while conformity to individuals, their personalities, and their need dispositions leads to individual efficiency.

Getzels and Guba identify a number of conflict situations that could potentially result from the organization's interaction with its human inhabitants. Among them are role-personality conflicts that result from a discrepancy between the pattern of expectations attached to a given role and the pattern of need dispositions of the role incumbent. An assistant principal with a high dependence orientation would find a role characterized by autonomous and independent action quite uncomfortable; teachers with a professional and technical need to interact with school policymakers who are defensive, authoritarian, and noncommunicative experience similar role-personality conflict. Multiple but conflicting expectations for the same role are another source of role conflict. Supervisors who are expected by some teachers to visit classes and by others to stay away experience conflict of this type. The young mother-teacher faces role conflict of this type as she struggles to justly fulfill two demanding roles. The school as an organization is frequently subject to role conflict of this type as it attempts to appease multiple and conflicting expectations from its many publics.

[37]Guba describes the process by which the terms *nomothetic* and *ideographic* were chosen for the theory as follows: "The terms 'ideographic' and 'nomothetic' were picked from *Roget's Thesaurus* by me one wintry afternoon when I had nothing better to do than to try to find some new and interesting terms to use in our theory. We justified this at the time by claiming that we had to find terms 'untainted' by value connotations."—E. G. Guba, "Development, Diffusion, and Evaluation," in T. L. Eidell and J. M. Kitchell (eds.), *Knowledge Production and Utilization in Educational Administration,* Eugene, Ore.: Center for the Advanced Study of Educational Administration, 1968, p. 38.
[38]E. W. Bakke, "Concept of the Social Organization," in Mason Haire (ed.), *Modern Organization Theory,* New York: Wiley, 1961, p. 60.

SUMMARY

We have, for illustrative purposes, discussed the school's life as something quite independent from that which results from those who live and work in the school. As the school "becomes alive," it takes on many of the characteristics of a human organism. As such, the school develops a unique organizational personality that is expressed by and, indeed, is imposed upon those who come to live and work within its boundaries. Further, in the absence of more than token human direction and control, the school pursues a series of satellite goals that revolve around the simple but omnipresent need for growth and survival.[39] Within this context the school's goals are generally pursued in a mechanical way, with changes occurring largely because the nature of growth and survival needs change. When changes do occur, they are seemingly unaffected by, and reflect little interest in, the wishes and requirements of the school's human inhabitants, except as such concerns contribute to the school's growth and survival. If left to its own whims, the school evolves into a monolithic structure that captures and uses its human participants to accomplish its, rather than their, ends. This phenomenon is illustrated by the *natural* tendency of schools to adopt conservative perspectives, to exert a major emphasis on maintenance activities, to avoid change, and thereby to avoid controversy and conflict. School conservatism is illustrated by the now-classic Mort studies, which showed a 50-year gap between an educational invention and widespread adoption of that educational practice.[40]

A fundamental concern of supervision is the question of whether schools use people to accomplish organizational ends or whether people use schools to accomplish human ends. This concern is placed in perspective by the following phrase from the *Cardinal Principles of Secondary Education,* 1918: "The objectives must determine the organization or else the organization will determine the objectives."

Human resources supervisors work to develop the human dimension in schools. They are concerned with the appropriateness of school goals, the welfare and growth of school workers, and, indeed, the intellectual, social, and emotional self-actualization of school clients. Such human concerns require the school as an organization to serve its students, unlike traditional supervisory patterns, which required individuals to serve the school.

The purpose of this chapter was to introduce those who supervise to the broader environment within which supervision takes place. The school was described as a complex organization that shares many characteristics of bureaucracy and professionalism. One hazard in viewing the school as a bureaucracy is to attribute to it degrees of rationality that do not match with reality. It was pointed out that schools are more accurately characterized as "satisficing" than as maximizing organizations, but this

---

[39]While *school growth* refers to extension of curricular offerings, school boundaries, size of staff, and the like, it also refers to increases in influence, status, and prestige. *Survival,* for schools, refers to continued community financial and moral support and the avoidance of conflict, controversy, and uncertainty, as well as guaranteed tenure for the present school establishment. Both can be maintained by giving only token attention to a quality educational program.

[40]The Mort studies are summarized in Paul R. Mort, "Studies in Educational Innovation from the Institute of Administrative Research: An Overview," in Matthew B. Miles (ed.), *Innovation in Education,* New York: Teachers College Press, 1964, pp. 317–328.

"satisficing" tendency does not prevent people from valuing and striving for excellence. Indeed, basic to the human resources view is the belief in the human capacity for setting goals, for striving for greater achievement even though people are subjected to "satisficing" limitations.

Professional elements and tendencies in schools were described and contrasted with bureaucratic elements by viewing the school as a structural-functional system. Though it is considered most appropriate for schools to be professionally oriented, a contingency approach to organization, relying on sociotechnical theory, was proposed. The school was then viewed as a social system, and key areas of conflict for supervisors were presented. Discussed were conflicts between professional and bureaucratic values, between the socializing tendency of organizations and individual personality, between ability and authority, and between autonomy and coordination.

STUDY GUIDE

Recall the concepts, ideas, and meanings associated with each of the following phrases and terms included in this chapter. Can you discuss each of them with a colleague and apply them to the supervisory context of your school? If you cannot, review them in the text and record the page number for future reference.

1. Ability-authority conflict _____
2. Axiomatic theory of organization _____
3. Bureaucratic dysfunction _____
4. Educational subsystem _____
5. Intensive technology _____
6. Maximizing _____
7. Nomothetic _____
8. Professional-bureaucratic conflict _____
9. Social system formulation _____
10. Structural-functional system _____
11. Unanticipated consequences _____
12. Autonomy-coordination conflict _____
13. Bureaucratically oriented school _____
14. Contingency approach _____
15. Ideographic _____
16. Long-linked technology _____
17. Mediating technology _____
18. Organizational subsystem _____
19. Satisficing _____
20. Sociotechnical theory _____
21. Technology of schools _____

EXERCISES

1. This chapter emphasizes the negative aspects of bureaucracy in schools. But bureaucracy provides us with benefits too. Consider, for example, an inexperienced teacher in conference with parents who are influential in the community (perhaps the local banker and spouse, a former teacher). How can the school as an organization with bureaucratic characteristics help provide this teacher with authority?

2. "People tend to seek not the best needle in a haystack, but rather one that satisfies the reason for their search." This metaphor was used to suggest the "satisficing" rather than maximizing nature of decision making in schools. Carefully observe one or two administrators or supervisors for a week. Describe the extent to which decisions they make are "satisficing."
3. Prepare a two-page case study involving supervisors and teachers in a situation that illustrates the ability-authority dilemma.

Chapter 4

BUILDING A CLIMATE FOR SUPERVISION

Before we begin this discussion of school organizational climate and its implications for supervision, let us examine some familiar groups and organizations. Take a moment to recall the one group or organization of which you were a member or that you know about that seemed best to encourage members to learn, solve problems, and take reasonable chances. Now let us reverse our thinking and recall the one group or organization that most hindered lealrning, problem solving, and moderate risk taking of members. If you did not choose a school group or organization in your analysis, try repeating the exercise limiting yourself to schools. Briefly describe the organizations or groups recalled. Who were the members? What was to be accomplished? How did the people work together? How did the people treat one another? What were the leaders like? Using the organizational climate questionnaire depicted in Exhibit 4-1, evaluate each of the organizations or groups recalled. Start first with the more effective learning organizations or groups. Circle the number for each category that best describes this organization. Now evaluate the less effective organization or group using check marks to indicate responses. Compare your circled and checked responses.

By describing organizations and groups that help and hinder learning and then evaluating them, you have been describing and measuring organizational climate. The seven item categories shown in Exhibit 4-1 are composed of several dimensions that social psychologists have found to be important in determining whether a climate is open (supportive) or closed (hindering). To obtain an overall climate score, simply total the score values given for each of the seven items. Remember to reverse the score given to item 1, conformity, for in this case low scores suggest a supportive climate. The higher the score, the more open or supportive the group or organization is. Now, using the item categories and scores, describe again the helpful and hindering organizations or groups you recall. You are now describing organizational climate in the language of social psychologists. Let us now examine the concept of organizational climate and its relationship to supervisory effectiveness more formally.

Introduction

For each of the seven organization climate dimensions described below place an (A) above the number that indicates your assessment of the organization's current position on that dimension and an (I) above the number that indicates your choice of where the organization should ideally be on this dimension.

1 Conformity The feeling that there are many externally imposed constraints in the organization; the degree to which members feel that there are many rules, procedures, policies, and practices to which they have to conform rather than being able to do their work as they see fit.

Conformity is not charac-   1 2 3 4 5 6 7 8 9 10   Conformity is very characteristic of this organization   teristic of this organization

2 Responsibility Members of the organization are given personal responsibility to achieve their part of the organization's goals; the degree to which members feel that they can make decisions and solve problems without checking with superiors each step fo the way.

No responsibility is given   1 2 3 4 5 6 7 8 9 10   There is great emphasis on
in the organization.   personal responsibility in the
organization.

3 Standards The emphasis the organization places on quality performance and outstanding production including the degree to which the member feels the organization is setting challenging goals for itself and communicating these goal commitments to members.

Standards are very low   1 2 3 4 5 6 7 8 9 10   High challenging standards
or nonexistent in the   are set in the organization.
organization.

4 Rewards The degree to which members feel that they are being recognized and rewarded for good work rather than being ignored, criticized, or punished when something goes wrong.

Members are ignored,   1 2 3 4 5 6 7 8 9 10   Members are recognized and
punished, or criticized.   rewarded positively.

5. Organization clarity The feeling among members that things are well-organized and goals are clearly defined rather than being disorderly, confused, or chaotic.

The organization is dis-   1 2 3 4 5 6 7 8 9 10   The organization is well-
orderly, confused, and   organized with clearly
chaotic.   defined goals.

6 Warmth and support The feeling that friendliness is a valued norm in the organization; that members trust one another and offer support to one another. The feeling that good relationships prevail in the work environment.

There is no warmth and   1 2 3 4 5 6 7 8 9 10   Warmth and support are
support in the organization   very characteristic of the
organization.

7 Leadership The willingness of organization members to accept leadership and direction from qualified others. As needs for leadership arise, members feel free to take leadership roles and are rewarded for successful leadership. Leadership is based on expertise. The organization is not dominated by, or dependent on, one or two individuals.

Leadership is not rewarded;   1 2 3 4 5 6 7 8 9 10 Members accept and reward
members are dominated or   leadership based on expertise.
dependent and resist
leadership attempts.

Exhibit 4-1 Organizational climate questionnaire. *(From David A. Kolb, Erwin M. Rubin, and James M. McIntyre,* Organizational Psychology in Experiential Approach, *3d ed., 1979, pp. 193–194. Reprinted by permission of Prentice-Hall, Englewood Cliffs, N.J.)*

WHAT IS ORGANIZATIONAL CLIMATE?

Since the climate of a school is a matter of impression, it is often difficult to define with precision. Climate might be viewed on the one hand as the enduring characteristics that describe a particular school, distinguish it from other schools, and influence the behavior of teachers and students, and on the other hand as the "feel" that teachers and students have for that school. Litwin and Stringer, for example, define climate as: "The perceived subjective effects of the formal system, the informal 'style' of managers, and other important environmental factors on the attitudes, beliefs, values, and motivation of people who work in a particular organization."[1]

According to this view, climate represents a composite of mediating variables that intervene between the structure of an organization and the style and other characteristics of leaders, and teacher performance and satisfaction.

THE IMPORTANCE OF CLIMATE

Many supervisors do not like to be cast into a leadership role that requires them to give attention to organizational climate. They prefer instead to devote full attention to what they feel really matters—the educational program and students. This concern is commendable, and indeed educational and instructional roles of supervision are most important. But supervisors will have a difficult time exercising this leadership without a sufficient supportive climate within which to work. Moreover, excluding or neglecting organizational climate in favor of educational tasks can actually limit the total amount of leadership talent available in the school.

The need for an organizational-climate emphasis is clear. A healthy climate frees supervisor and teacher to work more fully on educational matters. Further, a direct focus by supervisors on educational-leadership responsibilities is often viewed by teachers as authoritarian, and therefore the leadership initiatives of supervisors are limited. An organizational-climate emphasis, on the other hand, not only permits the supervisor to take a direct lead in educational matters when appropriate but draws out the leadership talents of others as well. Here leadership becomes a process rather than a set of prerogatives associated with the supervisor's role.

Direct instructional leadership is still at the core of the supervisor's role, but the focus is less on who assumes the role and more on whether it is indeed assumed. The supervisor may display instructional leadership directly or by working to see that leadership does emerge from within the teaching staff. Fundamental to this position is the belief that a major aspect of the supervisor's job is to provide the circumstances and climate for leadership.

THE SUPERVISOR AND SCHOOL CLIMATE

Climate is a necessary link between organizational structure and teacher attitude and behavior. George and Bishop, for example, found that formal structural characteristics

---

[1]George H. Litwin and Robert A. Stringer, Jr., *Motivation and Organizational Climate*, Boston: Harvard University, Division of Research, Graduate School of Business Administration, 1968, p. 5.

of the schools they studied had an important influence on the way in which teachers perceived the school's climate. The 296 teachers in their study were more likely to view the climates of bureaucratically oriented school districts as closed and constricting. Professionally oriented school districts, on the other hand, were viewed as being more trusting and open and as producing less anxiety in teachers.[2]

But climate would be of more interest to top administrators than to supervisors if it were primarily affected by organizational structure. Supervisors are interested because of the link that exists between leadership assumptions, characteristics, and behavior, and school climate, and indeed the link is strong. Halpin, for example, finds that it is the behavior of elementary school principals (the extent to which they are seen as aloof, emphasizing production and close supervision, setting an example through their own hard work, and showing consideration) that in a large measure sets a climate tone for a school.[3]

In a more direct investigation of leader behavior and organizational climate Litwin and Stringer found that by varying the leadership style in each of three simulated organizations, they were able to create three different climates, each with distinct implications for member performance and satisfaction.[4] In organization A the leader strongly emphasized structure, status, assigned roles, position authority, vertical communications, and a punitive system of rules and regulations. Organization A resembled the classical-management or bureaucratic view of management and organization. In organization B the leader strongly emphasized an informal, loose structure and promoted shared decision making, team work, and friendliness. This organization was fashioned pretty much in accordance with human relation beliefs. Organization C was also characterized by interpersonal support and cooperation, but here the leader provided an added emphasis on quality performance and encouraged creativity. Organization C approximated the human resources model. In each case the organizations varied in the mode of leadership provided by the designated leader.

Members in organization A viewed the climate as punitive and nonsupportive and as offering little chance for individual initiative. The leader was viewed as aloof, and interpersonal conflict was common despite efforts of the leader to suppress it. Members of organization B viewed the climate as warm, cooperative, participatory, tension-free, and friendly. Members of organization C viewed the climate as being somewhat cooperative and loosely structured but bounded by norms of responsibility, personal initiative, and risk taking. Though members found the organization rewarding, it was characterized by moderate conflict.

Each of the climates was, in turn, associated with quite different outcomes for the three organizations. Job satisfaction and performance were low in organization A. Performance was also low in organization B, but in this case innovation was moderately high and satisfaction very high. Organization C was characterized by very high performance and innovation and high satisfaction. These relationships are summarized in Table 4-1.

[2]J. George and L. Bishop, "Relationship of Organizational Structure and Teacher Personality Characteristics to Organizational Climate," *Administrative Science Quarterly,* vol. 16, pp. 467–476, 1971.
[3]Andrew W. Halpin and Donald B. Croft, *Organizational Climate of Schools,* Chicago: University of Chicago, Midwest Administration Center, 1963.
[4]Litwin and Stringer, op. cit.

TABLE 4-1
LEADERSHIP, CLIMATE, AND EFFECTIVENESS: LITWIN AND STRINGER

Leadership	Climate	Effectiveness
Organization A Bureaucratic leadership	Closed	Performance low Satisfaction low
Organization B Human relations leadership	Warm Supportive Friendly	Performance low Satisfaction very high Innovation high
Organization C Human resources leadership	Supportive Goal-oriented	Performance very high Satisfaction high Innovation very high

Supervisors frequently are not able to influence broader questions of organizational structure and function in schools to the extent they wish. But they can still exert a strong influence on school climate through the nature and quality of leadership they exercise.

ORGANIZATIONAL CLIMATE AND SCHOOLS

Two well-known constructs for conceptualizing organizational climate for schools can be found in the work of Matthew Miles[5] and of Andrew Halpin and Don Croft.[6]

Halpin, for example, views schools as being on a conceptual climate continuum that extends from open to closed.[7] This framework is not unlike that which considers individual personalities as being on a continuum from open-mindedness to closed-mindedness. At a very simple level, organization climate refers to the feeling that exists in a given school and the variability in this feeling as one moves from school to school. Halpin, in describing climate, notes that "as one moves to other schools, one finds that each has a 'personality' of its own. It is this 'personality' that we describe here as the 'organizational climate' of the school. Analogously, personality is to the individual what organizational climate is to the organization."[8]

The Organizational Climate Description Questionnaire was developed by Halpin and Croft as a means to measure and chart the difference in "feel" that characterizes individual schools. The instrument examines eight dimensions of organizational climate, four of which focus on teacher behavior and four on the behavior of the principal. These are presented in Table 4-2.

Each of the eight dimensions of climate is represented in the instrument as a subtest.[9] Various combinations of emphasis on each of the subtests, as perceived by the

[5]Matthew Miles, "Planned Change and Organizational Health: Figure and Ground," *Change Processes in the Public Schools,* Eugene, Ore.: The University of Oregon, Center for the Advanced Study of Educational Administration, 1965, pp. 11–34.
[6]Halpin and Croft, op. cit. For a condensed version see Halpin's *Theory and Research in Administration,* New York: Macmillan, 1967, pp. 131–249.
[7]The Halpin climate "continuum," as measured by the Organizational Climate Description Questionnaire, moves from open, through autonomous, controlled, familiar, and paternal, to closed.
[8]Halpin, *Theory and Research in Administration,* p. 131.
[9]Ibid., p. 150. The dimension that seems to have the strongest relationship to open climate is esprit.

TABLE 4-2
THE EIGHT DIMENSIONS OF ORGANIZATIONAL CLIMATE

	Intensity scale	
	Open	Closed

Teachers' Behavior

1. *Disengagement* refers to the teachers' tendency to be "not with it." This dimension describes a group which is "going through the motions," a group that is "not in gear" with respect to the task at hand. It corresponds to the more general concept of *anomie* as first described by Durkheim.* In short, this subtest focuses upon the teachers' behavior in a task-oriented situation. — | + +

2. *Hindrance* refers to the teachers' feeling that the principal burdens them with routine duties, committee demands, and other requirements which the teachers construe as unnecessary "busywork." The teachers perceive that the principal is hindering rather than facilitating their work. — | +

3. *Esprit* refers to morale. The teachers feel that their social needs are being satisfied, and that they are, at the same time, enjoying a sense of accomplishment in their job. + + | — —

4. *Intimacy* refers to the teachers' enjoyment of friendly social relations with each other. This dimension describes a social-needs satisfaction which is not necessarily associated with task-accomplishment. + | +

Principal's Behavior

5. *Aloofness* refers to behavior by the principal which is characterized as formal and impersonal. He "goes by the book" and prefers to be guided by rules and policies rather than to deal with the teachers in an informal, face-to-face situation. His behavior, in brief, is universalistic rather than particularistic; nomothetic rather than idiosyncratic. To maintain this style, he keeps himself—at least "emotionally"—at a distance from his staff. — | +

6. *Production emphasis* refers to behavior by the principal which is characterized by close supervision of the staff. He is highly directive and plays the role of a "straw boss." His communication tends to go in only one direction, and he is not sensitive to feedback from the staff. — | +

7. *Thrust* refers to behavior by the principal which is characterized by his evident effort in trying to "move the organization." Thrust behavior is marked not by close supervision, but by the principal's attempt to motivate the teachers through the example which he personally sets. Apparently, because he does not ask the teachers to give of themselves any more than he willingly gives of himself, his behavior, though starkly task-oriented, is nonetheless viewed favorably by the teachers. + + | —

8. *Consideration* refers to behavior by the principal which is characterized by an inclination to treat the teachers "humanly," to try to do a little something extra for them in human terms. + | —

*Emile Durkheim, *Le Suicide*, Paris, Libraire Felix Alcan, 1930, p. 277. *Anomie* describes a planlessness in living, a method of living which defeats itself because achievement has no longer any criterion of value; happiness always lies beyond any present achievement. Defeat takes the form of ultimate disillusion—a disgust with the futility of endless pursuit.

+ + Very high emphasis
+ High
— Low
— — Very low

Source: Andrew Halpin, *Theory and Research in Administration*, New York: Macmillan, 1967, pp. 150–151. Copyright © by Andrew Halpin. The intensity scale is an addition to the original Halpin table.

teachers responding to the instrument, reveal for the school a climate-similarity score that determines the relative position of the school on the open-to-closed continuum. The school with an open climate, for example, is characterized by low disengagement, low hindrance, very high esprit, high intimacy, low aloofness, low production emphasis, very high thrust, and high consideration. The closed school exhibits very high disengagement, high hindrance, very low esprit, high intimacy, high aloofness, high production emphasis, low thrust, and low consideration. Open- and closed-school climates are described by Halpin as follows:

> The Open Climate depicts a situation in which the members enjoy extremely high *Esprit.* The teachers work well together without bickering and griping (low disengagement). They are not burdened by mountains of busywork or by routine reports; the principal's policies facilitate the teachers' accomplishment of their tasks (low hindrance). On the whole, the group members enjoy friendly relations of intimacy. The teachers obtain considerable job satisfaction, and are sufficiently motivated to overcome difficulties and frustration. They possess the incentive to work things out and to keep the organization "moving." Furthermore, the teachers are proud to be associated with their school.[10]
>
> The Closed Climate marks a situation in which the group members obtain little satisfaction in respect to either task-achievement or social-needs. In short, the principal is ineffective in directing the activities of the teachers; at the same time, he is not inclined to look out for their personal welfare. This climate is the most closed and the least genuine climate that we have identified.[11]

The values associated with human resources supervision suggest that the work of the school needs to be accomplished within the framework of open climates. Attention to climate is particularly crucial in that the classroom door does not provide a sufficient buffer to protect the classroom from the prevailing school climate. Closed climates in organizations tend to breed closed learning climates. Open climates in organizations tend to breed open learning climates. A significant direction for leadership-supervisory behavior is moving toward the development and maintenance of the climate most conducive to dynamic instructional leadership.

ORGANIZATIONAL HEALTH: A SUPERVISORY GOAL

A similar but broader approach to understanding the prevailing flavor, attitude, sentiment, and orientation of a given school is that which Miles proposes as the concept of organizational health. Miles describes the healthy school as one that exhibits reasonably clear and reasonably accepted goals (goal focus); communication that is relatively distortion-free vertically, horizontally, and across boundary lines (communi-

[10]Ibid., pp. 174–175.
[11]Ibid., p. 180. We should caution at this time that the OCDQ was developed for use with elementary schools. Some controversy seems to exist over whether the instrument can be used in other school settings, but the instrument tends not to be valid for large secondary schools and perhaps (in our opinion) even for large elementary schools. As schools increase in size and/or complexity, the referent-point principal should perhaps be changed to someone closer to the teachers. See J. Foster Watkins, "The OCDQ—an Application for Some Implications," *Educational Administration Quarterly,* vol. 4, pp. 46–60, Spring 1968. See also Fred D. Carver and T. Sergiovanni, "Some Notes on the OCDQ," *Journal of Educational Administration,* vol. 7, no. 1, May 1969.

cation adequacy); equitable distribution of influence to all levels of the organization (optimal power equalization); and effective and efficient use of inputs, both human and material (resource utilization). The healthy school likewise reflects reciprocally satisfying vectors of influence between the inhabitants and the school (cohesiveness), a feeling of well-being among the staff (morale), self-renewing properties (innovativeness), and an active response to its environment (autonomy and adaptation). Finally, the healthy school maintains and strengthens its problem-solving capabilities (problem-solving adequacies).   *organizational*

Each of the 10 dimensions of health is described in detail below. They form a major share of the content that composes the process of supervision. From Miles, they are:[12]

1. *Goal focus.* In a healthy organization, the goal (or more usually goals) of the system would be reasonably clear to the system members, and reasonably well accepted by them. This clarity and acceptance, however, should be seen as a necessary but insufficient condition for organization health. The goals must also be *achievable* with existing or available resources, and be *appropriate*—more or less congruent with the demands of the environment.

2. *Communication adequacy.* Since organizations are not simultaneous face-to-face systems like small groups, the movement of information within them becomes crucial. This dimension of organization health implies that there is relatively distortion-free communication "vertically," "horizontally," and across the boundary of the system to and from the surrounding environment. That is, information travels reasonably well—just as the healthy person "knows himself" with a minimum level of repression, distortion, etc. In the healthy organization, there is good and prompt sensing of internal strains; there are enough data about problems of the system to insure that a good diagnosis of system difficulties can be made. People have the information they need, and have gotten it without exerting undue efforts, such as those involved in moseying up to the superintendent's secretary, reading the local newspaper, or calling excessive numbers of special meetings.

3. *Optimal power equalization.* In a healthy organization the distribution of influence is relatively equitable. Subordinates (if there is a formal authority chart) can influence upward, and even more important—as Likert has demonstrated—they perceive that their boss can do likewise with his *boss.* In such an organization, intergroup struggles for power would not be bitter, though intergroup conflict (as in every human system known to man) would undoubtedly be present. The basic stance of persons in such an organization, as they look up, sideways and down, is that of collaboration rather than explicit or implicit coercion.

4. *Resource utilization.* We say of a healthy person, such as a second-grader, that he is "working up to his potential." To put this another way, the classroom system is evoking a contribution from him at an appropriate and goal-directed level of tension. At the organization level, "health" would imply that the system's inputs, particularly the personnel, are used effectively. The overall coordination is such that people are neither overloaded nor idling. There is a minimal sense of strain, generally speaking (in the sense that trying to do something with a weak or inappropriate structure puts strain on that structure). In the healthy organization, people may be working very hard indeed, but they feel that they are not working against themselves, or against the organization. The fit between people's own dispositions and the role demands of the system is good. Beyond this, people feel reasonably "self-actualized"; they not only "feel good" in their jobs, but they have a genuine sense of learning, growing, and developing as persons in the process of making their organizational contribution.

[12]Miles, op. cit., pp. 18–21.

5. *Cohesiveness*. We think of a healthy person as one who has a clear sense of identity; he knows who he is, underneath all the specific goals he sets for himself. Beyond this, he *likes himself;* his stance toward life does not require self-derogation, even when there are aspects of his behavior which are unlovely or ineffective. By analogy at the organization level, system health would imply that the organization knows "who it is." Its members feel attracted to membership in the organization. They want to stay with it, be influenced by it, and exert their own influence in the collaborative style suggested above.

6. *Morale*. The implied notion is one of well-being or satisfaction. Satisfaction is not enough for health, of course; a person may report feelings of well-being and satisfaction in his life, while successfully denying deep-lying hostilities, anxieties, and conflicts. Yet it still seems useful to evoke, at the organization level, the idea of morale: a summated set of individual sentiments, centering around feelings of well-being, satisfaction, and pleasure, as opposed to feelings of discomfort, unwished-for strain, and dissatisfaction.

7. *Innovativeness*. A healthy system would tend to invent new procedures, move toward new goals, produce new kinds of products, diversify itself, and become more rather than less differentiated over time. In a sense, such a system could be said to grow, develop, and change, rather than remaining routinized and standard.

8. *Autonomy*. The healthy person acts "from his own center outward." Seen in a training or therapy group, for example, such a person appears nearly free of the need to submit dependently to authority figures, *and* from the need to rebel and destroy symbolic fathers of any kind. A healthy organization, similarly, would not respond passively to demands from the outside, feeling itself the tool of the environment, and it would not respond destructively or rebelliously to perceived demands either. It would tend to have a kind of independence from the environment, in the same sense that the healthy person, while he has transactions with others, does not treat their responses as *determinative* of his own behavior.

9. *Adaptation*. The notions of autonomy and innovativeness are both connected with the idea that a healthy person, group, or organization is in realistic, effective contact with the surroundings. When environmental demands and organization resources do not match, a problem-solving, restructuring approach evolves in which *both* the environment and the organization become different in some respect. More adequate, continued coping of the organization, as a result of changes in the local system, the relevant portions of the environment, or more usually both, occurs. And such a system has sufficient stability and stress tolerance to manage the difficulties which occur during the adaption process.

10. *Problem-solving adequacy*. Finally, any healthy organism—even one as theoretically impervious to fallibility as a computer—*always* has problems, strains, difficulties, and instances of ineffective coping. The issue is not the presence or absence of problems, therefore, but the *manner* in which the person, group, or organization copes with problems. Argyris has suggested that in an effective system, problems are solved with minimal energy; they stay solved; and the problem-solving mechanisms used are not weakened, but maintained or strengthened. An adequate organization, then, has well-developed structures and procedures for sensing the existence of problems, for inventing possible solutions, for deciding on the solutions, for implementing them, and for evaluating their effectiveness.

Each of the dimensions of organizational health for any school operates in a system of dynamic interaction characterized by a high degree of interdependence. Clear goal focus, for example, depends upon the extent to which the school communicates its goals and permits inhabitants to modify and rearrange them. At another level, a high degree of organizational health encourages school adaptiveness, while school adaptiveness contributes to, and is essential to, organizational health.

THE SYSTEM 4 CLIMATE: AN INTEGRATED APPROACH TO SCHOOL SUPERVISION

In 1961 *New Patterns of Management*[13] by Rensis Likert appeared as part of the general literature in supervision. The book made a significant and widespread impact on noneducational settings and a small but nevertheless significant inroad in the literature and in the practice of educational supervision. The significance of this book to educational supervision is that it offered for the first time an intergrated, research-based system of supervision applicable to schools. This system is based on the development of highly effective work groups who are committed to the goals of the school and who work toward these goals as a means to professional growth and development and personal self-fulfillment. These groups are linked together in an overlapping pattern that permits them to function, on the one hand, as relatively small and cohesive primary groups and, on the other hand, as dynamic contributors to, and influencers of, the total school enterprise.

A highly effective school work group is described as one that: (1) members perceive as supportive and that builds and maintains their sense of personal worth, (2) has high performance goals that are consistent with those of the school and/or the profession, (3) uses group decision making, and (4) is linked to other school groups through multiple and overlapping group structures.

From these ideas Likert was able to develop a theory of supervision that relies heavily on the concept of organizational climate as an intervening variable between what supervisors and administrators do and organizational effectiveness. The theory was described in Likert's 1967 book entitled *The Human Organization: Its Management and Value*.[14] Here Likert proposed four different climates known as management systems 1, 2, 3, and 4. The profile of organizational characteristics is the instrument used by Likert to measure the extent to which each of the climates is reflected in an organization or group. Such characteristics as leadership processes (from nonsupportive to supportive), motivational forces (low to high), communication processes (weak and inaccurate to strong and accurate), interaction and influence processes (cold and formal to warm and informal), decision-making processes (hierarchical to shared), goal-setting processes (hierarchical to shared), control processes (hierarchical to shared), and the nature of performance goals (low to high) are measured by the profile. Subscales and selected items from the profiles are shown in Table 4-3.

Respondents generally perceive high-performing groups or organizations as scoring toward the right end of the scale on each of the organizational variables and low-performing groups or organizations as scoring toward the left. Likert reports research that supports these perceptions and notes that as organizations move toward System 4, they are more productive, are characterized by high-performing work groups, have lower costs, have more favorable attitudes, and display improved

[13]Rensis Likert, *New Patterns of Management*, New York: McGraw-Hill, 1961. In the early chapters of *New Patterns of Management*, Professor Likert summarizes, synthesizes, and articulates hundreds of studies performed through the institute that have relevance to supervision. In the remaining chapters, Likert uses this mass of findings to develop and support a theory of supervision based on three fundamental principles: (1) the principle of supportive relationships, (2) the principle of group decision making and group supervision, and (3) the principle of high performance goals for individuals, groups, and the organization.
[14]Rensis Likert, *The Human Organization: Its Management and Value*, New York: McGraw-Hill, 1967.

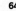

TABLE 4-3

SUBSCALES AND SAMPLE ITEMS FROM PROFILE OF ORGANIZATIONAL CHARACTERISTICS

Organizational variable	System 1 (Exploitive-authoritarian)	System 2 (Benevolent-authoritarian)	System 3 (Consultative)	System 4 (Participative)
1. Leadership processes used *a.* Extent to which superiors have confidence and trust in *subordinates*	Have no confidence and trust in subordinates	Have condescending confidence and trust, such as master has in servant	Substantial but not complete confidence and trust; still wishes to keep control of decisions	Complete confidence and trust in all matters
2. Character of motivational forces *a.* Underlying motives tapped	Physical security, economic needs, and some use of the desire for status	Economic needs and moderate use of ego motives, e.g., desire for status, affiliation, and achievement	Economic needs and considerable use of ego and other major motives, e.g., desire for new experiences	Full use of economic, ego, and other major motives, as, for example, motivational forces arising from group goals
3. Character or communication process *f.* Psychological closeness of superiors to subordinates. (How well does superior know and understand problems faced by subordinates).	Has no knowledge or understanding of problems of subordinates	Has some knowledge and understanding of problems of subordinates	Knows and understands problems of subordinates quite well	Knows and understands problems of subordinates very well
4. Character of interaction-influence process *a.* Amount and character of interaction	Little interaction and always with fear and distrust	Little interaction and usually with some condescension by superiors; fear and caution by subordinates	Moderate interaction, often with fair amount of confidence and trust	Extensive, friendly interaction with high degree of confidence and trust
5. Character of decision-making process *f.* To what extent are subordinates involved in decisions related to their work?	Not at all	Never involved in decisions; occasionally consulted	Usually are consulted but ordinarily not involved in the decision making	Are involved fully in all decisions related to their work

TABLE 4-3 (Continued)
SUBSCALES AND SAMPLE ITEMS FROM PROFILE OF ORGANIZATIONAL CHARACTERISTICS

Organizational variable	System 1 (Exploitive-authoritarian)	System 2 (Benevolent-authoritarian)	System 3 (Consultative)	System 4 (Participative)
6. Character of goal setting or ordering *b.* To what extent do the different hierarchical levels tend to strive for high performance goals?	High goals pressed by top, generally resisted by subordinates	High goals sought by top and often resisted moderately by subordinates	High goals sought by higher levels but with occasional resistance by lower levels	High goals sought by all levels, with lower levels sometimes pressing for higher goals than top levels
7. Character of control processes *a.* At what hierarchical levels in organization does major or primary concern exist with regard to the performance of the cnotrol function?	At the very top only	Primarily or largely at the top	Primarily at the top but some shared feeling of responsibility felt at middle and to a lesser extent at lower levels	Concern for performance of control functions likely to be felt throughout organization
8. Performance goals and training *a.* Level of performance goals which superiors seek to have organization achieve	Seek average goals	Seek high goals	Seek very high goals	Seek to achieve extremely high goals

labor-management relationships, with System 4 organizations achieving excellent records in each of these dimensions. The converse seems to be true for organizations displaying management systems that lie well toward System 1. We would, of course, expect similar responses from educators and similar findings in educational organizations.

The Profile of the School is a version of the Likert instrument specifically designed for the school context. Studies comparing this version with Halpin and Croft's Organizational Climate Description Questionnaire find that the two are similar (correlations of 0.59), with more open schools being Systems 3 and 4 and more closed schools, Systems 1 and 2.[15]

SHIFTING MANAGEMENT SYSTEMS

The management systems described in Table 4-3 are composed of individual characteristics and tendencies, each dependent upon the existence of others of a similar intensity.

[15] John W. Hall, "A Comparison of Halpin and Croft's 'Organizational Climates' and Likert and Likert's 'Organizational Systems,'" *Administrative Science Quarterly*, vol. 17, pp. 586–590, 1972.

As a result of this interdependence it is not likely, except for incidental responses, that a given school can be described as possessing some characteristics of System 1, others of System 2, and still others of System 4. Typically, a pattern of response to Table 4-3 would emerge for a given school that would clearly type the school into one or another system category. In explaining this phenomenon Likert observes: "The communications processes of System 1 are compatible with all other aspects of System 1 but are not compatible with any aspect of System 3 or System 4. The same is true of the decision-making processes and the compensation plans. *The Management system of an organization must have compatible component parts if it is to function effectively.*"[16]

It is not likely that enduring changes can be made, for example, in the levels of teachers' commitment to school goals without substantial changes in supervisory assumptions. People should expect to see the alteration of their supervisory assumptions reflected in each of the mediating variables, including the commitment levels of teachers. As a further illustration, it is not likely that supervisory efforts to improve the problem-solving capabilities of staff will be effective if each of the other variables that constitute this system is ignored. The hard facts of the matter suggest that a System 2 supervisor who wishes to adopt one dimension of System 4 will not have much success unless he or she adopts the other dimensions.

Systems 1 and 2

System 1 is referred to as exploitive-authoritarian and System 2 as benevolent-authoritarian. Differences between the two exist, but they are close enough to be described together. Supervisors (principals, teachers, and others) who adopt System 1 or System 2 perspectives rely on high-control methods; hierarchical pressures and authority; Theory X assumptions in regard to subordinates, domination, regulation, and distortion of communication channels; and programmed, delimited, and centralized decision making as they work to achieve school goals.

Systems 1 and 2 supervisors can expect from subordinates (administrators, teachers, students, and others) less group loyalty, lower performance goals, less cooperation, more conflict, less teamwork and mutual assistance among peers, more feeling of unreasonable pressure, less favorable attitudes toward supervisors and the school, and lower motivational potential for performance.[17] This response from the human organization of the school takes its toll in poor performance on each of the school-success variables.

Systems 3 and 4

System 3 is described as consultive, while System 4 is labeled participative. System 3 is somewhat descriptive of supervisory practice, which characterizes schools well on their way toward developing professional organization. It is a transitional management system that is often characterized as being "better than before" but still clings to many of the features of the earlier type of management. System 3 fails in attempting to maximize the achievement of school goals, student actualization, and teacher self-

---

[16]Likert, op. cit., p. 123.
[17]Likert, *The Human Organization*, p. 76.

fulfillment, but it at least performs satisfactorily in each of these pursuits while maintaining dimensions and features that are organizationally and administratively familiar.

System 4 is indeed close to our concept of human resources supervision. Administrators, teachers, and others who adopt this perspective rely on the principle of supportive relationships, on group methods of supervision, on Theory Y assumptions, on self-control methods, on ability authority, and on other principles of System 4. The human organization of the school reacts to this perspective by displaying greater group loyalty, high performance goals, greater cooperation, more teamwork and sharing, less feeling of unreasonable pressure, more favorable attitudes toward the supervisor and the school, and higher levels of motivation for performance.[18] The result, of course, is increases in the dimensions of school success. System 4 is, of course, an ideal difficult to achieve in practice. Therefore it may be more useful in actual situations to speak of *tendencies toward System 4* rather than speaking of actually meeting this goal.

CLIMATE AND LEARNING

In recent years the emphasis in climate has shifted from a management to a student orientation. One avenue of research in this tradition is identified with the Pupil Control Ideology Scale (PCI) developed by Willower and his associates.[19] This scale measures the basic assumptions and ensuing attitudes of teachers and supervisors toward students on a continuum from custodial to humanistic. "Custodial schools," identified by the PCI studies, tend to be rigidly controlled and concerned primarily with maintenance of order. Students do not participate in decision making and are expected to accept decisions without question. Further, students are viewed as being irresponsible, undisciplined, untrustworthy, and trouble-prone. Thus strong emphasis is given to controlling students through the development and articulation of punitive methods. "Humanistic schools," on the other hand, resemble more a community that includes students as fuller members and seeks their cooperation and interaction. Self-discipline is emphasized and learning is considered to be enhanced by student identity and commitment. In schools with humanistic climates teachers are likely to cooperate with one another in pursuit of learning objectives, to have high morale, and to enjoy a sense of task achievement as well as social interaction. In custodial schools characterized by the lack of these characteristics, students are likely to be more alienated, with the goals of order and discipline usurping those oriented more toward student achievement. Teachers are more likely to view the school as a battlefield.

In a study of 12 inner-London secondary schools Rutter, Maughan, Mortimer, and Ouston found that important differences in climate existed between more and less effective schools.[20] Effectiveness was defined as higher scores on national examinations, better behavior, and better attendance. In the more effective schools teachers worked

[18]Ibid., p. 76.
[19]Donald J. Willower, Terry I. Eidell, and Wayne K. Hoy, *The School and Pupil Control Ideology,* Pennsylvania State University Studies #24, State College, Pa.: Pennsylvania State University, 1967.
[20]Michael Rutter, Barbara Maughan, Peter Mortimer, and Janet Ouston, *Fifteen Thousand Hours: Secondary Schools and Their Effects on Children,* Cambridge, Mass.: Harvard University Press, 1979.

harder and had better attitudes toward learning, spent more time in actual teaching relied more heavily on praising students, and were better able to involve students as active learners. Further, more effective schools involved the students generally in the life of the school, gave students more responsibility, and made an effort to provide students with pleasant conditions and such conveniences as telephone use. All in all, the climate in effective schools was characterized by a positive attitude toward young people and toward learning.

SUMMARY

In this chapter the importance of organizational climate to school effectiveness was discussed. Climate was viewed as a combination of the enduring characteristics that describe a particular school and distinguish it from other schools, and the feeling teacher and student have for that school. Accordingly, climate represents a composite of mediating variables that intervene between initiating and school-effectiveness variables. It was pointed out that although supervisors have difficulty in affecting climate by initiating changes in organizational structure and function, they can exert direct influence on school climate through the leadership they provide. Bureaucratic leadership, for example, tends to be associated with relatively closed climate and low performance and satisfaction. Human relations leadership tends to be associated with a warm, supportive, and friendly climate and with low performance but high satisfaction and some innovation. Human resources leadership tends to be associated with a supportive, goal-oriented climate and high performance, satisfaction, and some innovation. Views of organizational climate, as conceptualized by Halpin and Croft and by Miles, were then presented as examples of ways of thinking and descriptive statements of climate components. Items from Likert's profile of organizational characteristics were then presented as a method for charting and monitoring school climate. This instrument sample was accompanied by a discussion of four organizational climates, Systems 1, 2, 3, and 4, each associated with a particular pattern of leadership. System 4 was then discussed as the ideal toward which human resources supervisors work. Finally, a discussion of the relationship between climate and learning was presented.

STUDY GUIDE

Recall the concepts, ideas, and meanings associated with each of the following phrases and terms included in Chapter 4. Can you discuss each of them with a colleague and apply them to the supervisory content of your school? If you cannot, review them in the text and record the page numbers for future reference.

1. Bureaucratic leadership _____
2. Climate defined _____
3. Closed climate _____
4. Effectiveness variables and climate _____
5. Healthy climate _____
6. Human relations leadership _____

7. Human resources leadership _____
8. Initiating variables and climate _____
9. Management systems _____
10. Mediating variables and climate _____
11. Open climate _____
12. Organizational Climate Description Questionnaire _____
13. Organizational health _____
14. Profile of organizational characteristics _____
15. Systems 1, 2, 3, and 4 _____

EXERCISES

1. Describe the climate of your school using the eight dimensions of organizational climate included in Table 4-2. Provide specific examples or describe specific critical incidents that illustrate each climate dimension.
2. Have a group of teachers from the same school fill out the sample profile of organizational characteristics provided in Table 4-3, indicating for each item the way their school actually is (real) and the way they would prefer it to be (ideal). Average responses, and develop a real and ideal profile for that school. How might such a profile be used as a planning device for the supervisor?
3. Compare organizational climate as conceptualized and operationalized by Halpin, Miles, and Likert. How are these views similar and how are they different? Using these views, develop a 10-item questionnaire that you believe summarizes the most important dimensions of organizational climate.
4. Repeat the exercise described in 2 above using the organizational climate questionnaire presented in Exhibit 4-1.

CHAPTER 5

LEADERSHIP BEHAVIOR AND SUPERVISORY EFFECTIVENESS

Leadership refers to the supervisor's ability to influence an individual or group toward the achievement of goals. Modes of leadership influence, however, vary. Sometimes supervisors develop a specific set of leadership tactics that involves behaving in a certain way or using a particular approach to decision making. This is the mode of influence on which we will concentrate in Chapters 5 and 6. We are concerned with the supervisor's involvement in the deliberate tactical planning of influence and in subsequent leadership behavior designed to influence. This ability to influence can be enhanced by learning about and increasing one's own leadership skills.

But groups are influenced and goals are achieved by more indirect and subtle supervisory actions as well. For example, sometimes what is appropriate in leadership is not how the supervisor behaves but what he or she stands for and the ability to communicate these values to teachers. Sometimes what is important are the values and intents that teachers infer from what supervisors actually do and say. Of issue as well is the nature of goals and objectives and the direction of supervisory influence. It is, of course, possible that a supervisor with highly developed leadership skills can actually promote the "wrong" goals or influence teachers in the "wrong" direction. These more qualitative aspects of leadership will be considered in Chapter 11, where we provide a substantive theory of leadership. In this chapter and the next let us focus primarily on the more instrumental aspects of leadership, specifically on the social and management skills, concepts, and theories that can help improve leadership skills.

The following questions are considered in this chapter: What assumptions do supervisors and others make about human nature and, particularly, the behavior of people in their world of work? How do these assumptions affect the supervisor's behavior? What are the effects of this behavior on the human organization of the school? What are the predominant behavioral orientations that supervisors and others bring to school problems? How do these orientations affect supervisory behavior? And, again, how does this behavior affect the human organization of the school? Human resources supervision is concerned with the worth, growth, and development of the human organization, for it is upon this growth that the success of the school enterprise depends.

MANAGEMENT PHILOSOPHY AND SUPERVISORY ASSUMPTIONS

Whatever a person does makes sense to that person. This explains why two educators with similar supervisory responsibilities in similar schools with similar goals and similar personnel when confronted with an identical problem may operate in dissimilar ways. Both believe that their own method of operation is the one suitable to the task and circumstances. How do supervisors, principals, teachers, and others come to establish styles of supervision?[1] These are partly the result of management philosophies and of supervisory assumptions that individuals have accumulated or learned over the years.

Teachers, for example, whose classrooms are characterized as "open" have learned to consider students differently from their counterparts with "controlled" classrooms. These teachers have different management philosophies and different conceptions of their roles and the roles of their students. This is true, too, for principals who operate open, as opposed to closed, schools.[2] Interestingly, in each case teachers often respond to the supervisor's expectations in such a way that they prove him or her correct. This simply reinforces that supervisor's use of a given supervisory style. Understanding this self-fulfilling prophecy is crucial to understanding the relationship between management philosophy and supervisory behavior.[3] Rensis Likert's study of supervisors of highly effective work groups in industry, for example, strongly suggests that subordinates generally respond positively to the supervisor's high evaluation and confidence in them and work harder to justify the supervisor's expectations.[4] In the next section we present and discuss Douglas McGregor's comparison of two ideal-type management philosophies, along with supervisory assumptions that emerge from these philosophies.[5] He describes them as Theories X and Y in order to minimize semantic and value confusion.

THEORY X AND SCHOOLS

McGregor's language may seem more descriptive of nonschool environments, but his ideas have wide application to schools.[6] Examine his assumptions and propositions

[1]By *supervisory* or *leadership style* we refer simply to predominant patterns of behavior associated with a given person, role, or school. Any given style permits and absorbs occasional departures in behavior, provided that it does not alter the prevailing or basic behavior pattern.
[2]"Open" and "closed" are used here within the framework of the Organizational Climate Description Questionnaire. See Andrew Halpin and John Croft, *The Organizational Climate of Schools,* Chicago: University of Chicago, Midwest Administration Center, 1963.
[3]An interesting application of the self-fulfilling prophecy is in the operation of controlled-environment examinations. When heavy cheating is expected, elaborate controls are implemented and the cheating rate will tend to rise. The rate declines as expectations for cheating decline and controls are minimized. For an extensive treatment of the self-fulfilling prophecy as it applies to teacher expectations of student performance, see Robert Rosenthal and Lenore Jacobson, *Pygmalion in the Classroom,* New York: Holt, 1968.
[4]Rensis Likert, *New Patterns of Management,* New York: McGraw-Hill, 1961. See, for example, Chap. 1.
[5]An ideal type represents a conceptualization of a number of interrelated ideas in a polarized fashion. While the risk of stereotyping is present in the use of ideal types, they are nevertheless most useful in describing and grouping phenomena. Therefore, no one individual or case may provide a mirror image for any ideal type, and it is recognized that ideal descriptions tend to overstate their arguments. But such individuals or cases may be usefully described as approximating one or another type.
[6]This discussion is based largely on Douglas McGregor, *The Human Side of Enterprise,* New York: McGraw-Hill, 1960. See also, Warren G. Bennis and Edgar H. Schein (eds.), *Leadership and Motivation: Essays of Douglas McGregor,* Cambridge, Mass.: M.I.T., 1966.

below, first in reference to school administrators, supervisors, and teachers, and then in reference to teachers and students.

Management Propositions—Theory X

1. Management is responsible for organizing the elements of productive enterprise—money, materials, equipment, people—in the interest of economic [educational] ends.
2. With respect to people, this is a process of directing their efforts, motivating them, controlling their actions, modifying their behavior to fit the needs of the organization.
3. Without this active intervention by management, people would be passive—rewarded, punished, controlled—their activities must be directed. This is management's task in managing subordinate managers or workers. We often sum it up by saying that management consists of getting things done through other people.

Supervisory Assumptions—Theory X

Behind this conventional theory are several additional beliefs—less explicit but widespread:

4. The average man is by nature indolent—he works as little as possible.
5. He lacks ambition, dislikes responsibility, prefers to be led.
6. He is inherently self-centered, indifferent to organizational needs.
7. He is by nature resistant to change.
8. He is gullible, not very bright, the ready dupe of the charlatan and the demagogue.[7]

One cannot avoid noticing that schools tend toward the pessimistic assumptions of Theory X. In answering the question of whether this pessimistic image of humanity is correct, McGregor suggests that human behavior in organizations is approximately what management perceives it to be. Social scientists who have confirmed management's Theory X suspicions are sure that this behavior is not a consequence of inherent human nature. In schools, such behavior on the part of students or teachers is in part a consequence of our administrative, supervisory, and educational philosophy, policy, and practice. Thus supervisory styles stemming from Theory X are based on mistaken notions of what is cause and what is effect. Fundamental to Theory X is a philosophy of direction and control. This philosophy is administered in a variety of forms and rests upon a theory of motivation that is inadequate for most adults, particularly professional adults, and indeed is quickly outgrown by students.[8]

The behavior typically manifested in Theory X assumptions is labeled by Argyris as Pattern A.[9] Pattern A takes two forms: hard and soft. In the school, the hard version is a no-nonsense approach characterized by strong leadership, tight controls, and close supervision by the teacher in a classroom setting and by the supervisor in a total school setting. The soft approach relies heavily on buying, persuading, or winning people through good (albeit superficial) human relations and benevolent paternalism to obtain

[7]These assumptions are quoted from McGregor's essay, "The Human Side of Enterprise," which appears in Bennis and Schein, op. cit., p. 5. The essay first appeared in *Adventure in Thought and Action*, Proceedings of the Fifth Anniversary Convocation of the School of Industrial Management, M.I.T., Apr. 9, 1957. We added the word "education" to item 1 in McGregor's list. The article has been reprinted in *The Management Review*, vol. 46, no. 11, pp. 22–28, 1951.

[8]We discuss the motivational assumptions that are the bases for Theories X and Y in a later chapter. See A. H. Maslow, *Motivation and Personality*, New York: Harper, 1954.

[9]Chris Argyris, *Management and Organizational Development*, New York: McGraw-Hill, 1971, pp. 1–26.

compliance and acceptance of direction from superiors. The emphasis in both soft and hard versions of Pattern A is on manipulating, controlling, and managing people. The assumptions supervisors hold remain the same regardless of whether the hard or soft approach is used.

There are many problems with Theory X and Pattern A as management systems in organizations in general, though the patterns seem more acute in the school. As basic philosophies, Theory X and Pattern A seem inconsistent with the hopes of teachers, administrators, and supervisors who are interested in raising the quality of life for young people in schools, and therefore they are not compatible with human resources supervision.

THEORY Y AND SCHOOLS

An alternate management philosophy based on more adequate assumptions of human nature is needed for schools to meet their professional growth commitment to teachers and to improve the intellectual, social, and emotional welfare of their young clients. This optimistic philosophy is called Theory Y after McGregor. Its main components are outlined below:

Philosophy and Assumptions—Theory Y

1. Management is responsible for organizing the elements of productive enterprise— money, materials, equipment, people—in the interest of economic [educational] ends.
2. People are *not* by nature passive or resistant to organizational needs. They have become so as a result of experience in organizations.
3. The motivation, the potential for development, the capacity for assuming responsibility, the readiness to direct behavior toward organizational goals are all present in people. Management does not put them there. It is a responsibility of management to make it possible for people to recognize and develop these human characteristics for themselves.
4. The essential task of management is to arrange organizational conditions and methods of operation so that people can achieve their own goals *best* by directing *their* own efforts toward organizational objectives.[10]

Indeed, there are formidable obstacles that stand in the way of full implementation of this theory in every cubic inch of our schools. We have made progress in this direction, even if it has been slow, but additional modifications will need to be made in the attitudes of the school establishment, its publics, administrators, teachers, and students alike.

Pattern B is the label that Argyris gives to behavior associated with Theory Y assumptions. Basic to Pattern B is the dependence upon building identification and commitment to worthwhile objectives in the work context and upon building mutual trust and respect in the interpersonal context. Success in the work and interpersonal contexts is assumed to be dependent on whether meaningful satisfaction for individuals is achieved within the context of accomplishing important work as well as upon authentic relationships and the exchange of valid information. "More trust, concern for feelings, and internal commitment; more openness to, and experimenting with, new ideas and feelings *in such a way that others could do the same,* were recommended if

[10]McGregor in Bennis and Schein, op. cit., p. 15. Again we add the word "educational" to item number 1.

valid information was to be produced and internal commitment to decisions generated."[11]

The differences between Theory X assumptions and behavior of the hard, or tough, variety and Theory Y assumptions and behavior are readily observable and understood. Theory X *soft* and Theory Y, however, are often deceptively similar. Theory X soft is consistent with human relations practices and Theory Y with human resources practices. These approaches are contrasted in Table 5-1.

INFANCY MANAGEMENT ASSUMPTIONS

A perhaps harsher analysis of assumptions inherent in management is offered by Argyris.[12] He notes that the ordinary worker (in the school's case teachers and students) is often considered to have little substantial ability for self-direction and self-discipline. Further, individuals largely prefer to be told what to do rather that to think for themselves, and when they do have ideas, they are generally naive or unrealistic. Gellerman, in interpreting the Argyris position, makes the following comments:

> Most organizations, especially at the lower levels, are geared for men who make a very childlike adjustment to life: They leave very little leeway for choosing, for using discretion, or for adapting rules to fit circumstances. Most employees are expected to do just as they are told and leave the thinking to the foreman, whose capacity for doing so is a perennially moot point among the people he supervises. In any case millions of grown men are required to spend forty hours a week suppressing their brainpower in order to maintain a system that is not nearly as efficient as it looks.[13]

The Argyris position is essentially that the human personality is not given sufficient opportunity to mature in most formal organizations. Schools in general do offer relatively more opportunities for personal growth than most other organizations. Yet proportionally—that is, when one considers that schools are essentially human organizations—*our record on this matter is less than impressive.*

In noting the distinction between the mature and immature personality, Argyris lists seven processes that normally occur as the infant grows into the young adult, as the young adult grows into full adulthood, and as the adult increases his or her capabilities and effectiveness over the course of his or her lifetime. The seven dimensions and directions of human growth follow:[14]

First, healthy human beings tend to develop from a state of passivity as infants to a state of activity as adults. They move from being stimulated, motivated, or disciplined to relying on self-initiative and self-determination. As they mature, they rely less on

[11]Argyris, op. cit., p. 18. Argyris does not recommend that people be completely open and trusting but that they be open to an extent that permits others to be open. He argues that trust and openness exist only in interpersonal relationships and, therefore, the question is, "How open is the relationship between person A and person B?" In Argyris's words, "To say what you believe is to be honest: to say what you believe in such a way that the other can do the same is to be authentic."

[12]This discussion is based largely on Chris Argyris, *Personality and Organization,* New York: Harper, 1957. See also, "Individual Actualization in Complex Organizations." *Mental Hygiene,* vol. 44, no. 2, pp. 226–237, April 1960; and *Integrating the Individual and Education,* New York: Wiley, 1964.

[13]Saul Gellerman, *Motivation and Productivity,* New York: American Management Associations, 1963, p. 73.

[14]Our discussion of the seven directions and dimensions of the mature personality follows closely that which appears in Argyris, "Individual Actualization in Complex Organizations," op. cit., pp. 226–227.

TABLE 5-1
SUPERVISORY ASSUMPTIONS

Theory X Soft *Human relations model*	*Theory Y* *Human resources model*
ATTITUDES TOWARD PEOPLE	
1. People in our culture, teachers and students among them, share a common set of needs—to belong, to be liked, to be respected.	1. In addition to sharing common needs for belonging and respect, most people in our culture, teachers and students among them, desire to contribute effectively and creatively to the accomplishment of worthwhile objectives.
2. While teachers and students desire individual recognition, they more importantly want to *feel* useful to the school and to their own work group.	2. The majority of teachers and students are capable of exercising far more initiative, responsibility, and creativity than their present jobs or work circumstances require or allow.
3. They tend to cooperate willingly and comply with school goals if these important needs are fulfilled.	3. These capabilities represent untapped resources that are presently being wasted.
KIND AND AMOUNT OF PARTICIPATION	
1. The supervisor's basic task (or in reference to students, the teacher's basic task) is to make each worker believe that he or she is a useful and important part of the team.	1. The supervisor's basic task (or in reference to students, the teacher's basic task) is to create an environment in which subordinates can contribute their full range of talents to the accomplishment of school goals. He or she works to uncover the creative resources of subordinates.
2. The supervisor is willing to explain his or her decisions and to discuss subordinates' objections to the plans. On routine matters, he or she encourages subordinates in planning and in decision making. In reference to students, the teacher behaves similarly.	2. The supervisor allows and encourages teachers to participate in important as well as routine decisions. In fact, the more important a decision is to the school, the greater the supervisor's efforts to tap faculty resources. In reference to students, the teacher behaves similarly.
3. Within narrow limits, the faculty or individual teachers who make up the faculty should be allowed to exercise self-direction and self-control in carrying out plans. A similar relationship exists for teachers and students.	3. Supervisors work continually to expand the areas over which teachers exercise self-direction and self-control as they develop and demonstrate greater insight and ability. A similar relationship exists for teachers and students.
EXPECTATIONS	
1. Sharing information with teachers and involving them in school decision making will help satisfy their basic needs for belonging and for individual recognition.	1. The overall quality of decision making and performance will improve as supervisors and teachers make use of the full range of experience, insight, and creative ability that exists in their schools.

TABLE 5-1 (Continued)
SUPERVISORY ASSUMPTIONS

Theory X Soft Human relations model	Theory Y Human resources model
EXPECTATIONS	
2. Satisfying these needs will improve faculty and student morale and will reduce resistance to formal authority.	2. Teachers will exercise responsible self-direction and self-control in the accomplishment of worthwhile objectives that they understand and have helped establish.
3. High faculty and student morale and reduced resistance to formal authority may lead to improved school performance. It will at least reduce friction and make the supervisor's job easier.	3. Faculty satisfaction and student satisfaction will increase as a by-product of improved performance and the opportunity to contribute creatively to this improvement.

Source: Adapted from Raymond E. Miles, "Human Relations or Human Resources?" *Harvard Business Review*, vol. 43, no. 4, pp. 148–163, 1965, esp. exhibits I and II.

supervision (teacher's, principal's, or parent's) to control them. Given clear expectations and the opportunity to develop commitment, mature adults act on their own.

Second, they move from a state of dependence upon others in infancy to an adult state of relative independence, and finally to interdependence. They are able to stand on their own feet and yet to acknowledge healthy dependencies. As part of this development, they internalize a set of values, which become the bases of their behavior.

Third, they tend to develop from being capable of behaving in only a few ways as infants to being capable of behaving in many different ways as adults. They actually prefer to vary their style and do not care for fixed or rigid job assignments. They prefer to develop their own means to achieve ends rather than to be limited by the *best* way as defined by the organization.

Fourth, they tend to develop from having unpredictable, shallow, casual interests of short duration as infants to having deeper interests as adults. The mature personality is characterized by responding to an endless series of challenges, and reward comes from doing something for its own sake. Adults need a work environment that is challenging to skill and creativity.

Fifth, healthy human beings tend to develop from having a short-term perspective as infants—one in which the present largely determines their behavior—to a much larger time perspective as adults—one in which behavior is affected by past events and future hopes.

Sixth, they tend to develop from being in a subordinate position in the family and society as infants to aspiring to occupy an equal and/or superordinate position in reference to their peers. They are willing to accept leadership from others if they perceive it as legitimate, but they find being "bossed" offensive.

Seventh, they tend to develop from a lack of awareness of self as infants to an awareness of, and control over, self as adults. They are sensitive about their concepts of self and aware of their individuality. They therefore experience with displeasure attempts to lessen their self-worth. They cannot be expected to simply do the work that is put before them. They need to experience ego involvement in their work.

School assumptions that require teachers and students to behave in ways that tend toward the infancy end of the Argyris continuum usually have negative consequences for the human organization and ultimately retard school effectiveness. Such assumptions are reflected administratively in the formal organizational structures of the school in directive leadership and in managerial control through budget, incentive systems, inspection, and review procedures. Argyris describes the effects of "infancy" managerial assumptions as follows:

> Healthy human beings (in our culture) tend to find dependence, subordination and submissiveness frustrating. They would prefer to be relatively independent, to be active, to use many of their deeper abilities; and they aspire to positions equal with or higher than their peers. Frustration leads to regression, aggression, and tension. These in turn lead to conflict (the individual prefers to leave but fears doing so). Moreover, it can be shown that under these conditions, the individual will tend to experience psychological failure and short-time perspective.[15]

Our focus in this discussion has been on adults in school organizations, but the analogy is perhaps more important in its application to students. Argyris has captured the function of American schools—to move youngsters from infancy to maturity, intellectually, socially, and emotionally. Let us examine some of the alternatives that teachers on the one hand and students on the other have in adapting to school environments that frustrate mature development.[16]

For teachers	For students
1. Leave the school. Absence and turnover.	1. Same.
2. Climb the organizational ladder into administration and supervision.	2. Submit and "play ball" with the system.
3. Become defensive, daydream, become aggressive, nurture grievances, regress, project, feel low self-worth.	3. Same.
4. Become apathetic, disinterested, non-ego-involved in the school and its goals.	4. Same.
5. Create informal groups for mutual protection from the organization.	5. Same.
6. Formalize into militant associations and unions.	6. Go underground or dissent in newspapers, organized demonstrations, student unions.
7. De-emphasize in their own minds the importance of self-growth and creativity and emphasize the importance of money and other material rewards.	7. De-emphasize intrinsic learning goals and other values and emphasize grades, credits, and the like, to beat the system.
8. Accept the above-described ways of behaving as being proper for their lives outside the organization.	8. The depressing aspect of this cycle of events is that youngsters may accept socialization into the value system of infancy management and thus reinforce and perpetuate the system for another generation.

[15]Ibid.
[16]The list that follows is an adaptation of one which appears in Argyris, "Individual Actualization in Complex Organizations," op. cit., p. 227.

Some writers maintain that what Argyris criticizes so vehemently is exactly what workers in organizations want. Dubin, for example, argues:

> The fact of the matter is this. Work for probably a majority of workers, and even extending into the ranks of management, may represent an institutional setting that is not a central life interest for its participants. The consequence of this is that while participating in work, a general attitude of apathy and indifference prevails. The response to the demands of the institution is to satisfy the minimum expectations of required behavior without reacting affectively to these demands.[17]

Of course not everyone is capable of mature behavior or is able to respond to Theory Y assumptions, but what Dubin fails to add is that this reaction is learned as a result of one's experience with organizations. People are not *inherently* removed from organizational life.

MISTAKES IN IMPLEMENTING THEORY Y

It is important to point out that Theory Y is not a universal theory of how to administer and supervise. A common misunderstanding is that Pattern B behavior, the behavior most closely associated with Theory Y, should be used at all times in all cases and that it elicits a uniformly positive reaction from subordinates. What is not understood is that Theory Y refers to the *inherent potential* and *capacity* of people rather than their present condition or their disposition at a given point in time.

Consider the example of motivation:

> Motivation in teachers depends upon a complex set of factors and conditions, many of which are well beyond the control of the school and the supervisor. One's set of values and work norms, for example, affects one's orientation toward his or her job. Some teachers will never be properly motivated to work and others will usually be motivated to work regardless of what supervisors do. Indeed a good rule of thumb is, if you want motivated teachers, hire motivated people if you can. Wisdom aside, we still face the problem of increasing the identity, commitment, and performance of large numbers of teachers already tenured on the job. The majority of teachers desire and seek satisfying work and will respond to human resources supervision. But many will not and alternate supervisory methods and procedures that suit these teachers will need to be provided. Human resources supervision is not an elixir to be administered indiscriminately to all. But it is a powerful conception of supervision which by using the concepts of motivation and job enrichment can markedly improve the identity, commitment, and performance of most teachers and the effectiveness of schools.[18]

Pattern A behavior, the behavior most associated with Theory X, is not in itself inconsistent with Theory Y. Supervisors need to behave in a variety of ways, sometimes

---

[17]Robert Dubin, "Person and Organization," in William Greenwood (ed.), *Management and Organizational Behavior Theories,* Cincinnati: South-Western Publishing Co., 1965, p. 487. See also George Strauss, "Some Notes on Power-Equalization," in Harold J. Leavitt (ed.), *The Social Science of Organizations,* Englewood Cliffs, N.J.: Prentice-Hall, 1963, pp. 45–59.

[18]Thomas J. Sergiovanni, "Human Resources Supervision," in T. J. Sergiovanni (ed.), *Professional Supervision for Professional Teachers,* Washington, D.C.: Association for Supervision and Curriculum Development, 1975, p. 30. Human resources supervision follows closely the premises of Theory Y. See also Edgar Schein, "The Hawthorne Studies Revisited: A Defense of Theory Y," in Eugene Cass and Frederick Zimmer (eds.), *Man and Work in Society,* New York: Van Nostrand, 1975, pp. 78–94.

in a rather direct fashion, other times in a supportive or considerate fashion, and at still other times in a manner described as participative or team building. No one best approach applicable to all situations exists, but rather the effectiveness of an approach is dependent upon its suitability to the situation at hand. But the approach or style suited to the particular situation at hand is different from one's overriding assumptions and the beliefs upon which one's behavior is based. In human organizations such as schools it is clear that leadership styles and other behavioral patterns, though they may vary depending upon the situation, are generated from within the broad perspectives of Theory Y.

DETERMINANTS OF SUPERVISORY PATTERNS

This chapter is concerned with the values, assumptions, and management philosophies that are a part of the supervisor's concept of self. As these dimensions are internalized, they largely determine dominant supervisory behavior patterns. Other forces, however, such as those that exist within the client and those that exist in the environment, contribute to selecting appropriate supervisory style. These forces are delineated and described in the following sections.[19]

Forces in the Supervisor

When supervisors face a problem, their approach, behavior, or style is largely affected by each of the following internalized forces:

1. *Value system.* How strongly does a supervisor feel that individuals should have a share in making the decisions that affect them? Or, how convinced is the supervisor that the official who is paid to assume responsibility should personally carry the burden of decision making? The behavior of the supervisor will also be influenced by the relative importance that he or she attaches to organizational efficiency, personal growth of subordinates, and company profits.

2. *Confidence in subordinates.* Managers differ greatly in the amount of trust they have in other people generally, and this carries over to the particular employees they supervise at a given time. In viewing their particular group of subordinates, managers are likely to consider their knowledge and competence with respect to the problem. A central question managers might ask themselves is, "Who is best qualified to deal with this problem?" Often managers may, justifiably or not, have more confidence in their own capabilities than in those of their subordinates.

3. *Leadership inclinations.* There are some managers who seem to function more comfortably and naturally as highly directive leaders. Resolving problems and issuing orders come easily to them. Other managers seem to operate more comfortably in a

---

[19]This discussion follows Robert Tannenbaum and Warren Schmidt, "How to Choose a Leadership Pattern," *Harvard Business Review,* vol. 36, no. 2, pp. 95–101, 1958. Tannenbaum identifies three forces that managers should consider in deciding how to manage: (1) forces in the manager, (2) forces in the subordinates, and (3) forces in the situation. See also Tannenbaum and Fred Massarick, "Participation by Subordinates in the Managerial Decision-making Process," *Canadian Journal of Economics and Political Science,* vol. 16, pp. 408–418, August 1950.

team role where they are continually sharing many of their functions with their subordinates.

4. *Feelings of security in an uncertain situation.* The manager who releases control over the decision-making process thereby reduces the predictability of the outcome. Some managers have a greater need than others for predictability and stability in their environment. This "tolerance for ambiguity" is being viewed increasingly by psychologists as a key variable in a person's manner of dealing with problems.[20]

Such an impressive list of internalized forces may provoke feelings of helplessness in supervisors, but each of these dimensions can be altered and modified. A first step toward this end is awareness and understanding. As supervisors come to understand the nature of the values, prejudices, and management styles that have become a part of their conscious or unconscious selves, they are in a better position to evaluate and change their present approach to supervision.

Forces in the Supervisory Environment

The organizational forces that we have described in Chapter 3 are a major influence on supervisory style. The organizational style of the school, the school's normative culture, its role expectations, its belief pattern, and its authority and power systems serve as boundaries that often delimit choice of supervisory action. Further, the nature of the problem, the consequences of the task, and the character of the goal are additional determinants of appropriate supervisory behavior. A teacher, for example, may be required by default to consult with students when class activities are varied and complex, but such consultation is little more than perfunctory when activities are routine and simple.

Forces in Others

The extent to which school supervisors may permit their respective clients to exercise more freedom and control over their own destiny and that of the school depends largely on the following conditions:

1. Whether the subordinates have relatively high needs for independence. (As we all know, people differ greatly in the amount of direction that they desire.)

2. Whether the subordinates have a readiness to assume responsibility for decision making. (Some see additional responsibility as a tribute to their ability; others see it as "passing the buck.")

3. Whether they have a relatively high tolerance for ambiguity. (Some employees prefer to have clear-cut directives given to them; others prefer a wider area of freedom.)

---

[20]Tannenbaum and Schmidt, op. cit. The label "manager" tends to have negative connotations to many school people but the descriptions are equally appropriate if one substitutes the term "school supervisor" for "manager."

4. Whether they are interested in the problem and feel that it is important.

5. Whether they understand and identify with the goals of the organization.

6. Whether they have the necessary knowledge and experience to deal with the problem.

7. Whether they have learned to expect to share in decision making. (Persons who have come to expect strong leadership and are then suddenly confronted with the request to share more fully in decision making are often upset by this new experience. On the other hand, persons who have enjoyed a considerable amount of freedom resent the boss who begins to make all the decisions alone.)[21]

Indeed the choice of one supervisory pattern over another is partly a function of forces in the client to be supervised, but this rationale should not provide a convenient "out" for those whose dominant supervisory patterns fall outside the range of human resources supervision.

Human resources supervision recognizes that forces in the client may require the supervisor to behave in a variety of ways. Highly dependent teachers may well need paternalistic supervisory environments, and uncommitted students will require closely controlled supervisory environments. Human resources supervisors, however, are not resigned to these patterns in that they do not accept dependency in teachers as being natural or inherent. Dependency of teachers and lack of commitment of students are perceived as symptoms of client immaturity and/or perhaps supervisory immaturity and organizational immaturity. With this perception, the human resources supervisor works to diminish client dependency and to increase client commitment, for in the synthesizing theory these are important means to affect the school-effectiveness variables positively.

We shall now discuss and explore different supervisory leadership behavior patterns and examine their effects on the human organization that constitutes the school.

LEADERSHIP AND SUPERVISORY BEHAVIOR OBSERVED

Jack Gibb, in writing for the American Association for Higher Education 1967 Yearbook, *In Search of Leaders,* identifies and describes two ideal types of leadership style used by school administrators. The emergence of one or another of these styles in a given individual largely depends upon how that individual feels about his or her own adequacy and how much he or she trusts others.

Gibb classifies the first view, sometimes described as authoritarian or paternalistic, as *defensive.* "Dynamically the view defends the administrator against his own fears and distrusts and against perceived or anticipated attack from the outside."[22] In this view, defensive leadership patterns are based on fear and distrust, thrive on the distortion of information, and use strategies of persuasion and high control.

[21]Ibid.
[22]Jack R. Gibb, "Dynamics of Leadership," in *In Search of Leaders,* Washington, D.C.: National Education Association, American Association for Higher Education, 1967, p. 56.

The alternative to defensive supervisory practices is described by Gibb as being *participatory*. The key to this leadership style is high trust and confidence in people. "The self-adequate person tends to assume that others are also adequate and, other things being equal, that they will be responsible, loyal, appropriately work-oriented when work is to be performed, and adequate to carry out jobs that are commensurate with their levels of experience and growth."[23]

Gibb's description of the two ideal types of supervisory behavior is not without substantial support in the literature of leadership-supervisory styles. The Gibb analysis, however, emphasizes the forces within supervisors that determine their behavior. We move now to examining this behavior and its effects on the school.

THE DIMENSIONS OF LEADERSHIP

The research tradition dealing with leadership style in educational and noneducational settings has identified two key dimensions of leadership. These dimensions have been given a variety of labels. Subtle differences may exist in the labels, but by and large experts agree that leadership style is defined by the extent to which the leader seems to show concern for, focuses on, or seems oriented toward getting work done or accomplishing tasks and the extent to which the leader seems to show concern for, focuses on, or seems oriented toward the needs or feelings of people and his or her relationships with them.

In this discussion we will use the phrases "task-oriented" (TO) to refer to tendencies the leader shows for work and "relations-oriented" (RO) for the leader's tendency to show concern for people in displaying leadership behavior. Each of these dimensions of leadership style is illustrated conceptually in Figure 5-1.

The horizontal marginal axis line (abscissa) that forms the base of the grid represents the extent to which the leader's behavior shows a concern for task accomplishment (TO), with high concern to the right and low concern to the left. You might estimate the extent to which your leadership style shows concern for task accomplishment by checking one of the numbers (1 to 9) on this line. The vertical

---

[23]Ibid., p. 62.

Figure 5-1 The leadership grid. *(From T. J. Sergiovanni and David Elliot, Educational and Organizational Leadership in Elementary Schools, Englewood Cliffs, N.J.: Prentice-Hall, 1975.)*

marginal axis line (ordinate) that forms the left side of the grid represents the extent to which the leader's behavior shows a concern for people and relationships (RO), with the top representing high concern and the bottom, low concern. Again, estimate the extent to which you show concern for people and relationships in expressing leadership by checking one of the numbers on this line. To find your location in the grid based on the estimates you have made, simply find the point where lines drawn from each of the numbers you checked would intersect. For example, if you checked a 7 on the TO line and 6 on the RO line, your position on the grid would be indicated by the x that appears on the grid.

THE MANAGERIAL GRID

A more descriptive attempt to conceptualize the task dimension and the people dimension of supervisory behavior has resulted in a formulation referred to as the *managerial grid*.[24] The grid focuses on five ideal-type theories of supervisory behavior, each based on the two dimensions that we have identified and discussed as crucial variables found in organizations: (1) task and (2) people. Blake and Mouton, the proposers of the grid formulation, show the relationship between the two variables and present the five ideal-type combinations of style in Figure 5-2.

Notice that the horizontal axis, concern for production, is similar to the task-oriented construct, and that the vertical axis, concern for people, to the relationship-oriented construct. By locating degree of intensity for each of these two

[24]Robert Blake and Jane Mouton, *The Managerial Grid*, Houston: Gulf, 1964.

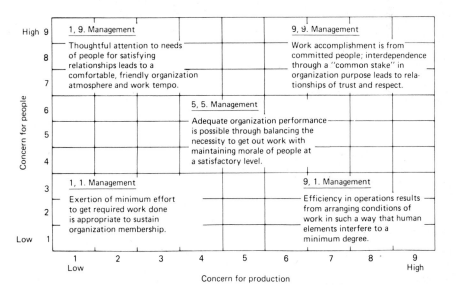

Figure 5-2 The managerial grid. *(From Robert Blake and Jane Mouton,* The Managerial Grid, *Houston: Gulf, 1964.)*

dimensions (from 1 to 9), we can see that the grid has potential for generating 81 different styles.

When asked to describe ideal leadership behavior in principals, teachers tend to express a preference for the integrated style that combines both TO and RO.[25] This preference seems to hold even though teachers may vary in terms of personality or need orientations. This observation lends support to the optimistic assumptions that make up the McGregor-Argyris management philosophy. That is, teachers seem able to describe ideal leadership behavior as emphasizing task—the organizational and structural aspects of the school—as well as providing for individual needs, regardless of their own personality shortcomings or strengths. Human resources supervision maintains that providing for needs of mature teachers is dependent upon efforts toward achieving school goals: the two dimensions then are viewed as interdependent, since goal achievement over time is dependent upon provision for teacher need, and teacher need over time is dependent upon the achievement of school goals.

REDDIN'S 3-D THEORY OF LEADERSHIP

The managerial grid is considered to be a normative theory of leadership in the sense that it prescribes the 9.9 image of leadership as the one best style. In this section we describe a more descriptive theory (Reddin's 3-D Theory), which shares many of the features of the managerial grid but assumes that no one best style exists.[26] Reddin views leadership style as consisting of a task and relationship emphasis similar to that illustrated previously in the quadrants of Figure 5-1.[27]

The lower-right-hand quadrant (TO high and RO low) represents a style of supervision that is characterized by a good deal of drive and emphasis on work and little overt concern for the relationship dimension. This is called the *dedicated* leadership style and is characterized by an emphasis on organizing, initiating, directing, completing, and evaluating the work of others.

The upper-left-hand quadrant (TO low and RO high) represents a style of supervision that emphasizes concern for people and little overt concern for the task dimension. This is called the *related* leadership style and is characterized by an emphasis on listening, accepting, trusting, advising, and encouraging.

The upper-right-hand quadrant (TO high and RO high) represents a combination approach to supervision, whereby people concerns are expressed through emphasizing

[25]This generalization of *ideal* style results from the Leadership Behavior Description Questionnaire research tradition of Ralph Stogdill and of Andrew Halpin. The Leadership Behavior Description Questionnaire was developed by the Personnel Research Board at Ohio State University and is published by the Bureau of Business Research at that university. See John K. Hemphill and Alvin E. Coons, *Leader Behavior Description,* Columbus: Ohio State University, Personnel Research Board, 1950. See also Andrew Halpin, *Theory and Research in Administration,* New York: Macmillan, 1967, p. 86. Halpin's efforts with the LBDQ and education are pioneering. See his *The Leadership Behavior of School Superintendents,* Chicago: University of Chicago, Midwest Administration Center, 1959. See also, "The Leader Behavior and Leadership Ideology of Educational Administrators and Aircraft Commanders," *Harvard Educational Review,* vol. 25, pp. 18–32, Winter 1955.
[26]W. J. Reddin, *Managerial Effectiveness,* New York: McGraw-Hill, 1970.
[27]This discussion follows that which appears in T. J. Sergiovanni, *Handbook for Effective Department Leadership: Concepts and Practices in Today's Secondary Schools,* Boston: Allyn and Bacon, 1977, p. 141. See also, Sergiovanni, "Leader Behavior and Organizational Effectiveness," *Notre Dame Journal of Education,* vol. 4, no. 1, 1973; and Sergiovanni and Elliott, *Educational and Organizational Leadership in Elementary Schools,* Englewood Cliffs, N.J.: Prentice-Hall, 1975, pp. 98–116.

meaningful work, and work concerns are emphasized by bringing together and stimulating committed groups of individuals. This is called the *integrated* leadership style and is characterized by an emphasis on interaction, motivation, integration, participation, and innovation.

The lower-left-hand quadrant (TO low and RO low) represents a style of supervision that expresses very little concern for either dimension. In a sense the leader removes himself or herself from both task and people. This is called the *separated* leadership style and is characterized by an emphasis on examining, measuring, administering, controlling, and maintaining.

The behavior indicators that Reddin suggests are associated with each of the four basic leadership styles shown in grid 4 in Figure 5-3.

Reddin proposes that the effectiveness of a given leadership style can be understood only within the context of the leadership situation. He assumes that related, integrated, separated, and dedicated are four basic styles only, each with an effective and an ineffective equivalent depending upon the situation in which it is used. These effective and ineffective equivalents result in eight operational leadership styles, as shown in Figure 5-4.

In Reddin's terms the basic *integrated* styles when displayed in an inappropriate setting might lead to *compromise* but when displayed in an appropriate setting lead to *executive* effectiveness. As *executives,* supervisors are seen as good motivators who set high standards, who treat teachers as individuals, and who prefer team approaches in operating their units. As *compromisers,* supervisors are seen as poor decision makers who allow pressures in the situation to influence them too much.

The basic *related* style expressed inappropriately may be perceived as *missionary* behavior, but when the situation is ripe for this style, *development* of people takes place. As *developers,* supervisors are seen as being primarily concerned with developing teachers as individuals and professionals. As *missionaries,* supervisors are seen as being primarily interested in harmony.

If supervisors behave in a *separated* way given appropriate conditions, they are displaying an appropriate *bureaucratic* response, but if their involvement in task or people or both is needed but not forthcoming, they are seen as *deserters.* As

	Related	Integrated
High	To listen	To interact
	To accept	To motivate
	To trust	To integrate
	To advise	To participate
	To encourage	To innovate
RO	To examine	To organize
	To measure	To initiate
	To administer	To direct
	To control	To complete
	To maintain	To evaluate
Low	Separated	Dedicated

Low ——————— TO ——————→ High

Figure 5-3 Basic style behavior indicators. *(From W. J. Reddin,* Managerial Effectiveness, *New York: McGraw-Hill, 1970.)*

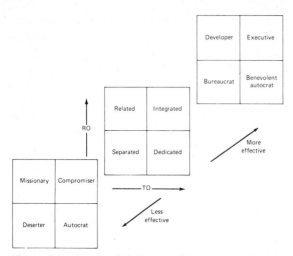

Figure 5-4 Reddin's 3-D Theory of Leadership. *(From W. J. Reddin,* Managerial Effectiveness, *New York: McGraw-Hill, 1970.)*

bureaucrats, supervisors are seen as being primarily interested in rules and procedures for their own sake and as wanting to maintain and control the situation by their use, and they are viewed as being conscientious. As *deserters,* supervisors are seen as being uninvolved and passive.

Dedicated supervisors who are inspirational and driving forces given appropriate circumstances are seen as *benevolent autocrats,* but when this style is displayed in inappropriate situations, they are viewed as interfering, dominant, and *repressive autocrats.* In the first instance supervisors are seen as people who know what they want and know how to get it without causing resentment. In the second instance they are seen as people who have no confidence in others, as unpleasant, and as being interested only in the immediate job.

At first glance the theory seems complex and the labels chosen by Reddin confusing and on occasion inappropriate. But the language system is worth deciphering, for the concepts and ideas basic to the theory are powerful and important. A key to this theory is the notion that the *same* style expressed in different situations may be effective or ineffective. For example, a supervisor who uses the integrated style with a teacher who is in need of personal support may be seen as *compromising* the personal dimension by not giving exclusive attention to the needs of the individual. This same supervisor who relies exclusively on support and understanding when a teacher is searching for a task solution to a problem may be seen as a *missionary* lacking in forceful leadership. This related style, however, would have been perceived as being most effective in the first instance.

UNDERSTANDING SITUATIONAL LEADERSHIP VARIABLES

The situational determinants of leadership style effectiveness are difficult to identify and formally catalog. Nevertheless, some useful generalizations can be made about situational variables and their relationship to leadership style. With a little practice one's ability to match appropriate style to situation can be improved considerably.

Generally speaking, we can assume that educational settings and particularly leadership situations in schools will only occasionally call for separated and dedicated styles, for in each of these cases the human dimension is neglected. This generalization is consistent with the human resources model for supervision. Occasions will exist when styles that show low concern for people are appropriate, but the focus of leadership *in general* will be in the related and integrated quadrants.

A number of exceptions to this generalization come to mind. In each case the job demands are such that the dedicated style, which emphasizes task but not people, will probably be most effective. One exception deals with routine situations where goals and objectives are simple, clear, and uncontroversial, and where the paths to reach the goal are few in number and clearly marked. Another exception relates to situations where very favorable leader-member relationships exist. Here, members trust the leader and are willing to follow him or her. A third exception relates to situations characterized by excessive interpersonal tension, confusion, and stress. Short-term success in these situations can be accomplished through use of the dedicated style. The leader's formal position in the school hierarchy is another important condition. When too much positional or hierarchical distance exists between leader and members, it is often less stressful for everyone if the leader uses a more directive or task-oriented style. Other important considerations that influence choice of style include time constraints and competency and motivational levels of teachers. These and other variables one must consider in matching style to situation are discussed in the next chapter, entitled "A Contingency Approach to Supervisory Leadership."

SUMMARY

Leadership is of particular importance to effective supervision. When compared with other conditions that influence the mediating variables, organizational structure and function, for example, leadership is more directly accessible to supervision. An important conceptual distinction was made between leadership and administrative behavior, but for operational purposes both were considered as variations in leadership style.

The importance of supervisory assumptions in influencing leadership style was emphasized by discussing McGregor's Theories X and Y and Argyris's infancy management assumptions. In addition, the assumptions basic to Theory X soft (human relations) were compared with those of Theory Y (human resources). It was pointed out that though Theory Y seems more clearly appropriate to human organizations such as schools, this does not preclude the use of a number of leadership approaches.

Forces in the supervisor, in the environment, and in subordinates were discussed as additional factors impinging upon choice of style. The leadership theories of Blake and Mouton (the managerial grid) and W. J. Reddin (3-D Theory) were then discussed. Both theories are concerned with the task and relationship emphasis of the supervisor. Each describes basic styles of leadership as comprising a mix of emphases. In 3-D Theory it was suggested that though four basic styles (dedicated, related, integrated, and separated) could be identified, no one best style appropriate for all cases existed. The dependence of leadership effectiveness upon the correct matching of style to the characteristics of the situation at hand was discussed. A number of situational leadership variables were suggested, and it was promised that they would be further delineated in Chapter 6.

STUDY GUIDE

Recall the concepts, ideas, and meanings associated with each of the following phrases and terms included in this chapter. Can you discuss each of them with a colleague and apply them to the supervisor context of your school? If you cannot, review them in the text and record the page number for future reference.

1. Dedicated style _____
2. Forces in the environment _____
3. Forces in others _____
4. Forces in the supervisor _____
5. Grid numbers _____
6. Infancy management assumption _____
7. Integrated style _____
8. Leadership definitions _____
9. Leadership quadrants _____
10. Managerial grid _____
11. Misunderstandings of Theory Y _____
12. Pattern A _____
13. Pattern B _____
14. Relations-oriented _____
15. Related style _____
16. Self-fulfilling prophecy _____
17. Separated style _____
18. Situational leadership variables _____
19. Theory X soft _____
20. Theory Y _____
21. 3-D Theory _____

EXERCISES

1. Contrast Theory X, Theory X soft, and Theory Y supervisory assumptions. Develop three teacher-evaluation policy statements with implementation guidelines—each based on one of the assumption sets.
2. Though the authors are committed to the values of Theory Y, they suggest that on occasions, *behavior* based on Theories X and X soft is justified. Provide examples suggesting when X or X soft behavior is appropriate.
3. Explain the differences between normative and situational theories of leadership.
4. List each of the behavioral indicators contained in Figure 5-2 on a separate sheet of paper, mixing the items so that they are not categorized. Role-play or actually ask teachers to select 5 of the 20 indicators that they expect supervisors to emphasize. Repeat this procedure with administrators and supervisors. Re-sort the selected indicators into the four grid categories. You should now have three sets of expectations for the supervisor's role. In what ways are these expectations similar and in what ways are they different? Where differences occur (role conflict), and how might they be resolved?

CHAPTER 6

A CONTINGENCY APPROACH TO SUPERVISORY LEADERSHIP

In Chapter 5 it was pointed out that no one best style of leadership could be identified but rather that effectiveness of style was determined by its appropriateness to the situation at hand. Indeed, any one style might be appropriate for situation A but not B and another for situation B but not A. Using Reddin's 3-D Theory of Leadership, we identified four basic styles, each with an effective and ineffective expression.[1] The styles, with their effective and ineffective counterparts, are summarized in Table 6-1.

In this chapter we are concerned with the identification of situational variables and with helping supervisors to match styles to situational demands. This is a contingency approach to supervisory leadership.

CONTINGENCY LEADERSHIP THEORY (FIEDLER)

A new theory of leadership effectiveness has emerged from some 15 years of research conducted at the University of Illinois through its Group Effectiveness Laboratory and

[1]W. J. Reddin, *Managerial Effectiveness*, New York: McGraw-Hill, 1970.

Table 6-1 Effective and Ineffective Expression of Leadership Style

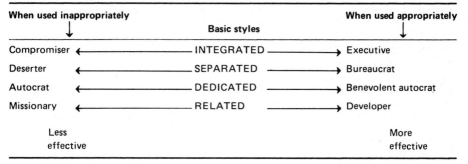

From W. J. Reddin, *Management Effectiveness*, New York: McGraw-Hill, 1970, p. 40.

from work done at the University of Washington since 1970. This theory, developed by Fred Fiedler and his associates,[2] stems from a research tradition primarily associated with that of small-group psychology. The theory suggests that both task-oriented and relationship-oriented leaders are able to perform effectively in a group given conditions appropriate to and supportive of their leadership style. Further, the theory accepts the style of the leader as a given, and therefore recommends that the arrangement of tasks and situations accommodate leader styles rather than that styles change to fit situations.[3] Fiedler would suggest, for example, that the supervisor who is effective on a one-to-one basis with teachers because of the increased status this arrangement provides but is ineffective working with teachers as a group (group situations often decrease status differences between designated leaders and followers) should arrange for a pattern of supervision that favors the first situation and avoids the second.

The task-oriented leader in Fiedler's research corresponds to the dedicated-leadership designation of Reddin's theory, and the relationship-oriented leader to the related designation. Fiedler does not examine the separated and integrated styles.

Fiedler's extensive research strongly indicates that task-oriented leaders perform best in group situations that are either very favorable or very unfavorable to the leader. Relationship-oriented leaders, on the other hand, perform best in group situations that are intermediate in favorableness. Favorableness is defined by the degree to which the situation enables the leader to exert influence over the group.

Three major situational variables seem to determine whether a given situation is favorable or unfavorable to the leader. In order of importance they are listed as follows: (1) leader-member relations, which in our case refers to the extent teachers accept, admire, like, and are willing to follow individual supervisors because of the kind of people they are and the relationship they have developed with the teachers; (2) task structure, which in our case refers to the extent the work of the unit or person being supervised is structured, how clearly the objectives are defined, and how limited the processes available for achieving these objectives are; (3) position power, which in our case refers to the amount of formal authority and status the supervisor has.

Fiedler's Contingency Model

A simplified version of Fiedler's contingency model is presented in Figure 6-1.[4] This figure shows the effectiveness of relationship-oriented leadership versus task-oriented

---

[2]See Fred E. Fiedler, *A Theory of Leadership Effectiveness*, New York: McGraw-Hill, 1967, for a comprehensive treatment of this theory. More popular versions of the theory are found in Fiedler's "Engineering the Job to Fit the Manager." *Harvard Business Review*, vol. 43, no. 5, pp. 115–122, September 1965: "Style or Circumstance: The Leadership Enigma." *Psychology Today*, vol. 2, no. 10, pp. 38–43, March 1969; and Fiedler and Martin Chemers, *Leadership and Effective Management*, Glenview, Ill.: Scott, Foresman, 1974. These references form the basis of the following discussion.

[3]Leadership styles are measured by an instrument that yields a Least Preferred Co-Worker (LPC) score for respondents. Using an Osgood Semantic Differential format, respondents are asked to describe their least preferred co-worker on each of 16 dimensions. Those who describe this worker in a relatively positive sense are typed as relationship-oriented, while those who describe him or her in a negative sense are typed as task-oriented. Fiedler presents impressive evidence supporting this method in Chap. 3 of his book, *A Theory of Leadership Effectiveness*.

[4]The contingency model is constructed by plotting correlations of leadership style against the taxonomy of group situations. The approximate median correlations between leader LPC score and group performance plotted for each group situation (Cells 1 to 8 in Fig. 6-1) are −.55, −.60, −.30, .43, .40; none available for Cell 6, .3, and −5.0. (Fiedler, *A Theory of Leadership Effectiveness*, p. 146.)

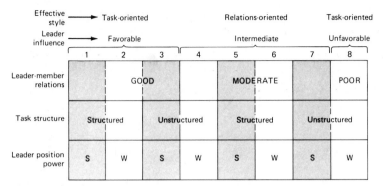

Figure 6-1 Fiedler's contingency theory of leadership.

leadership for group situations characterized by different combinations of leader-member personal relationships, task structure, and leader position power.

Eight group situations are identified and categorized according to whether they are high or low on each of the three critical dimensions that determine the favorableness of a given style. The group situations are arranged in declining order of the leader's influence, with Cell 1 providing the leader with the most influence and Cell 8 the least influence. The leader, for example, who is well liked by group members, who is working in structured tasks, and who has a great deal of authority can exert strong influence on the group, while the opposite, the leader who is not liked, who has an unstructured assignment, and who comes with little authority has difficulty in exerting influence.

The contingency model suggests that task-oriented leaders perform best in situations that provide them with substantial influence *and* in situations that provide them with very little influence. Relationship-oriented leaders, on the other hand, are most effective in mixed situations that afford them moderate influence over the group. Leadership contexts 1 to 3, for example, provide the leader with the most favorable opportunities to influence the group, and Fiedler finds that task-oriented leadership is the most effective style. Leadership context 8 provides the leader with the least amount of influence on group members, and again the task-oriented or directive style is found to be effective. The remaining four contexts, according to the contingency leadership theory, seem best suited to the relationship-oriented style.

When supervisors have the respect and good wishes of teachers and a great deal of formal authority to back them up, exerting influence is easy. Personal relationships with teachers are such that teachers are more willing to follow. In addition position power is such that teachers more readily yield to the supervisor the right to lead. Combine these with a structured task, as in context 1, which tends not to call for much participation anyway, and we have the perfect setting for more task-oriented or dedicated leadership. Contexts 2 and 3 are not quite as favorable as 1 but possess enough of the same ingredient to permit easy influence.

Contexts 4 to 7, on the other hand, each require the supervisor to earn the right to lead, to win the loyalty and commitment of teachers, or, as in contexts 4 and 7, where tasks are unstructured, to depend upon the knowledge and abilities of others in order to be effective. In each case related and integrated styles are found to be more effective. Context 8 is so unfavorable that, at least for a short period of time, the more directive task style is recommended. As the supervisor works to improve the situation so that it approximates context 4, his or her style needs to change accordingly.

THE HERSEY AND BLANCHARD MODEL

Hersey and Blanchard's model of contingency leadership is a useful and well-known construct for understanding and guiding supervisory leadership. Relying on the traditional four-quadrant format depicted in Figures 5-1 to 5-4, they suggest that the best leadership style is the one that matches the maturity level of followers. The essentials of their theory are shown in Figure 6-2. When the maturity level of followers is very low, they recommend that the supervisor use a direct and structured style characterized by high-task orientation and low-relationship orientation. As the maturity level increases in a particular individual, changes as individuals and groups change, or changes for an individual as the situation changes, supervisors should use a more integrated blend of task and relationship in their styles. A more participatory approach

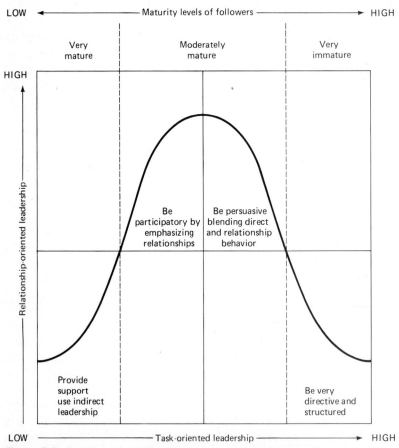

Figure 6-2 The Hersey and Blanchard model emphasizing maturity.

to leadership characterized by high-relationship orientation is recommended as maturity in followers continues to increase. And finally, for very mature followers who possess a great deal of self-responsibility or a great deal of knowledge about a particular event, a less directive and unobtrusive style is recommended. In the language of Hersey and Blanchard, the emphasis in leadership shifts from telling to selling, participating, and delegating as maturity in followers increases. They define maturity as "the capacity to set high but attainable goals (achievement motivation), willingness and ability to take responsibility, and education and/or experience of an individual or a group."[5] The Hersey and Blanchard theory has great appeal because it is easy to learn and makes intuitive sense.

THE ZONE OF INDIFFERENCE

All teachers do not have a uniform desire to participate in the decision-making processes of the school nor for that matter do all teachers wish to be involved in the same things. When the context of decision making is of little or no concern to a teacher (that is, when it is in his or her zone of indifference), a more task-oriented approach from the leader would be appropriate.[6] Teachers, for example, are not likely to be terribly interested in many of the purely administrative or technical aspects of operating a particular unit and would probably be pleased by a supervisor who can regulate them in a dedicated but unobtrusive way. Teachers often resent being involved in events and activities they consider to be unimportant. As one's zone of indifference with reference to a particular issue decreases, however, one's desire to be involved increases, and this necessitates use of the more related and integrated styles. These relationships are shown in Figure 6-3.

[5]Paul Hersey and Kenneth H. Blanchard, *Management of Organizational Behavior: Utilizing Human Resources*, 3d ed., Englewood Cliffs, N.J.: Prentice-Hall, 1977, p. 161.
[6]This discussion follows Sergiovanni and D. Elliott, *Organizational and Educational Leadership in Elementary Schools*, Englewood Cliffs, N.J.: Prentice-Hall, 1975, pp. 108–109.

Figure 6-3 The Zone of Indifference. *(Adapted from Robert Tannenbaum and Warren Schmidt, "How to Choose a Leadership Pattern,"* Harvard Business Review, *vol. 36, no. 2, 1957.)*

A broad range of styles exists between the two extremes of task orientation and relationship orientation. It is difficult to conceptualize leadership on the task and relationship continuum only. For example, as one moves to the extreme right on Figure 6-3 to where the supervisor defines limits and asks teachers to make decisions and to where the supervisor permits teachers to function within limits defined by agreed-upon goals and objectives, concern for task and concern for people are both present. These are the essential characteristics of the integrated style. Nevertheless, it seems appropriate to generalize that as the substance of decision making moves closer to the classroom activities of teachers and as proposed changes in operation and procedure require attitudinal and behavioral changes from the teachers, the zone of indifference is likely to decrease. Teachers will be more concerned with the issues at hand and will want to be involved. In such cases, leadership styles that include a generous component of relationship orientation (the related and integrated styles) are most likely to be effective. Moreover, the relationship between styles of supervision and the level of teachers' interest holds for the relationship between styles of supervision and the competency, maturity, and commitment levels of teachers. The more competent teachers are, given a particular set of problems or tasks, the more appropriate are related and integrated styles. The less competent teachers are, given a set of problems and tasks, the more appropriate is the dedicated style.

CONTINGENCY LEADERSHIP THEORY (VROOM)

One important characteristic of leadership style is the emphasis, or lack of emphasis, given to the participation of subordinates in decision making. Dedicated and separated styles tend not to emphasize participation. Related and integrated styles, on the other hand, tend to emphasize participation.

Victor Vroom's theory of leadership focuses on this one important dimension of leader behavior, the degree to which the supervisor should encourage participation of teachers in decision making.[7] In a typology similar to that proposed by Tannenbaum and Schmidt[8] as adapted in Figure 6-3, Vroom identifies five decision styles, or processes, that might be available for use by supervisors. This is a contingency approach in the sense that no one decision-making process is best under all circumstances and that the effectiveness of one's choice is dependent upon properties of the situation at hand. The decision styles are described as follows:

1. The supervisor solves the problem or makes the decision using information available at the time. This is an approach consistent with the dedicated style.

---

[7]See, for example, Victor Vroom, "A New Look at Managerial Decision-Making," *Organizational Dynamics,* vol. 1, 1973; Vroom and P. W. Yetton, "A Normative Model for Leadership Styles," in H. J. Leavitt and L. Pondy (eds.), *Readings in Managerial Psychology,* 2d ed., Chicago: University of Chicago Press, 1973; and Vroom, "Leadership Revisited," in Eugene Carr and Frederick Zimmer (eds.), *Man and Work in Society,* New York: Van Nostrand, 1975, pp. 220–234.
[8]Robert Tannenbaum and Warren Schmidt, "How to Choose a Leadership Pattern," *Harvard Business Review,* vol. 36, no. 2, pp. 95–101, 1957.

2. The supervisor obtains necessary information from teacher(s), then decides on the solution to the problem. The supervisor may or may not tell teachers much about the problem when obtaining information from them. The role of teachers in this case is in providing information—rather than generating or evaluating solutions. This approach combines aspects of the dedicated and separated leadership styles.

3. The supervisor shares the problems with relevant teachers individually, obtaining their ideas and suggestions without bringing them together as a group. Then the supervisor, at times being influenced by their advice and at other times, not, makes the decision. This approach combines aspects of the dedicated and related leadership styles.

4. The supervisor shares the problem with teachers as a group, obtaining ideas and suggestions, and then makes the decision, which may or may not reflect the influence of teachers. The approach combines aspects of the integrated and dedicated leadership styles.

5. The supervisor shares the problem with teachers as a group. Together they generate and evaluate alternatives and attempt to reach agreement on a solution. The supervisor does not try to pressure the group to adopt his or her solution and is willing to accept and implement any solution that has the support of the group. This approach combines aspects of the related and integrated leadership styles.[9]

The supervisor determines which decision style is best for a particular situation on the basis of answers to seven critical questions, each of which defines and helps diagnose aspects of the problem at hand. Depending upon how the critical questions are answered, the supervisor is able to determine the best decision styles for this situation. This process, along with the critical questions, is illustrated in the form of a decision tree in Figure 6-4.

Letters A through H representing the eight critical questions are arranged along the top of Figure 6-4 in a fashion that elicits "yes" or "no" responses. To use the model, start with the box on the left-hand side of the diagram and ask question A. The answer, either "yes" or "no," determines the path to take on the decision tree. Continue to the right until you encounter a second box. Answer the question associated with that box and continue the process until a terminal node is reached. At that node you will find a number designating a range of feasible decision styles. This number and the range of decision styles are listed below the decision tree and correspond to the five decision styles discussed previously.

As an example, assume that in starting with square 1 to the left of the model, the answer to question A is "no." The supervisor would then follow the "no" branch of the decision tree to square 2 and respond to question D. A "yes" response to this question leads to square 3 and question E. A "no" response to this question leads to a terminal node to the far right of the diagram. Here the supervisor finds the number 2, which prescribes the appropriate decision style range. Consulting the lower portion of Figure

[9]Adapted from Vroom, "Leadership Revisited," in Carr and Zimmer (eds.), op. cit., p. 225.

Critical questions:
- A. Is there a quality requirement such that one solution is likely to be more rational than another?
- B. Do I have sufficient info to make a high quality decision?
- C. Is the problem structured?
- D. Is acceptance of decision by subordinates critical to effective implementation?
- E. If I were to make the decision by myself, is it reasonably certain that it would be accepted by my subordinates?
- F. Do subordinates share the organizational goals to be attained in solving this problem?
- G. Is conflict among subordinates likely in preferred soltuions? (This question is irrelevant to individual problems.)
- H. Do subordinates have sufficient info to make a high quality decision?

Range of decision styles

1. (1, 2, 3, 4, 5)	7. (5)	13. (4)
2. (5)	8. (4)	14. (4, 5)
3. (1, 2, 3, 4, 5)	9. (3, 4)	15. (4, 5)
4. (1, 2, 3, 4, 5)	10. (2, 3, 4)	16. (5)
5. (1, 2, 3, 4)	11. (2, 3, 4, 5)	17. (5)
6. (5)	12. (2, 3, 4, 5)	18. (4)

Figure 6-4 Vroom: Decision process flow chart. *(Adapted from Victor Vroom and Arthur Jago, "Decision-Making as a Social Process: Normative and Descriptive Models of Leadership Behavior,"* Technical Report No. 5, *Organizational Effectiveness Research Programs, Office of Naval Research. N0014-67-A-0097-0027, A, 1974.)*

6-4, we find that the number 2 suggests *only* decision style 5, which urges the supervisor to share the problem with the group and seek a consensus solution. Beginning again at square 1 to the far left of the model, we find that a "yes" answer to question A leads to square 2 under question B and so on, until the process has continued through the decision tree to another terminal node.

Notice that in a number of cases several decision styles are listed. Vroom suggests that though the listed styles represent the feasible range of options available, the supervisor must still select one decision style for implementation. Each of the styles is arranged in *ascending* order of time required for implementation and *descending* order in terms of potential for *development* of teachers. Decision style 1 is most efficient in time but promises the least in developing teachers. By contrast, decision style 5 is most costly in time but has the most potential for developing teachers. Vroom suggests that one should select the decision style furthest to the left (closest to 1) from among those identified as feasible on the decision tree when time is scarce and furthest to the right (closest to 5) when time is plentiful.

In the case of schools where the development of human resources is particularly critical, the prudent supervisor will make every effort to choose decision styles closest to 5—that is, those with the greatest potential for developing teachers.

DEVELOPMENTAL SUPERVISION

Listed below are three groups of words: A, B, and C. They characterize ways in which a supervisor might work with teachers in improving instruction. Think about how you as a supervisor work with teachers in this capacity. If you are not a supervisor, think about the extent to which each of the three groups of words suggests how you might behave:

A	B	C
Presenting	Presenting	Listening
Directing	Clarifying	Encouraging
Demonstrating	Listening	Clarifying
Standardizing	Problem solving	Presenting
Reinforcing	Negotiating	Problem solving

Rate *each group* of words on a 6-point scale with 6 as the high to reflect the extent to which each group describes your supervisory style.[10]

Glickman has proposed a useful model of leadership called Developmental Supervision, which is designed specifically for application to the context of supervising teachers to improve instruction.[11] He identifies three basic leadership orientations: directive, collaborative, and nondirective. The words in group A describe the directive style, those in group B the collaborative, and those in group C the nondirective. Figure 6-5 depicts the three styles of supervision superimposed on the traditional four-quadrant leadership grid (see, for example, Figures 5-1 and 5-3). Use this figure to plot your A, B, and C scores. Note that high nondirective scores suggest a relationship style, high directive scores a task style, and high collaborative scores a team style.

Glickman proposes a contingency theory based on the premise that each of the styles of supervision might be appropriate or not giving characteristics of the specific situation at hand. He suggests that two major characteristics be considered: commitment levels of teachers and abstract levels of teachers' thinking. Commitment is an essential ingredient in the concept of maturity as proposed by Hersey and Blanchard. Commitment can be conceived of as a continuum from low to high.

Abstract thinking refers to "a teacher's ability to stand back from his or her classroom, to clarify his or her own instructions (management, discipline, record keeping, organization, and student attitudes), determine alternative solutions to these problems and then to plan a course of action. . . ."[12] Teachers high in the quality of abstract thinking are able to function more independently and with greater flexibility and complexity and are able to tolerate more ambiguity. In a fashion somewhat similar

---

[10]Only a general indication of supervisory style can be obtained from this rating procedure. The descriptions are based on the Supervisory Beliefs Inventory developed by Carl D. Glickman and Roy T. Tamashiro. See Carl D. Glickman, *Developmental Supervision,* Alexandria, Va.: Associatior for Supervision and Curriculum Development, 1981, pp. 12–14.

[11]Ibid.

[12]Ibid., p. 44.

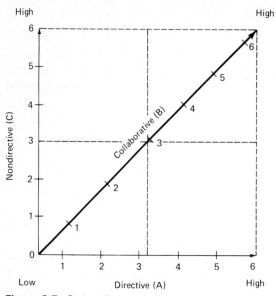

Figure 6-5 Styles of supervision.

to the Hersey and Blanchard[18] leadership model, Glickman proposes a contingency model as follows:

1. Use more directive supervision when teacher levels of commitment and abstraction are low.
2. Use more collaborative supervision when teacher levels of commitment are low but levels of abstraction are high or when levels of abstraction are low and levels of commitment are high.
3. Use more indirect supervision when teacher levels of commitment and abstraction are both high.

Note that as teachers become more "mature" on the two dimensions proposed by Glickman, the emphasis shifts from more control to less control by the supervisor.

JOB DEMANDS AND LEADERSHIP EFFECTIVENESS

An additional set of concerns for supervisors interested in selecting leadership strategies in a manner consistent with contingency theory is the unique characteristics that define the job or task at hand. Job demands vary as objectives and tasks change or as attention shifts from one set of problems or objectives to another. In one situation, for example, the supervisor might be more expert than teachers, and in another case, they may be more expert than the supervisor.

Reddin suggests that as a general guide, if the problem and objectives currently in focus result in the following job demands and conditions, then the related style will

---

[18]Hersey and Blanchard, op. cit.

probably be the most effective:[14]

- Teachers have high expertness or unusual technical skills.
- Teacher identification and commitment are necessary for success.
- The job is arranged in a way that teachers can largely decide how tasks will be accomplished.
- It is difficult to evaluate performance outcomes precisely.
- Teachers need to be creative and inventive in their work.

If the situation is such that the following job demands and conditions are present, then the separated style will probably be the most effective:

- The teacher's job is programmed in a routine fashion and requires the following of established procedures, curriculum formats, teaching strategies.
- The teacher's job is easy to perform and easy to regulate.
- Automatic feedback is provided so that the teacher can readily note her or his progress.
- Intellectual privacy and thinking are much more important than the teacher being actively involved in something.

If the situation is such that the following job demands and conditions are present, then the integrated style will probably be most effective:

- Teachers need to interact with each other in order to complete their tasks.
- Teachers are interdependent; the success of one depends upon the help of others, and vice versa.
- Successful completion of tasks requires that the supervisor must interact with teachers as a group.
- Several solutions are possible, and the number of solutions proposed and evaluated is improved by interaction among group members.
- Teachers can set their own pace as the group pursues its task.

If the situation is such that the following job demands and conditions are present, then the dedicated style will probably be most effective:

- The supervisor knows more about the task or problems at hand than the teachers do.
- Numerous unplanned and unanticipated events are likely to occur which require attention from the supervisor.

[14]Charting job demands and relating them to leadership styles is an integral part of Reddin, *Managerial Effectiveness,* New York: McGraw-Hill, 1970, pp. 69–88. This section follows T. J. Sergiovanni, *Handbook for Effective Department Leadership in the Secondary Schools: Concepts and Practices,* Boston: Allyn and Bacon, 1977, pp. 151–152.

• Teachers need to be given direction frequently in order for them to complete their task.

• The teacher's performance is readily measurable, and corrective actions by the supervisor are visible and can be easily evaluated.

NOTES ON CONTINGENCY THEORY

Contingency theories of leadership appear at the same time complex and accessible. On the one hand, they portray leadership effectiveness in a fashion that causes one to grasp for the security of styles and modes that are familiar, and on the other hand, their sophistication carries promises of success far beyond that which one might realistically expect. Nevertheless, contingency theories are an improvement over "one best style" theories. They are indeed complex but can be learned and used by most supervisors. They do promise much and therefore may well disappoint many users. On balance we believe that mastery and use of contingency theories can help improve effectiveness, particularly if supervisors keep in mind that the phenomena of leadership still remain somewhat of a mystery and that to date all theories are at best partial explanations, unable to account for all the forces impinging upon leader effectiveness.

One consequence of focusing on the behavioral aspects of leadership and on developing leadership strategies is that the substance of leadership decisions may get slighted. Leadership skills are important, but they cannot guarantee genuine leadership if the leader does not have a clear sense of purpose and direction.

A decisive factor that distinguishes a leader is his or her vision of, or belief in, what is possible. Besides having technical competence in management or supervisory skills, a leader possesses a deep sense of the significance of what the group is doing. In communicating that sense of significance, the leader enlists the commitment of the group to achieving those significant results. Among the military, that significance may center on the defense of democratic freedom or the defense of one's homeland. Among medical scientists, it may be the discovery of a new cure for cancer. Among government workers, the significance might center on the improvement of the quality of life for citizens in the community or even a simpler way to pay taxes. Usually what will gain the commitment of a group to its task is the general belief that its work makes a difference in the lives of other people.

What solidifies the group commitment to its work is the living out of the belief in its significance by the leader. If leaders do not practice what they preach, then the group loyalty to them and to the achievement of the significant results they talk about will evaporate. On the other hand, the moral persuasion of their consistent example will lead to greater identification with their vision of, or belief in, the significance of what the group is doing. Gradually the group will appropriate and internalize the motivation of the leader, especially when it coincides with sources of motivation in themselves that, perhaps, have lain dormant.

Usually the leader can communicate a sense of drama inherent in his or her vision of what is possible. Routine and repetition are what tend to deaden work and decrease enthusiasm. What once was challenging is reduced to habit, to an automatic response, to ordinariness. Frequently, it is the leader who will help the group recapture a sense of pride in its work or a sense of purpose, if not enthusiasm.

Perhaps an example can clarify. Consider what happens to the consciousness of an audience that is attending an exceptional dramatic performance. During and after the play they experience the value and significance inherent in many situations that they have come to accept as "ordinary." In the play, words, gestures, and decisions make a difference, sometimes a profound difference, in the lives of the characters. One word might save a life; if one gesture had been otherwise, it might have made all the difference; a door left open instead of closed might have changed the whole course of a character's life. What the characters in the play do or say has dramatic significance; the drama of human life gathers to a new fullness. Greatness, heroism, or evil is made vividly possible on the stage. The audience experiences the beautiful or tragic possibilities inherent in human life. They leave the performance with a more intense awareness of what might have happened or might be happening to their own lives.

Leaders tend to live with this more intense consciousness of the drama inherent in the human condition, of the significance of human choices, of the exciting possibilities challenging human imagination. This kind of dramatic consciousness illumines and suffuses the technical performance of their management or administrative tasks. They dwell on the significance of the task, appreciate the inherent drama in the accomplishment of the task, and communicate an appreciation and sense of excitement about the task to the group.

Supervisor leadership behavior in education, then, involves not only the supervisor's appreciation of the considerable human resources of subordinates but also the supervisor's own beliefs about, and vision of, the dramatic possibilities inherent in all educational activity. This vision, or set of beliefs, provides the substance of supervisory leadership. The forms of supervisory leadership will vary frequently, depending on the situation, but the substance or content of that leadership behavior will steadily flow out of the vision.

While the authors do not offer fully developed educational philosophy in this book, they do affirm the critical importance of it for supervisory personnel who wish to exert leadership. Without some basic vision of their own, it would seem impossible for supervisors to develop with subordinates a shared sense of purpose that flows out of the significance of what they are doing for and in the lives of students.

SUMMARY

This chapter examined contingency approaches to leadership effectiveness. Contingency theory assumes that no one best style of leadership suitable to all situations can be identified but rather that effectiveness of style is determined by its appropriateness to the situation at hand. The four basic styles proposed by Reddin and their effective and ineffective counterparts were then reviewed. Using Fiedler's contingency theory of leadership, the related (RO) and dedicated (TO) styles were selected for further examination. Leadership situations were defined by three critical variables—the quality of leader-member relationships, the extent to which the group task is structured or unstructured, and the position power of the leader. Using the three variables, we identified eight situations for leadership in descending order of ease of influence by the leader. It was determined that the dedicated style (TO) is more effective in situations that are favorable and unfavorable to influence by the leader. Situations characterized as only moderately favorable were associated with the related (RO) leadership style. The popular Hersey and Blanchard model of leadership emphasizing maturity was then summarized.

The zone of indifference of teachers was also discussed as a further consideration in choosing an appropriate style. The dedicated style was found more suitable for situations characterized by teacher indifference, but as decision making moved closer to areas considered more important to teachers, related styles were judged more appropriate. Competency, maturity, and commitment levels of teachers were cited as examples of additional contingency variables to be considered.

Vroom's contingency theory of leadership was then discussed as one approach that focuses on an aspect of leader behavior of particular importance to supervisors, the degree to which the leader should encourage participation of subordinates in decision making. Five decision styles were described, each effective in some situations but not in others. Vroom provides a methodology that uses a decision tree along which a subject is guided by answers to seven critical questions, for determining which decision style is most appropriate to the situation at hand.

Glickman's Developmental Supervision model, a contingency model designed specifically for the context of educational supervision, was then presented.

Still an additional set of concerns to be considered in using contingency theory is the unique characteristics or job demands that define the job or task at hand. Lists of job conditions typically associated with the related, integrated, separated, and dedicated leadership styles were provided. Some cautions in implementing contingency theory were then discussed.

Finally, visions or beliefs of leaders were highlighted as constant sources for leadership behavior. Their consciousness of the dramatic possibilities for human growth in any educational setting—or their philosophies of education—energize their leadership behavior in whatever styles the contingencies of the situation encourage them to adopt.

STUDY GUIDE

Recall the concepts, ideas, and meanings associated with each of the following phrases and terms included in this chapter. Can you discuss each of them with a colleague and apply them to the supervisory context of your school? If you cannot, review them in the text and record the page number for future reference.

1. Contingency theory _____
2. Decision styles _____
3. Decision-free _____
4. Dedicated style _____
5. Developmental supervision _____
6. Fiedler's theory _____
7. Integrated style _____
8. Job demands _____
9. Leader-member relation _____
10. Maturity _____

11. Position power _____
12. Related style _____
13. RO _____
14. Separated style _____
15. Situational favorableness _____
16. Situational variable _____
17. Task structure _____
18. Terminal node _____
19. TO _____
20. Vroom's theory _____
21. Zone of indifference _____

EXERCISES

1. Develop thumbnail sketches of four supervisors, each with leadership styles categorized as basically integrated, separated, dedicated, or related. Include in each sketch one or two examples showing situations where that supervisor's basic leadership style might be effective and situations where that style might be ineffective.

2. Identify two or three decision-making problems, and analyze each using Vroom's decision tree. How would your analysis differ if you were using Fiedler's contingency theory? Which of the two approaches do you find more useful?

3. Review the job demands listed under the chapter heading "Job Demands and Leadership Effectiveness." Which of the demands best characterizes your school? What implications would these demands have for your leadership style?

4. The leader's sense of purpose and mission is what elevates the mechanics of leadership (style, contingency theory, and so on) from mere social engineering to a human activity, and indeed this is the note upon which Chapter 6 ends. Where do you stand on the purpose and mission question? What hopes and aspirations do you have as a supervisor? Review your responses to these questions after reading Chapter 11.

CHAPTER 7

POWER, AUTHORITY, AND CONFLICT IN SUPERVISION

Though many seek power, few speak of it. Our democratic culture and egalitarian norms are such that the word "power," like "politics," has become tainted. Yet power is the energy upon which organizational decision making and functioning operate. Schools, like other organizations, require a reasonable amount of order and conformity. They represent organized ways in which to accomplish certain ends. Thus directions are given, actions coordinated, suggestions made, activities assigned, meetings held, standards set, programs adapted, performance appraised, resources distributed, and plans developed within an organized structure in a systematic attempt to effect the schools' purposes. Each of these tasks and functions requires exchanges in influence in order to obtain the compliance of one person to the wishes of another and to influence the decision-making process. In the first instance we speak of a deliberate attempt by one person to influence another or a group, and in the second instance, of a more general attempt to make an impact upon the functioning of the school through its decision-making processes.

In this chapter the phenomena of authority and the bases of social power available to supervisors and others are discussed. Though authority typically rests in the hands of a few, the bases of social power are more widely distributed and are accessible to many. Competing sources of authority and accessibility to bases of power often lead to competing claims of influence and to conflict between individuals. Therefore attention is also given to the development of conflict-management techniques. In addition a section on organizational politics and the management of political behavior in the school is included.

DEFINING POWER AND AUTHORITY

Power and authority are concepts often difficult to separate in practice, but useful differences exist between the two that can help in understanding their respective origins, expressions, and effects. Authority is the right to act or to require others to act on behalf of school purposes. Weber defines authority as the willing compliance of people based on the belief that it is legitimate for the designated leader to impose his or her will on subordinates.[1] The most common view of authority is that it is related to one's position and the inherent rights associated with that position.[2]

Power, on the other hand, refers to one's ability to influence the decision-making process. Sometimes this ability comes from authority associated with one's formal position in the hierarchy of the school but at other times from other sources. Indeed, often those with little authority exert considerable influence (power) on the decision-making processes of the school. Many supervisory roles are defined in such a manner that authority is weak. Chairpersons, curriculum coordinators, resource persons, and instructional supervisors might be examples. Contrast the authority that incumbents of staff-type roles have with that of superintendent for instruction, principal, general superintendent, and other line positions.[3] Lacking sufficient organizationally derived authority, supervisors are often required to look elsewhere in order to generate enough influence to affect educational decisions.

Since influence is a natural and important aspect of life in schools, supervisors need to understand the nature of authority—its many origins, form, operational feasibility, and acceptance. As schools have matured into complex professional organizations, newer forms of authority have emerged to challenge traditional authority sources. Entrepreneurial administrative behavior, the one-person show, hierarchical authority that rests largely in the position one occupies, and bureaucratic rules are seriously challenged by professional authority, ability authority, and authority owing to other sources.[4]

WEBER'S AUTHORITY TYPES

Max Weber distinguishes among three types of authority on the basis of their acceptance as a common value orientation for a particular group.[5] They are described as follows:

> *Traditional* This authority base is legitimized by the belief in the sancity of tradition. A given person or caste of people, usually on the basis of heredity, is preordained to rule over the others. The divine right of kings is a classical example of traditional authority. In contemporary organizations, the management caste treasures and passes on traditional

[1]Max Weber, *The Theory of Social and Economic Organization,* Talcott Parsons (ed.), A. M. Henderson and T. Parsons (trans.), Glencoe, Ill.: Free Press, 1947.

[2]Chester Barnard provides a contrasting view of authority. In his "acceptance theory" he assumes that authority comes from below rather than above. Authority in itself does not exist but is based on the willingness of subordinates to accept. Without acceptance, in his view, no authority exists. See, for example, Chester Barnard, *The Function of the Executive,* Cambridge, Mass.: Harvard University Press, 1938.

[3]Traditionally a distinction has been made between *line* and *staff* positions. Line authority is straightforward and consists of a direct superordinate-subordinate relationship between individuals. Staff authority is more complex and is designed to support line authority by advising administrators and teachers and by providing special services at the request of either administrators or teachers. Operationally the distinction is more muddled, as our discussion of social power and authority will reveal.

[4]See, for example, John Kenneth Galbraith, *The New Industrial State,* Boston: Houghton Mifflin, 1967, particularly pp. 68–75. See also Victor Thompson, *Modern Organization,* New York: Knopf, 1961, Chaps. 3 and 4.

[5]Max Weber, op. cit.

prerogatives which other employees are perceived not to have. This is particularly visible in patriarchal family businesses and in paternalistic schools.

Charismatic This authority base rests on a profession of faith which considers the pronouncements of a given leader to be inspired by supernatural powers. Disciples willingly follow the charismatic leader as they become converted to and champions of his cause. In contemporary organizations, the innovator, the champion of new educational and social movements, may be able to tap the charismatic power base. Charismatic movements eventually evolve into traditional or bureaucratic management systems.

Legal This authority base is legitimized by a formalistic belief in the supremacy of norms and laws. In legal systems, compliance occurs as a result of a body of impersonal and universal principles and rules rather than of loyalty to the traditional or charismatic leader. Legal authority forms the basis for the ideal bureaucratic organization.

The Weber formulation provides a background for most scholarly discussions of organizational authority and power. In recent years a fourth source of organizational authority has emerged—one based on professional norms and skill. Professional authority is similar to legal authority in that both are legitimized by codes, rules, and norms. This similarity is a major cause of conflict between the two. In schools organizational norms and rules often conflict with professional norms. Consider, for example, the guidance counselor who feels it unethical or harmful to disclose test scores to parents but who is required to do so by the school code or by administrative decree. We begin our discussion by examining two general types of authority in schools— formal and functional.

FORMAL AUTHORITY VERSUS FUNCTIONAL AUTHORITY

Peabody,[6] in summarizing the work of Weber, Urwick, Simon, Bennis, and Presthus, identifies four broad categories of authority: (1) authority of legitimacy; (2) authority of position, including the sanctions inherent in position; (3) authority of competence, including both technical skills and experience; and (4) authority of person, including leadership and human relations skills.[7] The Peabody summary appears in Table 7-1.

According to Peabody, bases of formal authority (hierarchical authority, legitimacy, position, and office) are distinguished from sources of functional authority. Examples of the latter are professional competence, experience, and human relations skills. Peabody examined and compared perceptions of the bases for authority in three public service organizations: a police department, a welfare office, and an elementary school. A summary of his findings appears in Table 7-2. An overview of this table indicates that teachers seem to value authority of competence over authority of person, position, or legitimacy. Peabody offers the following explanation:

Perhaps the most striking contrast between these three public service agencies was the relative importance attached to authority of professional competence in the elementary school. Almost half of the twenty-member school staff singled out this basis as compared with 22 per cent of the welfare workers and only 15 per cent of the police officers. In part

[6]Robert L. Peabody, "Perceptions of Organizational Authority: A Comparative Analysis," *Administrative Science Quarterly*, vol. 6, no. 4, March 1962.
[7]Ibid., p. 466.

TABLE 7-1
THE BASES OF AUTHORITY

	Formal authority		Functional authority	
	Legitimacy	Position	Competence	Person
Weber*	Legal		Rational authority	Traditional authority
	Legal order	Hierarchical office	Technical knowledge, experience	Charismatic authority
Urwick†		Formal, conferred by the organization	Technical, implicit in special knowledge or skill	Personal, conferred by seniority or popularity
Simon‡	Authority of legitimacy, social approval	Authority of sanctions	Authority of confidence (technical competence)	Techniques, persuasion (as distinct from authority)
Bennis§		Role incumbency	Knowledge of performance criteria	Knowledge of the human aspect of administration
Presthus¶	Generalized deference toward authority	Formal role or position	Technical expertise	Rapport with subordinates, ability to mediate individual needs

*Max Weber, *The Theory of Social and Economic Organization*, Talcott Parsons (ed.), A. M. Henderson and Talcott Parsons (trans.) Glencoe, Ill: Free Press, 1947, pp. 328, 339.
†L. Urwick, *The Elements of Administration*, London, 1944, p. 42.
‡Herbert A. Simon, "Authority," in Conrad M. Arensberg et al. (eds.), *Research in Industrial Human Relations*, New York, 1957, pp. 104–106; H. A. Simon et al., *Public Administration*, New York: Knopf, 1950, pp. 189–201.
§Warren G. Bennis, "Leadership Theory and Administrative Behavior: The Problem of Authority," *Administrative Science Quarterly*, vol. 4, pp. 288–289, 1959.
¶Robert V. Presthus, "Authority in Organizations," *Public Administration Review*, vol. 20, pp. 88–91, 1960.
Source: Robert L. Peabody, "Perceptions of Organizational Authority: A Comparative Analysis," *Administrative Science Quarterly*, vol. 6, no. 4, p. 467, March 1962.

this was related to the fact that 75 per cent of the school staff had had graduate training, including nine teachers with the equivalent of master's degrees or beyond. Furthermore, all school staff members except the secretary and the custodian belonged to two or more professional organizations, as compared with about half the members of the police department and about one-quarter of the welfare workers who belonged to one or more professional organizations. While the principal of this school played a more passive "democratic" leadership role than either the police chief or the district director, his position or the school administration as a whole was the next most frequently mentioned source of authority in the school. The diffusion of authority which seemed to characterize this school may be the dominant pattern of authority relations in such highly professionalized organizations as research institutions, psychiatric and medical clinics, and universities.[8]

[8]*Ibid.*, pp. 480–481.

TABLE 7-2
PERCEPTIONS OF THE BASES OF AUTHORITY IN THREE PUBLIC SERVICE ORGANIZATIONS

Bases of authority	Police department, % (N = 33)	Welfare office, % (N = 23)	Elementary school, %* (N = 20)
AUTHORITY OF LEGITIMACY			
Generalized legitimacy	12	9	10
Law, state legislation, city ordinances, the state, county, city	15	17	15
Administrative codes, rules, regulations, manuals	0	17	0
Governing boards, policies of board	0	0	10
AUTHORITY OF POSITION			
Top external executive or executives, organization as a whole†	0	17	15
Top internal executive, ranking officers, administration as a whole‡	27	13	30
Immediate supervisor	9	39	0§
Inherent in position or job characteristics	30	26	15
AUTHORITY OF COMPETENCE			
Professional or technical competence, experience	15	22	45
AUTHORITY OF PERSON			
Personal characteristics or way in which authority is exercised	42	13	15
Other sources	6	4	0
No source supplied	18	22	15

*Percentages total more than 100 percent because some respondents indicated more than one base of authority.
†The category of "top *external* executive" included the chief executives of the parent organizations, for example, the county manager, director of public welfare, city manager, and school superintendent.
‡The category of "top *internal* executive" included the police chief, the district director, and the principal.
§Coded as "top *internal* executive" in the case of the elementary school.
Source: Robert L. Peabody, "Perceptions of Organizational Authority: A Comparative Analysis," *Administrative Science Quarterly,* vol. 6, no. 4, p. 477, March 1962.

Of similar significance is the strong support among elementary school teachers for position authority as opposed to authority of person. Current supervisory trends do not substantiate this finding, and one can interpret the wide teacher recognition of position authority as a vestige of classical and contemporary supervision. Human resources supervision relies heavily on competence and person as sources of authority.

Though the bases of authority remain somewhat stable in human resources supervision, the authority actors change as function changes. Hartmann describes the fluid nature of functional authority as follows:

> One of the most important characteristics of functional authority is its relativity. Authority of this kind is always dependent on the successful accomplishment of given ends. Performance is the immediate judge and executioner of such authority.
>
> Actually, the concept of functional authority makes it hard to understand why there should be hierarchies at all. The functional interplay of the productive process has an intrinsic order inasmuch as the specific contributions of all productive agents are geared to the exigencies of the over-all task. But there is nothing intrinsic to these functions (qua functions) to suggest that they should be ranked in such a way that some of these contributions should be subordinate to others.[9]

The elimination of an educational hierarchy appeals to many, particularly to professionally oriented teachers. Hierarchy, however, does offer stability to schools and provides continuity over time. Human resources supervision recognizes and supports legitimate and position authority, but it stresses and attempts to develop competence and person authority. Mary Parker Follett captures the spirit of authority systems in human resources supervision as follows:

> Another corollary from this conception of authority and responsibility as a moment in interweaving experience is that you have no authority as a mere left-over. You cannot take the authority which you won yesterday and apply it today. . . . In the ideal organization authority is always fresh, always being distilled anew.[10]

THE EROSION OF AUTHORITY BASES FOR ADMINISTRATORS AND SUPERVISORS

Authority bases for those who administer and for those who supervise in our schools are changing, shifting, and, in many cases, diminishing. Particularly susceptible to change and erosion is the principal's position. The principal at one time proudly possessed rather strong credentials as the legal and legitimate head of the school, in having broad powers by virtue of his or her *position* to impose sanctions and rewards, in displaying superior *competence* as a remarkable teacher, and in being a rather persuasive, if not paternal, personality.

As the technical structure (the teaching and educational program structure) increases in complexity and diversification, teachers by virtue of competence and person authority have assumed more responsibility for these areas. This increase in educational sophistication has required administrative arrangements beyond the traditional definition of the principal's role. Thus new positions and new policies are formed or added (on legitimate and position-authority bases) above the principal's position and located in

[9]Heinz Hartmann, *Authority and Organization in German Management,* Princeton, N.J.: Princeton University Press, 1959, p. 284.

[10]Henry C. Metcalf and L. Urwick, *Dynamic Administration: The Collected Papers of Mary Parker Follett,* New York: Harper, 1942.

the central office. The former trend is suggested by growth of the teacher autonomy movement and the latter by increases in central office staffs.

THE BASES OF SUPERVISORY POWER

It seems useful to consider authority as a broad basis for action not directed at any one individual. Power, on the other hand, at least in an administrative sense, is directed at winning individual or group compliance to superiors in the organization.[11]

French and Raven identify and describe five bases for the social power that person O can exert over person P:

> (a) reward power, based on P's perception that O has the ability to mediate rewards for him; (b) coercive power, based on P's perception that O has the ability to mediate punishments for him; (c) legitimate power, based on the perception by P that O has a legitimate right to prescribe behavior for him; (d) referent power, based on P's identification with O; (e) expert power, based on the perception that O has some special knowledge or expertness.[12]

Reward power is a particular characteristic of benevolent but paternalistic administrative and supervisory environments in schools. Rewards, of course, need to be acceptable to teachers or to be desired by them. Pay increase, recognition, special favors, better schools, favorable work assignments and schedules, better equipment, and so on, are among the reward incentives available to administrators. Reward power may also provide relief from disagreeable circumstances. *Coercive power* is simply the ability to impose sanctions on teachers. Coercive power systems are the reverse of reward power systems. They often go hand in hand. The department budgets of chairpersons who comply with the wishes of the principal are increased. If they defy the wishes of the principal, their department budgets are cut, and so on.

Expert power, a concept very similar to the competence authority base, is the ability to command compliance on the basis of professional knowledge, information, and skills. Administrators and supervisors who are able to command the admiration and respect of others operate from a *referent power base.* This power source is often a result of expert power—that is, we respect and admire an individual's competence. Referent power is nevertheless conceptually independent of expert power. Many supervisors gain the support of others simply because they are admired as people.

Legitimate power refers to an administrative prerogative of command and influence as a right of the office. When the new teacher meets the superintendent at the September orientation tea, be assured that the new teacher understands fully (and understandably exaggerates) the concept of legitimate power.

[11]This definition is not limited to compliance between and among superordinates and subordinates. Teacher A may have a powerful influence on teacher B and thus be assured of teacher B's reliable compliance, yet both are officially at the same hierarchical level.

[12]J. R. P. French, Jr., and B. Raven, "The Bases of Social Power," in D. Cartwright and A. F. Zander (eds.), *Group Dynamics: Research and Theory,* 2d ed., Evanston, Ill.: Row, Peterson, 1960, p. 612. In more recent work Raven speaks of a sixth source of social power he calls *informational power.* See, for example, Raven, "Social Influence and Power," in I. D. Steiner and M. Fishbein (eds.), *Current Studies in Social Psychology,* New York: Holt, 1965, pp. 371–382.

BASES OF SUPERVISORY POWER, SATISFACTION, AND PERFORMANCE

In an attempt to answer the question "Why do people comply with the requests of supervisors, and how are these reasons related to organizational effectiveness and individual satisfaction?" Bachman, Bowers, and Marcus[18] examined the bases of supervisory power in five organizational settings. The investigators asked subordinates why they complied with their supervisor's wishes. Additional measurements were obtained for worker satisfaction and, in three of the organizations, for worker performance. Table 7-3 shows the mean ratings of bases of power for each of the five organizations on each of the five power variables. Note that power variables are adopted from French and Raven.

The investigators observe that the most important reason for complying with the wishes of superiors was response to legitimate power and expert power. Referent and reward power were cited less often, with coercive power the least likely reason for compliance. This trend seems more pronounced for organizations described as professional—the branch office, the college, and the insurance agency. Public schools would be expected to respond similarly.

Correlations between the five bases of supervisory power and measures of satisfaction with the supervisor or with the job appear in Table 7-4.

This table shows that expert power and referent power seem to provide the strongest and most consistent positive correlation with worker satisfaction. Coercive power, particularly for the educational organizations studied, draws the most negative correlation with satisfaction. The investigators summarize their findings as follows:

> This summary of data obtained in five organizational studies has provided a number of fairly consistent findings. (1) Legitimate power was rated one of the two most important

[18]Jerald D. Bachman et al., "Bases of Supervisory Power: A Comparative Study in Five Organizational Settings," in Arnold S. Tannenbaum (ed.), *Control in Organizations*, New York: McGraw-Hill, 1968, p. 229.

TABLE 7-3
MEAN RATINGS OF BASES OF POWER*

	Organizational Settings				
	1	**2**	**3**	**4**	**5**
Bases of power	**Branch offices**	**Colleges**	**Insurance agencies**	**Production work units**	**Utility company work groups**
Legitimate	4.1	3.6	3.3	3.4	4.7
Expert	3.5	4.1	3.8	3.4	3.0
Referent	2.9	3.5	2.5	2.7	2.1
Reward	2.7	2.3	2.8	2.8	2.7
Coercive	1.9	1.6	1.8	2.3	2.5

*All ratings have been adjusted so that a value of 5.0 represents the highest possible rating and 1.0 represents the lowest possible rating. Respondents in organizational settings 1, 2, and 5 used a ranking procedure; those in settings 3 and 4 used a procedure that permitted independent ratings of the five bases of power.
Source: Jerald D. Bachman et al., "Bases of Supervisory Power: A Comparative Study in Five Organizational Settings," in A. S. Tannenbaum (ed.), *Control in Organizations*, New York: McGraw-Hill, 1968, p. 234.

TABLE 7-4
CORRELATIONS WITH SATISFACTION MEASURES

	Organizational settings				
	1	2	3	4	5
Bases of power	Branch offices (N = 36)	Colleges (N = 12)	Insurance agencies (N = 40)	Production work units (N = 40)	Utility company work groups (N = 20)
Legitimate	−.57*	−.52	.04	.40†	−.35
Expert	.69*	.75*	.88*	.67*	.30
Referent	.75*	.67†	.43†	.57*	.11
Reward	−.57*	−.80*	.48*	.27	−.12
Coercive	−.31	−.70†	−.52*	.01	−.23

*$p < .01$, two-tailed.
†$p < .05$, two-tailed.
Source: Jerald D. Bachman et al., "Bases of Supervisory Power: A Comparative Study in Five Organizational Settings," in A. S. Tannenbaum (ed.), *Control in Organizations,* New York: McGraw-Hill, 1968, p. 235.

bases of power; however, it did not seem a consistent factor in organizational effectiveness, nor was it related significantly to total amount of control. (2) Expert power was the other very prominent basis of power, and it was strongly and consistently co-related with satisfaction and performance. Of the five bases, expert power was most positively related to total amount of control. (3) Referent power was of intermediate importance as a reason for complying with a supervisor's wishes, but in most cases it was positively correlated with criteria of organizational effectiveness. In two sites it was significantly and positively related to total amount of control. (4) Reward power was also of intermediate importance; in this case the correlations with organizational effectiveness and with total control were not consistent. (5) Coercive power was clearly the least prominent reason for compliance; moreover, this basis of power was often negatively related to criteria of effectiveness and in two cases negatively related to total amount of control.[14]

In another study using the French and Raven formulation, Bachman, Smith, and Slesinger[15] examined the relationship among bases for social power and satisfaction and performance in a professional sales office.[16] Correlations among worker perception of office-manager power, office mean-performance scores, and office mean-satisfaction scores are provided in Table 7-5. This table again suggests that referent power and expert power yield higher positive and significant correlations with performance and satisfaction, while reward, coercive, and legitimate power bases yield some significant but all negative correlations with performance and satisfaction. The investigators conclude the following:

Total control, performance, and satisfaction with the office manager were all relatively high for the office manager whose leadership was perceived as resting largely upon his skill and expertise (expert power) and upon his personal attractiveness (referent power). Converse-

[14]Ibid., p. 236.
[15]Jerald D. Bachman et al., "Control, Performance, and Satisfaction: An Analysis of Structural and Individual Effects," in Arnold S. Tannenbaum, op. cit., p. 213.
[16]The salesmen in this study earned from $10,000 to $25,000 per year prior to 1961. Thirty-six branch offices of a national firm were used.

TABLE 7-5
POWER, PERFORMANCE, AND SATISFACTION

Bases of manager's power	Mean standardized performance	Mean satisfaction with manager
Referent	.40*	.75*
Expert	.36*	.69*
Reward	− .55†	− .51†
Coercive	− .31	− .71†
Legitimate	− .17	− .57†

Note: Sell entries are product-moment correlation.
*$p<$ .05, two-tailed.
†$p<$ .01, two-tailed.
Source: Bachman et al., "Control, Performance, and Satisfaction: An Analysis of Structural and Individual Effects," in A. S. Tannenbaum (ed.), *Control in Organizations,* New York: McGraw-Hill, 1968, p. 213.

ly, the less effective office manager was one who appeared to rely more heavily upon the use of rewards and sanctions (reward power and coercive power) and upon the formal authority of his position (legitimate power) as a formal description of his role might indicate. At the level of interoffice comparison, this overall relationship was substantial and highly consistent.[17]

In examining the relationship between influence and satisfaction in secondary schools, Hornstein and his associates conclude:

These data, which are in full accord with the findings of previous studies, suggest that the effects of superior-subordinate relations in school systems are very much like those of various industrial, sales, and voluntary organizations. Teachers report greatest satisfaction with their principal and school system when they perceive that they and their principals are mutually influential, especially when their principal's power to influence emanates from their perceiving him as an expert. Moreover, this same principal-teacher relationship is associated with a perception of higher student satisfaction.[18]

They also note that teachers' perceptions of the principal's use of coercive power were highly related to their dissatisfaction with the principal and the school and with their perceptions of students' dissatisfaction with teachers.

In a Canadian study that investigated sources of power used by elementary school principals and their relationship to teachers' perceptions of satisfaction and perform-ance, Balderson notes:

Schools with principals whose power was perceived to rest on relevant expertise received *high* scores for teacher morale, teacher satisfaction with principal's performance, and the degree to which the principal favored (1) teacher doing an effective job helping students learn, (2) teacher experimenting with new ideas and techniques, and (3) teacher suggesting ideas to improve the school. In addition these schools also received *high* scores for the degree to which teachers feel their principals are open to their ideas and the degree to

[17]Bachman et al., op. cit., p. 225.
[18]Harvey A. Hornstein et al., "Influence and Satisfaction in Organizations: A Replication," *Sociology of Education,* vol. 41, no. 4, p. 389, Fall 1968.

which they feel their principals have delegated enough authority to teachers to enable them to do their work. Without exception, those schools with principals who were perceived to exercise coercion in attempting to influence teachers revealed the lowest scores on these measures.[19]

Studies of this sort make it difficult to determine cause and effect, but the relationship between expert authority and other factors associated with school effectiveness seems clear. Balderson concludes that "if we also note that supervisors are involved in the task of achieving better instruction by working through others, that is teachers, it seems evident from these data that the effectiveness of supervisory practice will be enhanced by the adoption of practices based on expertise,"[20] a view entirely consistent with human resources supervision.

It seems apparent that supervisory behavior that relies on functional authority and on expert and referent power bases will have positive effects on the human organization of the school. Such efforts should lead to positive effects on the school-effectiveness variables, which are outlined in the synthesizing theory of Chapter 2.

COMPLIANCE THEORY (ETZIONI)

We have given emphasis to one or another base for supervisory action, but a number of strategies, power bases, and authority systems may be appropriate, depending upon the nature of goals to be achieved and the tasks that constitute action toward the goals. The "goodness of fit" of a given compliance or *power* strategy depends upon three major variables: *goals, involvement,* and *task.* The four components are arranged in a formulation of compliance theory by Etzioni.[21] The components and characteristics derived from his compliance theory are summarized in Table 7-6.

[19] James H. Balderson, "Principal Power Bases: Some Observations," *The Canadian Administrator,* vol. 14, no. 7, pp. 3–4, 1975.
[20] Ibid., p. 5.
[21] Amitai Etzioni, *A Comparative Analysis of Complex Organizations,* New York: Free Press, 1961.

TABLE 7-6
THE COMPONENTS AND CHARACTERISTICS OF ETZIONI'S COMPLIANCE THEORY*

Component	Type A	Type B	Type C
Goal	Order	Economic	Cultural
Power	Coercive	Utilitarian	Normative
Involvement	Alienative	Calculative	Moral
Task	Routine	Instrumental	Expressive

*Order goals are oriented toward control of actors in the organization. *Economic goals* refer to increasing or maintaining output at favorable cost to the organization. *Cultural goals* refer to the socializing, institutionalizing, preserving, extending, and applying of value systems and life systems.
Source: Amitai Etzioni, *A Comparative Analysis of Complex Organizations,* New York: Free Press, 1961.

The appropriateness of a given compliance strategy will depend largely on organizational costs in relation to goal achievement. If, for example, the goal is order and the task a routine one, the most efficient compliance strategy is coercive. Yet before one chooses this strategy, one must be prepared to pay the price of alienating subordinates. If it is worth the price to accomplish the goal, then the coercive strategy (at least within the limits of this formulation) is legitimate. The key, of course, rests with the time variable. Any system can absorb short periods of alienation in subordinates, but over time, alienation results in a collapse of the system. Schools, for example, can hardly operate as dynamic learning institutions with alienated students, parents, or teachers.

The goals of schools are generally considered to be predominantly cultural in nature. The tasks of teachers and students are largely expressive in that they define, legitimize, and strengthen commitment to the cultural goals of the school. Expressive tasks and cultural goals require, according to this formulation, normative compliance strategies and obtain moral commitment from school inhabitants. One can argue that each of the three goals is legitimate for schools. Human resources supervision, however, although recognizing the occasional legitimacy of each, does not view them as equally balanced, but leans heavily on the cultural, normative, expressive, and moral compliance strategies.

THE SCHOOL AS A POLITICAL SYSTEM

Earlier in this chapter we spoke of the accessibility of power in schools to those willing and able to tap appropriate sources. It is true that persons with authority derived from their positions have a distinct advantage in acquiring and using some sources of power, but nevertheless power monopolies tend not to exist. Increased reliance on functional authority, participatory decision making, and other power-equalization strategies associated with human resources supervision has enabled teachers to become more powerful. Further, as schools move further away from bureaucratically oriented images of structure and teaching, power equalization increases.

As power equalization increases in the school, the *potential* for expressing political behavior increases. Political scientists tend to define politics as self-serving behavior, protecting one's own domain, building support through a constituency, influencing and maneuvering, and/or building coalitions.[22] The acquisition and maintenance of power seems central in their view. In contrast to this view we define *organizational politics*, after Robbins, as *internal* to the organization and as any behavior of an organizational member that is *self-serving*. In his words, "when individuals act to enhance their own position, regardless of costs to the organization or to others, they are acting politically."[23] In this context political behavior is often dysfunctional to the organization, though at times one's self-interest may coincide with organizational purposes.

[22]Political behavior associated with organizational politics differs from political behavior associated with government and political science in its broadest sense. The former is concerned with the activities of individuals inside the organization, the latter with external constituencies.

[23]Stephen P. Robbins, *The Administrative Process Integrating Theory and Practice*, Englewood Cliffs, N.J.: Prentice-Hall, 1976, p. 64. This discussion follows closely Robbins's ideas as expressed on pp. 64–66.

One can debate the benefits and evils of political behavior in schools. To simplify matters, schools benefit when the correspondence between self and organizational interests is great and suffer when this correspondence is slight. Though political behavior may be functional at a given point in time, it is too risky to be considered as a widespread strategy. Political behavior is based on self-interest rather than organizational norms, goals, and beliefs, and though benefits accrue when the two are matched, organizational goals are likely to be sacrificed if self-interest so mandates.

But political behavior exists nevertheless, and indeed its *potential* for expression in the school *increases* as power equalization increases and as roles become more ambiguous. Faced with the prospect of increases in political behavior in the school, administrators and supervisors can slow down or suppress such behavior by reversing the trend toward power equalization and by clarification of roles. But this suggests a return to more classically and bureaucratically oriented schools—a trend not palatable to those who advocate human resources supervision. A second alternate is to "manage" political behavior so that it becomes less popular and, to the extent that it exists, matches more closely school purposes.

In developing a concept of organizational politics, Rogers describes five systems found with various degrees of emphasis in all organizations: ideological, social, technical (educational), judicial (legal), and political.[24] These are illustrated in Figure 7-1. The systems are not operationally discrete but can nevertheless be readily differentiated. We suggest as a basic proposition that the more manifest the ideological, legal, educational, and social systems are, and the greater the degree of commitment to them, the less chance of dysfunctional behavior in the political system. Since many aspects of the legal system are fixed, or given, the relationship suggested above is likely to be stronger for the ideological, social, and educational systems.

To the extent that the propositions we propose are true, dysfunctional political behavior can be controlled by making more explicit and increasing commitment to the ideological, social, and educational systems. In the school, the ideological system comprises the assumptions, values, and beliefs that represent a platform from which organizational decisions are made. Theory Y assumptions, for example, as part of a school's management platform would belong in the ideological system. The social system (greatly affected by the ideological system and corresponding closely to the mediating variables described in the synthesizing theory of supervision discussed in Chapter 2) includes the attachments, relationships, loyalties, and norms that characterize the school's human organization. The greater the group loyalty, the greater the support and trust that exist within the group and between the group and administrators and supervisors, the less likely will dysfunctional political behavior be expressed. The educational system includes the intents, assumptions, values, and beliefs that compose the school's educational platform. The more agreement that exists over educational intents, the less likely will dysfunctional political behavior be expressed.

Though one might speak idealistically of eliminating political behavior in schools, realistically the emphasis should be more on creating a better match between such

---

[24]Rolf E. Rogers, *The Political Process in Modern Organizations,* New York: Exposition Press, 1971. This reference is the source for the discussion that follows.

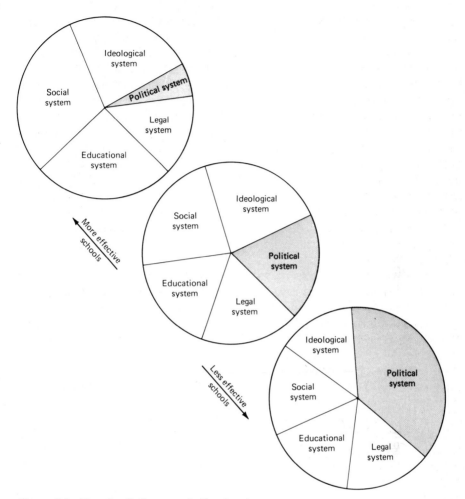

Figure 7-1 The school's five organizational systems.

behavior and the norms that constitute the school's ideological, social, and educational systems. The more explicit the norms and the greater the agreement between them, the more likely that self-interest will conform to school purposes than purposes to self-interest.

CONFLICT-HANDLING STYLES

As power becomes more widely dispersed in schools and political behavior becomes more manifest, the potential for interpersonal conflict increases accordingly. Like political behavior, conflict is now assumed to be a natural part of modern organization and indeed is at times credited with positive effects upon the organization. Positive effects aside, the school can hardly operate effectively in a state of siege, and therefore the resolution or management of interpersonal conflict and the cultivation of conflict-handling styles become a major concern of human resources supervision.

Following Blake and Mouton,[25] David Jamieson and Kenneth Thomas view conflict-handling styles as consisting of two critical dimensions. One dimension is concerned with the extent to which an individual attempts to satisfy the interest of the other party or partner in the conflict.[26] This is the *cooperative* dimension. A person's concern here can be described on a conceptual continuum ranging from uncooperative to cooperative. The second dimension focuses on the extent to which an individual emphasizes the satisfaction of his or her own concerns. This is the *assertiveness* dimension. A person's concern here can be described on a conceptual continuum ranging from unassertive to assertive. As illustrated in Figure 7-2, five specific conflict-handling styles, competing, accommodating, avoiding, collaborating, and compromising, can be identified from combinations of the two dimensions.

Each of the styles is based on certain assumptions and is characterized by distinctive actions.[27] Styles characterized as competing are based on assumptions that differences between people are natural and can be expected, that some people have knowledge and others do not, and that some issues are right and others wrong. Therefore the supervisor owes it to herself or himself to prevail in conflicts with others

[25]Robert Blake and Jane Mouton, *The Managerial Grid,* Houston: Gulf, 1964. See also Blake and Mouton, "The Fifth Achievement." *Journal of Applied Behavioral Science,* vol. 6, no. 4, pp. 413–426, 1970; and Blake, Mouton, and Herbert Shepard, *Managing Intergroup Conflict in Industry,* Houston: Gulf, 1964.
[26]David W. Jamieson and Kenneth W. Thomas, "Power and Conflict in the Student-Teacher Relationship," *Journal of Applied Behavioral Science,* vol. 10, no. 3, pp. 321–336, 1974.
[27]This discussion is based on Blake and Mouton, "The Fifth Achievement," *Journal of Applied Behavioral Science;* Jay Hall, *Conflict Management Survey,* Houston: Teleometrics, 1968; and David Kolb, Irwin Rubin, and James McIntyre, *Organizational Psychology: An Experiential Approach,* Englewood Cliffs, N.J.: Prentice-Hall, 1971.

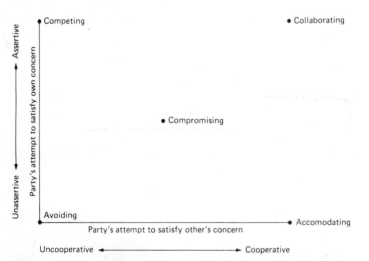

Figure 7-2 Conflict-handling modes, plotted according to party's attempt to satisfy own and other's concern, *(Reproduced by special permission from David W. Jamieson and Kenneth W. Thomas, "Power and Conflict in the Student-Teacher Relationships,"* Journal of Applied Behavioral Science, *vol. 10, no. 3, p. 326, 1974.)*

whose opinions and knowledge and goals are in doubt. Further, persuasion and force are acceptable tools in resolving conflict. Competing supervisors engage in a win-lose strategy and are quite willing to endanger some relationships and to sacrifice others in order to have their personal goals realized.

Accommodating supervisors, by contrast, feel that differences drive people apart and that good relationships cannot be ignored. The slogan of accommodating supervisors is, "To differ is to reject." Conflict requires that such supervisors sacrifice their personal convictions and goals in order to accommodate those of others and, if necessary, ignore differences in order to preserve harmony. Accommodating supervisors strive to maintain relationships at any cost.

Compromising supervisors feel that at times some parties (themselves included) are obliged to set aside their own view in the interest of the majority, and that people should be allowed to express their views but should not be allowed to block progress. Compromising supervisors will change course and alter plans if necessary but maintain enough consensus to keep moving, in the belief that motion is more important than destination and therefore that decisions should be made and purpose and direction compromised in order to maintain the consensus needed to keep moving.

Collaborating supervisors believe that differences are natural and healthy and view them as neither good nor bad. Conflict requires honest confrontation and objective problem solving. Such supervisors do not see an inherent difference in their personal goals and aspirations for the school and the view of others and are hopeful that both views can be integrated into some common good.

Avoiding supervisors see no virtue in conflict and do not personally face up to it. If avoiding supervisors cannot handle conflict in some impersonal manner (relying on rules and precedents for example), they are likely simply to withdraw from the situation.

It is difficult to decide which of the conflict-handling styles is best. Often different situations require different styles. *Constant* use of the accommodating, avoiding, or competing styles, however, is not likely to be very effective. Still, when the issues are important enough for one's view to prevail, or the situation is such that the other party is not sufficiently knowledgeable, the competitive style may be necessary. Sometimes the task or issues at stake are not important and much can be gained by emphasizing relationships, and here the accommodating style might be best. In sum, any of the conflict-handling styles might be appropriate in different circumstances.

SUMMARY

Power was described in this chapter as the energy upon which organizational decision making and functioning operate. Though many negative effects can be attributed to power abuses, care was taken to portray power, authority, and political behavior as in themselves neither good nor bad.

Authority was defined as the right to act or require others to act on behalf of school purposes. Authority is normally derived from one's position in an organization or status in a guild (profession) or social system. Power, on the other hand, refers to one's ability to influence the decision-making process. Though power is often derived from authority, other sources (expert and referent) were also cited.

Formal authority was differentiated from functional authority and various conceptualizations of authority were outlined. Among these were Weber's charismatic, traditional, and legal distinctions and Peabody's listing, which includes legal and position as examples of formal authority, and competence and person as examples of functional authority. The five bases of supervisory power were then discussed. These include legitimate, expert, referent, reward, and coercive. It was pointed out that expressions of power by supervisors based on expert and referent bases are positively associated with increased satisfaction and higher performance levels in subordinates. The association between use of power and level of identity of organizational members was then discussed in terms of Etzioni's compliance theory.

Power-equalization strategies such as shared decision making and reliance on functional rather than formal authority were associated with potential increases in political behavior of teachers. For organizational purposes, political behavior was described as any behavior of a teacher or other person that is self-serving. Such behavior was judged functional when matched to organizational purposes and dysfunctional when not. It was suggested in accordance with the ideas of Rolf Rogers that dysfunctional political behavior could be reduced by bringing greater commitment to the school's organizational philosophy and value system and to the intents, beliefs, and values that make up its educational platform. The chapter concluded with a discussion of five conflict-handling styles available to supervisors. These include competition, accommodation, compromise, collaboration, and avoidance.

STUDY GUIDE

Recall the concepts, ideas, and meanings associated with each of the following phrases and terms included in Chapter 7. Can you discuss each of them with a colleague and apply them to the supervisory context of your school? If you cannot, review them in the text and record the page number for future reference.

1. Acceptance theory _____
2. Assertiveness dimension _____
3. Authority _____
4. Coercive power _____
5. Compliance theory _____
6. Conflict-handling styles _____
7. Cooperative dimension _____
8. Educational system _____
9. Expert power _____
10. Formal authority _____
11. Functional authority _____
12. Ideological system _____
13. Legitimate power _____
14. Line authority _____
15. Organizational politics _____
16. Peabody's authority types _____
17. Political behavior _____

18. Political system _____
19. Power _____
20. Power and performance _____
21. Power and satisfaction _____
22. Power equalization _____
23. Referent power _____
24. Reward power _____
25. Staff authority _____
26. Weber's authority types _____

EXERCISES

1. In a typical elementary school setting the cast of characters might include teachers, students, custodians, principal-supervisor, parents, secretaries, and superintendent. What authority does each of these groups have over classroom decisions? How does this authority differ from the actual influence patterns (power) you observe?

2. Describe the political atmosphere in your school. Who are the main characters? What agendas do they have? How do they influence decision making? How does this political activity affect the supervisor's ability to use each of the five bases of supervisory power suggested by French and Raven?

3. Which of the descriptions of conflict-handling modes best fits the way you operate (or are likely to operate)?

CHAPTER 8

TEACHER MOTIVATION AND SUPERVISORY EFFECTIVENESS

Supervisors often ask why some teachers seem to work so hard and why others, by comparison, are relatively indifferent to their work or even seem dedicated to doing as little as possible. This question typically leads to speculations as to what supervisors can do to influence levels of commitment and the actual performance of teachers. Thankfully, the area of work motivation has been well researched and a number of theories have been developed that can help supervisors understand why commitment levels of teachers vary and what they can do to improve work performance.

The motivation issue is critical to supervision in two ways. First, the general climate of schooling in America today poses some unique problems. In the recent past, teachers were in short supply and teacher turnover was relatively high. Teachers were not quite as hesitant as they are now about moving to another school district in order to improve their financial condition, opportunity for promotion, job assignment, or job location. If a teacher had an undesirable position, the solution was to change jobs. Schools worked hard to compete for qualified teachers, and once they were hired, schools attempted to improve working conditions as a means to retain them.

We are now in a period of retrenchment and teacher surplus. In many parts of the country, good teaching jobs are already difficult to find, and teachers are increasingly less willing to move once they obtain employment. Low turnover poses a serious problem for schools. Dissatisfied teachers are less likely to leave. The reasons for staying on the job are too important. But if the reasons for staying are limited to job security and other bread-and-butter items, large numbers of teachers may remain on the job for the wrong reasons. As a result, instructional quality may be endangered. Motivation and commitment have always been important concerns to supervisors, but without the safety valve of turnover they become necessary concerns.

Staff stability raises as well the question of how to keep teachers in effective service in the same school or school district over the course of their careers. Effective service implies, of course, that a person keep up to date, and this has implications for supervision of staff development. But a further challenge is to keep teachers interested, motivated, and committed to work. The ideas presented in this chapter can help supervisors to maintain the continuing level of commitment needed from teachers.

The second point to consider is the importance of teacher motivation and commitment to the quality and continued growth of the school's human organization. This quality is reflected in a pivotal set of theoretical variables that stand between the decisions supervisors make about organizational matters and the resulting effects on the school. The link between supervisory actions and effects on the school, in other words, is *mediated* by several variables that constitute the school's human organization, and key among them are the motivational and commitment levels of teachers. This point may sound confusing now, but we will return to it in more detail in Chapter 10, where we provide and discuss an instrumental theory of supervisory leadership.

SOME BASIC ASSUMPTIONS

Before we begin a discussion of motivation and commitment, it is important to caution the reader about some points. Researchers and theorists have vested interests in their ideas, and thus in their enthusiasm they often seem to suggest that the theories they have developed apply to everyone in the same way all the time. Indeed, one criticism that can be made about the various theories of motivation is that they assume workers to be very much alike. Hence, though the theorists present different ways of looking at people at work, they assume that particular needs and wants are universal. Another criticism is that they assume that all situations are similar and therefore that motivational strategies, such as shared decision making, are applicable in all situations. These assumptions lead to the conclusion that "one best way" exists to motivate everyone.[1] A better perspective is to assume that motivation theories are modes of analysis that can help us to understand issues and to develop practices but that they cannot provide universal prescriptions applicable to everyone and in every situation. In this spirit, we will try to point out what the various theories can and cannot do and where they do and do not apply.

HUMAN MOTIVATION AND TEACHERS

Let us begin our inquiry into human motivation by examining needs of people at work. A commonsense approach to identifying human needs would undoubtedly reveal a list of factors such as air, water, shelter, food, protection, love, acceptance, importance, success, recognition, and control. This approach provides a random and undifferentiated list, and a significant effort is required to condense it into guidelines for supervisory behavior. Abraham Maslow, the distinguished psychologist, proposed a theory of human motivation that integrates the commonsense approach with human needs. His theory can help form an operational basis for supervisory behavior.

[1] For a discussion of this problem see, for example, David A. Nadler and Edward E. Lawler III, "Motivation: A Diagnostic Approach," in J. R. Hackman and E. E. Lawyler III (eds.), *Perspectives on Behavior and Organizations*, New York: McGraw-Hill, 1977.

THE MASLOW THEORY

Maslow's theory differs from other motivational formulations in that it does not consider an individual's motivation on a one-to-one basis or as a series of independent drives. Each of the human needs that the theory comprises is examined in relation to others, and they are classified and arranged into a hierarchy of prepotency. Thus before need B can be satisfied, one must first satisfy need A, and so on.

> Human needs arrange themselves in hierarchies of prepotency. That is to say, the appearance of one need usually rests on the prior satisfaction of another, more prepotent need. Man is a perpetually wanting animal. Also no need or drive can be treated as if it were isolated or discrete; every drive is related to the state of satisfaction or dissatisfaction of other drives.[2]

Maslow proposed a hierarchy of needs consisting of five levels. Specific need dimensions that compose each of the five levels are bound together by similarities in description, but, more importantly, by similarities in potency potential. Essentially, the most prepotent need occupies, and to a certain extent monopolizes, an individual's attention, while less prepotent needs are minimized. When a need is fairly well satisfied, the next prepotent need emerges and tends to dominate the individual's attention, while less prepotent needs are minimized. When a need is fairly well satisfied, the next prepotent need emerges and tends to dominate the individual's conscious life. Gratified needs, according to this theory, are not active motivators of behavior. Douglas McGregor describes each of the five Maslow levels and the prepotency feature of the theory simply and concisely as follows:[3]

Physiological Needs

> Man is a wanting animal—as soon as one of his needs is satisfied, another appears in its place. This process is unending. It continues from birth to death.
>
> Man's needs are organized in a series of levels—a hierarchy of importance. At the lowest level, but pre-eminent in importance when they are thwarted, are his *physiological needs*. Man lives for bread alone, when there is no bread. Unless the circumstances are unusual, his needs for love, for status, for recognition are inoperative when his stomach has been empty for a while. But when he eats regularly and adequately, hunger ceases to be an important motivation. The same is true of the other physiological needs of man—for rest, exercise, shelter, protection from the elements.
>
> *A satisfied need is not a motivator of behavior!* This is a fact of profound significance that is regularly ignored on the conventional approach to the management of people. Consider your own need for air: Except as you are deprived of it, it has no appreciable motivating effect upon your behavior.

Safety Needs

> When the physiological needs are reasonably satisfied, needs at the next higher level begin to dominate man's behavior—to motivate him. These are called *safety needs.* They are

[2]Abraham H. Maslow, "A Preface to Motivation Theory," *Psychosomatic Medicine,* vol. 5, p. 85, 1953. See especially his *Motivation and Personality,* New York: Harper & Row, 1954.
[3]Douglas McGregor, *The Human Side of Enterprise,* New York: McGraw-Hill, 1960, pp. 36–39.

needs for protection against danger, threat, deprivation. Some people mistakenly refer to these as needs for security. However, unless man is in a dependent relationship where he fears arbitrary deprivation, he does not demand security. The need is for the "fairest possible break." When he is confident of this, he is more than willing to take risks. But when he feels threatened or dependent, his greatest need is for guarantees, for protection, for security.

The fact needs little emphasis that, since every industrial employee is in a dependent relationship, safety needs may assume considerable importance. Arbitrary management actions, behavior which arouses uncertainty with respect to continued employment or which reflects favoritism or discrimination, unpredictable administration of policy—these can be powerful motivators of the safety needs in the employment relationship at *every level*, from worker to vice president.

Social Needs

When man's physiological needs are satisfied and he is no longer fearful about his physical welfare, his *social needs* become important motivators of his behavior—needs for belonging, for association, for acceptance by his fellows, for giving and receiving friendship and love.

Management knows today of the existence of these needs, but it often assumes quite wrongly that they represent a threat to the organization. Many studies have demonstrated that the tightly knit, cohesive work group may, under proper conditions, be far more effective than an equal number of separate individuals in achieving organizational goals.

Yet management, fearing group hostility to its own objectives, often goes to considerable length to control and direct human efforts in ways that are inimical to the natural "groupiness" of human beings. When man's social needs—and perhaps his safety needs, too—are thus thwarted, he behaves in ways which tend to defeat organizational objectives. He becomes resistant, antagonistic, uncooperative. But this behavior is a consequence, not a cause.

Ego Needs

Above the social needs—in the sense that they do not become motivators until lower levels are reasonably satisfied—are the needs of greatest significance to management and to man himself. They are the *egoistic needs,* and they are of two kinds:

1. Those needs that relate to one's self-esteem—needs for self-confidence, for independence, for achievement, for competence, for knowledge.
2. Those needs that relate to one's reputation—needs for status, for recognition, for appreciation, for the deserved respect of one's fellows.

Unlike the lower needs, these are rarely satisifed; man seeks indefinitely for more satisfaction of these needs once they have become important to him. But they do not appear in any significant way until physiological, safety, and social [needs] are all reasonably satisfied.

The typical industrial organization offers few opportunities for the satisfaction of these egoistic needs to people at lower levels in the hierarchy. The conventional methods of organizing work, particularly in mass-production industries, give little heed to these aspects of human motivation. If the practices of scientific management were deliberately calculated to thwart these needs, they could hardly accomplish this purpose better than they do.

Self-fulfillment Needs

> Finally—a capstone, as it were, on the hierarchy of man's needs—there are what we may call the needs for *self-fulfillment.* These are the needs for realizing one's own potentialities, for continued self-development, for being creative in the broadest sense of that term.
>
> It is clear that the conditions of modern life give only limited opportunity for these relatively weak needs to obtain expression. The deprivation most people experience with respect to other lower-level needs diverts their energies into the struggle to satisfy those needs, and the needs for self-fulfillmen remain dormant.

Although McGregor's analysis forces the needs into specific steps, Maslow considered all of them as being somewhat interdependent and, in fact, overlapping. It is nevertheless useful, at least conceptually, to consider human needs as being arranged into fairly delimited prepotency levels.

THE IMPORTANCE OF AUTONOMY

Some controversy exists as to whether needs that are at the lower levels of the hierarchy are ever activated enough to be considered work motivators. Porter,[4] for example, in adopting the Maslow hierarchy of needs for his research, has eliminated physiological needs from the list. Presumably, Porter feels that in our society this category lacks the prepotency to motivate behavior for most people. He substitutes instead a category of needs labeled "autonomy." The Porter modification seems to have particular relevance to education, for while physiological needs have tended to depreciate in importance,[5] teachers and students have expressed a demand for control over their work environment and, indeed, over their destiny. The need for autonomy that many educational participants express is based on the principle of self-government, self-control, and self-determination. Teachers, in particular, display formidable credentials in terms of professional expertness as justification for expression of this need.

In Figure 8-1 we use Porter's revision of the Maslow categories to illustrate the hierarchical relationships that constitute the theory of human needs.

THE PARTICIPATION AND PERFORMANCE INVESTMENTS

A basic principle in motivation theory is that people invest themselves in work in order to obtain desired returns or rewards.[6] Examples of that investment are time, physical energy, mental energy, creativity, knowledge, skill, enthusiasm, and effort. Returns or rewards can take a variety of tangible and intangible forms, including money, respect, comfort, a sense of accomplishment, social acceptance, and security. It is useful to

---

[4]Lyman Porter, "Attitudes in Management: Perceived Deficiencies in Need Fulfillment as a Function of Job Level," *Journal of Applied Psychology,* vol. 46, p. 375, 1962.

[5]Basic provision for needs at this level seems largely guaranteed in our society.

[6]This discussion of participation and performance investments follows closely that which appears in T. J. Sergiovanni and David Elliott, *Educational and Organizational Leadership in Elementary Schools,* Englewood Cliffs, N.J.: Prentice-Hall, 1975, p. 138. See also T. J. Sergiovanni, "New Evidence on Teacher Morale," *North Central Association Quarterly,* vol. 42, no. 3, pp. 259–266, 1968.

Motivational focus for:

1. Human resources supervision

2. Human relations supervision

3. Traditional supervision

Self-actualization

Autonomy

Esteem

Social

Security

Motivational potency

1. Higher-order needs

2. Support for second-level decision (performance)

3. To be earned on job

4. High motivational potential for professional teachers

1. Lower-order needs

2. Support for first-level decision (participation)

3. Considered as job givens

4. Low motivational potential for professional teachers

Figure 8-1 The hierarchy of needs: A motivational focus for supervision.

categorize expressions of investment in work as being of two types: first, a *participation* investment and second, a *performance* investment.

The participation investment is required of all teachers and includes all that is necessary for the teacher to obtain and maintain satisfactory membership in the school. Meeting classes, preparing lesson plans, obtaining satisfactory to good evaluations from supervisors, following school rules and regulations, attending required meetings, bearing her or his fair share of committee responsibility, projecting an appropriate image to the public—in short, giving a fair day's work for a fair day's pay. Teachers not willing to make the participatory investment in work find themselves unacceptable to administrators *and* other teachers. On the other hand, one cannot command teachers to give more of themselves—to go beyond the participatory investment. In return for the participatory investment, teachers are provided with such benefits as salary, retirement provisions, fair supervision, good human relations, and security. In a sense, we are describing the traditional legal work relationship between employer and employee. We can think of no great institution in our society and no great achievements that have resulted from merely the traditional legal work relationship. Greatness has always been a result of employers' and employees' exceeding the limits of this relationship.

The performance investment exceeds the limits of the traditional legal work relationship. Here, teachers give far more than one can "reasonably expect," and in return they are provided with rewards that permit them to enjoy deep satisfaction with their work and themselves. When we speak of motivation to work, we speak of providing incentives that evoke the performance investment from teachers. It is important to distinguish between the kinds of return or rewards that evoke each of these investments. One does not exceed the limits of the traditional legal work relationship for more rewards of the kind one has been receiving. Supervisors and administrators cannot buy this second investment with more money, privileges, easier and better working conditions, and improved human relationships. These are important incentives, as we shall see, but their potency is limited.

As we look to the needs hierarchy as a framework for prescribing the scope and content of supervisory behavior, it is helpful to visualize needs as falling into two categories: those described as lower-order needs (security, social, and, to some extent, esteem), and those described as higher-order (esteem, autonomy, and self-fulfillment), as illustrated in Figure 8-1. The lower-order needs are those which are available to teachers as they make the participation investment in schools. The school exchanges money, benefits, position, friendship, protection, interpersonal gratification, and the like, for satisfactory participation of teachers.

The higher-order needs are those whose fulfillment is exchanged for service that teachers give to the school and its clients as a result of the performance investment. Teachers tend not to be concerned with the pursuit of higher-order needs without consistent and considerable satisfaction of the lower-order needs. Since meaningful satisfaction of the esteem, autonomy, and self-fulfillment variety is intimately connected to performance, teachers will need to earn rewards of this kind through efforts toward the achievement of school goals. Supervisors who rely on reward structures characteristic of the higher-order needs are tapping potent motivational levels in teachers.

The motivational base for human resources supervision consists of needs of each of the five levels but focuses on those that we describe as higher order. The limited motivational basis for traditional and, to some extent, human relations supervision is totally inadequate for providing personal and professional growth opportunities that professionally oriented teachers seek.

COMPETENCE: PROFESSIONAL MOTIVE

Maslow's theory provides an integrated view of interdependent need structures, but some scholars have tended to focus on one need, often to the exclusion of other needs. Two such efforts seem to have particular relevance to understanding teacher behavior and teacher need. One effort explores in detail the competence motive—the desire for mastery—and the other, the achievement motive—the desire for success. The first effort, developed and popularized by Robert White,[7] presumes that people wish to understand and control their environment and wish to be active participants in this environment. This need is traced by White to early infancy and childhood experiences and is observed in the seemingly random and endless searching, feeling, tinkering, exploring, and investigating that characterize this age. White claims that the years 6 to 9 are critical ones in developing this motive. If early experiences prove successful, people are likely to continue developing and extending their competence motives. As adults, they behave in ways that permit them to test and reconfirm the adequacy of their competence. The competence test recurs as successes are compiled, and each new

[7]Robert W. White, "Motivation Reconsidered: The Concept of Competence," *Psychological Review,* vol. 66, no. 5, pp. 297–333, 1959.

test is usually at a level that is more challenging than that of a person's previous success.[8]

Many teachers have lost the capacity to strive for competence largely because of a history of failure. They are less ready to try something new or to undertake a more difficult assignment, for fear of additional failure. Schools benefit by developing and encouraging the competence motive, since teachers and other professional workers typically express a desire for job mastery and professional growth. A useful exercise for readers is to identify those aspects of the curriculum, the classroom management system, and the school management system that prohibit, delimit, or otherwise frustrate the opportunity for teachers and students to develop, express, and confirm the competence motive. When this motive is reinforced in teachers, personal satisfaction for the human organization and high-quality performance for the human school can be expected.

The second need, the achievement motive, is one studied intensively by David C. McClelland.[9] In commenting on McClelland's work, Gellerman describes a person who is "blessed" or "afflicted" with high need for achievement as follows:

> He tries harder and demands more of himself, especially when the chips are down. Consequently, he accomplishes more. We find, for example, that college students who have a strong achievement drive will usually get better grades than equally bright students with weaker needs for achievement. Executives "on their way up" in their companies are usually driven by stronger achievement needs than those who do not rise so quickly. The stronger the achievement drive, the greater the probability that the individual will demand more of himself.
>
> *Perhaps the most fascinating aspect of the achievement motive is that it seems to make accomplishment an end in itself.* If anything, it is the person who has little achievement motivation who expects a tangible reward for greater effort. While the achievement-motivated person does not spurn tangible rewards and even has a rather unexpected use for them, they are not really essential to him, either. He takes a special joy in winning, in competing successfully with a difficult standard; this means more to him than money or a public pat on the back. He is not an altruist: He simply finds enough delight in doing difficult things that he does not need to be bribed to do them.[10]

Teachers with a strong need for achievement have much to contribute to school effectiveness. They display an entrepreneurial behavior pattern that McClelland describes as being characterized by (1) moderate risk taking as a function of skill rather than chance, (2) energetic or novel instrumental activity, (3) individual responsibility and accountability for behavior, (4) the need for knowledge of results, and (5) anticipation of future possibilities.[11] As one would expect, teachers with a strong need for achievement demand a great deal from the school. They need opportunities to display the behavior manifestations that McClelland describes above and resist attempts to limit this behavior. Often if achievement needs cannot be expressed in the school, an

---

[8]As people perceive themselves as becoming increasingly competent, they evoke the self-fulfilling prophecy.
[9]David C. McClelland et al., *The Achievement Motive,* New York: Appleton-Century-Crofts, 1953; also, David C. McClelland, *The Achieving Society,* Princeton, N.J.: Van Nostrand, 1961.
[10]Saul Gellerman, *Motivation and Productivity,* New York: American Management Associations, 1963, p. 124.
[11]McClelland, *The Achieving Society,* p. 207.

individual seeks expression (1) organizationally in a "negative" fashion, (2) extraorganizationally in teacher associations and unions, or (3) in noneducational organizations and institutions. Teachers with a strong need for achievement can often be troublesome for many administrators and supervisors, but they have the potential to give fully and in a spirit of excellence to the school and its efforts.

MOTIVES OF SUPERVISORS

Although we are primarily interested in issues of motivation as they affect teachers at work, we are going to take a slight detour and examine the influence of motives on supervisors. Consideration will be given to three motives as they affect the helping relationship. The helping relationship example will be used because it is an important dimension of supervision. This example *symbolizes* as well that the entire discussion of motivation applies not only to teachers but to supervisors and others who constitute the human organization of schools.

Motives Influencing the Helping Relationship

The process of giving and receiving help and its successful outcome are strongly influenced by the basic motives each of the parties brings to this relationship. Though a number of motives are important, three have been identified as being particularly key in understanding the dynamics of the helping relationship: achievement, power, and affiliation motivation. As has already been described, the achievement motive is associated with persons wanting to take personal responsibility for their own success or failure, liking work situations where goals are clear and obtainable though reasonably challenging, and preferring frequent and unambiguous feedback that allows them to determine their success or failure rate in a continuous fashion.

Typically, supervisors with high achievement motivation are task-oriented, prefer short-range concrete targets to more ambiguous and long-range goals, like to be on top of things, and in seeking personal responsibility find it difficult to delegate authority or to come on strong in emphasizing human relationships for their own sake. A supervisor with a high need for achievement would likely be committed to building an achievement-oriented school with fairly high, visible, and detailed standards.

The power motive is associated with a desire to influence others and to maintain control of those aspects of the job that permit this influence. The word "power" typically conjures up negative images of one who uses her or his authority in an arbitrary way to manipulate people and events for self-satisfaction. But in fact the power motive can be harmful or helpful in supervision depending upon what other values and motives also come into play. A supervisor with a deep commitment to human values and to the democratic process will use the power motive constructively by facilitating, engaging people in decision making, clarifying, setting standards, and motivating people. This same power motive combined with highly authoritarian values, however, produces quite another picture of reality—one less attractive and certainly less effective.

Expressions of the affiliation motive in providing leadership and giving help can also be helpful or not depending upon other values and motives of the supervisor. The affiliation motive is reflected in the supervisor's concern for warm and friendly relationships with teachers. If the affiliation motive is all that is present, however, then the helping relationship may well be friendly but not very productive. Productivity requires that the teacher assume a great deal of initiative and responsibility for providing a focus to the helping relationship and for coming up with solutions. This motive combined with a moderate task and power emphasis, however, can provide the necessary interpersonal touch crucial to effective supervisory relationships.

George Litwin and Robert Stringer, Jr. suggest that from the way one answers the following questions[12] it is possible to gain insights into the importance to a person of the three motives. Take a moment and respond "yes" or "no" to each question:

1. When you start a job or task, do you stick with it?

2. Do you like getting involved with group projects, and are you sensitive to other people?

3. Do you like positions of authority where you can give rather than take orders? Do you try to take over?

4. Do you try to find out how well you are doing and keep track of the progress you are making?

5. Do you enjoy a good argument?

6. Do you try hard to get personally involved with your superiors?

7. Do you like fairly difficult and challenging situations?

8. Do you like and except responsibility? Do you set measurable standards for your performance?

9. Do you seem to be uncomfortable when you are forced to work alone?

10. Are status symbols important to you, and do you use them to gain influence over others?

11. Do you like to interact with other workers, and do you go out of your way to make friends with new workers?

12. Are you eager to be your own boss, even when you need assistance or when a group effort is better?

"Yes" answers to questions 1, 4, 7, and 8 suggest that you have a high need to achieve. These questions focus primarily on work situations with targeted outcomes involving moderate risk, in which you can monitor your own progress and have access to feedback. "Yes" answers to questions 3, 5, 10, and 12 suggest that you have a high need for power. They focus primarily on work situations that permit you to gain control and to influence others. "Yes" answers to questions 2, 6, 9, and 11 suggest that you

[12]The questions are adapted from George Litwin and Robert Stringer, Jr., *Motivation and Organizational Climate*, Boston: Division of Research, Harvard University, Graduate School of Business Administration, 1968, pp. 173–174. Reprinted by permission. Copyright © 1968 by The President and Fellows of Harvard University.

have a high need for affiliation. They focus primarily on work situations characterized by warm and supportive relationships.

Obviously, to obtain a more accurate assessment of the extent to which each of the three needs is important to you, one would need to use a more sophisticated technique than we have here. The typical method for assessing these needs, for example, is a projective technique involving the writing of stories and responses to work-oriented pictures. The stories are then carefully assessed for content suggestive of the three needs. Still, responses to the questions we have provided can give a rough idea of how important the needs are and, more importantly, help one to conduct further self-analysis.

Effective Helpers, Ineffective Helpers, and Nonhelpers

Of particular interest are the relationships that exist between the needs for achievement, power, and affiliation in supervisors and their subsequent effectiveness in giving help to teachers. One study[13] examining these needs within the helping relationship found that effective helpers were moderately motivated by needs for achievement, power, and affiliation. Ineffective helpers, on the other hand, were highly motivated by needs for achievement and power, but the affiliation need was quite low. And finally, nonhelpers were highly motivated by the need for affiliation, but power and achievement needs were quite low. Nonhelpers were described as not having had either a positive or a negative impact on the ability of the person receiving help to solve problems better. Helpers classified as ineffective actually made things worse.

These relationships are graphically illustrated in Figure 8-2. Notice that effective helpers were slightly below the mean for all subjects in the need for achievement but slightly above the mean for power and affiliation. Ineffective helpers, by contrast, were well above the mean on power and achievement and well below on affiliation. The nonhelper pattern, with affiliation dominating, is almost opposite to that for ineffective helpers. Of course, this study can only provide some general guidelines for the impact of motives on the helping relationship.

When they were asked to respond to a self-description semantic differential scale, effective helpers, ineffective helpers, and nonhelpers in this study viewed themselves quite differently. Nonhelpers viewed themselves as being more passive, democratic, submissive, following, guarded, quiet, timid, and self-conscious, and as preferring to listen. They did not see themselves as being very influential, articulate, or cynical. According to the researchers, the attitudes of nonhelpers as a group suggest they are accepting and democratic people who lack the self-confidence to influence others.

Ineffective helpers described themselves as being organized, impatient, open, and superior. The researchers suggest that the attitudes as a group reflect extreme self-confidence combined with self-importance and a lack of interest in others.

Effective helpers' descriptions of themselves were somewhere between the ineffective helper and nonhelper responses on all of the paired adjectives that constituted the scale, except for autocratic-democratic, organized-disorganized, and

---

[13]David A. Kolb and Richard E. Boyatzis, "On the Dynamics of the Helping Relationship," in David A. Kolb, Irwin M. Rubin, and James M. McIntyre (eds.), *Organizational Psychology: A Book of Readings,* Englewood Cliffs, N.J.: Prentice-Hall, 1971, pp. 331–355.

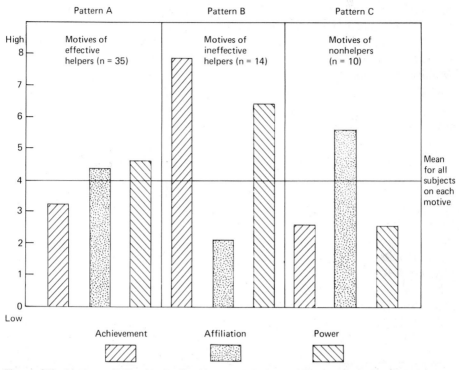

Figure 8-2 Motives of effective, ineffective and nonhelpers. *(Adapted from: David A. Kolb and Richard E. Boyatzis, "On the Dynamics of the Helping Relationship." In David Kolb, Irwin M. Rubin, and James M. McIntyre, Organizational Psychology: A Book of Readings, 3d ed. © 1979. Adapted by permission of Prentice-Hall, Englewood Cliffs, N.J.)*

humorous-humorless. On these items, they scored slightly more autocratic, more organized, and more humorous. It is clear from this study that effective helping requires more than just providing support and encouragement and being a good listener. Effective helpers were able to influence the outcome of events by taking the initiative and facilitating the learning of others. Focusing on the problems to be solved and the task to be accomplished were important to effective helping, but these behaviors did not dominate the supporter-facilitator roles of helpers.

It should be pointed out that too much emphasis on solving the problem itself or on completing the task at hand is really assistance, not help. The supervisor is not being helpful in the long run by providing answers and thus keeping teachers dependent on his or her help. Providing assistance is appropriate from time to time, but not as a dominant strategy or perspective.

The needs for achievement, power, and affiliation play an important role in determining how teachers are likely to react to supervisory efforts. Assume, for example, that each of the patterns of needs A, B, and C shown in Figure 8-2 represent the patterns of three teachers for whom you have supervisory responsibility. What reactions might you expect from each as you work with them in clinical supervision or in another mode of classroom supervision? What other factors might be taken into consideration in estimating reactions? Given these anticipated reactions, what might be some ways you would approach each of the three? Return to these questions after reading the rest of this chapter and share your ideas with a colleague or classmate.

Motivation-Hygiene Theory

An examination of human needs and important work motives such as achievement, competence, power, and affiliation provides us with important concepts. In this section a more operational approach to motivation-commitment is presented in the form of the motivation-hygiene theory as proposed originally by Frederick Herzberg and his associates.[14]

All the paragraphs that appear below are descriptions of important features of the motivation-hygiene theory. They are stated first, in an attempt to sketch out the nature, scope, and potency of the theory. Their description is followed by an analysis of theoretical and research findings that provide the origins of the theory.

1. There are certain conditions in work that teachers expect to enjoy. If these conditions are present in sufficient quantity, teachers will perform adequately, but only adequately. If these conditions are not present in sufficient quantity, teachers will be dissatisfied and work performance will suffer.

2. The conditions in work which teachers expect as part of the traditional legal work relationship are called *hygienic factors*. Their absence results in teacher dissatisfaction and poor performance. Their presence maintains the traditional legal work relationship but does not motivate performance. Hygienic factors are associated with the participation investment in work.

3. The factors which contribute to teachers' exceeding the traditional work relationship are called *motivators*. The absence of motivators does not result in dissatisfaction and does not endanger the traditional work relationship. Motivational factors are associated with the performance investment in work.

4. Motivational factors and hygienic factors are different. Motivation to work does not result from increasing hygienic factors.

5. Hygienic factors are associated with the conditions of work and are extrinsic in nature. Examples are money, benefits, fair supervision, and a feeling of belonging. Motivational factors are associated with work itself and are intrinsic in nature. Examples are recognition, achievement, and increased responsibility.

---

[14]Frederick Herzberg, Bernard Mausner, and Barbara Snyderman, *The Motivation to Work,* New York: Wiley, 1959; Frederick Herzberg, *Work and the Nature of Man,* New York: World Publishing, 1966. This discussion follows closely Sergiovanni and Elliott, op. cit., pp. 139–148. See also T. J. Sergiovanni and Fred D. Carver, *The New School Executive: A Theory of Administration,* 2d ed., New York: Harper & Row, 1980, Chaps. 5–8. The motivation-hygiene theory is not without its critics. See, for example, M. D. Dunnelle, J. P. Campbell, and M. D. Hakel, "Factors Contributing to Job Satisfaction and Job Dissatisfaction in Six Occupational Groups," *Organizational Behavioral and Human Performance,* vol. 2, pp. 143–174, 1967. For support, see D. A. Whitsett and E. K. Winslow, "An Analysis of Studies Critical to the Motivation-Hygiene Theory," *Personnel Psychology,* vol. 20, no. 4, pp. 391–415, 1967. Our review of motivation-hygiene studies leads us to conclude that the theory is indeed appropriate for white-collar and professionally oriented workers but less appropriate for other workers.

6. Hygienic factors are important, for their neglect creates problems in the work environment. These problems can result in dissatisfaction and lowered performance. Taking care of the hygienic factors prevents trouble, but these factors are not potent enough to motivate people to work, to evoke the performance decision.

7. Hygienic factors meet the human need to avoid unpleasantness and hardship. Motivational factors serve the uniquely human need for psychological growth.

8. Satisfaction at work is not a motivator of performance per se, but results from quality performance. Administrators and supervisors should not use satisfaction as a method of motivating teachers, but satisfaction should be thought of as a goal that teachers seek, one that is best obtained through meaningful work.

9. Administrators and supervisors who use job satisfaction to motivate teachers are practicing human relations. This has not been proven to be an effective approach. Human relations emphasize the hygienic factors.

10. Administrators and supervisors who consider job satisfaction as a goal that teachers seek through accomplishing meaningful work and who focus on enhancing the meaningful view of work and the ability of teachers to accomplish this work are practicing human resources supervision. This has been proven to be an effective approach. Human resources development emphasizes the motivational factors.

11. True, not all teachers can be expected to respond to the motivation-hygiene theory, but most can.

In summary, the theory stipulates that people at work have two distinct sets of needs. One set of needs is best met by hygienic factors. In exchange for these factors, one is prepared to make the participatory investment—to give a fair day's work. If hygienic factors are neglected, dissatisfaction occurs, and one's performance on the job decreases to a level below the acceptable. Another set of needs is best met by the motivational factors that are not automatically part of the job but that can be built into most jobs, particularly those found in elementary schools. In return for the motivational factors, one is prepared to make the performance investment, to exceed the limits of the traditional legal work relationship. If the motivational factors are neglected, one does not become dissatisfied, but one's performance does not exceed that typically described as a fair day's work for a fair day's pay.

The Motivation-Hygiene Factors

Hygienic factors are those largely extrinsic in nature and associated with our lower-order needs, and motivational factors are those largely intrinsic in nature and associated with our higher-order needs. Now let us examine the factors themselves.

Motivation-hygiene theory results from the research of Frederick Herzberg.[15] The model for his research is an interview method whereby workers are asked to describe job events associated with satisfaction and dissatisfaction at work. Further, the effects of these feelings and events on one's performance at work are examined. Dozens of

[15]Herzberg et al., *The Motivation to Work.*

studies have been conducted using this approach with a variety of workers, from scientists to assembly-line workers, in a number of countries.[16]

In the majority of cases, studies reveal that traditional linear notions regarding satisfaction and dissatisfaction at work are in need of modification. Traditionally, it has been assumed that if a cause of dissatisfaction is identified, elimination of this cause results in job satisfaction and motivated workers. Teachers unhappy with school policies, the kind of supervision they are getting, money matters, and class scheduling will move to a state of satisfaction and motivation if these deficiencies are remedied. Motivation-hygiene studies by and large show that this is not the case. Remedying the deficiencies that cause dissatisfaction brings a person up to a level of minimum performance that includes the absence of dissatisfaction. Satisfaction and motivation are the results of a separate set of factors. The factors associated with satisfaction, but not dissatisfaction, are called motivators because of their ability to stimulate performance. The factors associated with dissatisfaction, but not satisfaction, are called hygienic because of their ability to cause trouble if neglected.[17]

> The Motivation-Hygiene theory of job attitudes began with a depth interview study of over 200 engineers and accountants representing Pittsburgh industry. These interviews probed sequences of events in the work lives of the respondents to determine the factors that were involved in their feeling exceptionally happy and conversely exceptionally unhappy with their jobs. From a review and an analysis of previous publications in the general area of job attitudes, a two-factor hypothesis was formulated to guide the original investigation. This hypothesis suggested that the factors involved in producing job satisfaction were separate and distinct from the factors that led to job dissatisfaction. Since separate factors needed to be considered depending on whether job satisfaction or job dissatisfaction was involved, it followed that these two feelings were not the obverse of each other. The opposite of job satisfaction would not be job dissatisfaction, but rather *no* job satisfaction; and similarly the

[16]See, for example, Frederick Herzberg, *Work and the Nature of Man*, New York: World Publishing, 1966.
[17]Frederick Herzberg, "The Motivation-Hygiene Concepts and Problems of Manpower," *Personnel Administration*, vol. 27, no. 1, p. 3, 1964.

TABLE 8-1
THE MOTIVATION AND HYGIENE FACTORS*

Motivation (Found in the work itself)	Hygiene (Found in the environment of work)
Achievement	Salary
Recognition	Possibility of growth
Work itself	Interpersonal relations (subordinates)
Responsibility	Interpersonal relations (superiors)
Advancement	Interpersonal relations (peers)
	Supervision—technical
	Company policy and administration
	Working conditions
	Personal life
	Status
	Job security

*The factors were identified and reported by Herzberg in F. Herzberg et al., *The Motivation to Work*, New York: Wiley, 1959.

opposite of job dissatisfaction is *no* job dissatisfaction—not job satisfaction. The statement of the concept is awkward and may appear at first to be a semantic ruse, but there is more than a play with words when it comes to understanding the behavior of people on jobs. The fact that job satisfaction is made up of two unipolar traits is not a unique occurrence. The difficulty of establishing a zero point in psychology with the procedural necessity of using instead a bench mark (mean of a population) from which to start our measurement has led to the conception that psychological traits are bipolar. Empirical investigations, however, have cast some shadows on the assumptions of bipolarity; one timely example is a study of conformity and noncomformity, where they are shown not to be opposites, but rather two separate unipolar traits.

The factors Herzberg associates with motivation and hygiene are shown in Table 8-1. The findings of his original study are illustrated in Figure 8-3. Factors to the right of the zero line contribute predominantly to satisfaction, and factors to the left of this line contribute predominantly to dissatisfaction. The longer the line associated with a factor, the more often respondents cited this factor as contributing to job feelings. The

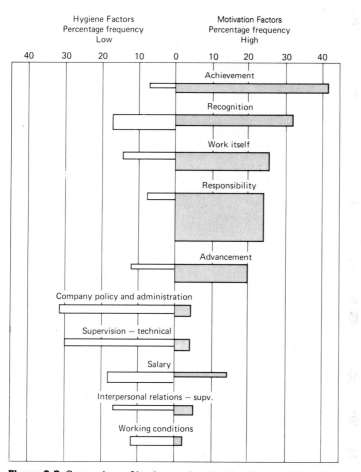

Figure 8-3 Comparison of hygiene and motivation factors. *(From Frederick Herzberg et al., The Motivation to Work, New York: Wiley, 1959.)*

greater the width of the line—in the diagram a box—the longer the duration of the attitude. Thus while respondents cited achievement more often than responsibility as a source of positive feelings about a job, when responsibility was cited, the feeling lasted longer than in the case of achievement.

Achievement, recognition, work itself, responsibility, and advancement are the factors identified by Herzberg as contributing primarily to satisfaction. Their absence tends not to lead to dissatisfaction. These are the motivators—the rewards that one seeks in return for the performance investment.

Policy and administration, supervision, salary, interpersonal relationships, and working conditions are the factors that Herzberg identifies as contributing primarily to dissatisfaction. These are the hygienic factors—conditions that workers expect in return for a fair day's work.

In the separate teacher study illustrated in Table 8-2 achievement and recognition were identified as the most potent motivators.[18] Responsibility, although a significant motivator, appeared in only 7 percent of the events associated with satisfaction. We do not take advantage of the motivational possibilities of responsibility in education—this factor is relatively standardized for teachers, in that responsibility does not vary much from one teacher to another. Work itself did not appear significantly more often as a contributor to satisfaction. Apparently, elements of the job of teaching as we currently know it are inherently less than satisfying. Among these are routine housekeeping, attendance, milk money, paperwork, study hall, lunch duty, and the like. The negative

[18]Thomas J. Sergiovanni, "Factors Which Affect Satisfaction and Dissatisfaction of Teachers," *The Journal of Educational Administration*, vol. 5, no. 1, pp. 66–82, 1967.

TABLE 8-2
PERCENTAGES FOR THE FREQUENCY WITH WHICH JOB FACTORS CONTRIBUTED TO HIGH ATTITUDES AS COMPARED WITH LOW ATTITUDES FOR TEACHERS

Job factors	Percentage of highs NR = 142	Percentage of lows NR = 142	P
1. Achievement	30*	9	.01
2. Recognition	28*	2	.001
3. Work itself	11	8	
4. Responsibility	7*	1	.05
5. Advancement	0	1	
6. Salary	2	3	
7. Possibility of growth	6	2	
8. Interpersonal relations (subordinates)	7	20*	.01
9. Interpersonal relations (superiors)	3	4	
10. Interpersonal relations (peers)	1	15*	.001
11. Supervision—technical	1	10*	.01
12. School policy and administration	2	13*	.01
13. Working conditions	2	6	
14. Personal life	0	5*	.05
15. Status	0	0	
16. Security	0	1	

N = 72 teachers; NR = number of responses
*Significant factor.

aspects of police, clerk, and custodial roles seem to neutralize professional teaching and guidance roles for these professionals. Poor interpersonal relations with students; inadequate, incompetent, insensitive, and close supervision; unfair, rigid, and inflexible school policies and administrative practices; poor interpersonal relations with other teachers and with parents; and incidents in their personal lives were the job factors found to contribute significantly to teachers' dissatisfaction.

Herzberg found in his original study with accountants and engineers[19] that, although recognition and achievement were mentioned most often as motivators, the duration of good feelings associated with these rewards was very short. Work and advancement seemed to have medium effects, but good feelings associated with responsibility lasted more than twice as long as those associated with work and advancement, and more than three times as long as those from achievement and recognition. Negative feelings associated with neglected hygienic factors were generally of short duration.

Teachers as Individuals

The motivation-hygiene theory provides simplified answers to rather complex questions. This is a bold theory that provides broad and general guidelines to administrators and supervisors interested in evoking the performance investment from teachers.[20] Its boldness and its broad propositions require intelligent caution in the application of the theory to practice. For example, while the theory suggests that by and large only the satisfiers motivate, it would be wrong to conclude that some people are not motivated by the dissatisfiers. Some individuals are indeed motivated by the dissatisfiers, but under ordinary circumstances it is not natural to be so motivated. The implication is that healthy individuals respond to the motivation-hygiene dynamic, while those less healthy do not. Further, healthy individuals who are deprived of work satisfactions on the job will seek these satisfactions elsewhere—at home through family membership, hobbies, community activity, sports, and the like. Attention to these aspects of life is important to all of us, but the world of work seems the more natural place for professional workers to find satisfaction for their needs of esteem, competence, achievement, autonomy, and self-fulfillment

Teachers who seem more interested in hygienic factors than motivational factors can be categorized as follows: (1) those who have the potential for motivation seeking but are frustrated by insensitive and closed administrative, supervisory, and organizational policies and practices; (2) those who have the potential for motivation seeking, but who decide to channel this potential into other areas of their lives; and (3) those who do not have the potential for motivation seeking on or off the job. Those in the second and third groups use their jobs as a means to achieve goals not related to the school.

The second group includes many teachers whose goals are buying a second car or a vacation house, supplementing their spouse's income to achieve a higher standard of

[19]Herzberg et al., *The Motivation to Work*.
[20]This discussion of teachers as individuals follows closely Sergiovanni and Elliott, op. cit., p. 147. See also T. J. Sergiovanni, "Human Resources Supervision," in Sergiovanni (ed.), *Professional Supervision for Professional Teachers*, Washington, D.C.: Association for Supervision and Curriculum Development, 1975, pp. 19–21.

living, putting their spouse or children through college, and so on. Men in this group often use the teaching occupation as a means to step into another job, such as coaching, counseling, or administration.[21]

The third group includes individuals who seem fixated at lower need levels. In a sense, they could be described as obsessed with avoiding unpleasantness and discomfort to the point that they have not developed the ability to seek satisfaction through the motivators and at higher need levels. Many psychologists regard this obsession as a symptom of poor mental health; if this is the case, then selection procedures should be devised to identify and filter out teachers of this type. Tenured teachers of this type will need to be heavily supervised.

Teachers who have the potential for motivation seeking, but elect to seek satisfactions of this kind outside of the school are by and large good teachers who give honest labor in exchange for what they hope to gain from the school. Extraordinary performance is lacking among them, however, for such teachers do not have a strong commitment to the school and its purposes. Teachers of this kind will be with us for a long time, but they cannot be depended upon to substantially upgrade the nation's schools or to display much interest in becoming full partners in the school enterprise unless they can become attracted to the motivational factors. Teachers who are interested primarily in hygienic factors but have potential for being influenced by the motivation factors can make significant contributions to the school's work if supervised kindly, but firmly and competently, or when combined with motivation seekers in schools with differentiated roles and responsibilities for teachers. Hygienically oriented teachers who have the potential for motivation seeking but are frustrated by the school and its administration are unfortunate casualties. When we deny teachers opportunities to channel motivation expressions they desire, we not only waste valuable human resources but deny youngsters important opportunities for growth in their schooling. In general, hygienically oriented teachers think of their jobs too much in terms of salary, working conditions, supervision, status, job security, school policies and administration, and social relationships.

EXPECTANCY THEORY OF MOTIVATION

One approach to motivation that takes into account differences in the desires and needs of others and that does not prescribe a one best motivational strategy but that shares

---

[21]Simpson and Simpson maintain that semiprofessional women are far less committed to work careers than are most men of comparable attainments. They note that "a fairly mild economic pressure is often enough, however, to keep them [women]at work. Relatively few of them would face utter destitution if they stopped work. The pressure is more often the desire to maintain a standard of comparative luxury, to help the family move into a larger house, or to save toward the children's college education. . . . Work for women is no longer considered a tragedy; it is an acceptable alternative but it is not the first choice for many."

They further note: "It is true that educated women whose husbands' incomes are high often re-enter the labor force after their children are beyond early childhood, and many of these appear to be motivated by a wish for self-expression apart from economic consideration. But the need for self-expression which these women say they feel appears to be occasioned more by the boredom of finding themselves with an empty nest rather than by strong identification with the world of work." Richard L. Simpson and Ida Harper Simpson, "Women and Bureaucracy in the Semi-Professions," in Amitai Etzioni (ed.), *The Semi-Professionals and Their Organization*, New York: Free Press, 1969, pp. 217–218.

some features of the motivation-hygiene theory is Vroom's expectancy theory of motivation.[22] Vroom's is a contingency theory in that he views motivation as a response in a person's needs to a specific goal that person seeks. Performance on the job, in his view, is a means by which the person can achieve a personal goal. This view is consistent with human resources supervision in that it assumes that performance is a means to satisfaction rather than satisfaction being viewed as a means to performance. Since personal goals for individuals are likely to vary, no one set of motivational factors is identified. The basic components of expectancy theory are illustrated in Figure 8-4.

Basically, individual motivation is viewed as a function of a person's perception that his or her increased performance will result in certain rewards that will help him or her attain personal goals. If a teacher's goal is to be more influential in educational decision making (to attain more expert power), motivation will depend upon that teacher's perception that increased performance (volunteering for difficult curriculum work and doing a good job of it) will lead to appropriate rewards (winning the professional respect of colleagues) that will enable the teacher to achieve this goal. By the same token, another individual with personal goals of group acceptance may not be motivated to volunteer for additional work, and if assigned work, may not be motivated to perform in an extraordinary way unless that behavior is associated with group acceptance.

Since personal goals differ, rewards that appeal to some teachers may not appeal to others. It is therefore necessary, on the one hand, to individualize rewards to match personal goals that are consistent with those of the school and, on the other hand, to help build greater consistency between personal and school goals. Further, the relationship between individual performance, organizational rewards, and personal goals is not always clear to teachers, and clarification of their parts by supervisors may be necessary.

In further developing the expectancy approach Nadler and Lawler provide three concepts as key building blocks of the theory:

1. *Performance-outcome expectancy.* Every behavior has associated with it, in an individual's mind, certain outcomes (rewards or punishments). In other words, the individual believes or expects that if he or she behaves in a certain way, he or she will get certain things.
2. *Valence.* Each outcome has a "valence" (value, worth, attractiveness) to a specific

[22]Victor H. Vroom, *Work and Motivation,* New York: Wiley, 1964. See also Vroom, "Organizational Choice: A Study of Pre- and Post-Decision Processes," *Organizational Behavior and Human Performance,* vol. 1, pp. 212–225, 1966; and J. Galbraith and L. Cummings, "An Empirical Investigation of the Motivational Determinants of Task Performance: Interactive Effects Between Instrumentality—Valence and Motivation—Ability," *Organizational Behavior and Human Performance,* vol. 2, pp. 237–257, 1967, for studies that substantiate aspects of Vroom's theory.

Figure 8-4 An expanded model of expectancy theory.

individual. Outcomes have different valences for different individuals. This comes about because valences result from individual needs and perceptions, which differ because they in turn reflect other factors in the individual's life.

For example, some individuals may value an opportunity for promotion or advancement because of their needs for achievement or power. Others may not want to be promoted and leave their current work group because of needs for affiliation. Similarly, a fringe benefit such as a pension plan may have great valence for an older worker but little valence for a young employee on his or her first job.

> **3.** *Effort-performance expectancy.* Each behavior also has associated with it, in the individual's mind, a certain expectancy or probability of success. This expectancy represents the individual's perception of how hard it will be to achieve such behavior and the probability of his or her successful achievement of that behavior.[23]

Nadler and Lawler conclude that, in general, a person will be motivated to behave in a certain way when she or he believes that this behavior will lead to a specific outcome, when the outcome has a positive value, or when he or she feels able to perform at the desired level (Will I be able to do what is required if I try? If I am able to perform appropriately, what will happen? Why do I want to try? That is, how important are likely outcomes to me?). Nadler and Lawler would add effort and ability to the basic expectancy model. Their expanded view is shown in Figure 8-4. Nadler and Lawler provide the following suggestions to supervisors wanting to use the expectancy theory in practice:[24]

1. Figure out what outcomes (personal goals) each teacher values. Don't assume that everyone wants the same thing. Responsibility, for example, is considered to be an important motivation factor in the motivation-hygiene theory but some teachers may prefer a more easy-going and less stressful environment which permits them to enjoy personal relationships on the job. The same strategy may be used by a supervisor (team teaching or family grouping, for example), but the desired outcomes for teachers may be different. Teacher A might be interested in the team approach because it provides for desirable social interaction; while Teacher B shares a similar interest in the team approach because of desires for increased responsibility.

2. Determine the kind of outcomes you desire. Supervisors need to have some image of the good life; some set of standards which specify what they are trying to accomplish. This image and standard provide the basis for determining the direction of motivational efforts.

3. Make sure that desired outcomes and desired ways of behaving for teachers are within their reach. Realistic objectives which reflect ability and disposition levels of teachers are important. Remember, if a new way of behaving requires too much perceived effort or is not likely to be seen as within reach, teachers will not be motivated.

4. Pay attention to how tasks, jobs, and roles are designed. (One source of desired

---

[23]David A. Nadler and Edward E. Lawler III, op. cit., p. 28.
[24]Ibid, pp. 30–32.

outcome is the work itself. The expectancy theory model supports much of the job enrichment literature in saying that by designing jobs which enable people to get their needs fulfilled, organizations can bring about higher levels of motivation.)

We will consider this point further when we explore the concept of job enrichment and its implications for supervisory effectiveness in the next section. In sum, expectancy theory recognizes that people at work have different abilities, needs, goals, and aspirations. This implies that supervisors need to take a more individualized perspective in motivating teachers and need to develop flexible strategies that permit choices. Finally, note that in expectancy theory job satisfaction is derived from performance. Similarly, in motivation-hygiene theory intrinsic satisfaction is derived from performing the work itself. Satisfaction from achievement, recognition, and responsibility is earned as a result of accomplished work. This thinking (improved performance leads to satisfaction) is an important improvement over human relations theories (which tend to assume that job satisfaction itself is linked to improved performance) and is essential to the human resources approach to supervision.

THE CONCEPT OF JOB ENRICHMENT

Supervisors have long known that how the work of teaching is organized, the structures provided within which teachers must function, and the resulting meanings that teachers attached to their work are important. In recent years this thinking has been formalized and developed into the concept of job enrichment. One very promising avenue of research on job enrichment and its link to motivation and commitment is that of Hackman and Oldham.[25] These scholars have developed a theory of job enrichment that has been successfully applied in practice. In a very real sense, the concept of job enrichment draws upon all of the other theories of motivation presented and shows how they might actually be implemented in practice.

Hackman and Oldham have identified three psychological states they believe are critical in determining a person's motivation for and satisfaction with a job:

Experienced meaningfulness:
The individual must perceive his or her work as worthwhile or important by some system of values held.

Experienced responsibility:
The individual must believe that he or she personally is accountable for the outcomes of efforts.

Knowledge of results:
The individual must be able to determine, on some fairly regularly basis, whether or not the outcomes of his or her work are satisfactory.[26]

[25]J. R. Hackman and G. Oldham, "Motivation Through Design of Work: Test of a Theory," *Organizational Behavior and Human Performance*, vol. 16, pp. 250–279, 1976.
[26]J. R. Hackman, G. Oldman, R. Johnson, and K. Purdy, "A New Strategy for Job Enrichment," *California Management Review, vol. 17, no. 4 p. 57.*

Hackman and Oldham maintain that when the three states are present in an individual, she or he feels good and performs well. Further, the presence of good feelings at any one time prompts the person to continue to perform well in an effort to earn more of these feelings in the future. Thus the three psychological states are the basis of "internal motivation." Internal motivation is important to supervisors, for we seem to have less and less to give of an external nature (money, benefits, etc.).

Five job characteristics have been identified that evoke these psychological states. Three of the characteristics—skill variety, task identity, and task significance—cumulatively determine *meaningfulness*. Autonomy, a fourth job characteristic, is associated with feelings of responsibility. Feedback, a final job characteristic proposed by Hackman and Oldham, is associated with *knowledge of results*.

The job enrichment model suggests that in teaching, jobs that require different activities in carrying out the work and the use of a variety of teacher talents and skills (skill variety); require that teachers engage in holistic or complete and identifiable tasks (task identity); are viewed by teachers as having a substantial and significant impact on the lives or work of other people (task significance); provide substantial freedom, independence, and direction to individual teachers in scheduling work and in deciding classroom organizational and instructional procedures (autonomy); and provide teachers with direct and clear information about the effects of their performance (feedback) are likely to evoke the psychological states of meaningfulness, responsibility, and knowledge of results. These in turn will result in high work motivation, high-quality performance, high job satisfaction, and low absenteeism among teachers.

This job enrichment model is depicted in Figure 8-5. Note that in addition to job dimensions, psychological states, and outcomes, an "implementing concepts" panel is provided. These are the suggestions the researchers offer to supervisors interested in building more of the job dimensions into work. As one can see, teaching has advantages over other fields of work in that many of these implementing concepts are already in evidence and the others can be easily introduced.

The principle of "combining tasks" suggests that to the extent possible, fractionalized aspects of teaching should be put together in larger, more holistic, modules. Comprehensive curriculum development strategies, interdisciplinary approaches, and team-group teaching modes all contribute to the combining of teaching and curriculum tasks. Combining tasks not only increases skill variety but one's identification with the work as well.

Establishing "client relationships" is easy in that generally teachers and students already work in close contact with each other. Nevertheless, some patterns of organization and teaching encourage a more impersonal relationship between teachers and students than would seem desirable. Missing as well is a closer relationship with parents—the legal clients of school services. Face-to-face contact with clients (students and parents) provides a natural avenue for obtaining feedback and encourages the development and use of a variety of skills.

Forming "natural work units" has some interesting implications for supervision and teaching. The intent here is to increase one's sense of ownership and continuing responsibility for identifiable aspects of the work. The self-contained elementary school

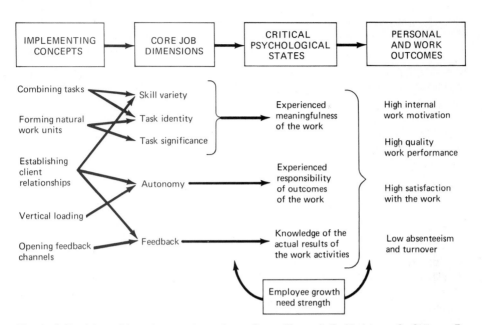

Figure 8-5 Job enrichment concepts and practices. *(From J. R. Hackman, G. Oldham, R. Johnson, and K. Purdy, "A New Strategy for Job Enrichment." © 1975 by The Regents of the University of California. Reprinted from* California Management Review, *Vol. XVII, no. 4, p. 64, by permission of The Regents.)*

classroom comes closer to this concept than does the departmentalized and quick-moving secondary teaching schedule. But even in this setting, the building of teaching teams that plan and work together and whose members share a common responsibility with students is often lacking.

"Vertical loading" suggests strategies that bring together teaching and planning. Providing teachers with more control over schedules, work methods, evaluation, and even the training of less experienced teachers might be examples of vertical loading. One might include as well giving teachers some budgetary control that allows them discretion in allocating available funds.

"Opening feedback channels" is another way of saying that the more supervisors are able to let teachers know how well they are doing, the more highly motivated they will be. Indeed, motivation and satisfaction are neglected benefits of teacher-evaluation strategies designed to provide teachers with helpful feedback. We have in mind here such strategies as clinical supervision, peer supervision, target setting, and other similar formats. A better approach still in providing teachers with feedback is to create ways in which feedback occurs naturally from teachers' day-to-day activities and from working closely with colleagues.

Job enrichment theory suggests that virtually every decision supervisors make about school and classroom organization, curriculum development and implementation, materials selection, and teaching itself has implications for building motivation and commitment of teachers.

A FINAL CAUTION

We began this chapter by suggesting that no one best way exists to motivate everyone and in every instance. This principle applies as well to the concept of job enrichment. Note, for example, in Figure 8-5 the boxed statement "employee growth need strength." Need strength refers to the extent people will seek personal accomplishment, are interested in learning and self-development, and want to be stimulated and challenged. Workers whose growth need strength is not high will not respond favorably to enriched jobs and will complain of being pushed too far. Most teachers have some potential for high-growth need strength, but for many the spark has become dim and may now even be nonexistent. Often this loss of need strength is not the individual's fault but results from previous experiences with organizations. What should one do in this case? We believe that supervisors still should provide teachers with enrichment opportunities in the hope that the need-strength spark may be rekindled. For the rare few who will not and are not able to respond, job enrichment strategies will not be appropriate. It would be better, in these cases, to rely more heavily on lower-order needs and hygiene factors. For these teachers, motivation strategies based on one of the human relations or traditional supervision approaches might be appropriate. Thankfully the number of teachers who need to be placed in this discouraging category is small.

SUMMARY

This chapter focused on the human organization of the school. The human organization was considered as the connecting link between how supervisors think, believe, and behave and school progress toward the achievement of its goals. The highly motivated teacher was listed as a high-priority concern of supervisors, and it was argued that quality education is largely dependent upon the presence in schools of competent administrators, teachers, and students who are internally committed and motivated to work.

  Maslow's theory of human motivation was then discussed. Needs were classified into a hierarchy of prepotency with lower-order needs identified as security, social, and aspects of esteem and higher-order needs as esteem, autonomy, and self-fulfillment. In addition to "professional" needs, achievement and competence were discussed because of their particular relevance to teachers.

  Needs of supervisors and their relationship to supervisory styles were considered. Of particular interest is the influence of supervisor needs for achievement, power, and affiliation on the helping relationship.

  Teachers were described as being faced with two levels of decisions in their jobs—a participation-level decision and a performance-level decision. The participation-level decision was described as the decision to continue in the traditional legal work relationship that exists between employer and employee, and the performance-level decision as a commitment to exceed this relationship. The motivation-hygiene theory, as developed by Herzberg, was then described as a means to identify motivating factors associated with the performance decisions and hygiene factors associated with the participatory decisions. Motivation factors are concerned with aspects of the work itself, such as the amount of achievement and recognition available to teachers. Hygiene factors, on the other hand, are related to the work context and include security and general working conditions.

The discussion of the motivation-hygiene theory concluded with the caveat that though by and large only the motivation factors motivate, it would be wrong to conclude that some people are not motivated by the hygiene factors. Vroom's expectancy theory of motivation was then discussed as being a theory that is able to account for individual differences. Vroom's is a contingency theory in that he views motivation as a function of a person's perception that his or her increased performance will result in certain rewards that will help him or her attain personal goals. The chapter concluded with a consideration of job enrichment research with implications for practice in supervision.

STUDY GUIDE

Recall the concepts, ideas, and meanings associated with each of the following phrases and terms included in this chapter. Can you discuss each of them with a colleague and apply them to the supervisory context of your school? If you cannot, review them in the text and record the page number for future reference.

1. Achievement motive _____
2. Autonomy _____
3. Competence motive _____
4. Expectancy theory _____
5. Helping relationship _____
6. Hierarchy of prepotency _____
7. Higher-order needs _____
8. Hygiene factors _____
9. Job context _____
10. Job enrichment models _____
11. Lower-order needs _____
12. Maslow's theory of motivation _____
13. Mediating variables _____
14. Motivation factors _____
15. Motivation-hygiene caveats _____
16. Motivation-hygiene theory _____
17. Need deficiency _____
18. Participation investment _____
19. Performance investment _____
20. Power motivation _____
21. Staff stability _____
22. Vroom's definition of motivation _____
23. Work itself _____

EXERCISES

1. Using the Maslow needs hierarchy, give specific examples of ways in which schools can help teachers to meet each of the five needs. As administrators and supervisors, consider the motivation question using Maslow's theory. What implications does the prepotency feature of the theory have?

2. Describe one or two teachers whom you know who are making only the participation decision at school. Contrast this with teachers who are making the performance decision.
3. What cautions should you keep in mind in developing motivational strategies based on Herzberg's motivation-hygiene theory?
4. Which of the three supervisory motives are most important to you? List examples of your behavior that correspond to each of the motives.
5. List 10 characteristics of the job of teaching that can be improved or "enriched." Use the job enrichment model provided in Figure 8-5 as a guide.

CHAPTER 9

SUPERVISION AND GROUP EFFECTIVENESS

How can supervisors judge the extent to which groups for whom they have responsibility are working effectively? One logical answer to this question is, by examining the outcomes or products of the group. What is the group supposed to be accomplishing and to what extent is it accomplishing these aims? If accomplishment is evidenced, then the group is judged to be *efficient.*

The problem with ending our analysis here is that efficiency is only one component of effectiveness. The other component is growth. Any effective group accomplishes not only its task today but improves its ability to accomplish even more difficult and more varied tasks tomorrow. Efficiency criteria are bounded by short-term time frames and locked into small-scale objectives. Effectiveness, on the other hand, is concerned with the long-term ability of a group to accomplish its goals and with its capacity for self-growth and development. Some studies have shown, for example, that giving prime attention to group efficiency and thus neglecting other factors results in short-term increases in group productivity. But over time, the work group not only loses its productive edge but actually becomes less productive[1]

EVALUATING GROUP EFFECTIVENESS

Judging group effectiveness, therefore, requires that we look beyond efficiency to how the group actually functions and to the extent functioning style contributes to long-term group growth. W. J. Reddin considers the eight functional characteristics listed below as critical dimensions of group effectiveness:

1. The amount of enthusiasm and commitment that exists for group goals and purposes.

2. The quantity and quality of member contributions to the group.

[1]See, for example, Nancy Morse and E. Reimer, "The Experimental Change of a Major Organizational Variable," *Journal of Abnormal and Social Psychology,* vol. 52, pp. 120–129, 1956.

↓ START ↓ HERE	A	B	C	D
PURPOSE (READ ACROSS) ———————➤	( ) There was little interest in getting the job done.	( ) There was more interest in harmony than in getting the job done.	( ) There seemed more interest in argument than in getting the job done.	( ) There was little consistent focus on the problem.
NEXT SEVEN ITEMS				
INDIVIDUAL TOTAL	( )	( )	( )	( )

Exhibit 9-1 Team analysis key. *(Copyright, © W. J. Redden, 1967, Managerial Effectiveness Ltd., Fredericton, New Brunswick.)*

3. The quality of listening by members to one another.

4. The amount of creativity exhibited in problem solving.

5. Ways in which conflict and disagreements are handled within the group.

6. The quality and nature of leadership that exists.

7. The methods and means of making decisions.

8. The ways in which the groups evaluates its performance.[2]

In this chapter we consider the relationship between effective supervision and group effectiveness. This relationship is important because, increasingly, supervision involves working with teachers within the context of groups. Such important supervisory responsibilities as facilitating peer-colleague supervision and clinical supervision, for example, are group dependent. Increasingly, staff-development programs and curriculum-development projects require extensive group work. And finally, a noticeable renewed interest in team, family, and group teaching raises the imporance of group effectiveness for supervision. But before we proceed, let us take a moment to address the present effectiveness of a group for which you have a responsibility or of which you are a member. (If you are presently taking a university course and have recently engaged in a class project requiring group effort, you might want to use this setting for your evaluation.) Recall the actual members of the group and how they typically work together. Now bring to mind a specific assignment or set of tasks on which the group has actually worked. Use this specific occasion as the basis of your analysis.

You are now ready to assess the group using the eight critical dimensions provided

---

[2]Team Style Diagnosis Test, Fredericton, New Brunswick: Managerial Effectiveness, Ltd., © by W. J. Reddin and used with his permission.

E	F	G	H	TOTALS
( ) There was much attention to following procedures and established patterns.	( ) There was much attention to the development of a team.	( ) There was a clear-cut attempt to stay directly with the problem.	( ) There was an enthusiastic team attempt to look at the problem as broadly and deeply as possible.	= 10
				= 10
				= 80

earlier. You will be using a modification and abbreviation of the Team Analysis Key (Exhibit 9-1) which is part of the Team Style Diagnostic Test developed by Reddin.[3] This modification allows you to evaluate a group on the basis of Reddin's eight critical dimensions but utilizes only one set of item descriptors concerning only the criterion goals and purposes. (The complete Reddin materials provide a separate set of items for each of the eight criteria of group effectiveness.) To the left of Exhibit 9-1 is listed the critical dimension of goals and purposes. To the right of this dimension appear eight alternative descriptions of group functioning. Select the three descriptors that best indicate how your group functioned on the occasion being evaluated. Now assign 10 points across the three descriptors selected, to indicate their relative accuracy in describing the group. Use any possible combination (8-1-1, 2-6-2, 3-3-4, 0-10-0, 1-3-6, etc.) providing that 10 points are distributed.

You are now ready to assess the group using the other seven critical dimensions: member contributions, quality of listening, creativity in problem solving, management of conflict, leadership quality, decision making, and evaluation of performance. To assist in your assessment first examine the item descriptors Reddin provides for goals and purposes and identify in each key words or phrases. Item A, for example, suggests "lack of interest" and Item B suggests "harmony." The array of key words and phrases for Items A through H are as follow:

A	B	C	D	E	F	G	H
lack of interest	harmony	arguing	lack of focus	procedural orientation	development orientation	on task	team work

Use these item descriptors to evaluate your group on each of the remaining seven dimensions scoring in the same fashion as you did for goals and purposes. Imagine the items and descriptors being arranged in the form of a grid. Total your scores in each column by summing the values given for each category A through H. Keep in mind that

[3]Copyright by W. J. Reddin and used with his permission.

this adaptation of the Team Analysis Key is designed to provide only a rough evaluation of group functioning and more importantly is *intended to raise the issue of group effectiveness and its characteristics.* A more functional evaluation would necessitate using the entire Team Style Diagnosis Test package and the complete Team Analysis Key. We will return to the Team Analysis Key and explain your scores for A through H later in this chapter. Let's now examine some of the characteristics of groups at work.

THE IMPORTANCE OF GROUP SUPERVISION

The person-to-person pattern of supervision has been the predominant supervisory method since the beginning of schooling in America. Since teachers usually worked alone and in physical environments which encouraged isolation, supervisors functioned on a person-to-person basis as they moved from class to class and from teacher to teacher. Two problems exist in person-to-person supervision: (1) this pattern resembles an inspectorial system and, as such, typically evokes negative responses from teachers and (2) this pattern locks in a one-way client-consultant relationship, with teachers always assuming the role of client and supervisors always assuming the role of consultant. Group patterns of supervision minimize power visability as they replace inspection with problem solving. Further, the supervisory relationship is considered an interchangeable one with actors assuming client or consultant roles as circumstances warrant and as functional authority changes. In recent years group supervision has gained more prominence. Much of this prominence can be traced to wider acceptance of the concepts of colleagueship and to such practices as peer and clinical supervision.

GROUP DEFINED

Let us begin our inquiry into group effectiveness by examining just what constitutes a group and why people seek membership in groups. Cattell describes a group as "an aggregate of organisms in which the existence of all is utilized for satisfaction of the needs of each."[4] Bass defines a group as a collection of persons which is mutually reinforcing.[5] Groups are characterized by the extent to which participants find group membership rewarding. In return for some form of need satisfaction, group members are expected to provide the group with loyalty, effort, and interest. An awareness of the relationship between rewards and investments is fundamental to understanding groups. Individual group participants will tend to become marginal group members or to withdraw from the group when the rewards they receive cease or become out of proportion to their contributions to the group. Further, some individuals abandon group membership when the group is no longer potent enough to provide the kind of need satisfaction that they require. This relationship is not a balanced one. Investors must perceive that the rewards they earn as a result of their active membership exceed

[4]Raymond Cattell, "New Concepts of Measuring Leadership in Terms of Group Syntality," *Human Relations*, vol. 4, pp. 161–184, 1951.
[5]Bernard Bass, *Leadership, Psychology and Organizational Behavior*, New York: Harper & Row, 1960, Chap. 3.

their investment in the group.[6] As indicated in Figure 9-1, investors need to get more out of group membership than they put into the relationship. This critical principle seems to defy the laws of logical mathematics, but thankfully, psychological rewards do not follow such laws.

Many departments and other units in schools might be better characterized as collections of individuals rather than as a group.[7] Though strictly speaking a collection of teachers may qualify as a physical group if they are in the same area of the building or as a department or grade-level group if they all teach in the same academic level or area, they do not qualify as a psychological group. In a psychological group, members share common purposes, interact with one another, perceive themselves to be a group, and obtain satisfaction of their needs as a result of group membership.

When a department or unit gets together, we can only be sure that a physical group is assembled. If only some of the teachers share common goals, interact with one another, share a group identity, and get needs met as a result of membership, then we have a psychological group within a physical group. Psychological groups are concerned with both "body and spirit"—physical groups are concerned only with body. Perhaps the deciding factor for most teachers as to whether they are merely physical members or are psychological members of a group is whether their needs are met as a result of group membership. Teachers will tend to become marginal group members or withdraw from the group when rewards cease or when rewards are not worth the contributions they are currently making to the group. In return for rewards teachers are expected to provide the group with loyalty, effort, and interest.

The development of a unit into a psychological group is a critically important first step, but in itself it is not enough. Psychological groups are not necessarily effective work groups. Consider, for example, a group of teachers who share a common purpose, *the maintenance of things the way they are;* who interact regularly, *to discredit attempts to change their school;* who identify as a group, *the regulars;* and who find

[6]Homans refers to this phenomenon as the "theory of distributive justice." See, for example, Leonard Sayles and George Strauss, *Human Behavior in Organizations,* Englewood Cliffs, N.J.: Prentice-Hall, 1966, p. 99. The theory works in either direction—the group ceases its reward-granting behavior when it no longer values or requires the commitment of individuals, and individuals cease their commitment when rewards, in their view, are not sufficient to warrant their commitment.
[7]See, for example, T. J. Sergiovanni, *Handbook for Effective Department Leadership,* Boston: Allyn and Bacon, 1977, pp. 97–138.

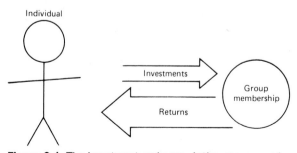

Figure 9-1 The investment exchange. Active group membership ceases (or becomes marginal) when investments in the group are equal to or exceed returns for members.

group membership comforting and satisfying, *sort of a mutual protection society.* This group indeed qualifies as a psychological group but probably does not qualify as an effective work group.

A physical group is a collection of individuals. A psychological group is a collection of individuals who share common purposes, interact with one another, perceive themselves to be a group, and who find group membership rewarding. Effective work groups are always psychological groups, but psychological groups are not always effective work groups. In an effective work group the purposes that members share are consistent with school objectives, and interaction between and among members is usually concerned with job-defined tasks, purposes, and activities. There is high identity with and commitment to school objectives, and task effectiveness is high.

PROPOSITIONS ABOUT GROUP FUNCTIONING

Let us consider several general propositions and assumptions that are basic to understanding groups.

1. Groups exist because they have to exist. Group life is a natural form of social organization for human beings. We influence groups and are influenced by groups throughout our lives. In the long run, more harm is done when schools work to frustrate and discourage group activity (among teachers *and* students) than when schools allow groups free expression.

2. Groups are neutral. In and of themselves, groups are neither good nor bad. While school groups can be powerful forces that work to achieve school goals, they can be equally powerful in working against school goals. For example, a teaching faculty with high morale may obtain satisfaction by working to frustrate school goals—and perhaps by discrediting the principal in the bargain—or by working to enhance school goals. Indeed, many student groups receive satisfaction in their dedication to frustrate the school's operation, while others are equally satisfied working for or with the school.

3. Groups have unique "personalities" which are conceptually similar to individual personalities. This group personality stems from and is composed of characteristics that individuals bring to the group. Thus, two school faculties or two departments with similar goals differ markedly because their membership differs.

4. As part of the group's personality, a group culture emerges that includes norms of behavior and a value system or belief pattern that are unique to the group. This belief pattern provides the cement that holds the group together and that regulates group behavior. We refer to the belief pattern as the group's *dynamic center.* A zone of freedom exists that permits individuals to stray somewhat from the dynamic center but still maintain group membership (see Figure 9-2). When group members move beyond the zone of freedom, they cross the group's boundary and forfeit membership. The closer a group member is to this dynamic center, the more influential that person will be. In Figure 9-3 we show various positions of group membership and levels of

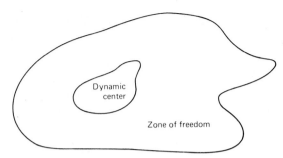

Figure 9-2 The group and its boundaries. *(From Harold Wilson et al., "The Group and Its Leaders," unpublished manuscript, Columbus: Ohio State University, Center for Educational Administration, Department of Education, 1963.)*

agreement in relation to the group's dynamic center. One who holds marginal membership in a group can improve his or her position by adopting more of the group's culture, thus moving closer to the dynamic center, or by moving the dynamic center of the group closer to himself or herself. This second strategy is difficult in that those who are removed from the dynamic center are often perceived by other group members as having little influence.

5. Individuals behave differently when they assume roles as group members from the way they behave when they operate as free agents. Groups influence people. As a result of this influence, people behave differently—they react to group pressure. This phenomenon is suggested by Heron when he contrasts the actions and demands of workers as groups with their desires as individuals:

> The opinion polls almost always show that the most prominent desires of the individual employee relate to the most important thing in the world—*himself*, his personality, his recognition, his security, and his progress. He wants recognition, for his skills, his suggestions, his attention and energy, his performance and production.
>
> But when he gets together with his fellow workers—who want exactly the same things—they agree almost unanimously to demand standard wage rates for all workers on the same job, the prohibition of piecework and incentives, and uniform increases in all wage rates.

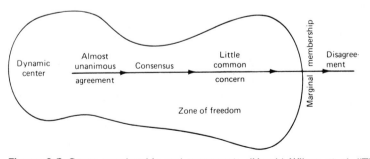

Figure 9-3 Group membership and movement. *(Harold Wilson et al., "The Group and Its Leaders," unpublished manuscript, Columbus: Ohio State University, Center for Educational Administration, Department of Education, 1963.)*

He wants fair treatment, as an individual, in job assignments and promotions. He resents favoritism or any process of selection which seems to overlook his abilities and gives the foreman job to someone less competent. He wants to be rewarded for his merit.

But in united action with his fellow workers he will demand that in promotions, layoffs, or rehirings, the principles of seniority shall strictly apply. He will stand on this demand with almost emotional devotion.[8]

As a result of this phenomenon, one may conclude that group pressures result in group conformity. Conformity in turn stifles creativity and individual expression. Therefore, as this agrument develops, groups have negative and frustrating effects on individuality. Indeed, groups do have enormous potential for applying normative pressure to individuals. Further, these pressures often require some conformity from group members. Conformity, however, if viewed moderately, is the strength in groups that supervisors should seek. Conformity is not inherently bad. Indeed, a group norm may be one of creative expression by its members. Thus members conform by expressing their individuality. This position is effectively argued by Cartwright and Lippitt as follows:

It is important, first, to make a distinction between conformity and uniformity. A group might have a value that everyone should be as different from everyone else as possible. Conformity to this value, then, would result not in unformity of behavior but in nonuniformity. Such a situation often arises in therapy groups or training groups where it is possible to establish norms which place a high value upon "being different" and upon tolerating deviant behavior. Conformity to this value is presumably greater the more cohesive the group and the more it is seen as relevant to the group's objectives.[9]

6. Goals held for the group but not by the group tend to be rejected by the group. The zone of freedom for a group is similar to the concept of self for individuals. A behavioral change for individuals is best accompanied by broadening one's concept of self to include the change. Groups change by broadening zones of freedom to include new alternatives. Even the most forceful leadership is frustrated if it overlooks this important concept.

GROUP-EFFECTIVENESS INDICATORS

In this section characteristics that describe the ideal group and components of group effectiveness are presented. This ideal model should serve as a goal for supervisors to pursue as they work with school groups, and the effectiveness model suggests how this ideal might be accomplished.

[8]Alexander Heron, *Why Men Work,* Stanford, Calif.: Stanford University Press, 1948, p. 20.
[9]Dorwin Cartwright and Ronald Lippitt, "Group Dynamics and the Individual," *International Journal of Psychotherapy,* vol. 7, no. 1, p. 95, 1957.

This group maximizes its effectiveness, according to Likert, when it is character-ized as follows:[10]

1. The members are skilled in all the various leadership and membership roles and functions required for interaction between leaders and members and between members and other members.
2. The group has been in existence sufficiently long to have developed a well-established, relaxed working relationship among all its members.
3. The members of the group are attracted to it and are loyal to its members, including the leader.
4. The members and leaders have a high degree of confidence and trust in each other.
5. The values and goals of the group are a satisfactory integration and expression of the relevant values and needs of its members. They have helped shape these values and goals and are satisfied with them.
6. Insofar as members of the group are performing linking functions, they endeavor to have the values and goals of the groups which they link in harmony with one another.
7. The more important a value seems to the group, the greater the likelihood that the individual member will accept it.
8. The members of the group are highly motivated to abide by the major values and to achieve the important goals of the group.
9. All the interaction, problem-solving, decision-making activities of the group occur in a supportive atmosphere.
10. The group is eager to help each member develop to his or her full potential. It sees, for example, that relevant technical knowledge and training in interpersonal and group skills are made available to each member.
11. Each member accepts willingly and without resentment the goals and expectations that he or she and the group establish for themselves.
12. When necessary or advisable, members of the group will give other members the help they need to accomplish successfully the goals set for them. Reciprocal help is a characteristic of highly effective groups.
13. The supportive atmosphere of the highly effective group stimulates creativity. The group does not demand narrow conformity as do the work groups under authoritarian leaders.
14. There is strong motivation on the part of each member to communicate fully and frankly to the group all the information which is relevant and of value to the group's activity.
15. There is high motivation in the group to use the communication process so that it best serves the interests and goals of the group.
16. Just as there is high motivation to communicate, there is correspondingly strong motivation to receive communications.
17. In the highly effective group there are strong motivations to try to influence other members as well as to be receptive to influence from them.

It seems useful to differentiate between two major sources of rewards for group members. One reward source is the mutual satisfaction, or reinforcement, that individuals get from interacting with other individuals. The more satisfaction for group members as a result of this interaction, the higher the interaction effectiveness of the group. Interaction effectiveness is an important characteristic of a psychological group. Another source of rewards for group members comes from actual implementation of the group's purposes. The more satisfaction for group members as a result of doing the

[10]Abridged from Rensis Likert, *New Patterns of Management*, New York: McGraw-Hill, 1961, p. 166. Likert's list is much more illustrative and comprehensive.

task, the higher the task effectiveness of the group. Task effectiveness and interaction effectiveness compose group effectiveness. The more satisfaction for group members as a result of interaction effectiveness and task effectiveness, the higher the group effectiveness.[11]

The Components of Group Effectiveness

Interaction effectiveness refers to the quality of group sentiment that exists for a given group. It includes such evasive concepts as morale, cohesiveness, communication ease, and so on. Bass suggests that this dimension of group effectiveness can be assessed by (1) the amount of harmony present and the absence of conflict, (2) the amount of satisfaction for members as a result of interaction, and (3) the perceived congruence between actual and expected relations among group members.[12]

Interaction effectiveness is facilitated by a number of variables, each having the strength to increase the potential for group members to interact. For example, collections of individuals about the same age, with similar educational backgrounds, and with similar interests will tend to have high interaction potential. The more homogeneous the group, the higher the interaction potential of the group. Exposure to contact, size, and pressures to participate are other variables affecting interaction potential.[13] Perhaps the most indicative factor of interaction potential is mutual predictability among group members. That is, a given group member is able to predict what other group members will do. The higher the mutual predictability among group members, the higher the interaction level of the group.

Consider, for example, a group of special teachers in an elementary school. One would suppose that this group, being somewhat homogeneous, manageable in size, having frequent opportunities for exposure to each other, and possessing common sentiments in terms of educational philosophy and school organization, would enjoy high interaction effectiveness. It is more difficult, however, to predict whether this group—or any other school group, for that matter—will use its energies, its power, its pressures, and its unique reward system on behalf of the school's purposes. Perhaps this group of special teachers will harness its energies to provide the very best services that it can to the school. Or perhaps this same group may decide that it is more rewarding to be a thorn in the principal's side. Another possibility is that this group may simply enjoy its unique informal reward system at the expense of doing more than a minimum job, if it does a job at all.[14]

The direction and orientation of a school group hinge on another aspect of group effectiveness, the accomplishment of task. *Task effectiveness* refers to activity that

---

[11] The notion of group effectiveness containing a task dimension and an interaction dimension is borrowed from Bernard Bass. Bass feels that *either* dimension or both dimensions may result in group effectiveness. Our view is that *both* dimensions are necessary for group effectiveness. Bernard Bass, *Leadership Psychology and Organizational Behavior*, New York: Harper & Row, 1960, Chap. 3. This discussion follows that which appears in Thomas Sergiovanni, "Group Effectiveness: Human Relations Is Not Enough," *Illinois Elementary Principal*, pp. 15–17, September 1967.

[12] Bass, op. cit., p. 46.

[13] See James G. March and Herbert A. Simon, *Organizations*, New York: Wiley, 1958, pp. 68–71, for an interesting and comprehensive discussion of factors that affect frequency of interaction.

[14] Dubin discusses subversive, cooperative, and neutral groups in his analysis of informal organization. Robert Dubin, *Human Relations in Administration*, 2d ed., Englewood Cliffs, N.J.: Prentice-Hall, 1961, pp. 84–87.

promotes, defines, clarifies, pursues, and accomplishes relevant school goals. It is described in terms of the rewards that group members get from doing or completing a task. Challenging work; responsibility; intrinsic satisfaction; autonomy; feelings of success, achievement, and competence; recognition for task efforts; bolstering of self- and group esteem; and individual and group status are words and phrases that best describe the flavor of the reward system that characterizes task effectiveness.

A group whose primary reward system rests with task effectiveness will have at its disposal an arsenal of weapons to encourage, to motivate, and perhaps even to pressure group members to work on behalf of the school and its purposes. On the other hand, a group deprived of the reward system resulting from task effectiveness may divert its efforts away from work-centered activities and tend to concentrate on seeking satisfaction solely from the interaction-effectiveness domain. The group, not the job, becomes the focus of an individual's attention. Group norms that conflict with the purposes of the school may be established. Conformity to the group and its norms becomes necessary if one wishes to benefit from the group's reward system. This conformity may require that teachers not exert more than a minimum effort in their jobs.[15] Such groups take a passive, rather than negative, stand in relation to school purposes and tasks. They expend energies, talents, and efforts primarily to maintain the group as a source of personal enjoyment for members. We conclude that groups high in interaction effectiveness but low in task effectiveness not only tend to be lacking in function, but may indeed be dysfunctional.

Interaction effectiveness and task effectiveness are not at opposite ends of a continuum. The effective group is highly successful in its task endeavors and uses its interaction potential on behalf of the task. Such a group would tend to reap rewards (acceptance, affiliation, belonging, and security, for example) while at the same time deriving satisfaction from getting a job done. This combination would best describe group effectiveness.

THE SUPERVISOR AS KEY

Supervisors are frequently in a position to make group effectiveness a reality. Their position is unique in that they affect *both* task and interaction effectiveness. They can foster interaction effectiveness by recognizing informal groups, by helping to initiate and promote interaction patterns within and between groups, and by planning formal groups in terms of their interaction potential. Much can be done by deliberately linking subgroups so that together they constitute an identifiable whole and develop a sense of cohesiveness as a faculty.[16]

Interaction effectiveness tends not to be potent enough, however, to provide the

---

[15]The rate-buster phenomenon and the sanctions that follow have been well documented in industry. We suspect that the analogy works for education, too. For example, elementary school teachers often mentioned that too much effort, too many displays, noticeable project work, elaborate bulletin boards, taking work home, and other signs of rate busting frequently result in informal and formal sanctions from the group.
[16]Rensis Likert, op. cit., proposes a plan of organization that is characterized by overlapping work groups, linked together by individuals who serve the original group but are also represented in groups at the next level. Likert's notion represents a proposal for organizing schools and other agencies on the basis of group structure.

kinds of rewards that nourish professional individuals. Professionals tend to need and actively seek the kinds of satisfaction that only task effectiveness can bring. Admittedly there are exceptions to this tendency. Some teachers tend not to be professionally oriented and may seek only relatively shallow levels of need fulfillment. These types would be quite content with the limited rewards available from interaction effectiveness.[17] Other teachers and teacher groups may focus on interaction effectiveness by default—that is, because this is the only source of rewards left open to them.

The implementation of group task effectiveness requires that supervisors encourage groups, formal and informal, to identify with and accept the school, its tasks, and its purposes. Task identification appears to be related to the extent to which individual teachers and groups of teachers are given responsibility and autonomy for participating in decision making and for participating in the development and implementing of teaching programs. Further, task identification appears to be related to the extent to which individuals perceive that they have opportunities to develop their professional skills. These variables are likely to increase opportunities for individual, group, and professional success.[18] Promoting task identification requires that supervisors, principals, and others be committed to faculty and student involvement and collaborative management, and that they willingly appreciate the authority that teachers and other school members bring to the school.

Group Effectiveness Summarized

The relationship between interaction effectiveness and task effectiveness in school groups is initially one of dependence. The consistent accomplishment of group tasks requires the establishment of interaction effectiveness. Once initial group effectiveness is achieved, the relationship changes to one of interdependence. That is, task effectiveness over time depends upon sustained interaction effectiveness, and sustained interaction effectiveness depends upon task effectiveness. The components of group effectiveness are summarized in Figure 9-4.

Interaction effectiveness, according to the model, is largely dependent upon communication frequency. The more homogeneous the group, the more opportunities for group-member contact; and the greater the mutual predictability among group members, the greater the frequency of communication. It should be noted that when creativity is valued as a group goal, more heterogeneity will need to be introduced, even at some loss to interaction frequency.[19] The rewards available to teachers through interaction effectiveness are feelings of affiliation, acceptance, and security. These rewards tend to focus on personal and need satisfaction but tend not to directly effect organizational need satisfaction.

The key component of task effectiveness is task identification. As group members identify with the task goals of the group, performance increases. March and Simon

---

[17]See our discussion of the motivation-hygiene theory that appears in Chap. 8 and our caveat regarding the universal application of human resources supervision in Chap. 1.

[18]March and Simon, op. cit., p. 77

[19]Heterogeneous groups are preferred when tasks are extremely complex, when time is plentiful, when the consequences of error in judgment are grave, and when creativity is desired. Homogeneous groups are preferred when time is scarce, when production is important, when tasks demand cooperation, and when problems are routine. See Bernard Bass, *Organizational Psychology*, Boston: Allyn and Bacon, 1965, pp. 204–213.

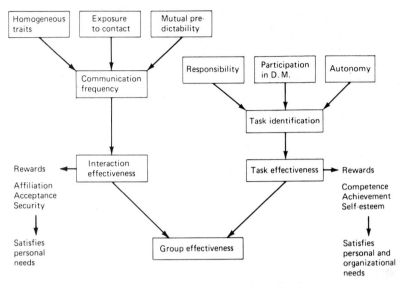

Figure 9-4 Basic components of the concept of group effectiveness.

suggest that the greater the amount of perceived autonomy and responsibility of group members, and the more opportunities that exist for participation of group members, the greater the task identification of the group. Rewards available to teachers through task effectiveness are feelings of competence and achievement and the bolstering of group and individual self-esteem. This reward system is unique in that the basis for personal need satisfaction is the satisfying of organizational needs. Task effectiveness and interaction effectiveness constitute group effectiveness.

GROUPS IN ACTION

This section examines the group in action by describing phases that groups must transcend if they are to successfully accomplish their work. This is followed by an analysis of leadership functions as they apply to groups. A taxonomy and description of roles that may be assumed by group members is then presented.

Group Phases

It is useful to visualize the group as having certain fundamental interpersonal needs much like those associated with the individual personality. Groups and individuals must provide for these needs before they can function properly. Schutz identifies group and individual needs as follows: "There are three fundamental interpersonal needs—*inclusion, control,* and *affection*—and in order for an individual to function optimally he must establish and maintain a satisfactory relation in all three areas."[20] Individuals need to include others and to be included, to control others and to be controlled, to love

---

[20]William Schutz, "The Ego, FIRO Theory and the Leader as Completer," in Luigi Petrullo and Bernard Bass, (eds.), *Leadership and Interpersonal Behavior,* New York: Holt, 1961, p. 57.

others and to be loved, and the exact mix of needing or wanting to express each of these variables differs for each person. Indeed, inclusion, control, and affection are phases through which groups must successfully pass if they are to be characterized by sustained effectiveness in accomplishing their goals. The phases are arranged into a relatively loose hierarchy, with the attention of the group being given first to inclusion, then to control, and finally to affection. Problems associated with each of these are never solved by the group but are at least reasonably settled. This settling is not unlike a simmering pot, which is characterized by relative stability but is subject to a periodic eruption of bubbles. The phases, indeed, overlap (Figure 9-5), with the group generally moving forward but occasionally vacillating from one phase to another.

Each of the phases is examined separately below:

Inclusion A group needs to define its boundaries and to work to include people within them. The inclusion phase requires that the group knows who is in the group and who is not. Further, in view of the group's dynamic center, the group must communicate and delineate to members an expression of required behavior and forbidden behavior. Part of this phase includes identifying and articulating group goals and subsequently testing members to see if they are in agreement with these goals. The group works to win commitment from its members or excludes those who express disinterest in its goals. This exclusion may be physical, if possible, or mental, if necessary.

Control Once the inclusion phase of group activity has been relatively settled, the group turns its attention to matters of control. Members need to decide problems of leadership, solve status arrangements, assign and agree upon roles to be played, distribute and consolidate power, provide for a workable and acceptable chain of command, and otherwise arrange themselves. While the control phase may not solve manifest control problems, hidden agenda problems, and other interpersonal problems, it works to solve them for the moment—to contain them. Whether such problems stay solved or not depends upon a group climate that is supportive, open, cooperative, and honest.

Affection The inclusion and control phases of group activity are seldom characterized by tranquility. Defining the dynamic center of a group and delineating its borders require a great deal of interpersonal expenditure. The control phase seems always characterized by tension. People are hurt as a result of the inclusion and control phases, and the group must heal its wounds if it is to function properly. The affection phase, then, is characterized by working to build a cohesiveness based on acceptance, forgiveness, and love.

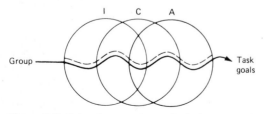

Figure 9-5 Natural group phases: Inclusion, control, and affection.

The Hidden Agenda

Much of the group's activity, as it works through the inclusion, control, and affection phases, can be scheduled on the group's agenda and carried out through formal or overt procedures. A substantial amount of this activity, however, takes the form of an undercurrent that permeates the group's life. The official reasons for people coming together to form a group—the publicly stated and agreed-upon tasks to be accomplished—are referred to as the group's *public agenda*.[21] Beneath the public agenda there are a number of hidden agendas, often ignored but nevertheless most powerful, that are not openly recognized. Such private agendas are held by group members, group leaders, and, indeed, the group itself. Bradford describes the hidden agenda as follows: "Unlabled, private and covered, but deeply felt and very much the concern of the group, is another level. Here are all of the conflicting motives, desires, aspirations and emotional reactions held by the group members, subgroups, or the group as a whole that cannot be fitted legitimately into the accepted group task. Here are all of the problems which, for a variety of reasons, cannot be laid on top of the table."[22]

Hidden agendas are an issue in each of the phases of group activity, but their influence is most strongly felt in the control phase. Hidden agendas need to be dealt with in one way or another. At one extreme they can be smothered or steam-rollered by strong leadership, and at the other extreme they can be brought to the surface and "understood," as can happen in human-encounter or sensitivity groups.

Bradford offers a number of suggestions for supervisors in confronting the problem of handling hidden agendas. Among them are (1) to be aware of, to look for, and to recognize hidden agendas—those of the supervisor and those of other group participants; (2) recognize that the group works continuously and simultaneously at both levels—hidden and public; (3) to work to bring hidden agendas to the surface; but (4) to be sensitive to the group's readiness to force some hidden agenda items, for many have potential for hurting the group more if they are made public; (5) to accept hidden agendas without evoking feelings of guilt; (6) to help the group work out methods of solving or settling hidden agendas in the same way that they develop methods of handling their surface agenda; and (7) to help the group evaluate its progress in handling hidden agendas.[23]

FUNCTIONAL ROLES OF GROUP MEMBERS

The question of leadership is one that cannot be avoided for long in an examination of groups. Traditionally, the group leader is considered the key determiner of a group's effectiveness. Good leaders, according to this view, are those who point direction for group activity, clarify goals, make relevancy judgments as they guide group discussion, keep people on the track, are the agenda watchdogs, push for full participation, and

---

[21]This discussion follows that which appears in Leland P. Bradford, "The Case of the Hidden Agenda," *Adult Leadership*, pp. 3–7, September 1952.
[22]Ibid., p. 3.
[23]Ibid., p. 7.

force decisions. Good leaders get things done! Their tools are their official role as chairpersons, an acceptable agenda, group know-how, and guided discussion.

Human resources supervision suggests that designated group leaders (teachers, chairpersons, supervisors, consultants, principals, and so on) come to conceive of their role primarily as one of providing service rather than direction to the group. For example, while traditional supervisory patterns require that the leader get things done (presumably by using the group and its resources), human resources supervisors work to help the group accomplish its tasks. Within this context, leaders do not merely solve the group's problems but focus on the group solving its problems; they do not merely move the group forward but help the group as it moves forward. But somebody must get the group going, must initiate discussion, define problems and goals, evaluate, summarize, monitor, provide information, and the like. Indeed, the group will not accomplish its goals without these and other leadership roles being fulfilled. Human resources supervisors are concerned with these roles but hold no monopoly on them. *Leadership functions are considered to be the responsibility of the entire group— not just of the designated leader.* The discussion that follows focuses on leadership and other group roles that are needed in effective groups rather than on who should assume what role. Roles are best assumed by those most capable of assuming them.

Group roles are often classified into three broad categories depending upon whether they support group task effectiveness, support group interaction effectiveness, or exist solely for the satisfaction of the role incumbent. The first category, group task roles, includes roles that facilitate and coordinate the selection and definition·of a common group problem and help in solving this problem. The second category, group-binding or group-maintenance roles, includes roles that are oriented to the functioning of the group as a group. The third category, individual roles, includes roles not primarily directed toward the group or the task but toward the individual participant.

Kenneth Benne and Paul Sheats provide an extensive taxonomy of the three functional roles that is useful in categorizing "Who does what?" in a group and in evaluating group processes. The roles they discuss are listed below:

Group Task Roles	Group Maintenance Roles	"Individual Roles"
Initiator-contributor	Encourager	Aggressor
Information seeker	Harmonizer	Blocker
Opinion seeker	Compromiser	Recognition seeker
Information giver	Gatekeeper	Self-confessor
Opinion giver	Standard setter	Playboy
Elaborator	Group observer	Nominator
Coordinator	Follower	Help seeker
Orientator		Special interest
Evaluator-critic		Pleader
Energizer		
Procedural technician		
Recorder		

Groups need to work for balance among the three types of roles. Surely task roles depend upon maintenance roles, and maintenance roles are legitimized and become purposeful as a result of task roles. Our "hidden agenda" discussion explains why individual roles are played in groups. A mature group permits its members to occasionally assume individual roles. Sustained behavior of this type by one or another group member suggests malfunctions in the group's climate. The more information members have about the group and their own performance in groups, the more likely they are to improve their performance.

DO GROUPS MAKE BETTER DECISIONS?

Throughout this chapter we have suggested that effectiveness is only one concern in group supervision. This still remains an important point as we conclude the chapter. Supervisors work in a group context because they are expected to by teachers. They realize as well that the group context provides a host of benefits in the areas of morale, building commitment and promoting self-growth and development. But the question remains—Do groups make better decisions? Are groups more efficient? Norman R. F. Maier's studies suggest that the decision-making assets of a group are:[24]

1. The total amount of knowledge and information available is greater. That is, the group as a whole has more information than does any of its members.
2. The total number of approaches to a problem is greater. Further, group interaction can actually stimulate creative thinking.
3. Decisions are likely to be more readily accepted as participation of members in group problem solving increases.
4. Members are likely to understand better the basis for a decision.

He notes, however, that these assets must be balanced against the following liabilities:

1. Social pressures, which members feel as they strive to be good members, can encourage them to hold back on disagreements.
2. A bias toward consensus exists as groups function. Typically, both positive and negative comments accompany proposed solutions or alternatives. But once a solution receives about 15 more positive than negative comments, it is likely to be accepted regardless of its quality.
3. It is easier for a dominant individual to emerge who can unduly influence group decisions.
4. Where power is distributed relatively equally among some subgroups or among individual group members, conflict increases and often the goal of winning one's point of view takes precedence over obtaining a best solution to a problem.

Given these assets and liabilities, it is difficult to reach a conclusive position with regard to the issue of efficiency and group decision making. By and large experts seem to suggest that group decisions are indeed better, although there are exceptions. Often, the most informed individual in a group can make a better decision if left alone. Indeed, group pressure can bring this person down to the group level. But it seems clear that for the most part decision-making efficiency improves within the group context.

[24]Normal R. F. Maier, "Assets and Liabilities in Group Problem Solving: The Need for an Integrative Function," *Psychological Bulletin,* vol. 74, no. 4, pp. 239–249, 1967.

COOPERATION AND COMPETITION AMONG GROUPS

As supervision takes on more of a group character, the issues of cooperation and competition become very important. What happens, for example, when one group of teachers involved in clinical supervision finds itself in competition with another group involved in another approach to supervision? Or what happens when one teaching team committed to approach A finds itself in competition with another team committed to approach B? Often such rivalry is nothing more than good-natured fun that has positive effects for everyone. But if genuine competition emerges (if one group will be declared the winner and the other the loser), serious problems quickly follow.

The effects of intergroup competition within and between groups is a thoroughly researched area. In summarizing a number of studies Schein describes the effects as follows:[25]

A. What happens *within* each competing group?

1. Each group becomes more closely knit and elicits greater loyalty from its members; members close ranks and bury some of their internal differences.
2. Group climates change from informal, casual, playful, to work and task oriented; concern for members' psychological welfare declines while concern for task accomplishment increases.
3. Leadership patterns tend to change from more democratic to more autocratic; the group becomes more willing to tolerate autocratic leadership.
4. Each group becomes more highly structured and organized.
5. Each group demands more loyalty and conformity from its members in order for it to be able to present a "solid front."

B. What happens *between* the competing groups?

1. Each group begins to see the other groups as the enemy.
2. Each group begins to experience distortions of perception. It tends to perceive only the best parts of itself, denying its weaknesses, and tends to perceive only the worst parts of other groups, denying their strengths; each group is likely to develop a negative stereotype of the other.
3. Hostility towards the other group increases while interaction and communication with the other group decreases; thus it becomes easier to maintain negative stereotypes and more difficult to correct perceptual distortions.
4. If the groups are forced into interaction, each group is likely to listen more closely to its own representative and not to listen to the representatives of the other group, except to find fault with the presentation; in other words, group members tend to listen only to that which supports their own position and stereotypes.

Intergroup competition has some beneficial effects *within* groups. The sense of battle builds cohesiveness and provides an incentive to focus on tasks. But as one group becomes more effective as a result of competition, the faculty as a whole becomes less effective and the result is a less effective school overall. In battle, for every winner there is a loser. The consequences of winning and losing as a result of competition are described by Schein as follows:

C. What happens to the *winner*?

1. The winner retains cohesion and may become even more cohesive.

[25]Edgar H. Schein, *Organizational Psychology.* © 1965, pp. 81 and 82. Reprinted by permission of Prentice-Hall, Englewood Cliffs, N.J.

2. The winner tends to release tension, lose its fighting spirit, become complacent, casual and playful.

3. The winner tends toward high inter-group cooperation and concern for members' needs, and low concern for work and task accomplishment.

4. The winner tends to be complacent and feel that winning has confirmed the positive stereotype of itself and the negative stereotype of the enemy.

D. What happens to the *loser*?

1. If the situation permits, there is a strong tendency for the loser to deny or distort the reality of losing; instead the loser will find psychological escapes such as "the supervisor was biased," "the principal really didn't understand our solution," "the rules of the game were not clearly explained to us."

2. If loss is accepted, the losing group tends to splinter, unresolved conflicts come to the surface, fights break out, all an effort to find the cause for the loss.

3. The losing group is more tense, ready to work harder, and desperate to find someone or something to blame: the leader, the person who decided against them, the rules of the game.

4. The loser tends toward low inter-group cooperation, low concern for members' needs and high concern for recouping by working harder.

5. The loser tends to learn a lot about itself as a group because positive stereotypes of itself and negative stereotypes of the other group are upset by the loss, forcing a re-evaluation of perceptions; as a consequence, the loser is likely to reorganize and become more cohesive and effective, once the loss has been accepted more realistically.

The positive effects of intergroup competition may outweigh the negative on some occasions and in the short run. But as a long-term strategy intergroup cooperation makes more sense. Intergroup cooperation requires that supervisors see themselves as a cadre of individuals committed to team leadership rather than as isolated local supervisors concerned exclusively with the self-interests of their particular group. The supervisor's commitment, in other words, is to educational leadership that is targeted at the school as a whole. In this effort, greater emphasis needs to be given to total school effectiveness and how a group contributes to it. Groups should be rewarded on the basis of their contributions to the total school effort rather than only on their own effectiveness. Opportunities for interaction and communication should be provided to enable groups to discuss intergroup problems with the aim that the groups will be better coordinated. Opportunities for rotation of members among groups should be provided to stimulate mutual understanding and empathy.

SIZING UP YOUR GROUP

Earlier in this chapter we suggested that a group could be evaluated by examining eight critical items:

1. The amount of enthusiasm and commitment that exists for group goals and purposes.

2. The quantity and quality of member contribution to the group.

3. The quality of listening by members to one another.

4. The amount of creativity exhibited in problem solving.

5. Ways in which conflicts and disagreements are handled within the group.

6. The quality and nature of leadership that exists.

7. The methods and means of making decisions.

8. The ways in which the group evaluates its performance.

Using an adaptation and abbreviation of Reddin's Team Analysis Key, you were asked to evaluate a group with which you were familiar on each of the eight dimensions. You totaled each of columns A through H to obtain eight scores. Each of the scores represents a particular mode of group functioning. Score A, for example, describes the group in *flight.* The group functional modes are described below and identified by the appropriate letter:

A. The group in *flight* is a group that displays little energy in getting the job done. Conflict is kept at a minimum because of the energy it requires. Creativity and contributions are low, and leadership appears to be absent. Usually the decision is, in effect, not a decision but a rewording of the problem as it originally existed. There is rarely any effort made to evaluate or improve group performance. When a group operates in this way, the supervisor usually functions as a *deserter.*

B. The *dependent* group is a group whose byword is harmony. More attention is paid to avoiding conflict than to discussing problems. Most of the contributions are ones with which everyone can be expected to agree, and creative ideas are blocked when they are seen as possible criticisms of members or the group as a whole. Disagreements, even when obviously functional, are avoided. Leadership sometimes evolves, but it is usually friendly and weak. Evaluation of the group's efforts is usually in the form of compliments. When a group operates in this way, the supervisor usually functions as a *missionary.*

C. The *fight* is a group characterized by conflict and argument. The conflict is not functional, as contribution and creativity are usually blocked by arguments of group members. Leadership is dominated by one or two individuals, often those with the loudest voices. Disagreements between individuals sometimes become personal rather than based on the issues. Evaluation of the group's efforts usually amounts to attacks on group members. When a group operates in this way, the supervisor usually functions as an *autocrat.*

D. The *mixed* group is a group that attempts to compromise between getting the task done and sparing people's feelings. The result is less effective. The group lacks focus on problems. Its members' comments are often irrelevant, and attempts at leadership usually fail. Disagreement exists but serves no useful purpose. Leadership is often absent when it is needed and often present when it is not needed. Evaluation is weak. When a group operates in this way, the supervisor usually functions as a *compromiser.*

E. The *procedural* group is a group that follows procedures and established patterns. Creativity and contributions, although forthcoming within defined procedures, are sound. Members listen politely, and disagreement is handled in a formal manner. Leadership is routine; evaluation usually amounts to a comparison of the group's effort to the efforts of other groups. Evaluation is, however, functional. When a group operates in this way, the supervisor usually functions as a *bureaucrat.*

F. The *creative* group is a group that focuses primarily on developing its members and its ideals. Much attention is paid to the minority opinion and to attempts to incorporate the ideas of all members in the decision. Disagreement, although rare, is looked into closely, so that benefit is derived from it. Evaluation of the group's effort is usually aimed at improving group creativity. When a group operates in this way, the supervisor usually functions as a *developer.*

G. The *productive* group is a task-oriented group whose primary concern is the immediate task. Contributions come from those who push for their own ideas. Disagreement occurs frequently but is usually useful. Discussions about productivity may be dominated by a few members, but their leadership is beneficial. Evaluation is usually focused on making the group more efficient. When a group operates in this way, the supervisor usually functions as a *benevolent autocrat.*

H. The *problem-solving* group is a group that attempts to examine problems as broadly and deeply as possible and thus reach an optimal solution to which all are committed. Due consideration is given to both the task at hand and the feelings of group members. Ideas are of high quality and are highly relevant to the task. When a group operates in this way, the supervisor usually functions as an *executive.*

Some groups may operate closely to one of Reddin's descriptions most of the time, but probably most groups shift operating styles occasionally on certain issues. The problem-solving, productive, creative, and procedural groups are indeed very different in operating styles, but nevertheless each is effective in its own way. On the other hand, the mixed, fight, dependent, and flight groups, although different in operating styles, are each relatively ineffective. The contingency variables associated with choice of leadership styles presented in Chapter 6 can help supervisors to select a team mode and group operating style most consistent with the problems, tasks, and circumstances facing the group at a given time.

SUMMARY

Groups are a natural, necessary, and important part of the organizational life of schools. In this chapter group supervision was offered as an alternative to person-to-person supervision as a means to more effectively achieve school purposes. Three types of groups were identified: physical groups, psychological groups, and effective work groups. Physical groups were defined as collections of individuals. Psychological groups were defined as collections of individuals who share common goals, interact with one another, view themselves as a group, and obtain satisfaction from group membership. Effective work groups were defined as psychological groups whose common purposes are consistent with those of the school.

Several propositions about group functioning were discussed, including such concepts as group necessity, neutrality, personality, culture, and normative structure.

The characteristics of an effective work group, as proposed by Likert, were then presented as ideal standards for group supervision. Two key components of group effectiveness, interaction effectiveness and task effectiveness, were identified. Factors contributing to the establishment of these components and the supervisor's role in maintaining and developing them were proposed.

The discussion then shifted to the group in action. Inclusion, control, and affection were offered as the natural cycle through which groups must travel before being able to work fully on tasks. The "hidden agenda" was then discussed as an example. It was suggested that leadership functions and roles as opposed to leadership prerogatives associated with one's position are emphasized in effective groups. A list of critical group task, maintenance, and self roles was then discussed. A discussion of cooperation and competition among groups followed. Critical to this discussion was an analysis of the costs and benefits of group competition. The chapter concluded with guidelines for sizing up a group and for determining its effectiveness. These guidelines were related to Reddin's 3-D Theory of Leadership presented in Chapters 5 and 6.

STUDY GUIDE

Recall the concepts, ideas, and meanings associated with each of the following phrases and terms included in this chapter. Can you discuss each of them with a colleague and apply them to the supervisory context of your school? If you cannot, review them in the text and record the page number for future reference.

1. Affection phase _____
2. Competition _____
3. Control phase _____
4. Cooperation _____
5. Creative group _____
6. Effective work group _____
7. Group dynamic center _____
8. Group maintenance roles _____
9. Group task roles _____
10. Group supervision _____
11. Hidden agenda _____
12. Inclusion phase _____
13. Individual roles _____
14. Interaction effectiveness _____
15. Investments returns _____
16. Leadership function _____
17. Likert characteristics _____
18. Marginal membership _____
19. Person-to-person supervision _____
20. Physical group _____
21. Problem-solving group _____
22. Psychological group _____
23. Sizing up the group _____
24. Task effectiveness _____
25. Zone of freedom _____

EXERCISES

1. How would you describe the group life in your department, unit, or school? How would your group measure up to the characteristics of group effectiveness suggested by Likert?

2. In sizing up your group, in what ways do you find it to share characteristics and features of the eight group types suggested by Reddin? Which of the four effective group types best fits your own leadership inclinations?

3. What are the consequences for a supervisor who fails to recognize the natural group tendencies that exist in school

4. What are the consequences for a supervisor who recognizes natural group tendencies in schools but who views them as undesirable and therefore works to subvert or discourage group activity?

5. Write a one-page description of a conflict incident among groups. Using Schein's discussion of the benefits and costs of conflict, list those that were in evidence in the conflict incident you described.

PART TWO

DEVELOPING A RELEVANT THEORY OF SUPERVISORY PRACTICE

INTRODUCTION: REQUIREMENTS FOR A USEFUL THEORY OF SUPERVISION

We are at an important juncture in the development of supervisory thought and practice. Presently, supervision enjoys unprecedented interest from an array of sources. State departments of education throughout the country are increasing supervisory services. Certification requirements for the licensing of administrators and supervisors are being evaluated, with greater emphasis being given to supervisory competencies. State legislators ponder legislation that would require state and local educational authorities to give greater attention to staff development, in-class assistance to teachers, and the evaluation of teaching. The Association for Supervision and Curriculum Development is giving more of its attention and resources to the "S" in its name. Programs of the National Curriculum Study Institute and the National Academy of School Executives reflect a greater concern for supervisory functions and responsibilities—a trend noticeable as well in the meetings of state and local professional organizations. One might well question whether this new attention is sufficient in quality of resources and efforts (it isn't!) but still recognize that the interest itself is a significant and bright sign.

Similar progress has been made within the academic community. As Robert H. Anderson suggests:

> . . . a mere decade has seen supervision emerge as a major force, perhaps we should rather say resource, in the significant improvement of educational services. Although the number of books and articles currently available on the topic of supervision may not be much greater than was the case in early 1970s, there is no doubt that the quality and usefulness of the newer materials are much greater. For one thing, scholars have produced sounder theory, especially with respect to the nature of effective organizations and processes of organizational change, and much more is understood about how the growth and development of adult human beings can be influenced and promoted within organizational settings. The emergence of *clinical* supervision as a central focus has greatly stimulated both theory and practice. The welcome revival, at a far higher level of discourse, of the old

debate about science versus art in supervision has produced new insights into the many dimensions of supervision[1]

As in the case with advances in the policy and practices areas of supervision, the scholarly ferment of which Anderson speaks is a healthy and hopeful sign of progress but still falls short of what is needed to develop supervision as a mature field of professional practice. Important to the maturing of any professional field is the development of a sound theoretical basis for action. That is why attention to theory is so important and why this part of the book entitled "Developing a Relevant Theory of Supervisory Practice" is included in the third edition. The long-term prospects for developing a mature field of professional practice are directly linked to the development of a strong theoretical foundation. The purpose of this foundation is to inform professional intuition and to guide practice. Theory, therefore, is not just an issue for academics but is of vital concern to those interested in improving professional practice.

THE INADEQUACIES OF THEORY IN SUPERVISION

Despite its importance, historically supervisory theory has not been found to be very appealing. There are good reasons for this halfhearted reception. Theory has not been of much use to practitioners. The reason for this discouraging news can be explained by the unique requirements education makes on theory. The test for a useful theory in education is that it informs the intuitions of professionals at work and helps them to make better decisions. In this endeavor, educational practice remains a fairly artistic enterprise but one informed by theory. But what is our present state? By and large, theories are developed and scientific principles are established with the intent that professional intuition is to be replaced. To understand this position and its problems we need to give some attention to the nature of science and applied science and to the unique requirements of work in education.

SUPERVISION AS A UNIQUE FIELD OF STUDY AND PRACTICE

Just what is our scientific heritage in education? The "experimenting society" is the term Campbell uses to describe scientific activity. In his view, growth and development of knowledge results from a series of trial-and-error processes involving the comparison of hypotheses with experimentally induced results.[2] Scientific inquiry seeks to ascertain and discover the facts on the one hand and to construct hypotheses and theories on the other. Theory building seeks to predict occurrences of events and outcomes of experiments and to explain facts that are discovered by establishing causal change between and among them.[3]

What is the aim of science? Stated simply, the aim of science is to establish truth

[1]Robert H. Anderson, "Creating a Future for Supervision," in T. J. Sergiovanni (ed.), *Supervision of Teaching*, 1982 Yearbook, Association for Supervision and Curriculum Development, Alexandria, Va., 1982, p. 182.
[2]P. J. Campbell, "Evolutionary Epistemology," in P. A. Schilpp (ed.), *The Philosophy of Karl Popper*, LaSalle, Ill.: Open Court Press, 1974, pp. 413–463.
[3]George Henrik von Wright, *Explanation and Understanding*, Ithaca, N.Y.: Cornell University Press, 1971.

and refute conjecture; to bring about oneness of thought through systematic experimental research; to find the right answer, the correct explanation, and the best way. The truth of fact is supreme in science. Throughout the scientific process the scientist must be scrupulous in separating fact from value, and where values come into play, they are to be treated as variables to be experimentally defined and manipulated as one would other variables.

What about applied science? Does this term more adequately describe the supervisory sciences? Applied science is the direct application of scientific truth and scientific theory to problems of professional practice. An assumption basic to applied science is that a one-to-one correspondence exists between scientific knowledge and professional practice. What is the aim of applied science? The aim is to establish the one best analysis of a problem, the one best way to practice given existing scientific knowledge. The truth of analyses and the truth of methods based on facts are supreme in applied science.

The images of science and applied science have great appeal in our society. If we view supervision as a true science, then we would need only to describe, explain, analyze, and predict. We would do this by applying the scientific approach of accuracy, reliability, objectivity, and neutrality. We could then identify and articulate clear-cut and indisputable principles to guide supervisory actions. At last, we would get our work down to a "science." Supervisors would need only to master a set of procedures and by repeating them would get the desired results every time.[4] Respect and power would come from such a development, but unfortunately this is not to be for supervision. Neither treating supervision as a science nor treating it as an applied science will enable us to to master the complexities of supervisory work.

Educational supervision is a distinct enterprise. Two important characteristics of this distinctiveness are its applied nature and human activity. Having both applied and human characteristics places unique requirements on inquiry and on the development or prescriptions for practice. "Applied" suggests that knowledge from a discipline is utilized toward some end. Further, in the pursuit of this end action takes place: decisions are made and implemented. Thus applied fields can be described as having purposive and practical qualities, as being concerned with practice toward some end.

Supervision is not merely concerned with ends in an instrumental sense but is concerned with better ends. Supervisory policy, for example, speaks to what ought to be and directs its analysis to uncovering and discovering the conditions under which this "ought" is to be realized. Supervisory practice, on the other hand, is the science and art of developing and implementing effective and satisfying ways to achieve desired ends. Improving schools and the teaching within them gives supervisory policy and practice normative qualities that must of necessity become an important part of inquiry, analysis, and practice. In short, supervision is the science and art of designing courses of action aimed at changing existing situations into preferred ones.

Supervision, as is the case with other human fields, has some "artificial" qualities as well. By artificial we mean that behavior in schools and reality are often human

[4]Elliott Eisner, "An Artistic Approach to Supervision," in T. J. Sergiovanni (ed.), *Supervision of Teaching*, 1982 Yearbook, Association for Supervision and Curriculum Development, Alexandria, Va., 1982, p. 58.

inventions governed by perceptions, values, and beliefs as much as they are made up of objective data gained from the use of scientific laws. Thus phenomenological and cultural concerns are important. Despite the fact that objective reality exists and is worth pursuing, reality is also a state of mind whose validity and meaning are determined by the private world within which each of us lives. Reality is also created and validated in our interaction with others, and this interaction network constitutes a cultural web of which we are a part.

In its scientific sense, for example, supervisory behavior can be defined as actions identified and described beyond interpretive disputes. Mary, a supervisor, might behave in a certain way, and after careful recording of this behavior indisputable conclusions might be reached, such as Mary was autocratic or task-oriented when she gave directions to teachers John and Bill. Behavior so described can be called "brute" data[5]—it has certain characteristics and configurations that can be documented and described fairly systematically. Mary tells John and Bill exactly what she expects and precisely what standards are to be met. The issue, of course, is exactly what Mary's behavior means. Meanings implicit in supervisory behavior are beyond the reach of mere descriptions and objective measurements. Indeed, the same act may have quite different meanings to different people or to the same people in different situations. John, for example, might view Mary's behavior as being overbearing, bossy, or dictatorial. Perhaps his professional ego is hurt or perhaps he feels that directive behavior is not an appropriate way to manage professionals such as teachers. Bill, on the other hand, considers Mary's identical behavior to be courageous, and he responds with admiration. Mary, he concludes, has high standards, cares about the school and him, gives a great deal of herself, and expects a great deal in return. He likes knowing where Mary stands and is motivated by her high standards and expectations. In this case Mary's actual behavior is clearly secondary to the meanings raised in the consciousness of John and Bill. When focusing on Mary's behavior in a descriptive sense, we are emphasizing the configurations of leadership but not its meaning, the brute data that constitute events in action but not sense data embedded in our consciousness, and descriptions of leadership but not understandings and interpretations. The key to the human side of life is that events have meanings. Understanding in the human side of life requires that events be interpreted and make sense.

In sum, traditional conceptions of theory and practice have not been able to capture the complexity and sensitivity needed to accommodate the purposive, practical, and human qualities of supervisory policy and practice. Nevertheless, some theoretical framework is needed, some systematic mode of analysis, some series of cognitive maps that can help in understanding and informing supervisory practice. A theory is needed that can accommodate itself to practice. Such a theory would seek truth in an effort to expand the knowledge base of a particular discipline but would seek to inform practice as well. The concept of a theory of practice represents a promising attempt to develop such a theoretical formulation.

[5]Charles Taylor, "Interpretation and the Sciences of Man," *The Review of Metaphysics*, vol. XXV, no. 1, Sept/ 1971, pp. 3–51.

DEVELOPING A THEORY OF SUPERVISORY PRACTICE

Our purpose in this book is not to provide a developed theory of practice but to argue for its need and to suggest some of its essential characteristics. We do not have such a theory yet, though this book represents some of its features. A theory of practice would be concerned with four key questions: What *is* reality in a given context? What *ought* to be reality? What do events that constitute this reality *mean* to individuals and groups? Given these three dimensions, what should supervisors *do?*

Traditionally, scientific inquiry and practice in applied fields have been concerned only with the first and last questions, what are fact and reality, and, given these absolutes, what should be done in practice. But theories of practice emphasize more increasing understanding and making sensible decisions given unique circumstances than establishing facts for their own sake. Knowing what leadership style works most efficiently in a particular situation, for example, is quite different from deciding which style a supervisor should use. It is because of this that practical reasoning differs from scientific reasoning. Practical reasoning seeks understanding, whereas scientific reasoning seeks verification of facts.

The question of what is, however, remains important in a theory of practice. Supervisors are indeed interested in accurate and reliable descriptions of the real world and how it works. With respect to supervisory behavior, for example, relationships must be explained, linked together, and predicted. Laws and rules that govern behavior must be sought. No progress can be made if the themes of prediction and explanation, the hallmarks of traditional scientific inquiry, are not included. But in the theory of practice, the ledger is incomplete without the normative side of science. A theory of practice is therefore concerned as well with what ought to be. What cultural imperatives should determine action? What values should be implied? Theories of practice are designed to improve things, to bring about higher standards, to cause people to strive for a better life. Much debate exists on the role of values in any scientific endeavor. Skeptics often point to the difficulty in establishing the truth of value assertions. Part of this difficulty is the insistence that the same definitions of truth used in traditional science be used for value assertions. Paul Taylor points out that the truth of value assertions is different. In his words, "A factual assertion is truth if it corresponds to the way the world is regardless of whether we want the world to be that way. . . . A normative assertion is true, on the other hand, only because we have decided to adopt a standard or rule as applicable to what we are making the assertion about. We must decide what ought to be the case. We cannot discover what ought to be the case by investigating what is the case."[6]

And finally, the third question, What do "is" and "ought" mean? must be considered. If theories are concerned with useful knowledge, they should be concerned as well with knowledge that makes sense to people. It is for this reason that a theory of practice must move beyond the mapping of the abstract to the mapping of reality as viewed in different contexts and by different people. No human event studied in abstract is the same as in use. The art of supervision becomes apparent as the three

---

[6]Paul W. Taylor, *Normative Discourse,* Englewood Cliffs, N.J.: Prentice-Hall, 1961.

questions are brought together in the analysis of supervisory problems and in the guiding of supervisory practices.

THE THEORETICAL BASES OF THIS BOOK

Each of the parts of this book emphasizes different aspects of a theory of supervisory practice, but throughout we have tried to provide an integrated analysis. Part Two includes two chapters: Chapter 10, "An Instrumental Theory of Supervisory Leadership," and Chapter 11, "A Substantive Theory of Supervisory Leadership." As is implied by the word "instrumental," Chapter 10 deals primarily with the first question of what is reality and with which scientific laws exist to help inform supervisory practice. It represents a summary of the book's first nine chapters and brings together an array of social science theories already discussed in these chapters into an integrated whole. The second question, dealing with value dimensions, is included in this analysis as well. Human resources theory is not just based on social science facts but represents a set of beliefs about and a commitment to the human species.

Chapter 11 proposes a substantive theory of leadership. Substantive, by contrast to instrumental, refers to content and purpose. Instrumental aspects of supervisory leadership might be viewed as the armature of a sculpture. Substantive aspects, on the other hand, give the sculpture a unique personality and an identity. Substantive aspects are much more concerned with issues of "ought" and meaning than they are with questions of what is. Remember that supervisory practice is a field characterized by purposes, human activity, and practical action. The theoretical perspectives provided in Chapters 10 and 11 are intended, therefore, to bring together the instrumental and the substantive in an effort to inform practice in supervision.

CHAPTER 10

AN INSTRUMENTAL THEORY OF SUPERVISORY LEADERSHIP

Developing a useful theory of supervisory practice requires that attention be given to both instrumental and substantive aspects of leadership. Instrumental aspects are more tactical and refer to the development of means to achieve particular ends. Substantive, by contrast, refers to the content of leadership itself, to its purpose and value and the meanings that leadership acts communicate to others. Issues of effectiveness and efficiency are important in instrumental considerations, whereas issues of value and worth are important in substantive considerations. Of course, distinctions between instrumental and substantive aspects are only possible in books and in classroom seminar discussions. In the real world of supervisory practice substantive and instrumental considerations go hand in hand. Every instrumental leadership act has substantive meaning whether it is actually intended to or not. The example provided in the introduction to Part Two involving Supervisor Mary illustrates this point. Regardless of Mary's intentions, her leadership behavior communicated different meanings to teachers John and Bill. Still, for our purposes, a conceptual distinction between substantive and instrumental aspects is useful. It reminds us of the several dimensions that should be considered in understanding leadership and helps us to note omissions and deficiencies in conceptualizations of supervision.

Part One of this book, "Human Resources Supervision and Organizational Leadership," was primarily concerned with instrumental leadership. It sought to identify aspects of the general social science and management science literature that could be helpful in informing supervisory practices in education. Our strategy in preparing that section was twofold. On the one hand we sought to provide a useful inventory of scientific findings covering an array of topics (organizational behavior, school climate, leadership, politics and power, teacher motivation and satisfaction, conflict, and group processes) of importance to supervision. One purpose of this inventory was to provide a theoretical basis from which supervisory practices might be informed and supported.

In recognition of the fact that quality supervision is more than the articulation of social science findings, Part One emphaszied as well what ought to be by proposing images of the good life in supervision. Human resources supervision is social science and more. It reaches into the realm of philosophy in search of humanistic values, and these values share equally with social science findings as cornerstones for the theory.

In Chapters 1 through 9 the integration of fact and value is noticeable. On the one hand, leadership theory is presented as a neutral conception that provides definite links to how supervisors behave and the achievement of certain desired objectives. On the other hand, we suggested that the correct leadership response is the one that over the long-haul enriches people and improves the quality of life that exists in the school. Motivation theory is discussed as a set of brute facts, but a distinct value commitment overrides the discussion, which reminds supervisors of their responsibility to enrich the lives of the people with whom they work.

Despite the fact that human resources supervision is as much a value statement as it is a behavioral science theory, Part One tends to emphasize the latter. Of prime interest has been the identification and articulation of social and management science knowledge found to be of most use to developing effective supervisory programs and for specifying links between leadership behavior and increased effectiveness. Typically, effectiveness was defined in a fairly mechanical way. By contrast, much less attention was given to such substantive issues as overall purpose, sense of mission, and the educational content of supervision —issues to be discussed at length in Parts Three and Four of the book.

In this chapter the inventory of scientific findings presented in Chapters 1 through 9 is summarized and synthesized in the form of an instrumental theory of supervisory leadership. To balance this view, a more substantive theory of supervisory leadership is provided in Chapter 11. Chapter 11 provides as well an introductory perspective to Parts Three and Four: "Human Resources and Educational Leadership" and "A Human Resources Approach to Staff Development, Clinical Supervision, and Teacher Evaluation." It is the integration of instrumental and substantive issues that gives full meaning to human resources theories and practices.

THE IMPORTANCE OF THEORY

The effective supervisor needs to practice his or her profession from a foundation of concepts and ideas strong enough to stand the test of time and powerful enough to account for a variety of situations, many of which will be new and unfamiliar. Consider, for example, the differences between training and education. Training is a process of accumulating a series of programmed behaviors that can be applied with reliability to a series of highly predictable situations. The preparation of masons, refrigerator repairers, and computer console operators is characterized by training. Jobs suitable for training can be precisely defined and analyzed, and a best way can be determined for implementing each job's activities.

Education, by contrast, is a process of accumulating understandings and interpretations of knowledge. Definitive answers are not provided in education, but rather the emphasis is on acquiring knowledge paradigms, value perspectives, structures, concepts, and ways of thinking that help the educated person to generate pertinent strategies for new and often unfamiliar situations.

Some aspects of supervision, charting classroom interactions using the Flanders method, for example, are quite programmed and suitable to training. But supervision is largely a varied, situational, and unpredictable discipline. It is difficult to generate universal laws and principles of procedure for supervision, and for this reason the supervisory setting is more suitable to education than training. Conceptual considerations and theoretical frameworks are not only powerful and economical ways to understand supervisory problems and practices but are necessary components of the supervisor's education.

Theories are modes of thinking that lead to the generation of propositions amenable to testing either in the laboratory or in practice. In developing an instrumental theory for human resources supervision, our intent is to construct a systematic conceptual framework to assist readers in increasing understanding of present practice and in generating additional practices.

Many view theory as a set of abstractions that occur in some mysterious way, from which principles are derived that seem only remotely related to practice. In fact, however, theory is usually derived from practice. Practices become established sometimes as a result of hunches and often as a result of trial and error. Those who observe practice fairly systematically form additional hunches about the relationship between and among practices. Hunches can lead directly to propositions and principles relating to practice, but as hunches are formalized and linked together, they become the basis for theory. Propositions and principles are derived from theory, and their testing in the laboratory or real world leads to the establishment and extension of practice. The cycle continues with practices leading to new hunches, more theory, additional propositions, testing, and further modification and extension of practice.

SKILL LEVELS FOR SUPERVISORS

Scholars have attempted to identify the traits of successful supervision and more recently have turned their attention to identifying competencies for successful supervision. The complex, varied, and unpredicatable nature of supervision, however, has made such attempts difficult. Adequate maps of successful supervision remain elusive.

An alternate strategy is to focus less on traits and competencies and more on skills and their related domains of knowledge. Katz has identified three basic skills upon which he believes successful supervision rests—technical, human, and conceptual.[1] The skills are actually quite interdependent but can be treated separately for analytical purposes. Each of the skill domains applies to educational and organizational leadership roles of supervisors as well.

Technical skills assume ability to use knowledge, methods, and techniques to perform specific tasks. The mechanics associated with writing a lesson plan, developing a study unit, equipping a learning-resource center, purchasing laboratory equipment, preparing a meeting agenda, scheduling a cycle of clinical supervision, and filling out an annual report might be examples of technical skills.

[1]Robert L. Katz, "Skills of an Effective Administrator," *Harvard Business Review,* vol. 33, no. 1, pp. 33–42, 1955.

Human skills refer to one's ability and judgment in working with and through people. This skill requires self-understanding and acceptance as well as consideration for others. Its knowledge base includes an understanding of, and facility for, leadership effectiveness, adult motivation, attitudinal development, group dynamics, and the development of human resources.

Conceptual skills refer to the supervisor's ability to view the school, the district, and the educational program as a whole. This skill includes the effective mapping of the interdependence between the components of the school as an organizational system, the educational program as an instructional system, and the human organization as a functioning human system. Understanding the interdependencies that exist between establishing a humane organization, articulating a humane administrative-supervisory system, and developing a humane educational program is an example of conceptual skill.

Katz argues that, though each of the skill levels is universally present in administrative and supervisory positions, conceptual skills are emphasized more by administrators and technical skills more by supervisory personnel, who are for the most part concerned with the day-by-day work of the school. This relationship is illustrated in Figure 10-1.

Notice that regardless of level a common and strong emphasis is required on human skills. Part One of this book, "Human Resources Supervision and Organizational Leadership," gives strong attention to the knowledge domains associated with this skill level. The conceptual skill level, particularly important to Chapters 9 and 10 and to Part Three, "Human Resources and Educational Leadership," is strongly emphasized throughout the book. The theme that human organization, human supervision, and human educational programs are interdependent and inseparable is an example. Some attention is given to technical skills, particularly in Part Four, "Human Resources Approach to Staff Development, Clinical Supervision, and Teacher Evaluation," but this attention is limited by the need to relate technical skills to specific supervisory situations—a task better accomplished through class discussion and simulation and in-service education programs.

A SYNTHESIZING VIEW OF SUPERVISION

What follows in the form of an instrumental theory of supervision represents a blueprint for the development of subsequent chapters as well as a basis for developing supervisory strategies. The theory proposed is one that depends heavily upon a number of formulations, concepts, and ideas discussed in Chapters 1 through 9 that are

Figure 10-1 Skills needed at various levels.

synthesized and related to provide an integrated and systematic effort toward improving supervisory effectiveness.

The theory identifies and describes three sets of variables. One set is the *initiating* variables. Initiating variables are what supervisors start out with. They include the assumptions, values, and beliefs which determine the leadership style and pattern and the priorities of supervisors and the kinds of decisions they are likely to make. With regard to organizational structure, for example, how supervisors view and use rules and regulations, the decision-making traditions and procedures they establish, and the patterns of authority they develop and enforce are considered initiating variables.

Reactions of persons influenced by the initiating variables make up the second set of variables referred to as *mediating*. The third set, the *effectiveness* variables, represents the "output" that results from school efforts and activities. These are the key components of the school's human organization.

The following list of variables is not conclusive or exhaustive but represents examples that fall into each of the three categories. In each case the emphasis is on teachers and other adults, but the categories and the theory itself apply to students as well.

EXAMPLES OF INITIATING VARIABLES

1. Assumptions that supervisors hold in reference to their peers, subordinates, and themselves.

2. Administrative and supervisory behavior patterns that are consistently displayed by supervisors.

3. The nature of the authority system that prevails in the school and the resulting strategies for compliance used by supervisors.

4. The nature of goals and directions for the school and patterns for the emergence of these goals.

5. Character of motivational topics and motivational strategies used by supervisors.

6. The supervisor's view of change and the articulation of his or her change-agent role.

7. The structure and functioning of decision making.

8. The supervisor's perspectives on the organizational character of the school or unit. Consider, for example, the emphasis the supervisor gives to each of the following:
   a. Formalization (the extent to which the supervisor emphasizes rules and regulations.)
   b. Stratification (the importance the supervisor places on status systems and the rights of those in superordinate positions.)
   c. Centralization (the extent to which the supervisor emphasizes shared decision-making, as opposed to superordinate decision-making, prerogatives.)

d. Productivity (the emphasis the supervisor gives to the number, but not necessarily the quality, of units processed. The number of learning objectives, the number of students served, the amount of time spent, and the number of months gained could be considered as examples.)

e. Efficiency (the extent to which the supervisor emphasizes quantity of output at least cost. Large classes and lecture methods are more efficient means to cover text material than small classes.)

f. Adaptability (the emphasis the supervisor gives to school responsiveness to changing needs and requirements of students, advances in educational technology and pedagogy, and changes in community. Individualized instruction, team teaching, and active participation of parents and students are often common indicators of adaptability.)

g. Complexity (the extent to which the supervisor relies on the personal and professional expertness of subordinates and respects their stature as educational specialists.)

h. Job satisfaction (the emphasis the supervisor gives to providing teachers and other organizational members with opportunities for achieving *intrinsic* satisfaction at work.)

EXAMPLES OF MEDIATING VARIABLES

1. Attitudes that teachers and other employees have toward their jobs and toward their superiors, peers, and subordinates.

2. The extent to which the staff is committed to school goals and purposes.

3. Levels of performance goals held by teachers and other educational workers.

4. Levels of group loyalty and group commitment that exist in the school.

5. The extent to which teachers have confidence and trust in themselves, their peers, and their superiors.

6. The extent to which teachers feel that they have control over their immediate work environment and can meaningfully influence the larger school environment.

7. The extent to which a system for communications exists at all levels of the school enterprise and in all directions.

EXAMPLES OF EFFECTIVENESS VARIABLES

1. Performance levels of teachers and other employees.

2. Performance growth levels of teachers and students.

3. Personal growth levels of teachers and students.

4. Absence and dropout rate of the students.

5. Quality of school-community relations.

6. Quality of teacher-management relations.

7. Levels of intrinsic job satisfaction for teachers.

TRADITIONAL SUPERVISORY PATTERNS

Confusion often results when one attempts to map the relationships that exist between variables of one set and those of other sets. Indeed, the relationships between and among these sets of variables are just beginning to be understood. A common practice, which is now considered to be suspect, is for supervisors to work from initiating variables directly to effectiveness variables. This practice is associated with the classical scientific-management (and the now-popular neoscientific-management) approach to supervision and is illustrated as follows:

Initiating ⎯⎯⎯⎯⎯⎯⎯⎯⎯⎯⎯⎯⎯⎯⎯⎯⎯⟶ Effectiveness
variables   variables

Social science theorists seem now to suggest that the attainment of effectiveness variables is dependent upon the health of the school's human resources as reflected in teachers' skills, loyalty, trust, support, commitment to objectives, and motivation to work. This requires that supervision be concerned with conscious and direct efforts to influence the mediating variables.

HUMAN RESOURCES SUPERVISORY PATTERNS

Patterns of supervision associated with human resources are based on the premise that consistent and long-term achievement of school success is dependent upon the positive presence of the mediating variables.

The human organization of schools, which includes the quality of communications, group loyalty, levels of job satisfaction, and commitment to task, for example, exerts a direct influence over the determining of the nature and quality of school success. In turn, these mediating variables are influenced and determined by the nature and quality of attitudes, practices, and conditions that the initiating variables comprise. For conceptual purposes the variables are arranged unilaterally, but in practice they are interactive. We usually speak of the initiating variables affecting the mediating, but overlook the influence of the mediating on the initiating variables. This interacting relationship can be viewed as follows:

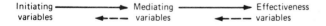

Initiating ⎯⎯⎯⟶ Mediating ⎯⎯⎯⟶ Effectiveness
variables ⟵ ⎯ ⎯ variables ⟵ ⎯ ⎯ variables

The direct approach may be illustrated by a principal who, in attempting to improve learning experiences for youngsters, wishes to adopt innovation A for his or her school. This principal may, by behaving in an administrative way, choose to use hierarchical position and legal prerogative to require this change (he or she might proceed with the adoption of the change over the summer recess and present the new teaching pattern, innovation A, to the teachers upon their return in the fall), or might, by behaving in a supervisory way, approach the human organization concerning the problem of improving learning experiences for children with an expectation of the professional response of others to this problem.

The first approach—the strategy that moves directly from the intervening variable set to the school-success variables—risks creating apathy or alienation in the human organization. Teachers will tend not to identify with changes imposed on them from above. The effectiveness of the school, therefore, may actually be reduced rather than improved as originally intended by our fictitious principal. A well-meaning administrator who ignores the human organization often finds that his or her efforts are unappreciated as well as ineffectual in terms of school performance.

The key to understanding the theory is to differentiate between long- and short-term effectiveness. Often, working directly from initiating to effectiveness variables is more effective in the short run than working to effect changes in the mediating variables. But over time, this strategy can result in serious erosion of the school's human organization. Consider, for example, the now-classic Morse and Reimer study,[2] which analyzed the effectiveness (the productivity and well-being of the human organization) of employees subjected to two different styles of supervision. Group 1, subjected to a style of supervision described as hierarchical by the investigators, outdistanced Group 2, subjected to a participatory style, in productivity, but showed a commensurate decline in the quality of its human organization. Over time, this erosion of the human organization in the hierarchically controlled environment took its toll in performance. In commenting on this phenomenon, Likert notes that that "the attitudes, loyalties, and motivation which improved the most in the participatory program and deteriorated the most in the hierarchical controlled program are those which these studies have consistently shown to be most clearly related *in the long run* to employee motivation and productivity.[3]

Human resources supervision, that which fully coordinates, develops, and utilizes the resources of the human organization, requires an investment in time by school officials before appreciable results can be realized. As the mellowing process sets in, the school's investment in its human organization will likely show improvement in each of the effectiveness variables.

THE THEORY ILLUSTRATED

The accompanying flowchart (Table 10-1) suggests samples of alternative attitudes and ways of behaving for those who supervise in schools, as well as several organizational styles that schools may adopt. The potential effects of each of these initiating variables on a host of mediating variables are described. And finally, changes that can be expected to result in the school-effectiveness variables are indicated. The theory, as illustrated in Table 10-1, formed the basis for Part One of this book. Each of the concepts that compose the theory is cross-referenced to concepts discussed in Chapters 1 through 9. As you read the flowchart highlighting key characteristics of the theory, note that

---

[2]Nancy Morse and E. Reimer, "The Experimental Change of a Major Organizational Variable," *Journal of Abnormal and Social Psychology,* vol. 52, no. 1, pp. 120–129, 1956.
[3]Rensis Likert, *New Patterns of Management,* New York: McGraw-Hill, 1961, p. 68.

TABLE 10-1
A SYNTHESIZING THEORY OF SUPERVISORY EFFECTIVENESS

Initiating variables	Supervision: Classical	Contemporary	Human resources	How the mediating variables are affected	Results: Types 1-3	Quality of effectiveness variables	Low / Medium / High
							Overtime
1. Administrative and supervisory assumptions (McGregor)	Theory X (p. 71)	Consistent choice ———	Theory Y	Type 1 (p. 192) →		Low	
				Type 3 (p. 193) →		High	
Management assumptions (Argyris)	Infancy assumptions (p. 74)	———————	Growth assumptions	Type 1 →		Low	
				Type 3 →		High	
2. Administrative and supervisory orientation: Style propensity (Gibb)	Defensive	———————	Participatory	Type 1 →		Low	
				Type 3 →		High	
Value system	School / Community / Society / Individual	———————	Individual / Society / Community / School	Type 1 →		Low	
				Type 3 →		High	
Skill level (Katz)	Technical only (p. 181)	———————		Type 1 →		Low	

187

TABLE 10-1 *(continued)*

Initiating variables	Supervision			How the mediating variables are affected	Quality of effectiveness variables
	Classical	Contemporary	Human resources	Results: Types 1-3	Low / Medium / High
		Human only ⟶		Type 2 ⟶	Medium
			Technical / Human and conceptual ⟶	Type 3 ⟶	High
3. Administrative and supervisory behavior:					
Social system (Getzels)	(p. 181) Nomothetic ⟶			Type 1 ⟶	Low
	(p. 50) Ideographic ⟶	Transactional ⟶		Type 2 ⟶	Medium
				Type 3 ⟶	High
Managerial grid style (Blake and Mouton)	9, 1. ⟶	1,9. ⟶		Type 1 ⟶	Low
	(p. 83)		9,9. ⟶	Type 2 ⟶	Medium
				Type 3 ⟶	High
Contingency leadership theory (Fiedler, Reddin)	Separated and/or Task (p. 84, 91) ⟶	Related ⟶	Contingency with related and integrated prominent ⟶	Type 1 ⟶	Low
				Type 2 ⟶	Medium
				Type 3 ⟶	High
Patterns of supervision (Likert)	Man-to-man style of supervision (p. 152)		Group supervision ⟶	Type 1 ⟶	Low
				Type 3 ⟶	High

TABLE 10-1 *(continued)*

Initiating variables	Supervision — Classical	Supervision — Contemporary	Supervision — Human resources	How the mediating variables are affected {Results: Types 1-3}	Quality of effectiveness variables {Low Medium High}
4. Authority systems (Thompson)	Legally defined authority based on position-hierarchy			→ Type 1	→ Low
	(p. 106)	Organizationally defined authority based on ability		→ Type 3	→ High
Peabody formulation	Formal authority		Functional authority		
	Legitimacy Position			→ Type 1	→ Low
	(p. 108)	Competence Person		→ Type 3	→ High
Power base (French and Raven)	Legitimate Coercive Reward			→ Type 1	→ Low
	(p. 110)	Expert Referent		→ Type 3	→ High
Compliance system (Etzioni)	Coercive			→ Type 1	→ Low
		Utilitarian		→ Type 2	→ Medium
	(p. 114)	Normative		→ Type 3	→ High
5. Motivational perspective					
Maslow theory of human motivation	Security (p. 124)			→ Type 1	→ Low

189

TABLE 10-1 *(continued)*

Initiating variables	Supervision			How the mediating variables are affected {Results: Types 1-3}	Quality of effectiveness variables {Low Medium High}
	Classical	Contemporary	Human resources		
		Social and Esteem →		Type 2 →	Medium
			Esteem / Autonomy / Self-Actualization →	Type 3 →	High
Motivation-hygiene theory (Herzberg)	Coercive (p. 134) →			Type 1 →	Low
		Hygiene →		Type 2 →	Medium
			Motivation and Hygiene →	Type 3 →	High
Expectancy theory (Vroom)	Satisfaction = production (p. 140) →			Type 2 →	Medium
		Production = satisfaction →		Type 3 →	High
6. Change strategy	Coercive (p. 143) →			Type 1 →	
		Avoidance →		Type 2 →	
			Participative →	Type 3 →	High
Change perspective	Extrapersonal political view →			Type 1 →	Low
		Interpersonal human relation view →		Type 2 →	Medium
			Intrapersonal paradigm shift view →	Type 3 →	High

TABLE 10-1 *(continued)*

Initiating variables	Supervision — Classical	Contemporary	Human resources	How the mediating variables are affected	Results: Types 1-3	Quality of effectiveness variables	Low / Medium / High
7. Manifestation of organizational style, managerial emphasis on mechanistic or organic, bureaucratic or professional (Hage)	Mechanistic Formalization Stratification Centralization Production Efficiency ($)		Organic	Type 1 → Low			
	(p. 37)	Adaptability Complexity Job satisfaction		Type 3 → High			
8. Management system (Likert)	System 1 System 2 (p. 63)	System 3 System 4		Type 1 → Low Type 2 → Medium Type 3 → High			
9. Organizational climate (Halpin and Croft)	Closed (p. 58)	Open		Type 1 → Low Type 3 → High			

across the top are listed the three variables of concern: the initiating variables, how the mediating variables are affected by the initiating variables, and the resulting quality of school effectiveness. The initiating variables are further subdivided into schools of thought, or supervisory theories, with which they are most associated. Supervisory assumption, for example, might be associated with rational-bureaucratic, human relations, or human resource theories. Mediating variables, listed to the right of initiating variables in Table 10-1, are affected by initiating variables in three ways represented as Types 1, 2, and 3. The mediating variables in turn influence the quality of school effectiveness. That is, over time, the school may exhibit high, medium, or low effectiveness depending upon the reaction of the mediating variables to those listed as initiating. Quality of school effectiveness is listed to the extreme right of Table 10-1.

Further discussion of the mediating variables and the types of reactions they provide to what the supervisor initiates are described below.

Mediating Variables—Type 1 Reaction[4]

Type 1 reactions—those prompted by rational-bureaucratic supervisory patterns—are typically characterized by considerable teacher job dissatisfaction with working conditions, supervision, school policies, and administration. Further, dissatisfaction with job security, with interpersonal relations with peers and subordinates, and with superiors, status, and salary can be expected. Some of these factors are symptomatic of a supervisory climate that encourages alienation of the teaching staff. Supervisors do not work deliberately to cause Type 1 reactions. Such reactions are usually unanticipated consequences of ignoring the human organization of the school. The Type 1 reaction results, over time, in lower levels of performance; resistance to change; higher turnover; antiorganizational, informal group activity; and formal labor problems for the school.

Mediating Variables—Type 2 Reaction

Human relations supervisory patterns evoke Type 2 responses from teachers. The Type 2 reaction involves a feeling of apathy toward the welfare of the school and toward the vigorous pursuit of school goals. Supervisors who emphasize a socially oriented group life characterized by high morale, good feelings, and low tension often elicit this response. Teachers are relieved from job dissatisfaction, performance expectations are low, work pressure is eliminated, and security is guaranteed. Yet teachers feel no compulsion to exert commitment, energy, and effort beyond that which is minimally required to carry on day by day. Little opportunity exists for teachers to grow personally and professionally and to enjoy deep satisfaction from their work.[5] Supervisors who evoke a Type 2 reaction from teachers often fail to distinguish

[4]The evidence does not substantiate a link between morale—that is, satisfaction—and performance—that is, productivity—unless satisfaction is dependent upon performance. See, for example, Bernard M. Bass, *Organizational Psychology*, New York: Allyn and Bacon, 1965, p. 38.

[5]Type 2 response is characterized by the relative absence of dissatisfaction, combined with little opportunity for achieving satisfaction. The phenomenon is discussed in detail in Chap. 8. See, for example, Frederick Herzberg, Bernard Mausner, and Barbara Synderman, *The Motivation to Work*, New York: Wiley, 1959.

between using people and working with people to achieve school goals. This is a confused pattern, characterized by ambivalence and uncertainty.

Mediating Variables—Type 3 Reaction

Human resources supervisory patterns—those that work to achieve school-effectiveness variables through encouraging the growth and development of the human organization—evoke responses from subordinates that are labeled Type 3. This type of response is characterized by high commitment to the work of the school, high loyalty to the school and to the membership subunit, high performance goals, and a desire, combined with an opportunity, for personal and professional growth. Job satisfaction centers around growth opportunities, achievement, recognition, responsibility, and advancement. The reward system that encourages Type 3 responses depends heavily upon achievement.[6] Supervisory behavior that evokes a Type 3 response from the human organization is most associated with school effectiveness.

CAUTIONS IN IMPLEMENTING HUMAN RESOURCES SUPERVISION

Enthusiasm is both virtuous and dangerous. One purpose of this book is to promote enthusiasm for the concept of human resources supervision. We have argued that human resources supervision is not only humane and fitting for educational organizations with their "people intensive" characteristics and distinctively human undertakings but that this view is supported by a formidable body of theory and research and enjoys claims of success from practitioners in many fields. But why the caution?

It would be a mistake, we believe, to view the assumptions, concepts, and practices associated with human resources supervision as universally applicable. Human beings are much too complex for that sort of blanket prescription.

Consider, for example, the problem of motivation and human resources supervision. A distinct and powerful point of view of motivation was presented in Chapter 8. Documentation for this view was provided on three counts—value system, theory, and empirical evidence. Though the point of view will be applicable to most teachers, still, many will not respond. One's set of values and work norms, for example, affects one's orientation toward a job. Some teachers will never be properly motivated to work and others will usually be motivated to work regardless of what supervisors do. Indeed, a good rule of thumb is, if you want motivated teachers, hire motivated people, if you can. The majority of teachers, however, desire and seek satisfying work and will respond to human resources supervision. But many will not, and alternative supervisory methods and procedures that suit these teachers will need to be provided. In such cases, patterns of supervision associated with rational-bureaucratic or human relations theory may well be appropriate.

Human resources supervision is not an elixir to be administered indiscriminately to all. But it is a powerful conception of supervision that, by using the concepts of motivation and job enrichment, can markedly improve the identity, commitment, and performance of most teachers and the effectiveness of schools.

[6]See footnote 4.

A further note—though supervisors may find many teachers to whom the theory will not apply, they need to be careful if this number increases. The problem may well be with the teachers the supervisors encounter, but, on the other hand, it could be with the supervisors and their perceptions of teachers.

SUMMARY

Many scholars have proposed theories and models that have the potential to be used in a powerful way by those who supervise in the nation's schools, but no one schema has been offered as a general theory of supervision. Chapter 10 builds upon the work of scholars from a variety of social science fields by integrating and synthesizing their ideas into an instrumental theory of supervisory effectiveness. The theory identifies and relates three sets of variables: initiating (supervisory and organizational), mediating human organization), and school effectiveness, which permit the conceptual mapping of effective supervision.

The concepts, models, and schemata that comprise the initiating variables in the theory were the focus of Chapters 2 to 7. Chapters 8 and 9 dealt with the mediating variables and the school-success variables.

STUDY GUIDE

Recall the concepts, ideas, and meanings associated with each of the following phrases and terms included in this chapter. Can you discuss each of them with a colleague and apply them to the supervisory context of your school? If you cannot, review them in the text and record the page numbers for future reference.

1. Conceptual skills _____
2. Educating supervisors _____
3. Effectiveness variables _____
4. Human organization _____
5. Human skills _____
6. Initiating variables _____
7. Mediating variables _____
8. Middle-range theories _____
9. Synthesizing theory of supervision _____
10. Technical skills _____
11. Theory _____
12. Training supervisors _____
13. Type 1 reaction _____
14. Type 2 reaction _____
15. Type 3 Reaction _____

EXERCISES

1. Paul Mort is often quoted as having said, "Action without theory is like a rat scurrying through a maze." Another favorite quote of theorists is, "There is nothing as practical as good theory." In your own words, develop a working definition of theory. Give examples of how theory is dependent upon practice.

2. Develop a list of competencies for two or three supervisory roles (perhaps department chairperson, elementary school principal, and central office director of instruction). Sort the competencies for each role into each of the three skill levels—technical, human, and conceptual. Compare your analyses of supervisory skills with the discussions in this chapter.

3. Develop a paragraph or two describing three real or imagined teachers, one whose reaction to organizational life is Type 1, another whose reaction is Type 2, and a third, Type 3. To what extent are these reactions related to administrative, organizational, and supervisory characteristics as described in the synthesizing theory, and to what extent are these reactions related to other factors? Other factors might include the teacher's interest in teaching, the teacher's personality, or perhaps competing demands from forces outside the school.

CHAPTER 11

A SUBSTANTIVE THEORY OF SUPERVISORY LEADERSHIP

Is it conceivable that a supervisor can master all the social and management science wizardry presented so far in this book, become an expert in articulating leadership skills, and still not contribute to quality schooling? The answer to this question is yes! Mastering management and leadership skills is important but is not enough to ensure that supervisors will be able to build school excellence in the form of human and educational quality.

Recent studies of leadership activity and leadership effectiveness suggest that beyond maintaining routine competence in their organizations, leaders do not make much of a difference.[1] One well-known theorist, James G. March, argues that leaders are interchangeable (assuming equal basic managerial competence among them), with no one making a more significant impact on the organization than others.[2] He uses a metaphor of a light bulb to illustrate his point—light bulbs are necessary but indistinguishable from one another. Any one that is manufactured to standard will do the job as well as any other. Taken to heart, this research indicates that while competent supervisors are necessary to ensure things will work in schools, they appear not to make much a difference beyond a minimal level of satisfactory school performance.

Competent leadership is defined in these analyses as the mastery and articulation of basic management routines and leadership skills. Knowing how to arrange and prepare for a group session, mastering a contingency theory of leadership, and being able to articulate effectively conflict management techniques would be examples of such routines and skills. Though it is difficult to link these skills with excellence, incompetence or nonexistent skills leads to less effective supervision and schooling. Thus *leadership skills represent a critical foundation for excellence.* But going beyond these satisfactory conditions to excellence requires that supervisors give attention to the

[1]Henry Mintzberg, *The Nature of Managerial Work,* New York: Harper & Row, 1973.
[2]James G. March, "How We Talk and How We Act: Administrative Theory and Administrative Life," David D. Henry Lecture, Urbana-Champaign: University of Illinois, Sept. 25, 1980. This essay appears as Chap. 2 in T. J. Sergiovanni and J. E. Corbally (eds.), *Administrative Leadership and Organizational Cultures,* Urbana: University of Illinois Press, forthcoming, 1983.

more substantive aspects of leadership, the theme of Chapter 11. Consider, for example, the observation of Mary Parker Follett on the subject:

> But let us look further at the essentials of leadership. Of the greatest importance is the ability to grasp a total situation. The chief mistake in thinking of leadership as resting wholly on personality lies probably in the fact that the executive leader is not a leader of men only but of something we are learning to call the total situation. This includes facts, present and potential, aims and purposes and men. Out of a welter of facts, experience, desires, aims, the leader must find the unifying thread. He must see the relation between all the different factors in a situation.

She continues:

> The leader then is one who . . . can organize the experience of the group and thus get the full power of the group. The leader makes the team. This is pre-eminently the leadership quality—the ability to organize all the forces there are in an enterprise and make them serve a common purpose. Men with this ability create a group power rather than express a personal power. They penetrate to the subtlest connections of the forces at their command, and make all these forces available and most effectively available for the accomplishment of their purpose.[3]

Since Follett made these comments in 1933, you can see that the idea of giving attention to substantive issues in leadership may be neglected but certainly is not new.

STRATEGIC AND TACTICAL REQUIREMENTS OF LEADERSHIP

Quality in leadership requires that balanced attention be given to both strategic and tactical requirements. Balancing the two can often be difficult, but it is clear that the emphasis in leadership today is on the tactical. Strategy is defined as the science and art of obtaining and employing support for policies and purposes and for devising means for accomplishing long-term goals. Tactics, by contrast, involves smaller-scale objectives, decisions, and actions that serve a larger purpose and refers to methods and means of less magnitude.

One of the reasons why tactical aspects of leadership are strongly emphasized is that they reflect the broader management culture of western society. Such values as efficiency, specificity, rationality, measurability, and objectivity combined with beliefs that good management is tough-minded are part of this culture. Results-oriented management is the slogan, the bottom line is worshiped, and the direct, in-control manager is admired. Leadership is broadly defined as achieving objectives effectively and efficiently. Leadership theory puts the emphasis on the leaders' behavior and on results. The metaphors of the battlefield are often used to remind us that one must be hard-nosed and that the going is tough. Evaluation is quick and to the point and success is determined on the basis of short-term accomplishments.

Missing from an emphasis of tactical concerns are holistic values of purpose,

---

[3]Mary Parker Follett, "The Essentials of Leadership," in Howard Merril (ed.), *Classics in Management*, New York: American Management Associations, 1970, pp. 199–300.

goodness, and importance. Missing is an emphasis on long-term quality schooling and a long-term commitment to the quality of the human organization.

Strategic and tactical requirements of leadership are compared in Table 11-1. Proper balance requires that tactical requirements be clearly linked to and dependent upon the strategic. They represent short-term and highly focused managerial expressions that characterize day-by-day leadership activity. Separated from the strategic, they are ends in themselves devoid of the purpose and meanings needed for quality leadership and quality schooling.

Let us take as an example the important tactical skill of mastering a contingency approach to leadership, characterized by careful reading of situations and by applying the right doses of the correct mix of leadership style. Combine this skill with a

TABLE 11-1
TACTICAL AND STRATEGIC REQUIREMENTS OF LEADERSHIP

Tactical Requirements of Leadership	Strategic Requirements of Leadership
1. Ask what should be done now to achieve objectives. An atomistic or task-specific view is important	Ask what is good in the long-haul. A holistic view is important.
2. Develop a contingency perspective for education supervision, management, and the organization that permits altering arrangements to suit unique short-term circumstances.	Develop an enduring philosophy of education supervision, management, and organization to ensure consistency and to give a proper purpose and meaning to events.
3. Emphasize leadership styles that are carefully and skillfully matched to task requirements.	Emphasize leadership qualities that reflect and nurture this philosophy.
4. Develop operating structures, procedures, and schedules for implementing purposes.	Develop an overall plan or image that provides a frame for implementing purposes.
5. Decisions should be governed by stated objectives.	Decisions should be governed by purposes and philosophy.
6. The outputs to be achieved are important. Be concerned with structures and results.	The meaning of events to people is important. Be concerned with processes and substance.
7. The development and articulation of sound techniques are key to success.	Sensitivity to and involvement of people are key to success.
8. Quality control is a result of careful planning and organizing of the work to be done and/or providing continuous evaluation.	Quality control is a state of mind that comes from loyal and committed people who believe in what they are doing.
9. Evaluation should be short term to determine if specific objectives are being met and to enable the provision of systematic and continuous feedback.	Evaluation should be long term to determine more adequately the quality of life in the school and to assess effectiveness more holistically.
10. A basic corollary: *Strategic requirements should never be sacrificed in favor of tactical requirements.*	

supervisor who has certain purposes, beliefs, and commitments to what the school is and can be and who can communicate these in a fashion that rallies others to the cause, and we are achieving proper balance. One would not want to choose between the tactical and the strategic, but if we had to make such a choice, our vote would be with the latter. What a leader stands for is more important than what he or she does. The meanings a leader communicates to others are more important than his or her specific leadership style.

THE 10-P MODEL OF QUALITY LEADERSHIP

Leadership skills are important, constitute the tactical side of the quality equation, and are critical components of instrumental theories of supervisory leadership. *Leadership antecedents, leadership meanings, and leadership as cultural expression* are important too. They constitute the strategic side of the quality equation and are critical components of substantive theories of supervisory leadership. From leadership skills, meanings, antecedents, and culture can be extracted 10 principles of quality leadership. The principles are depicted in Figure 11-1. The 10 principles bring together instrumental and substantive issues to form the basis for human resources supervision.

There is always a risk in reducing the subtle and complex to a handful of abbreviated and specific principles. We accept this risk in order to provide busy professionals with a useful and easily remembered framework. The risk will be reduced if we agree that the 10 principles are not meant to be recited as a litany but are offered to bring to one's consciousness a cognitive map of the requirements for quality in leadership.

Prerequisites refers to the various leadership skills needed to develop and maintain basic leadership competence. Such skills as mastering and using various contingency leadership theories, conflict management tactics, team management principles, shared decision-making models, and group processes techniques are examples of basic

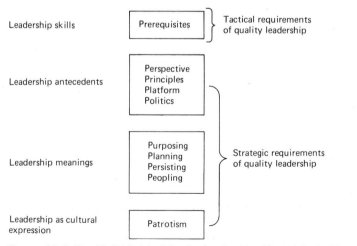

Figure 11-1 The 10-P Model of Quality Leadership. *(Copyright © Thomas J. Sergiovanni.)*

leadership requirements. Leadership skills are tactical in the sense that they are situationally specific, of short duration, and focused on specific objectives or outcomes. Successful leadership is not likely to be within the reach of those who are not competent in the basic leadership skills. But competence and excellence are different. To move beyond routine competence one must shift attention from the tactical to the strategic. Much of the emphasis given in Chapters 1 through 9 relates to the important leadership skills that are prerequisites to excellence. The remaining nine quality principles are strategic in nature. They give meaning and direction to the leadership skills. Parts Three and Four of this book give prime attention to these strategic principles.

The next four quality principles are leadership antecedents in the sense that they represent conditions, feelings, assumptions, cognitive maps, and attitudes of the leader that determine his or her reality and that guide his or her leadership decisions, actions, and behavior. As antecedents vary among leaders, so do leadership quality and meaning.

Perspective refers to the ability of the leader to be able to differentiate between the tactical and strategic and to understand how they are related. A leader with perspective brings a broader, patient, more long-range view to his or her leadership events and outcomes and the determining of worth.

What the leader stands for and believes in about schooling, the place of education in society, how schools should be organized and operated, and how people should be treated constitute the guiding principles that bring integrity and meaning to leadership. Leaders stand for certain ideals and principles that become cornerstones of their very being. In a recent *Wall Street Journal* Gallup poll, for example, integrity was the factor considered most important by chief executives of 282 of the nation's largest firms in describing characteristics of subordinates considered most important for advancement. The number one failing of weak managers, by contrast, was limited point of view. That integrity was considered to be the most important factor suggests that the leader values something important and is able to communicate this value to others.

Platform refers to the articulation of one's principles into an operational framework. Platforms are governing in the sense that they represent a set of criteria and an implicit standard from which decisions are made. One's teaching platform governs the decisions one makes about teaching and provides a set of ideals that make teaching decisions sensible to a person. Educational and management platforms, so essential to quality in leadership, operate in much the same way.

Politics is the final leadership antecedent to be considered. At its simplest level, leadership can be defined as the ability of an individual to influence another individual or group in a manner that helps to achieve certain desired goals. Power is an essential ingredient in the leadership act. Power, defined simply, is the ability to act to produce an effect. Power and leadership go hand in hand. Indeed, in schools political behavior is a key ingredient in successful leadership. Public schools, like other areas of public administration, are political organizations characterized by multiple interest groups, unclear and competing goals, diffuse sources of power, and ambiguous lines of authority. Unlike the simple business firm or owner-operated store, the supervisor typically cannot exercise direct authority to obtain compliance or cooperation from others. Often, groups to be influenced are outside the school itself or are outside the administrator's or supervisor's legal authority. Typically, the supervisor must obtain voluntary cooperation, support, and goodwill from others to get things done.

Sensitivity to *politics* and knowledge that the supervisor is typically dependent upon the good wishes and voluntary compliance of others if he or she is to be effective in the long-haul is a necessary leadership antecedent.

Key to quality in leadership and quality in schooling is that teachers and others find their work to be interesting, satisfying, and meaningful. Meaning suggests as well that they believe in what they are doing and appreciate its importance to the school, to society, and to themselves. Leadership meanings can be summed in four additional quality principles: purposing, planning, persisting, and peopling.

Purposing breathes life and meaning into the day-by-day activities of people at work in schools. It helps people to interpret their contributions, their successes and failures, their efforts and energies in light of the school's purposes. Through this process, seemingly ordinary events become meaningful, with subsequent motivational benefit to the school. In addition, purposing is the means by which leaders bring to the forefront of school activity the leadership antecedents of principle and platform. Purposing represents as well the rallying point for bringing together all human resources into a common cause.

Planning is the articulation of purpose into concrete but long-term operational programs. Planning sketches out the major structures and design to be implemented, the major steps to be taken, and the major milestones to be achieved. The time frame is long range, and planning as a strategic requirement of leadership should not be confused with such tactical requirements as management by objectives, the specification of short-term outcomes or results, or the various scheduling devices such as Gantt or PERT. Despite the usefulness of such tactics in the short range, they can mislead if they are not part of a more long-range plan.

Persisting refers to the attention leaders give to important principles, issues, goals, and outcomes. Symbolically how a supervisor uses time is a form of administrative attention that communicates meanings to others in the school. It is assumed by most that a supervisor gives attention to the events and activities he or she values. As others learn the value of this activity to the leader, they are also likely to give it attention. Administrative attention, then, can be considered as a form of modeling for others who work in the school. Through administrative attention, the leader contributes to setting the tone or climate of the school and communicates to others the goals and activities that should receive high priority.

The social-psychological effects of administrative attention tend to occur whether or not they are intended. An elementary school principal might, for example, espouse an educational platform that suggests a deep commitment to building a strong educational program sensitive to individual needs of students, taught by a happy, committed faculty, and supported by his or her school community. But this platform is likely to be ignored in favor of the one that students, teachers, and parents infer on the basis of administrative attention. Protestations to the contrary, if most of the principal's time is spent on the many trivial activities associated with routine administrative maintenance, observers will learn that "running a smooth ship" is the goal of real value to the principal and school.

Peopling recognizes that little can be accomplished by the leader without the good wishes of others. More than mere compliance from others is necessary if excellence is sought. Instead, the leader seeks to fine-tune and match more closely the goals, objectives, and desires of people with those of the organization. Growth and development of the human organization enjoys equal status, as a tactical objective, with increased school outputs. Indeed, lower levels of school achievement might well be appropriate in the short term if human values would otherwise be endangered. When considered in the long term, an undisputed link exists between the satisfaction and development of the human organization and increased organizational performance, both in quantity and quality. Peopling is a key strategic requirement of quality leadership. Accepting short-term gains that compromise the quality of life in schools that people enjoy simply does not make strategic sense.

When leadership skills, antecedents, and meanings are successfully articulated into practice, we come to see leadership as less a behavioral style or management technique and more as a cultural expression. Here a set of norms, beliefs, and principles emerge to which organizational members give allegiance. These represent a strong bond, which brings people together to work on behalf of the school. Indeed, a culture emerges that details what is important and provides guidelines that govern behavior. The quality principle of *patriotism* is key to viewing leadership as a cultural expression. In highly effective organizations workers share a set of common beliefs and reach a set of common agreements that govern what will be done and how it will be done. Members express loyalty or patriotism to this way of life. Organizational patriots are committed to purposes, work hard, believe in what they are doing, feel a sense of excitement about the organization and its work, and find their own contributions to the organization meaningful if not inspirational.

LEADERSHIP IN HIGH-PERFORMING SYSTEMS

The recent research of Peter Vaill, which seeks to identify leadership characteristics associated with high-performing systems, corroborates many of the quality-leadership principles as well.[4] He defines high-performing systems as those that are performing excellently against a known external standard, are performing excellently against what is assumed to be their potential level of performance, are performing excellently relative to where they were at some earlier point in time, are judged qualitatively by informed observers to be doing substantially better than other comparable systems, are doing whatever they do with significantly less resources than it is assumed are needed, are perceived as exemplars of the way to do whatever they do, and are perceived to fulfill at a high level the idelas of the culture within which they exist. From his research Vaill identifies three characteristics of leaders common to all the high-performing systems he studied:

1. Leaders of high-performing systems put in extraordinary amounts of time. They work hard. They demonstrate that they care. Their consciousness is dominated by the issues and events in the system of which they are a part.

[4]Peter Vaill, "The Purposing of High Performing Systems," paper presented at conference entitled "Administrative Leadership: New Perspectives on Theory and Practice," Urbana-Champaign: University of Illinois, July 1981. This essay appears as Chap. 6 in Sergiovanni and Corbally, op. cit.

2. Leaders of high-performing systems have very strong feelings about the attainment of the system's purposes. They care deeply about the system. This includes its structure and conduct, its history, and its future security. They care deeply about the people in the system. They want the system to be successful. They want the system to make a respected contribution to society. They want the system to contribute to the quality of life of people who are involved in it. Their feelings are evidenced in the way they talk about the system and in the way in which they behave in the system.

3. Leaders of high-performing systems focus on key issues and variables. They understand the concept "management of attention" and recognize the importance of modeling organizational purposes and values. They focus on what is important and are able to rally others to this purpose.

Vaill believes that it is this time-feeling focus, when brought together within the lifestyle of the leader, that results in a qualitative difference between competence and excellence in leadership. He points out that leadership or management style, described in its instrumental sense (cold-warm, task-relationship, democratic-autocractic), is not the determining factor in a high-performing system, although style may be more important in low- or average-performing systems. He concludes from his research that leaders who strive for excellence should "seek constantly to do what is right and what is needed in the system (Focus). Do it *all out* in terms of your energy (Time). Put your whole psyche into it (Feeling)."[5] It is these factors that provide constant purposing to the system. In high-performing systems, to reiterate a basic axiom of this substantive theory, *what the leader stands for and communicates to others is more important than how he or she behaves given any particular set of circumstances.*

In his recent study of 80 highly successful chief executive officers of public and private organizations Warren Bennis notes that they all seemed to possess the following characteristics: ability to create and communicate a compelling vision of a desired future state *(vision)*, the ability to communicate this vision and to obtain support from a variety of constituencies (communication and alignment), the ability to maintain the group or organization's direction even when the going gets rough (persistence, consistency, focus), the ability to create environments that can draw together the necessary commitment and abilities to bring about desired results (empowerment), and the ability to find ways for the group or organization to monitor its performance and compare its results with intents (organizational learning).[6] In his words, "Nothing serves an organization better . . . than leadership which knows what it wants, communicates those intentions successfully, empowers others, and knows when and how to stay on course and when to change,"[7] qualities well beyond the mastery of instrumental leadership skills.

---

[5]Vaill, op. cit.
[6]Warren Bennis, "Transformation Power and Leadership," paper presented at conference entitled "Administrative Leadership: New Perspectives on Theory and Practice." Urbana-Champaign: University of Illinois, July 1981. This essay appears as Chap. 4 in Sergiovanni and Corbally, op. cit.
[7]Ibid.

The Importance of Purposing

Vaill's research is particularly illuminating in understanding the importance of purposing to leadership excellence. In his words, *"The definition and clarification of purpose is both a fundamental step in effective strategic management, AND it is a prominent feature of every high performance system I have investigated."* He considers purposing to be *"that continuous stream of actions by an organization's formal leadership which have the effect of inducing clarity, consensus, and commitment regarding the organization's basic purposes."*

Purposing provides content and substance to the day-by-day leadership acts of supervisors and gives meaning and importance to the day-by-day work of teachers. Purposing seeks to identify and communicate what the school is about, what people believe in, and what they are trying to accomplish. No matter how skillful a supervisor is at being a good manager-leader, excellence requires that upon this base be built a substantive commitment to educational matters. It is the statesmanship responsibilities of the supervisor's role that are key, and this is the theme of Parts Three and Four.

Robert H. Anderson speaks similarly to those issues as follows:

> For supervision to become the force it deserves to be in improving schools, there must be a clear understanding of *and commitment* to educational goals on the part of supervisors. In seeking to conceptualize the operational essentials for effective supervision, therefore, we are obliged to connect all elements and activities to the goals that provide direction to everyone's work. . . . the very center is the district's goal structure.
>
> Sometimes a school's goals are at best implicit, or they are stated mostly as platitudes that have little operational meaning to either the teachers or the students. However, educators are fast coming to appreciate the importance of setting down clear and inclusive statements of the goals towards which everyone in the school district should be working, along with references to specific objectives, indicators of attainment, and performance standards that help to illuminate the way. Inasmuch as each school has its own culture and its own unique mission within the larger goal structure, it is important for the school staff not only to understand and embrace that larger goal structure but also to engage in a more particularized goal-setting process for themselves and to select foci and priorities for each year's efforts.[8]

Throughout the process of strategic goal setting and the subsequent development of tactical strategies and plans by teachers as described by Anderson, it is important to remember that the true meanings and purposes—those that will actually get attention from teachers—are those communicated symbolically as the supervisor emphasizes leadership meanings by practicing the principles of purposing, planning, and persisting. These in turn are effected by the leadership antecedents of perspective, principles, and platform. Symbolized aspects of leadership are more powerful determiners of the actual goals of the school than are the more formal and instrumental supervisory processes and techniques used for development of goals and objectives.

---

[8]Robert H. Anderson, "Creating a Future for Supervision," in T. J. Sergiovanni (ed.), *Supervision of Teaching,* 1981 Yearbook, Association for Supervision and Curriculum Development, Alexandria, Va., 1982.

THE JAPANESE EXPERIENCE

Increasingly, American management theorists have looked to Japanese management for insights that might be incorporated into our way of doing things. The Japanese management success is already a modern legend, and Japanese economic productivity and quality standards are admired and envied throughout the world. What is their secret? Have they developed superior management tactics and techniques? Can their secrets be discovered and borrowed? When novices embark on this journey to study, learn, and emulate the secrets of successul Japanese management, they soon find that such popular management techniques as quality-control circles and the *ringi* system of decision making are important but are not particularly key.

The use of quality-control circles is a management technique for sharing responsibilities with workers for locating and solving problems that interfere with organizational creativity, productivity, and job satisfaction. It is estimated that more than 100,000 such circles are registered in Japan and perhaps more than 1,000,000 others exist.[9] Quality-control circles typically consist of 2 to 10 employees who meet regularly to examine work-related issues. They then decide on specific issues to study, launch action-research projects aimed at solving defined problems or resolving issues, and make suggestions to management. Their suggestions are taken quite seriously, and typically result in better performance and, more importantly, better commitment from workers. In a sense, the quality-control circle makes every employee a manager, with resulting motivational effects that come from this increased vested interest in the enterprise.

The *ringi* system refers to an elaborate decision-making network requiring approval of new ideas from sources throughout the organization. It is characterized by the circulation of plans, proposals, or papers *(ringisho)* to various individuals at various levels in the organization and the affixing of stamps or seals indicating their approval of the plan. Following Kazuo Noda,[10] the system can be described as follows. Plans are typically drafted by individuals low in the organization and sponsored by middle-level management. One subtle reason for this procedure beyond seeking input from lower levels is that newer members of the organization are socialized into the organizational culture as modifications are suggested to their plans by those at other levels. Plans are circulated and changed until they fit the organizational culture. This technique permits new ideas to be presented to those at other levels and provides the means for superiors to give feedback to those lower in the organization. Final plans are usually a compromise between traditional organizational expectations and new ideas proposed by those lower in the organization.

Before the *ringisho* is forwarded to upper levels it receives careful and lengthy horizontal consideration. Consensus at this level is symbolized by the affixing of seals and stamps to the *ringisho*. Finally it is sent forward for approval by those at upper

[9]William Ouchi, *Theory Z: How American Business Can Meet the Japanese Challenge*, Reading, Mass.: Addison-Wesley, 1981, p. 262.
[10]Kazuo Noda, *Nihon no juyaku* (Big Business Executives in Japan), Tokyo: Diamond Press, 1960, pp. 115–117, as described in William Brown, "Japanese Management: The Cultural Background," *Momenta Nipponica*, vol. 21, pp. 47–60, 1966.

levels. The *ringisho* moves slowly up the line, with modifications occurring along the way. Finally the chief executive approves the *ringisho* by affixing a final seal. Advocates of the *ringi* system point out that though consensus builds slowly, once a decision is made support is strong and widespread. Americans, by contrast, typically make quick decisions but then have subsequent difficulty implementing them because of support and commitment problems.

Quality-control circles and the *ringi* system are good ideas worth emulating here, but the Japanese success story is not a result of better tactical or technical skills as much as it is a result of a better view of what is important in management and a better appreciation of the human element. The Japanese believe in and are generally better at articulating all of the 10 quality leadership principles, not just the prerequisites. This observation is firmly and convincingly documented in two books on the topic: William Ouchi's *Theory Z: How American Business Can Meet the Japanese Challenge* and Richard T. Pascale and Anthony G. Athos's *The Art of Japanese Management*.[11] Theory Z is primarily the application of the basic values of McGregor's Theory Y to the organizational level. Unlike Theory Y, which details a set of management assumptions to guide managerial action, Theory Z speaks to a culture, a way of life that exists at the organizational level. Its building blocks are trust and loyalty to the organization, a commitment to one's job, and a sense of dedication that stems from an organizational philosophy that gives direction to organizational actions and provides meanings to organizational members.

Similarly, Pascale and Athos derive a theory of management that emphasizes heavily the cultural aspect of leadership and organization. They propose a framework consisting of seven dimensions: three "hard" (strategy, structure, and system) and four "soft" (staff, style, skills, and subordinate goals). The hard dimensions, emphasized heavily in American management theory and practice, refer to the basic organizational leadership and to management skills and techniques with which we are all familiar. They are the tactical requirements of leadership and constitute *prerequisite* leadership principles. By contrast, the soft dimensions are more cultural and humanistic and are more like the remaining nine quality principles presented in this chapter. Pascale and Athos note that the soft dimensions share *equal status* with the hard in Japanese management and in a number of successful American firms as well.

Both books derive their theories of excellence from studies of successful Japanese *and* American organizations. Although irreconcilable cultural differences exist between the Japanese and the American way, the successful American organizations studied had more in common with their Japanese counterparts than with less successful American organizations.

It is interesting that though much of the success of Japanese management is cultural, history tells us that modern concepts of management were introduced into Japan by Americans shortly after World War II. Indeed, Joseph Juran, an American management theorist, is often regarded as the father of Japanese quality-control techniques.[12] Juran was a consultant to Japanese management in 1954. One of the

---

[11] William Ouchi, op. cit., and Richard T. Pascale and Anthony G. Athos, *The Art of Japanese Management*, New York: Simon & Schuster, 1981.
[12] Norihiko Nakayama, "Using Japanese Quality Control," New York: American Management Associations and Technology Transfer Institute, Dec. 19, 1980.

pioneers in the Japanese quality-control circle movement was W. E. Deming. His involvement dates back to 1949. Today the Deming Prize is given to recognize outstanding contributions of Japanese quality-control circles.[13]

Our Tacit Understanding of Excellence

The Japanese evidence is impressive, but we do not have to look to successful Japanese management to corroborate or validate the 10-P Model of quality leadership. Enough evidence in its favor exists here in the United States, and indeed the best proof of the 10 principles rests in our own experiences and intuitions. Take a moment to recall experiences in which one group, team, unit, or organization of which you were a member, when compared with all others from you personal experience, was the highest performing. You might go all the way back to your teen years and recall a childhood or high school gang, or perhaps refer to your experiences as a family member, as a member of some social group or fraternity, your military service, or your experiences on a sports team or sandlot group. Perhaps your attention will focus more on the world of work, and you might recall some job you had, either recent or past, that included membership in a particularly high-performing group. Whatever the case, recall how the system operated. How did you feel about membership in the group? What made you work so hard? What accounted for your enthusiasm? Why did you enjoy being associated with the group? What was the system trying to accomplish? How loyal were you and why? How meaningful was your membership and why? Chances are pretty good that your analysis of this system highlights many of the quality leadership "P's" proposed here. Repeat this exercise, this time limiting yourselves to schools and work groups within schools with which you are familiar even though you may not have been a member. Recall the one most effective, most excellent, highest performing from among all your experiences with schools and school groups. Describe the system, what it valued, and how it worked. Take the time to sketch out some ideas on a sheet of paper. Again, compare your analysis with the quality leadership P's. You should find a remarkable resemblance between the two.

Debates over such issues as skills versus meanings or tactics versus strategy can be misleading. The issues of concern should be ones of balance and integration. It is clear that at present in educational administration and supervision, the leadership emphasis is not balanced but tilts too much in the direction of leadership skills and the prerequisite management techniques they suggest. Proper balance must be restored, for no matter how important instrumental leadership theories are, substantive theories are directly linked to excellence in supervision.

In bringing about a balance between the two, the function of leadership skills is not to stand alone or even to be "added in" but to be integrated into a larger focus. This integration is suggested in the following quality leadership equation:

$$QL = LS(LA + LM + LCE)$$

Notice that quality leadership (QL) results from the compounding effects of leadership skills (LS) *interacting with* leadership antecedents (LA), meanings (LM), and cultural

[13]Ouchi, *Theory Z*, op. cit., p. 264.

expression (LCE). In the 10-P Model of quality leadership is offered as an interdependent and interlocking network. Though conveniently sorted into four categories of skills, antecedents, meanings, and cultural expression, human resources supervision is the result of their integration in practice.

SUMMARY

In this chapter a substantive theory of supervisory leadership was presented. Substantive theories differ from instrumental theories in that they are concerned with leadership purposes and meanings rather than just processes. Strategic and tactical requirements for leadership were contrasted, and the 10-P Model of quality leadership (prerequisites, perspective, principles, platform, politics, purposing, planning, persisting, peopling, and patriotism) was proposed and explained. The model was examined in light of the human resources theorist and of current developments in Japanese management. The chapter concluded with an examination of our tacit understanding of excellence. Throughout the chapter it was argued that leadership skills are important to leadership quality but in themselves are not sufficient. The formula $QL=LS(LA+LM+LCE)$ was proposed to suggest that such skills need to be integrated with antecedents, meanings, and cultural expression as the art of human resources supervision is articulated in practice.

STUDY GUIDE

Recall the concepts and meanings associated with each of the following phrases and terms included in this chapter. Can you discuss them with a colleague and apply them to the supervisory context of your school? If you cannot, review them in the text and record the page number for future reference.

1. Leadership as cultural expression _____
2. Leadership meanings _____
3. Leadership skills _____
4. $QL=LS(LA+LM+LCE)$ _____
5. Quality-control circle _____
6. *Ringi* system _____
7. Strategic requirements _____
8. Tacit understanding _____
9. Tactical requirements _____
10. The 10-P Model _____
11. Theory Z _____

EXERCISES

1. Refer to the section on tacit understanding of quality leadership. How did you respond tacitly to leadership quality? How does this understanding compare with the 10-P Model of quality leadership?
2. Use the contrasts between strategic and tactical requirements of leadership as depicted in Table 11-1 to evaluate the emphasis on leadership in your school. Select a time frame of 1 to 2

weeks for your analysis. Keep a log of leadership incidents categorized into tactical and strategic. Which receives the greatest emphasis?

3. "What the leader stands for and communicates to others is more important than how he or she behaves given any particular set of circumstances." Prepare two statements, one in support and the other against this axiom. Share your arguments with one or two others. What would be a more moderate position one might take on this issue?

PART THREE

HUMAN RESOURCES AND EDUCATIONAL LEADERSHIP

INTRODUCTION: SUPERVISING THE HUMAN CURRICULUM

Parts One and Two of this book deal with the exercise of organizational leadership. They attempt to point out those supervisory behaviors that lead to self-fulfillment of all organizational inhabitants. Many behavioral dynamics described in Part One can be applied to actual instructional practices in the classroom. Granting that a school were now willing to adopt the supervisory processes described in Parts One and Two we must take up more precise educational concerns with which supervisors must deal. That is, what essential educational considerations should be uppermost in the supervisor's work with teachers and students?

While the authors propose a process of supervision that promotes the fuller development of all the human resources of the school community, they also assume that supervisors are concerned with more than process. That is to say, supervisors ought to have some ideas of their own about how education *ought* to be—how, for example, a good course might be structured, or how educational programs ought to nurture a variety of learning experiences. To be sure, the supervisor will not be the only source of ideas in the school. On the other hand, the supervisor ought to be working from some informed basic operational convictions about what constitutes good educational practice.

Assuming that human resources supervision is essential for developing a more humane school, what central ideas about the nature of human growth, the nature of learning, the nature of educational programs, and indeed the essential purposes of schooling will guide the supervisor? Without turning this book or a supervision course in which it might be used into a series of discourses on educational philosophy or curriculum development, the authors nonetheless believe that those preparing for or engaged in supervisory roles must articulate their convictions on these central issues. What follows in Part Three is a series of chapters that pose critical educational questions for supervisory personnel. Their responses may be tentative and open to modification by discussions and experimentation with their colleagues in the schools.

But supervisors should nonetheless develop some provisional principles by which to chart the course of their supervisory practice.

The questions posed in these chapters assume that readers have already been exposed to some treatments of the basics of curriculum development, learning theory, and educational philosophy. Our intention is to focus the reader's attention on some of the more important educational questions supervisors will face. There will be issues left out—for example, those issues relating to human development and the appropriate curricula for different stages of growth as outlined by Piaget, Bruner, Kohlberg, and Fowler.[1] Neither will we discuss supervising teachers and programs with a specialized focus, such as those dealing with special education or early childhood education. What is discussed in this section, however, would have relevance in that it touches upon some essential questions facing all supervisors.

Our contention is that supervisory behavior, whether exercised by a building principal, a department chairperson, a central office staff person, or a teaching colleague, is beginning to be seen as the locus for upgrading the educational achievement of a particular school. Individual teachers will take responsibility for continuing their efforts at improving program and instructional effectiveness. But supervisory personnel as individuals, and more so as teams, will be the key people in improving the whole school or the whole system's educational effectiveness.

To be sure, we have moved beyond the days when teachers were grossly underprepared in their own education for the tasks of teaching. In those days, the supervisor was expected to continue, through in-service and informal guidance, the education of those teachers. Today, teachers are better prepared than ever before. The tight job market has further squeezed out the less competent in the teaching profession.

Nevertheless, the schools as educational communities are floundering. Outstanding teachers are there in the school, but as a whole, faculties in many schools are being accused of not getting the essential job done. Supervisory personnel will be called on more and more to bring about significant improvement in the educational effectiveness of the whole school enterprise. If this is to happen, then people in supervisory capacities will have to roll up their sleeves and mobilize the talent, imagination, and enthusiasm of the faculty and help them pull together as a team, or as clusters of teams, to bring about schoolwide or systemwide improvements.

One of the perspectives of Part One of this book is that organizations and bureaucracies are not necessarily bad things. If one knows how they work, then one can use the organization and bureaucracy to do what they were set up in the first place to do. A school as an organization or bureaucracy brings together very talented and very committed people and brings together resources—money, learning materials, libraries,

---

[1] Jean Piaget, *The Language and Thought of the Child*, New York: Harcourt, Brace, 1926, *The Child's Conception of the World*, New York: Harcourt, Brace, 1928, and *The Science of Education and the Psychology of the Child*, New York: Viking, 1970; J. S. Bruner, J. J. Goodnow, and G. A. Austin, *A Study of Thinking*, New York: Wiley, 1956; L. Kohlberg, "Stages of Moral Development as a Basis for Moral Education," in C. Beck, B. Crittenden, and E. Sullivan (eds.), *Moral Education*, New York: Newman, 1971, and "Development as the Aim of Education," *Harvard Educational Review*, pp. 42, 449–496, 1972; James W. Fowler, "Stages in Faith: The Structural-Developmental Approach," in Thomas C. Hennessy (ed.), *Values and Moral Development*, New York: Paulist Press, 1977.

and labs—so that this organization can do what an individual teacher is unable to do. Yet teachers behave frequently as though they want as little to do with the organization as possible. Usually because of some hurtful or frustrating experiences with administrators, teachers become more and more individualistic. They set up their classroom as a private kingdom and work overtime to protect that private domain.[2]

That kind of individualism is necessary in a bureaucracy gone mad, and some large urban systems seem to be moving in that direction. Yet that very isolationism cuts the teacher off from the potential enrichment of her or his work by preventing the sharing of ideas and resources that a large system makes possible.

Supervisors, because of their positions between teachers and the higher-level administrators, can intervene and interpret for both levels. They can effect the sharing of ideas and resources both vertically and horizontally in the organization, which will enrich the educational environment. In our opinion, no other person is in a better position to do this. Hence our repeated claims, especially given circumstances in the schools today and in the future, that supervisory leadership is the key to improved educational activity in the schools.

As people with supervisory responsibility move into the contemporary arena of education, they will find educational purposes and programs of every shape and hue. In order to assist others in bringing clarity to their thought and work, supervisors will have to have some clarity of their own. They will have to have taken time to step back from the everyday concerns of the school and the classroom to develop frames of reference and basic operating principles that will guide and make sense out of their everyday experience. The following chapters try to develop some of these frames of reference and principles that would allow the supervisor to exercise educational leadership.

Chapter 12 locates the supervisor in the midst of controversies that daily divide or accentuate divisions between teachers and other school personnel, not to mention school boards and parent groups. These controversies deal with the purposes, organization, and curriculum of schools. Where does the supervisor stand on these issues, and how will that stance affect his or her supervisory practice?

Chapter 13 highlights the importance of the supervisor's *platform*—that constellation of assumptions and beliefs about children and youth, about learning, program development, school climate, and the purposes of schooling. Some sources for the development of a platform are suggested.

Chapter 14 suggests critical questions supervisory personnel need to ask about curricular programs and the environment of learning. In working with individual teachers, departments, or schoolwide curriculum committees, as well as school administrators, supervisors enjoy unique advantages for creative intervention and advocacy.

In Chapter 15, the question of student and program evaluation occupies center stage. The role of supervisors in assisting in the development of useful forms of student and program evaluation is developed.

---

[2]Cf. Ann Lieberman and Lynne Miller, "The Social Realities of Teaching," *Teachers College Record,* vol. 80, no. 1, 1978.

CHAPTER 12

THE CONTROVERSIAL CONTEXT OF SUPERVISION

When even slight cultural shifts are taking place in any society, they are bound to affect the education of the young. Changes in clothing style or work habits of adults will lead some in the schools to tighten controls lest the young be infected by the invasion of these subversive attitudes. Other educators will claim that youth must be prepared for changing times and therefore will openly discuss the advantages of these cultural innovations. We can, perhaps, recall with amusement the battles over women's voting rights or the early efforts of labor to unionize, and how many arguments raged in faculty lounges and school board meetings over the potentially good or evil influences these controversial changes would have on the education of youth.

Over the past two decades, however, schools at the local, state, and national levels seem to have been the center of controversy over a constellation of dramatic shifts in our culture. Integration, busing, teacher strikes and collective bargaining, lawsuits over student rights, drugs, the counter culture, prayer in the classroom, civil rights, and nonviolent social activism—these and many other easily recognizable phenomena have started debates and not a few riots, and have cost teachers and administrators their jobs and some students their lives. There is not a great deal that anyone in education can do about social and cultural shifts of this magnitude—to prevent, control, or resolve them. Most of them will be resolved or absorbed in a disjointed and haphazard political give-and-take between various groups in the community. Educators can play a part in this give-and-take, dealing with individual students or groups of students or their parents or adults in the neighborhood as problems arise. But educators do no control these cultural shifts and so, more often than not, are primarily in a reactive position.

ORGANIZATIONAL CONTROVERSY

There are, however, many things that educators, collectively and individually, do control. Class schedules, variable instructional space, variable grouping of students, variable staff assignments, budget allocations, weekly and yearly calendars, curriculum design, and pedagogy—these and other organizational variables can be arranged in a variety of constellations to serve a variety of purposes.

However, not everyone agrees as to the one best fit between all of these variables. The disagreement almost always goes beyond efficiency considerations to more philosophical opinions. Let us consider a few of the controversies, examine some of the underlying pros and cons, and then indicate some implications for supervisory behavior.

One basic controversy deals with the structuring of space in schools. What is the most appropriate size and setting for instruction? The structuring of space for instruction or for learning is found on a continuum from a totally self-contained classroom with one teacher to a totally open school or campus, with the larger community seen as a legitimate place for learning and instruction. In between these two extremes, one finds more variety: schools with self-contained classrooms for different subject areas, each equipped with its own instructional resources; some self-contained classrooms for some subjects and some open areas for other subjects, where students are freer to move around among different small groups or to work at different tasks; some schools with only open-space learning areas, but which are themselves self-contained buildings or on self-contained campuses; and some schools that have partially open campus arrangements on a regular basis for learning and instruction in the community.

Underlying the choices for one or another use of space for learning and instruction are some assumptions and beliefs about teaching, about learning, about discipline, about child and adolescent development, about a lot of things. These assumptions operate below the surface until someone changes the space arrangement. Then all kinds of charges are made: "Kids will waste time." "It will be too noisy." "I won't be able to take attendance." "Kids need to be working on the same thing together." "No, this creates teamwork." "Kids will spend all their time at McDonald's." These assertions may or may not be true. But they indicate how strongly people feel about such a seemingly simple variable as space.

And, indeed, they might well feel strongly about this issue, for it raises several other issues such as: If instruction and learning can legitimately take place in a variety of settings, then perhaps there are a wide variety of ways to teach and ways to learn; if that is so, then the stress on the relative uniformity of teaching and uniformity of classroom size and class times may be inappropriate and, indeed, counterproductive. But if there is no uniform model for teaching and no uniform setting for learning, then who is to say what *is* legitimate or appropriate teaching or what setting *is* legitimate or appropriate? And if we do not know the answers to those questions, or if we know that the answers are not *educational* answers but political answers, then what are supervisors supposed to do?

Supervisors were always thought to know what constituted good teaching; and, since their observations were always made during a traditional class period in a traditional classroom, they knew the best way to make use of *that* space. But what if there is no classroom as such to visit? What if the teacher being supervised is working in a very large, open-space room with four other teachers, and they interchange groups and teaching tasks and are always moving about this large room dealing with seven or eight groups of students of different sizes and different ages working on different tasks? How does the supervisor, using the traditional checklists, evaluate this teacher?

Suppose, for example, you are supervising a mountain-climbing project with 15 students. You are out in the mountains with them, hiking up narrow paths and clinging to cliff faces all day long. This is quite different from supervising learning activities in a biology laboratory. Imagine all the ways in which the style and method of supervising the mountain-climbing project differ from classroom supervising.

Or suppose you are supervising a wide diversity of "intensive education" experiences, which take the form of mini-courses. These mini-courses cover, unlike more standard courses offered in any large senior high school, field experiences such as working in orphanages, the city tax office, an architect's office, the water board offices. Are there uniform categories you could use to assess whether genuine learning was taking place in all of these field experiences? How would you validate these categories? What would be appropriate instructional strategies in each one of these field experiences?

Besides the fights over appropriate instructional space, other organizational controversies present the supervisor with further questions about his or her behavior. Assume that you are a new supervisor in an elementary school. Instead of traditional grade divisions, students are grouped in multiage, multigrade groups. This multigrade grouping or nongraded grouping is based on the mastery of certain skill levels, and promotion or advancement is not from one grade to another but from the mastery of certain skill-related tasks or constellation of such tasks to new learning tasks. Some students might achieve mastery and advance to another group within 1 year. Others might take 3 years.

You are accustomed to a more standard supervisory situation: one teacher in one classroom all day long. When you had post-class-visit conferences with your teachers in the other schools, it was fairly easy to point out strengths and weaknesses in that setting. But now, the teacher you are observing is dealing with learning-activity packets in small groups of students, giving 5 minutes of instruction, and then leaving the students free to teach one another and to work on their own as she moves on to another small group. Even to keep her in view, you have to move around the different configurations of movable partitions and bookcases that act as partial space dividers in the large room. Should you follow her around, trying to catch some of her oral instructions to the small groups? Should you sit in on one of the small groups after she has gone to see how well it is doing? Suppose the room is noisy. Is that good or bad? Some students leave the room without asking anyone's permission. What do you think about that? As you retreat to your office to prepare for your afternoon conference with this teacher, where will you begin?

When the conference begins, you discover that this teacher is part of a team working with a master teacher. Two of the other people in the large room were volunteer parents. This teacher's work was focused on a follow-up exercise to a multimedia presentation given by the master teacher that morning. After faking your way through the conference, you sit back and try to sort out all the questions chasing each other around in your head: In order to evaluate this teacher, do I need to evaluate how the whole team works? Suppose the master teacher is dull. How does that affect the reaction of the students to the other teachers? This teacher I've just spoken with had a very specific task to do—explain the instructions on the learning packet to each group. The two volunteers were to drift around and answer other questions and, when necessary, help a group work through the learning task. Now suppose this teacher is really good at giving instructions but weak in other teaching skills. How will he or she know that? Does the master teacher vary the tasks of the team? And the noise in that room! Can children actually learn anything with everyone talking like that and people getting up and leaving the room? Perhaps they can, but how do I find that out if teachers don't give out grades in this arrangement? Well then, how does one tell the smart ones from the dumb ones? Do kids get marked for effort or only for achievement?

Anyway, the teacher seemed pleased that you visited her learning area. She said that you were the first one to observe her teaching in the 3 years since her first teaching assignment. Now, what is your next move?

This hypothetical situation is closer to reality for more and more supervisory personnel. With diversification of staff roles, no one person is the supervisor in a school, nor is one uniform method applicable to such diversified staff roles. With diversification of instruction settings, a standard supervisory process can no longer be uniformly applied to each setting. With diversification of pacing and grouping (multiability, multiage, large-small, etc.) and instructional strategies designed for different learning styles, learning packages, or diversified contracts, and with more and more emphasis on individualized learning and education by appointment, it becomes clear that supervisory personnel, at whatever level, have to be extremely flexible and adaptive in trying to assess where the real learning might be taking place.

Not only does the supervisor need flexibility, he or she also requires a discriminating sense of judgment. Simply because schools have developed more complex and diversified organizational structures, processes, and programs does not mean that "anything goes." Being a supervisor does not mean accepting any type of activity, no matter how sloppy or disorganized, as legitimate educational activity under the rubric of experimentation or "field education" or individualized learning. Unstructured, unsupervised, aimless "free time" during the class day may be called "independent study," but sometimes that means a few extra hours for teachers to sip coffee in the faculty lounge and a few extra hours of playtime for students. Some free play is certainly appropriate for students of any age. But don't label that time with some grandiose title such as "advanced research time" or "independent exploratory module for creative inquiry" (in the daily schedule abbreviated to IEMFCI). In other words, the supervisor should exercise discretion in deciding whether some teacher and student activities are as appropriate as others. Sixty percent of the school day devoted to free play, for example, would seem unacceptable under normal conditions. Granted that there are exceptions to every general rule of thumb; nonetheless, the supervisor has to be able to say "no" to certain proposals or activities. In themselves they may be worthwhile, but at a given time and place, they may be less appropriate educational activities than others.

This leads to the sticky question of the basis for decision making. Assume that you are supervising a group. Frequently the group will choose to make the decision. They will agree unanimously to do something a certain way, and you agree with their decision. Sometimes the group is not clear which decision to make. You as supervisor take them through a problem-solving exercise, and they then see what the solution should be. Sometimes, however, the group will be divided on a decision, but the decision must be made. They agree to abide by your decision as long as you can give some reasons for your decision. That situation arises frequently in a school setting. And that situation calls upon you to decide on your strongest convictions as an educator.

As was said in the chapters on leadership, leadership through supervision requires a vision of what is possible, a belief about what is best or better in educational activities, a clear view of the purposes of education, and a willingness to stand by those convictions. Having convictions as a supervisor does not mean that one imposes them autocratically on one's subordinates. A person can have convictions and respect the convictions of others who disagree. Neither does having convictions about purposes and activities in education imply a necessary disdain for research and experimentation. Without some provisional convictions about what is important in education, however, a supervisor's interaction with subordinates turns to jelly; it becomes dominated by the wishes or convictions of the subordinates or by the least common denominator among their convictions. Supposedly, one gets appointed to supervisory roles because of some demonstrated competence as an educator, competence that flows out of a sense of purpose. One does not surrender that sense of purpose when moving into a supervisory position. Instead, that sense of purpose can be the key source of the supervisor's effectiveness.

CURRICULUM CONTROVERSY

Besides various controversies surrounding the efficacy of various organizational arrangements in the school, supervisory practice takes place amidst the crosscurrents of curriculum controversies. For the sake of clarification we will consider three sets of arguments going on in almost any school. Protagonists or debaters will not usually fit into one camp exclusively on every issue. The position or point of view is seldom proposed in its pure form; it is more a question of emphasis. By highlighting each position or school of thought in what follows, however, we wish to provide the prospective supervisor with some analytical lenses for interpreting why educators espouse some educational activities and oppose others. We also wish to challenge the readers to examine their own convictions. Where do they stand on these issues? How will their supervisory behavior be influenced by their convictions? What supervisory style will be most consistent with each of the differing schools of thought?

We will group the controversies in three sets of arguments:

Arguments between behaviorists and humanists

Arguments between those advocating a child-centered program and those advocating a society-centered school

Arguments between academicians and moralists

By lumping many positions together in paradigmatic groups or schools, we are obviously overlooking their many and varied nuances. We do so only to emphasize, by oversimplification, some of the larger differences between the various groupings. It is our belief that none of the six schools in their pure form provides sufficient basis for a total educational program. It would be difficult to find a school anywhere that reflected only one of the six positions. Neither could one find any theoretician who would advocate any one of the six positions in a pure form.[1]

Behaviorists versus Humanists

Two competing groups of thinkers and educators who have influenced both teaching methodology and program design can be listed as behaviorists and humanists. The scholars in both schools express a variety of points of view, but they clash on essentials. The behaviorists attempt to establish empirically verifiable links between teacher-student interaction, prescribed course sequences, and logical and rationally definable states of knowledge or student learning. In contrast, the humanists insist that personal, moral, aesthetic, and intellectual development involves internally dynamic processes of growth far more complex than the mechanistic, stimulus-reinforcement model of the behaviorists. The behaviorists are concerned much more with statistically valid research on the improved effectiveness of instruction in reaching predefined cognitive under-standings and skill levels. The humanists reply that reality is too multidimensional to be treated in this reductionist fashion. They contend that learning, as it relates to the total developing consciousness of the individual, is too multidimensional and idiosyncratic to be profitably analyzed by limited statistical correlations, which cannot capture the simultaneous and preconscious nature of learning that is continuously taking place. And even if the behaviorists could analyze learning behavior at this complex level through computerized measurement of multiform simultaneous responses that children have to instructional exercises and curricular materials, the humanists would consider this an unneccessary proof of the unique individuality of every student, which they hold to be self-evident already.

Some behaviorists, like Benjamin Bloom, do not appear to be as narrow-minded as some humanists might think they are. Instead, they have taken a rather hardheaded approach to learning and seem to be saying, "Look, I can't study everything all at once; instead, I am trying to take a look at the possibility of children mastering some skills and basic understandings. Yes, probably, there *are* any number of other variables involved in learning, and there is more complex learning going on all the time inside students. But there are some students who don't acquire mastery of even some very basic skills that form the building blocks for more complex learnings—skills such as the use of language syntax and reading. I'm trying to discover effective ways to promote mastery at least in these areas. Our research seems to show that if you alter the time requirements, improve instructional communications, and specify precisely what it is you are trying to get students to do so that *they* know when they're making progress, we can demonstrate cognitive and emotional growth."[2]

With that kind of interpretation, the humanists can have very little to argue with,

---

[1]Much of what follows dealing with these six competing schools of thought is adapted from Robert J. Starratt, "Curriculum Theory: Controversy, Challenge, and Future Concerns," in William Pinar (ed.), *Heightened Consciousness, Cultural Revolution and Curriculum Theory,* Berkeley, Calif.: McCutchan, 1974, pp. 17–23. Reprinted by permission of the publisher. A differently nuanced treatment of conflicting positions in the curriculum field can be found in Elliot W. Eisner and Elizabeth Vallance (eds.), *Conflicting Conceptions of Curriculum,* Berkeley, Calif.: McCutchan, 1974.

[2]Cf. Benjamin S. Bloom, "An introduction to Mastery Learning Theory," presented at the AERA Symposium entitled "Schools, Society, and Mastery Learning," New Orleans, Feb. 28, 1973, as part of the Proceedings of the AERA Annual Meeting. See also James H. Block (ed.), *Mastery Learning: Theory and Practice,* New York, Holt, 1971.

as long as the behaviorists do not then universalize or absolutize their research findings as the *one* or *complete* explanation of all human learning, or claim that their definitions of specific behavioral outcomes encompass the whole range of possible or desirable learning outcomes.

Nor is the charge that behaviorists are concerned with mere training as opposed to education entirely fair. Again, it depends on whether the behaviorists will admit that they have carved out a limited domain of the educational enterprise while insisting that their work deserves attention as *at least one way* of approaching some *fundamental* learning problems. The willingness to leave their effort open to the judgment of empirical evaluation, moreover, is often more than can be said for the proposals of some humanists.

Humanists, in differing from behaviorists, tend to affirm human spirit, higher forms of intelligence, imagination, creativity, and feeling as well as lower-level intellectual activities as legitimate components of learning activities. Learning that involves interpersonal relations, self-image, creative expression, exploration of feelings, discussions of conflicting values—all of these—must be relatively open-ended types of learning, the results of which cannot be preprogrammed. *Man: A Course of Studies* would be an example of a humanist, rather than a behaviorist, type of curriculum.[3] The behaviorist would criticize this curriculum because the course objectives were not specified in terms of student behavior and because the organization of the lessons is not logically linked together in a sequence in which each lesson builds on the concepts and skills developed in the previous lesson.

Whether one exercises a supervisory role from the central office or in a classroom, one's convictions about the issues of this debate will color one's behavior. As a teacher supervising student learning activities, will you insist on carefully articulated student learning objectives? Will they *all* be spelled out in empirically observable and behaviorally specific detail, or will some be more general or open-ended? If you are a department chairperson supervising the teaching of the members of your department, what pedagogical principles will you insist on, if any? And what will your approach be to your own supervisory behavior—will your own supervisory goals be spelled out in observable activities? If you have strong convictions about the efficacy of behavioral objectives, how will you deal with teachers who have equally strong convictions about humanistic pedagogy? Consensus-building exercises may carry you only so far, and then the philosophical convictions may sharply diverge.

Personal Freedom versus Social Adaptation

Another dispute, which has continued for years and is still continuing, involves those who would focus primarily on the individual personal freedom of the student, and those who would focus on social adaptation and citizenship. The heavy emphasis by some on individualized instruction, on letting the student choose when and what he or she will study on the basis of his or her own interests and curiosity, tends to relegate social requirements such as cooperation with legal structures and parental authority to the background. On the other hand, those who argue for social adaptation and the

---

[3]Cf. Elliot W. Eisner's analysis of this curriculum in Elliot W. Eisner and Elizabeth Vallance (eds.), *Conflicting Conceptions of Curriculum*, Berkeley, Calif.: McCutchan, 1974, pp. 193–200.

development of good citizenship can appear to minimize attention to the need for personal freedom of conscience, for affective relationships, and for individual self-fulfillment.

We can perhaps evaluate the argument by pointing to the philosophical roots of these differing points of view.[4] The personal-freedom group seems to side with the philosophical position of Jean Jacques Rosseau. Rousseau, with his "noble savage" concept of man, conceives of man as inherently good, noble, and innocent but as eventually being corrupted by society, its rules and regulations, its taboos and neurotic fears, its compromises, and its hypocritical social roles and mores. If parents, educators, government authorities, and other adults with power would leave children alone, children would naturally develop their healthy emotions of affection, trust, and compassion and a sense of justice. Many of these assumptions seem to be present in the writings of the personal-freedom group.

The social-adaptation group seems, on the other hand, to side more with the philosophical position of Thomas Hobbes. Hobbes considered man to be inherently selfish and aggressive. In order for men to live together in society with some kind of order and peace, individuals had to surrender, through a social contract, some of their own freedoms to the state, so that they in return, would be protected from exploitation at the hands of others. Although they do not put it so explicitly, the social-adaptation group seems to assume that society has the right to expect schools to indoctrinate youth into the requirements of adult life, to channel them into socially productive work roles, and to condition them for the responsibilities of parenthood, voting, material consumption, and middle-class social behavior.

To one who observes in passing the actual practice in large public junior and senior high schools, this conflict is sometimes glaringly evident. The social system of the school (the system of sanctions, discipline, rewards, rules and regulations, and legal and professional authority)—what some have called the hidden curriculum—is thoroughly Hobbesian in tenor, while the curriculum-instruction system is often based primarily, though implicitly, on Rousseau's image of man. Usually the social system within the school completely undermines whatever impact the curriculum might have in developing curiosity and free inquiry. Students grow cynical about teachers' exhortations to creativity and autonomy when they are forced to request a pass to go to the bathroom.

Ironically enough, we find someone like Jonathan Kozol bitterly criticizing the romantics who follow A. S. Neil in their efforts to promote freedom and spontaneity in youth. He does not disagree that these are ideals that in an ideal world would be worthwhile; rather, he claims that Summerhill-type schools are havens for the spoiled children of the wealthy, who do not have to face up to the harsh reality of an oppressive environment. Kozol's type of "free school," on the contrary, would provide a strict and demanding environment, for that is the only way the children of the poor can be toughened and trained to deal politically with the discriminatory use of power against them.[5]

The education-for-ecstasy people, the schools-without-failure people, appear to

[4]Regarding the philosophical positions, see John E. Longhurst, *Essay on Comparative Totalitarianisms: The Twin Utopias of Hobbes and Rousseau,* Lawrence, Kan.: Coronado Press, 1966.
[5]Jonathan Kozol, *Free Schools,* Boston: Houghton Mifflin, 1972; and Jonathan Kozol, *The Night is Dark and I Am Far from Home,* Boston:Houghton Mifflin, 1975.

speak from an upper-middle-class and utopian bias that refuses to acknowledge that the exercise of freedom requires *constant* political negotiation, or that there is a paradoxical principle operative in society—namely, that to ensure the basic freedom of individuals, laws, sanctions, and institutions must be established that by their nature, demand that the individual negotiate his or her behavior according to *their* ground rules and not his or her own spontaneous desires. As Schwab cogently remarks:

> A curriculum based on a theory about individual personality which thrusts society, its demands, and its structures far into the background or which ignores them entirely can be nothing but incomplete and doctrinaire, for the individuals in question are in fact members of a society and must meet its demands to some minimal degree since their existence and prosperity as individuals depend on the functioning of society.[6]

One can agree with the individual-freedom group's criticism of the misuse of authority, power, and laws in education without accepting the *abolition* of authority, power, and law: reform yes, deschooling no.

While cautioning against an exclusive concentration on individualized personal growth to the neglect of the complementary social-adaptation orientation, one must agree with Harold Shane[7] that what is presented in educational literature as teaching the democratic process reflects the *folklore* of democracy, not its reality as it is practiced in this country. Such naiveté among educators receives support from social theorists such as Talcott Parsons and his followers, who assume a basic rationality in their analysis of social dynamics.[8] Parsons seems to assume that decision making follows the logic of the scientific method and technological efficiency and that social change takes place primarily in a rational fashion.

A rather different perspective of social change and the art of politics, however, derives from viewing it through the conflict model. From this vantage point, social change occurs only when those who have less power confront those who have more power and, through legal and political strategems or through more aggressive means, wrest some of it away from them.[9] In our country, moreover, the concrete practices of our economic system seem to dominate government and politics much more than the ideology of egalitarian democracy does. Most Americans in their public lives are constantly engaged in power trade-offs and in highly competitive quests for personal gains, and will use every trick in the political game to attain those ends—egalitarianism be damned. Ask the critical thinkers among minorities what democracy means to them, and they will tell you it is the pious rhetoric used by the majority to cloak their entrenched opposition to increased political and economic equality for minorities.

Those interested in the social-adaptation goals of education, therefore, must strive for an honest appraisal of how free-enterprise economics has distorted the democratic

[6]Joseph J. Schwab, *The Practical: A Language for Curriculum,* Washington, D.C.: National Education Association, Center for the Study of Instruction, 1970, p. 23.

[7]Harold G. Shane, "Looking to the Future: Reassessment of Educational Issues of the 1970's," *Phi Delta Kappan,* vol. 54, no. 5, p. 332, January 1973.

[8]Talcott Parsons, *Essays in Sociological Theory,* New York: Macmillan, 1959.

[9]Ralph Dahrendorf, *Class and Class Conflict in Industrial Society,* Stanford, Calif.: Stanford, 1959; Paulo Freire, *Pedagogy of the Oppressed,* New York: Herder & Herder, 1970.

ideals of this country. These educators need to be more aware of the need for constant reformation of the political process to protect the rights of all segments of our society. The personal-freedom group very seldom alludes to the need for young adults to act responsibly as *citizens,* to promote the welfare of all members of the community, to engage in an ongoing reform of the political process. The wealthy, perhaps, can withdraw into a private world to tend to their health gardens and frivolities, but schools should not contribute to a withdrawal of the majority of citizens from active participation in the political process.

Supervisors frequently find this conflict impinging on their workday. The vice-principal in charge of discipline is usually after younger teachers who do not hand in attendance records. He or she comes to you, the supervisor, asking you to "straighten these teachers out." At the same time, you recognize the importance of a teacher's gaining the trust of the children. They may need some time to work out a system with the children that conforms to school regulations but that does not put the teacher in the role of police officer. Other teachers may need some firm advice about their blatantly unprofessional attitudes toward a reasonable concern for order. The supervisor cannot take a different position on this issue every day. Rather, the supervisor needs to take the leadership in getting these conflicting positions out in the open and helping the faculty and administration develop realistic policies that all can accept and live by.

Academicians versus Moralists

Finally, a third major conflict in the schools takes place between academicians and moralists. The academicians tend to come from within the classical liberal arts tradition and would promote hardheaded intellectual rigor, logical rationality, and concentration on the traditional disciplines, such as the natural and social sciences and the humanities. The moralists would claim that education's primary task is to build character and maturity and to build virtuous and healthy men and women, and that schools should therefore engage students, by example and by practice, in efforts to clarify and appreciate values, to develop heroic and altruistic attitudes, and to accept responsibility for their personal and public lives.

The academicians have always found champions among college and university professors, from the Committee of Seventeen to the promoters of the "structures of the discipline" of the last decade. The great headmasters of the private Ivy League prep schools, as well as progressive educators of the twenties and thirties who talked about "educating the whole child," and, more recently, people such as Carl Rogers or Arthur Foshay or Lawrence Kubie, could broadly be considered in the moralist school. To make their point about the questionable exclusive concentration on the academic disciplines, the moralists can point to what Kubie calls "the idiot-savant, a man who is a scholar in his field, but humanly speaking an ignoramus. . . ."[10] The academicians counter that their job is not to play baby-sitter, handholder, or amateur counselor, but that the

[10]Lawrence S. Kubie, "Research in Protecting Preconscious Functions in Education," in Harry Passow (ed.), *Nurturing Individual Potential,* Washington, D.C.: Association for Supervision and Curriculum Development, 1964, p. 31.

primary purpose of schooling is to develop the mind and an appreciation for human achievements in the scholarly and cultural fields—let parents, psychologists, and clergymen look to the moral development of youth. Foshay seems to strike a healthy balance in his curriculum proposals for the seventies, although he does seem to promote the naive concept of democracy, based on the folklore of democracy, mentioned earlier.[11]

Once again, supervisory personnel can easily get caught in this crossfire. Having counseled a teacher that a certain book was acceptable for supplementary reading, you may find yourself embroiled in a controversy with the school board, which claims that the book is dangerous to the morals of the children. Or, you may tear your hair out trying to convince a teacher that she or he needs to spend time after class talking with a student who is having a particularly difficult time at home with alcoholic parents. The teacher, on the other hand, may insist that if the child were *really* interested in learning compound sentence structure, she would not let the unpleasantness at home get in the way.

Again, the supervisor needs to be clear about his or her own beliefs on this issue. These will obviously influence the ways in which certain behavior of subordinates is perceived, valued, and rewarded.

SUMMARY

In this chapter we have attempted to situate the supervisory process in a realistic educational context. Anyone in a supervisory position in schools or school systems will be expected to take a stand on some fundamental organizational and curricular issues. Taking a stand on issues, however, does not mean autocratically imposing those positions or beliefs on subordinates. Rather, the supervisor's own clarity on the pros and cons of a controversy should enable subordinates to reach some agreement about their behavior.

Some controversies involve organizational aspects of the school, such as space and time utilization, diversified groupings, open classrooms, weekly and yearly calendars, and diversified staffing. Any one of these organizational variables can drastically affect the style and methodology of supervisory behavior. Some organizational changes will call for totally new supervisory strategies for educators.

Other controversies revolve around the school purpose and curricular emphases. Various proponents of one position or another can be grouped—though awkwardly in many instances—into arguing camps: the behaviorists versus the humanists, the personal-freedom advocates versus the social-adaptation advocates, and the academicians versus the moralists. Supervisors will act differently in their relationships with subordinates depending on where they stand on these issues. Frequently, supervisors will be called upon to negotiate between different factions in the school that cannot resolve their differences on these issues. By being able to clarify what some of the underlying assumptions are behind these different positions, the supervisor may enable

---

[11]Arthur W. Foshay, *Curriculum for the 70's: An Agenda for Invention,* Washington, D.C.: National Education Association, Center for the Study of Instruction, 1970.

people in the school to come to some working agreements about what will be acceptable behavior of teachers in the school.

STUDY GUIDE

Recall the concepts and meanings associated with each of the following phrases and terms included in this chapter. Can you discuss them with a colleague and apply them to the supervisory context of your school? If you cannot, review them in the text and record the page number for future reference.

1. Academicians _____
2. Behaviorist views _____
3. Curriculum controversy _____
4. Humanist views _____
5. Moralists _____
6. Organizational controversy _____
7. Personal-freedom views _____
8. Social-adaptation views _____

EXERCISES

1. What is the basic difference between an organizational controversy and a curriculum controversy?
2. As a teacher who supervises student learning, how would your supervisory behavior differ between *(a)* supervising a biology laboratory and *(b)* supervising a 3-day mountain-climbing expedition with the students?
3. Role-play the situation on page tk, with the roles of teacher, vice-principal for discipline, and supervisor all holding conflicting organization and curriculum positions.
4. Analyze three controversies during the past 2 years that have taken place in the schools in your state or hometown, according to the organization or curriculum distinctions of this chapter. Then list the implications, if any, for supervisory personnel.

CHAPTER 13

THE SUPERVISOR'S EDUCATIONAL PLATFORM

Supervisory personnel can expect to face a wide variety of educational settings in today's schools. Even within the same school system, one can find traditional schools and highly innovative schools. Because of strongly felt expectations about education in the community, many school systems have purposely designed a variety of programs and settings in order to provide families with clear options for the education of their children. Educators moving between or within school systems will be required to shift gears and adjust, for example, to different systems of discipline, grading, scheduling, and class grouping. Supervisory personnel, therefore, must develop versatility in their methods of supervision in order to match their methods to the educational setting.

This increased demand for versatility can be very unsettling. Supervisors accustomed to one method of supervision that seems effective in one particular school setting may have so identified sound pedagogy and effective learning experiences with that one setting they cannot imagine any other setting being equally effective. Frequently one way of organizing a schedule or a system of grading or a mixture of courses is defended with metaphysical certitude as the only valid and effective way in which children and youth can learn. Or, among supervisors, one supervisory strategy assumes a rigid orthodoxy, and it is believed that this strategy must be applied to any and all educational settings.[1]

How, then, can one avoid either extreme of this dilemma? Does one become a total relativist, accepting any form, method, pedagogy, or school organization as being as valid as any other? Or does one choose one way as *the* one way to educate? Educators can easily get caught up in running battles with their colleagues, with parents, and with the school board on this issue as long as they stick to the *surface* realities. What is needed is some firm footing in principle. Some have called our often unexpressed constellation of principles a platform.[2] Just as a political party is supposed to base its

---

[1] Cf. Chap. 16 for comments about the new orthodoxy on teaching effectiveness.
[2] Decker Walker, "A Naturalistic Model for Curriculum Development," *School Review*, vol. 80, no. 1, 1971.

decisions and actions on a party platform upon which it seeks election, so, too, supervisory personnel need a platform upon which, and in the light of which, they can carry on their work. With a clearly defined platform, they can begin to take a position relative to educational practices, looking beyond the surface behavior to probe for the real consequences of a variety of school practices.

To talk about the educational platform behind supervisory practice, however, raises the question of authority once again. The synthesizing theory of supervision places great stress on understanding how mediating variables within the school organization influence the effectiveness, or output, variables.[3] This theory criticizes the "direct" approach of supervision, where, for example, a principal moves from desire for an innovation (initiating variable) to mandating of the attitudes, opinions, or competencies of the teachers (mediating variables). If now we advocate that the supervisor clarify his or her *own* educational platform, does this mean that his or her own platform will be imposed on the school?

On the contrary, if the supervisor is to draw out the genuine talent and leadership of subordinates as we propose in human resources supervision, the supervisor needs to know what his or her own basic opinions, values, beliefs, and principles are. Without any commitment to some basic educational idea, how can the supervisor or the subordinate develop some sense of direction as they work together to achieve their educational goals? Having a platform of one's own does not necessarily mean that the supervisor is the *most* knowledgeable instructional expert. Indeed, we propose that the role of teachers as instructional leaders should be supported, with supervisors exercising more managerial or growth-inducing leadership. On the other hand, the supervisor can best assist subordinates in clarifying what their educational platform is or ought to be only if the supervisor has clarified his or her own.

To be more specific, then, what does an educational platform consist of? It consists of a series of assumptions or beliefs usually expressed in declarative, or sometimes normative, statements. These assumptions or beliefs deal with the way children and youth grow, with the purposes of schooling, with the nature of learning, with pedagogy or teaching, with educational programs, and with school climate.

In the previous chapter we examined what amount to platform positions on the purposes of schooling. These platform positions result in very observable structures, programs, and behaviors within the school. Classroom control, or discipline, for example, will differ considerably between schools and teachers who espouse the platform of social adaptation at the expense of personal growth and freedom and those who espouse the platform of personal freedom at the expense of social adaptation. Or to put it more clearly, when personal growth is defined as identical with social adaptation, then uniform compliance with school rules and regulations will tend to be interpreted as primary evidence that children's personal growth is proceeding on a schedule. Or in a school stressing academic achievement the reward system of grades, teacher approval, awards banquets, and so on, will focus on that to the neglect of recognition for achievements in other areas, for instance, those of social, moral, and personal growth. Frequently, a supervisor may encounter a policy dispute that actually

[3]Cf. Chap. 10.

stems from a conflict between the administration's platform position on the purposes of schooling and that of teachers, or between platform positions of teachers on the same faculty.

One way of bringing such conflicts into the light for rational discussion is for the supervisor to clarify the assumptions and beliefs that lie behind these disagreements. Normally, such discussions disclose the legitimacy of the other point of view and lead toward a more balanced integration of competing platforms. In other words, the supervisor can bring people out of their entrenched positions, dissolving "either-or" thinking and opening the way to a "both-and" platform position that allows for a differentiation that complements rather than excludes other points of emphasis.

What follows are three examples of at least partially developed platforms. They tend to focus on the primary emphasis of the platform. The first example places the central focus of the platform on the individual student and her or his growth in the schooling process. The second example exhibits an emphasis on predetermined learnings. The third example highlights the socialization function of the school.

HUMAN GROWTH PLATFORM

1. The student is unlike input factors in system designs of industrial or military organizations, for instance, a piece of steel that arrives at the "input station" all neatly measured and stable. Steel, wood, and stone do not grow and change during the very time when the production worker is trying to manipulate them. Students do.

2. The school makes a difference in a child's growth, but not *that* much difference. If the school were nonexistent, other influences and experiences would "educate" the child. Besides, human beings are dynamic and constantly growing. The school simply speeds up the growth process and channels it in supposedly beneficial directions, rather than leaving the student to random, trial-and-error growth.

3. Curricular-instructional programs should be designed in conformity to the growth patterns of students. The human growth needs of students should never be subordinated to objectives dictated by the needs of society and the demands of the disciplines. Theoretically, these three concerns—human growth, achievement of disciplined skills and knowledge, and fulfillment of social responsibilities—should not be in conflict. In practice, however, they frequently are in conflict, and the concern for human growth usually is the one to be sacrificed.

4. The educator's primary function is to become obsolete. The job of the educator is to so influence students that the students will gradually but eventually reach the point where they do not need the teacher, where they can pursue their own learning on the basis of their acquired knowledge and skills.

5. *Active* pursuit of knowledge and understanding, an actual dialogue with reality, will produce the most significant and long-lasting types of learning. Whenever possible, therefore, the student must actively search, actively inquire, actively discover, and actively organize and integrate. The teacher's job is to guide and direct this activity toward specified goals.

These five basic assumptions place the individual student at the heart of this platform. In order to clarify this platform, the following diagrams attempt to sketch in broad strokes a picture of this growing human being.

Figure 13-1 attempts a rudimentary, three-dimensional model of growth that emphasizes the individual's gradual increase in freedom to explore his or her world. Initially, the behavior of infants is almost entirely dominated by their biological needs, such as needs for food, warmth, sleep, and basic sensory stimulation. As these needs are regularly taken care of, and as infants become able to provide for these needs themselves, they have more time and energy to seek more complex sensory stimulation and to move away from purely self-centered concerns toward whatever makes up their environment. Their environment, they discover quite early, is made up of people and things. Animals populate their early "people world," but gradually they, too, become part of the nonhuman world. The exploratory behavior of infants is called *reality-oriented behavior* because through it, they move toward discovering things and people in their *own* right and not simply as gratifiers of their physical needs. As they move toward things and people in their own right, infants discover that reality is quite complex—that they have to deal with each situation and each person in different ways at different times.

As individuals mature physically, they discover that they can, and are expected to, manage many of the things that parents and siblings provided in their infancy, such as feeding, washing, dressing, returning toys to the toy closet, and so forth. Moreover, they are allowed more freedom to explore their environment, first outside their crib and playpen, then outside the house, and eventually outside the neighborhood. This

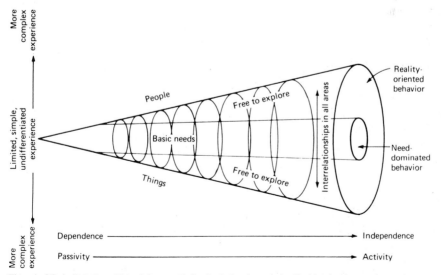

Figure 13-1 Relationship of free activity to behavior controlled by basic needs.

pattern of continued movement away from dependency toward independence to interdependence, and from passivity to increased activity, is basic to the process of maturing, of becoming a developed human, and this process involves both emotional and cognitive development as well as physical development. And, unless severe physical or emotional restraints are imposed on individuals, they will develop along these lines naturally. There is a natural internal dynamism in human beings toward this kind of growth.

Figure 13-2 attempts to indicate the development of habits, skills, and understandings that allow individuals the freedom to explore and participate in their environment. By mastering and internalizing any skill, individuals no longer have to consciously think about each minute part of the behavior involved in the performance of a skill. Rather, it becomes natural, like breathing or walking, and thus the conscious energies of individuals are freed to explore new areas of their environment, which they gradually assimilate into new skills, new understandings, and new interpretive maps of their environment. As they develop these skills and understandings, they are increasingly able not merely to explore the environment but to interact with it—to develop deeper friendships, for example, or to take on part-time jobs, or to solve problems in school assignments.

These basic learnings include social skills, such as learning appropriate manners for different occasions, learning something about sex, age, and authority role-relationships, learning to delay gratification in order to achieve a higher goal, and so forth. Other basic learnings involve physical skills, such as manual dexterity, visual and auditory perceptual differentiation, correct speech habits, athletic skills, and so forth. Besides developing symbolic skills, methodologies for inquiry, and attitudes and values, individuals accumulate a repertory of personal meanings. These are derived from experiences whose intensity left a lasting, and frequently highly emotion-laden, impression. Finally, the emergining self concept lies at the heart of the developing core of individuals and suffuses all of their accumulated learnings. Together, these elements of the developing core of the person determine the quality and degree of the freedom of individuals to participate in their human environment.

These growth processes can level off after a while, as the result of a variety of circumstances. Everyone is familiar with people who have stopped growing—who simply do not go beyond a certain point either in exploring their universe or in pursuing more intense human experiences. When people stop growing, their experience of their environment levels off, and they settle into a daily routine where things seldom change.

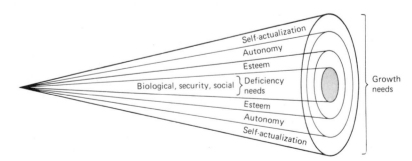

Figure 13-2 Developing freedom to explore and participate in the human environment.

Again, the stress of this platform is on the intrinsic dynamism of human growth. A corollary of this stress is that teachers should appeal to the natural curiosity of students, presenting them with exciting and imaginative learning tasks that will immerse the student in learning activity. Rather than continuously imposing the teacher's own agenda, leaving the student in a passive state while the teacher engages in the activity that the *student* should be performing, this platform emphasizes that the drive to learn and grow is already there in the student. This is not to say that the demands of the logical sequence of learning activities within a specified discipline of knowledge will be ignored. But much more leeway will be given to students to rummage about within the discipline of knowledge, frequently leapfrogging over logical steps to new insights and discoveries. Students can go back and fill in what they have left out; indeed, frequently they will come to recognize this need on their own. The emphasis is, however, on giving the students their head, encouraging them as they experience the excitement of the search or the puzzle. Obviously this leads to another corollary: the necessity of a highly individualized form of instruction, using learning-activity packets, exploratory projects, and expressive activities, and employing a variety of media adapted to different learning styles.

One can go on from this basic platform emphasis to postulate the kind of learning environment that this emphasis would require, including teacher-student relationships, student groupings, daily and weekly schedules, grading systems, learning materials, and so on.

BASIC COMPETENCY PLATFORM

1. The purpose of schooling is to ensure a minimal competency in prescribed skills and understandings for all children. Enrichment of students' learning beyond these minimum competencies is an important but secondary aim of schooling.

2. Schools can make a great difference in the achievement of these minimum competencies; people who do not achieve them end up as unproductive citizens living on the margin of society.

3. Present and future civic and employment demands point to the absolute necessity of acquiring basic competencies. Mastery of these competencies will assist the person in other areas of personal and social growth.

4. The educator's job is to construct an highly organized environment to promote the gradual mastery of basic competencies in reading, writing, computation, and scientific processes. This implies a careful definition of learning objectives for each major unit of an intentionally sequenced series of learnings, careful assessment of entry-level skills and understandings with built-in correction of start-up deficiencies, careful monitoring of student progress with built-in remediation phases, a requirement of mastery before moving on to the next unit, and a sequential progression to broader and deeper levels of mastery of the competencies as defined by graduation requirements.

5. Almost all students, except a small percentage of more severely handicapped children, are capable of mastery levels of learning in these minimum competencies, given sufficient time and appropriate instruction.

6. The most significant factor in learning is "time on task." This means that much of class time will be spent on drills and exercises that strengthen the target competency, that additional time will be afforded to those students needing it, and that daily homework will be assigned on the target competency.

7. While one approach to learning a competency may be initially stressed, alternative methodologies will be employed for students experiencing difficulty.

8. Higher-level learnings and cultural enrichment activities will tend to receive less attention, especially in the earlier grades, except for those students who have achieved mastery of the minimum competencies.

9. Classroom discipline will be controlled more by the intense concentration on the learning task than by teachers' imposition of punishments and repetition of rules.

10. All the reward systems of the school should serve to promote academic achievement as the highest priority. Rewards for other desirable behaviors or achievement should hold second place to this priority.

DEMOCRATIC SOCIALIZATION PLATFORM

1. The primary aim of education is to enable the individual to function in society. Assuming a democratic society, the school should promote not only those qualities necessary for survival (employment, getting along with people, managing one's financial affairs, being a responsible family person, etc.) but also those qualities necessary for a healthy democratic society (political involvement that seeks the common good, willingness to displace self-interest for a higher purpose, skills at community building and conflict resolution, an understanding of how the political process works and how to influence public policy, etc.).

2. The school should intentionally arrange itself so that learning takes place primarily in a community context. Students should be taught to collaborate on learning tasks rather than engage in competition against one another. Team projects, peer tutoring, group rewards, and discussion of community problems should have priority even while encouraging the development of individual talents. Individual talents, however, should be prized more for what they contribute to the community than for the exclusive enrichment of the individual.

3. Learning is best nurtured in a community context. Language skills are developed by regular and varied group communication. A sense of history and culture is nurtured by a focus on the group's history and culture. Psychological needs such as self-esteem and assertiveness are best met through active involvement in the community. Acceptance of differences and the development of individuality are negotiated best within a sense of belonging to a community. Values, laws, and social customs are best taught within the context of the community.

4. The educator stands within the learning community and yet holds a special place of authority. The educator facilitates and directs the learning tasks of the younger members of the community but allows the agenda of community dynamics to intrude on the more academic tasks when the need arises.

5. Teachers and students function best when they work in relatively small, relatively self-contained, relatively autonomous learning communities. Hence, those schools with large enrollments should be broken down into manageable learning communities that allow for closer and more continuous contact between a team of teachers and their students.

6. The curriculum should be controlled by a set of schoolwide learning outcomes for each year, but the learning community should have considerable autonomy in the ways it achieves these outcomes. The team of teachers should be accountable for promoting required learnings but should be allowed to devise the particular learning activities that best respond to the students in their communities.

7. Wherever possible, the learning communities should be involved with the large civic community through parental involvement, by using the civic community as a learning laboratory, by discussing problems in the civic community, and by promoting ideals of community service.

THE SUPERVISOR'S PLATFORM

In stressing the importance of the supervisor's explicating his or her own platform, we realize that it may or may not come out as clearly as the three contained in this chapter. On the other hand, the effort to elucidate one's platform is of primary importance to the supervisor's task. Without sufficient clarity on what one really believes is important in schooling, it will be difficult to assist teachers in clarifying what their educational platforms are. As we will see in subsequent chapters,[4] the process of clinical supervision we propose involves this clarification process. If the teacher is to profit from the interaction with the supervisor and to move clearly and decisively toward sharply focused growth objectives, then the effort at platform clarification, and perhaps at platform amplification, will be one of the supervisor's primary concerns.

What are some practical guidelines, then, that might assist supervisors to draw up their platform? First we will look at some of the key ingredients that should make up an educational platform and then add some that belong specifically to a supervisor's educational platform.

We can identify 10 major ingredients that should be included in any educational platform.[5] Using these as benchmarks, supervisors could identify the key elements of their own platforms and those of teachers they supervise.

---

[4]See Chaps. 16–19.
[5]We have been helped in identifying these ingredients by the categories used by Zvi Lamm in *Conflicting Theories of Instruction*, Berkeley, Calif.: McCutchan, 1976. We have modified these categories and the interpretation Lamm gives them, however. In his provocative treatment, Lamm attempts to expound the logic behind what amounts to three educational platforms. Unfortunately, in our opinion, he has so stereotyped two of them as to render his analysis inapplicable for our purposes.

1. The aims of education—Here, the treatment of the schools of thought discussed in the previous chapter would help to clarify where one stood in terms of one's emphasis. Here it would help to set down, in order of priority (if possible), the three most important aims of education—not simply education in the abstract, but education for the youngsters in our school system.

2. Major achievements of students this year—Bringing these aims down to more specific application, identify the major achievements of students that one deals with desired by the end of the year. (For example, some might put down mastery of some academic skills up to a certain level; others might put down the acquisition of certain basic principles that would govern behavior; others might put down more personal achievements, such as increased self-awareness or self-confidence, or trust and openness.)

3. The social significance of the student's learning—Here one might find that he or she emphasizes learning for entering the world of work; others might focus more on the utilization of learning for good citizenship; still others might focus on the acquisition of the cultural heritage of our civilization. This element may also draw a response that denies any direct major social significance to the student's learning because of a predisposition to view the individual in a highly individualistic sense.

4. The image of the learner—This element tries to uncover attitudes or assumptions about how one learns. Is the learner an empty vessel into which one pours information? Some may view the learner in a uniform way—as though all learners are basically the same and will respond equally to a uniform pedagogy. Some may use "faculty" psychology to explain how students learn. Still others will differentiate among various styles and dispositions for learning that point to a greater emphasis on individualization of learning.

5. The value of the curriculum—This element touches upon attitudes about what the student learns. Some will say that the most important learnings are those most immediately useful in "real" life. Others will say that any kind of learning is intrinsically valuable. Others would qualify that latter position and consider some learnings, such as the humanities or the school subjects to be intrinsically more valuable, because they touch upon those more central areas of our culture. Others would claim that the learning of subjects has value only insofar as it sorts out people of different abilities and interests and channels them in socially productive directions. Some might even claim that the curriculum helps youngsters to understand God better.

6. The image of the teacher—What basically is a teacher? Is a teacher an employee of the state, following the educational policies and practices dictated by the local, state, and federal government? Or is a teacher a professional specialist whom a community employs to exercise his or her expertise on behalf of youngsters? Or is a teacher a spokesperson for tradition, passing on the riches of the culture? Or is a teacher a political engineer, leading youngsters to develop those skills necessary for the reform of their society? This element tries to elicit assumptions about the role of the teacher.

7. The preferred kind of pedagogy—This element should be fairly clear. Will the teacher dominate the learning experience? Some assume that inquiry learning is the best way to teach. Others assume that each discipline lends itself better to some forms of pedagogy. Some would opt for a much more permissive, student-initiated learning enterprise. While there would understandably be some reluctance to focus on *one* pedagogical approach to the exclusion of all others, nonetheless, we usually tend to settle on two or three as the more effective approaches.

8. The primary language of discourse in learning situations—This element frequently concerns the levels and quality of learning involved.[6] Does the language focus on precision of verbal definitions or the precise measurement of phenomena, or does it rather stress imaginative relationships? Frequently the difference between the question "How do you feel about that?" and the question "What do you think about that?" reveals a basic orientation toward the kind and level of learning being emphasized. Frequently a metaphor that is used gives away some underlying attitude, whether it be concerned with exact precision, the moral use of knowledge, or artistic sensibility.[7]

9. The preferred kind of teacher-student relationship—This element involves the quality of interpersonal relationships preferred by the teacher and student. Some would prefer a very caring kind of relationship in which the "needs of the whole child" are attended to. Others would prefer much more distance, leaving the personal needs of the students for someone else to attend to, stressing more the academic discipline. Still others would be very nondirective, allowing the spontaneous, felt needs of the child to direct the relationship, with the teacher being more of a resource person. Others might prefer a group orientation in which the teacher works primarily to facilitate the work of the group.

10. The preferred kind of school climate—Here, some of the organizational considerations touched upon in the previous chapter would come into play. This element concerns a constellation of factors such as schoolwide and classroom discipline, student pride in the school, faculty morale, the openness of the school community to divergent lifestyles, expressive learnings, and individualistic ways of thinking and behaving. Some would opt for order and predictability. Others would prefer a more relaxed climate, perhaps more boisterous but also more creative and spontaneous. This element would be very much related to what is valued in the curriculum and to the social consequences of learning.[8]

It becomes obvious as one tests out one's assumptions under each of the categories listed above that there tends to be an intrinsic logic to them. That is, there tends to be a consistency between assumptions about the nature of the learner and the preferred kind of teacher-student relationship, which in turn relates logically to one's

---

[6]Benjamin S. Bloom, *Taxonomy of Educational Objectives: The Classification of Educational Goals, Handbook I: Cognitive Domain,* New York: McKay, 1956.

[7]Dwayne Huebner, "Curriculum Language and Classroom Meanings," in James B. Macdonald and Robert R. Leeper (eds.), *Language and Meaning,* Washington, D.C.: Association for Supervision and Curriculum Development, 1966, pp. 8–26.

[8]The material in Chap. 16 very much relates to questions about school climate, although there the focus is primarily on the classroom setting rather than the schoolwide setting.

beliefs about the aims of education.[9] As one clarifies one's assumptions, beliefs, and opinions under each of these 10 categories, the platform one uses in one's everyday actions in the school should begin to become apparent. That is to say, we usually make practical decisions about our professional practice as educators based upon convictions, assumptions, and attitudes which are not that clearly or frequently articulated. Nevertheless, they do influence, some would even say dominate, our actions. By bringing these convictions, assumptions, and attitudes out into the open for our own reflection, we can evaluate their internal consistency and cogency. We can also check whether we are satisfied with our platform, or whether, perhaps, we have not taken important factors into consideration. By clarifying the underlying rationale for our actions, we might see a need to grow in specific areas in order to increase our effectiveness as well as to broaden our human capacities.

Two other categories round out the supervisor's platform. That is to say, the above analysis of key elements in a platform has been dealing with an educational platform. This educational platform focuses on what one believes ought to happen in a process of formal education. It could belong to a teacher, a student, an administrator, or a supervisor. The supervisor can elaborate his or her own educational platform, but it becomes complete when the supervisor adds his or her convictions about how the activity of supervising is supposed to help such a platform influence the realities of a school. The two categories that concern supervision are the following: the purpose of supervision and the preferred process of supervision.

11. The purpose or goal of supervision—Some would answer from a neoscientific orientation. Others would speak from a human relations perspective. Still others would utilize the human resources rationale.

12. The preferred process of supervision—Some would express a preference for the clinical supervision approach.[10] Others would prefer a more permissive process that does not involve any evaluation or feedback but only periodic reports by the teacher on what is being done in the classroom.

Again, the point of clarifying one's convictions and unspoken assumptions about the nature of supervision is to open the door for growth, for the sharing of ideas, and for supervisory performance that operates out of a clear sense of direction. Ideally, these last two elements of the supervisor's platform should perhaps be written down at the beginning, before one reads this book, and then at the end, after one has read the book. If the analysis of supervision presented between these covers has an effect, it would show up in the differences between the two platform statements.

APPROACHES TO PLATFORM CLARIFICATION

Many supervisors may find the initial efforts at platform clarification very frustrating. It is not something they do often, and there can be a feeling of awkwardness. Yet

[9]Again, we wish to acknowledge Lamm's *Conflicting Theories of Instruction* as the recent reminder of the logic inherent in our educational platforms.
[10]See Chaps. 16–19.

everyone has an unexpressed platform. Were a sensitive observer to follow the supervisor around for a day or two on the job, it would be relatively easy to guess that supervisor's belief about how youngsters learn best, about what is important to learn, about good teaching and inferior teaching, and so on. Our actions usually reveal our assumptions and attitudes quite clearly.

Many will find the orderly process of filling out where one stands on the 12 elements of the platform the most convenient approach to take. The categories provide guidance in identifying the essential characteristics of one's platform. One can also check the internal consistency between statements under each category.

Others will prefer a less structured approach, letting their assumptions come out as they are felt and recognized, rather than having to force them into categories with which they are uncomfortable.[11] They will have a more difficult time expressing their platform, perhaps, but this approach may be far more rewarding for them.

Sometimes it helps to find a quiet place and to write down one's reflections. Normally, these will come out in a jumble, in no particular order of priority. Once we have written down the elements of our platform, we can with further reflection begin to group them in clusters and place them in some order of importance. Almost everyone with any experience in education, however, will feel several times during this exercise the need to qualify and nuance those general statements. "Which teaching strategy I'd use in a given situation depends a lot on a youngster's background. But by and large, I'd choose this approach." "While I'd place my major emphasis on mastery of basic intellectual skills, I still think it's important to spend some time teaching kids good manners." "I almost always prefer to start a lesson with a colorful advance organizer. That usually stirs up the pupils' curiosity. But there are times when I run plain, old-fashioned memory drills."

Others will find the writing exercise too tedious and will seek out a colleague to discuss this whole question. The free flow of shared ideas frequently stimulates the process of clarification. In those instances, having a tape recorder along may help for subsequent transcription of the conversation. Others may find a combination of dialogue and writing the better way. Still others may go to a formal statement of goals that the school or system has in print to begin the process. By studying the goals and *probing the assumptions behind them*, the supervisor may discover areas of disagreement or agreement.

COMPARING PLATFORMS

However one goes about clarifying his or her platform initially, two other steps will prove helpful. After the first tentative statement of the platform, the supervisor should compare his or her platform with those of two or three colleagues, to test out areas of agreement or disagreement. Sometimes this may lead to modification of one's platform. It may also lead to a greater acceptance of diversity of perspectives. It certainly will help supervisors to build teamwork. Knowing the biases behind one

---

[11]People in this group may identify with many of the sentiments expressed in William Pinar (ed.), *Curriculum Theorizing: The Reconceptualists*, Berkeley, Calif.: McCutchan, 1975. The authors there break new ground, using different categories to lend intelligibility to their educational platform.

another's approach will enable them to work together in areas where they agree or might complement one another.

When the supervisors have discussed their platforms together, they should then compare them with the school's or the system's platform. That may not exist in a written document, but, as in their own cases, it exists implicitly in the operational policies of the school or school system. Frequently, they may find some genuine discrepancies between what the goal statements profess and what the school practices. Bringing those discrepancies to light, in itself, would be a service to the school. The purpose of examining against each other the expressed and unexpressed (but operative) platforms of the school, however, is aimed more at a comparison between the school's platform and the supervisor's platform. If they find striking divergences between them, then the supervisors will have to seek some means of reconciling the divergences, or of modifying one or the other to make them more compatible.

The point of this exercise is not to introduce frustration and cynicism but on the contrary to reduce it. It may be that the platform of the school and that of the supervisor are incompatible. In our opinion, the supervisor should leave the school in that case, and go to one that is more compatible. But if the supervisor or supervisory group in a school or school system are to exercise their potential influence in upgrading the quality of education, then they must be generally in agreement with the platform of the school or school system Where that agreement exists, then supervisors can work with teachers and programs to achieve commonly agreed-upon goals. This does not mean uniformity in its oppressive sense. Rather, the supervisors can mobilize the talent and enthusiasm of the teachers, along with the technical support system of the school to move in an agreed-upon direction.

SUMMARY

In this chapter we have taken up the concept of the educational platform. When three examples of educational platforms were given, it became apparent that a platform is made up of those basic assumptions, beliefs, attitudes, and values that are the underpinnings of one's behavior as an educator.

Some time was spent suggesting ways in which supervisors could draw up their own platform. Ten essential elements to the platform were outlined, with two additional ones added for supervisors. With these as guidelines, supervisors can then begin to draw up their own educational platform. Again, the logic and basic intelligibility that flows from platform clarification to one's supervisory practice was stressed as the point of the whole exercise.

With this as a foundation, we can now move on to other concerns for the supervisor's exercise of educational leadership.

STUDY GUIDE

Recall the concepts and meanings associated with each of the following phrases and terms included in this chapter. Can you discuss them with a colleague and apply them to the supervisory context of your school? If you cannot, review them in the text and record the page number for future reference.

1. Basic competencies platform _____
2. Democratic socialization platform _____
3. Educational platform _____
4. Human growth platform _____
5. Mastery learning _____
6. Ten elements of an educational platform _____
7. Time on task _____
8. Two elements of a supervisor's platform _____

EXERCISES

1. Identify the assumptions behind the three platforms proposed in this chapter.
2. In your experience with teachers, pick out two whom you know pretty well and try to write down their platforms according to the 10 categories.
3. Identify an experience of conflict between a teacher and a supervisor where the conflict was rooted in differing platforms.
4. Write out your platform only for your own eyes. After you have completed it, ask yourself whether it would differ much if you had to show it to your superintendent.

CHAPTER 14

CURRICULUM CONCERNS FOR SUPERVISORY LEADERSHIP

The thesis of Part Three of this book is that educational supervision deals not only with the school as an organization but as an organization established for the purposes of education. Educational supervision, therefore, of necessity involves the supervisor in educational theory, in regard to both the general purposes of education and the means to achieve these purposes, the curriculum-instructional program. In this chapter we wish to summarize some of the more important issues supervisors face when, in their interaction with subordinates, they move into the arena of curriculum and instruction.

Curriculum has been often separated from instruction, or pedagogy, for purposes of analysis, research, and evaluation, as well as for professional course work in graduate schools. The supervisor, however, will most often encounter it in its living form, that is, embodied in the behavior of a teacher. Yet what the supervisor encounters in the instructional behavior of the teacher may not be immediately intelligible beyond a surface impression of the teacher's physical actions and interactions with students. Without some frames of reference provided either by the teacher or by his or her own study and experience, the observer may not be able to interpret the significance of the sequence of class activities, or why the teacher chose to introduce the topic in such and such a manner.

One way of attempting to understand curriculum and its influence in what goes on in the classroom is to review the textbook and other materials being used in the class.[1] Another way, which gets one closer to the reality of what one is supposed to be supervising, is to study the teacher's lesson plans, not only for that day, but for the classes that follow. While these two steps are helpful, the observation and analysis of the actual instructional activity lie at the heart of the activity of educational supervision. It is in this instructional activity that the supervisor sees the teacher putting into action the teacher's integration of his or her educational platform with the

---

[1]A helpful overview of approaches to evaluating curriculum materials can be found in Michael Eraut, Len Goad, and George Smith, "The Analysis of Curriculum Materials," University of Sussex, Occasional Paper 2, Education Area, 1975.

goals of the school, the goals of this course, the specific objectives of this particular unit or lesson, and his or her knowledge of the ability, interests, and personalities of the students in the class. All these influences are uniquely synthesized, integrated, and molded and then put into action in the teacher's instructional activity. Therefore, one observing that activity somehow has to be very sensitive to the intentions of the teacher to see how the activity of the teacher reflects this complex integration or synthesis. In other words, the supervisor must try to observe how the curriculum or the teacher's perception of it is, in fact, one of the controlling influences in what the teacher *does* in that classroom.

CURRICULUM-INSTRUCTIONAL ACTIVITY

The term curriculum has many definitions, as does the term instruction. For our purposes, we will define *curriculum* as that which the student is supposed to encounter, study, practice, and master!in short the stuff of what the student learns. That can be many things, from a basic skill such as counting numbers, to spelling 100 words correctly, to memorizing the multiplication tables, to understanding the biological explanations of photosynthesis, to playing the piano, to writing verse, to comparing Plato's *Republic* with Augustine's *City of God* in a doctoral dissertation. We acknowlege that there is always a hidden or informal curriculum being taught in the classroom as well as elsewhere in the school. But we wish here to restrict curriculum to the formal or overt curriculum.

Instruction we will define as that process by which the student is led to encounter the curriculum to the desired degree of mastery. Not only must the instructional process lead the student to the curriculum, it must so structure that encounter that the student does not move on to something else before a predetermined level of mastery is achieved. Instruction, then, can be something a teacher does, or it can be built into a programmed textbook or into a computer or a learning packet.

In general, we will speak of curriculum as "what is to be learned" and instruction as "how it is to be taught." One must be aware, however, that these are loose and pragmatic ways of speaking. To say that instruction means how something is to be taught can be misleading. For example, someone could say: "I learned that by hard work, by breaking that problem down myself into the small pieces until I could find where the loose wire was. . . . I taught myself how to do that." In that instance there was no external instructor. In a sense, the person instructed herself. Or perhaps the person had earlier learned a generalizable problem-solving skill that in turn taught her a way of attacking other problems. In that instance, what she learned (the problem-solving skill) taught her in subsequent experiences *how* to learn other things. For our purposes, however, we will use instruction primarily to refer to a process in which a teacher is interacting with a student.

OBSERVING INSTRUCTIONAL ACTIVITY

Now, let us suppose you are having a busy day supervising. You visit the classes of five physics teachers. You discover that each teacher is using quite different methodologies.

One teacher has his class divided into small groups and they spend most of the class discussing how best to go about studying the wave versus the particle theories of light. In another, the teacher is showing an animated cartoon that illustrates the different properties of light but concludes by leaving the students in a quandary over which theory of light is correct. In another class, the teacher is relating Newtonian particle physics to individualistic theories of society, and contrasting that with field theory physics and more communal views of society; toward the end of class the students get into a lively discussion of the low level of student morale and the prevailing tendencies of people at the school to "do their own thing." In the fourth class you find the students in the physics laboratory performing an experiment with a ripple tank, carefully following the instructions in their lab books and recording their measurements carefully in their notebooks. There is no class discussion; the teacher merely walks around the lab, occasionally pointing out a faulty measurement notation or telling one student team to stop "goofing off" or he will send them to detention hall. In the fifth class the students have been reading a biography of Isaac Newton and the teacher has assigned teams to prepare a model replication of Newton's laboratory. The class begins with the teacher questioning the students about the antecedent scientific knowledge to which Newton had access that might have shaped much of Newton's approach to his experiments.

You come back to your office at the end of the day with a half hour before you must leave to referee a basketball game in the league quarterfinals. Tomorrow you are scheduled for individual conferences with all the teachers you have observed today. Besides all the routine aspects of class management such as the lighting, ventilation, noise levels, pupil attentiveness, and so forth, what will you say about the approach the teacher is using, especially as that relates to the curriculum that is supposed to be taught? Granting the observable strengths and weaknesses of each teacher in putting on the instructional performance (self-confidence, good tone of voice, good use of questions, etc.), can you say that one approach was better than another? If you say none of the approaches is necessarily better, do you mean that they are all interchangeable, that it does not really matter which approach one uses? Or does each approach come out of a different idea of what the curriculum is or is supposed to be? Are these approaches mutually exclusive? Is the content learned in one approach totally different from the content learned in another? Or are there some common learnings one finds embedded in each approach? Is it fair, however, to give one departmental exam covering material taught in such divergent ways? How would these students score on a national physics test? Does it make much difference to you if the teacher does not care that much about national test scores? Before you begin to put some order into these bewildering issues, the bell rings and you must dash over to the gym to catch the bus for the basketball tournament.

Let us leave our distraught supervisor and return to our more dispassionate and reflective environment to put some order, sequence, and logic into this task. For example, what were some of the questions that did *not* occur to our frantic supervisor? It might be a good test of our own frames of reference if we were to pause at this point, close the book, and place ourselves in the situation, without the press of time and the basketball game distracting us. Perhaps we could generate 10 other questions of major importance. After we put them down in the haphazard order in which they occur to us, we might order or group them in some sequence, e.g., moving from the more abstract to the more particular, or from those dealing with curriculum to those dealing with student achievement, to those dealing with the teacher's platform, and so on.

OTHER QUESTIONS

An exercise such as the above will yield a variety of results. One salutary effect of going through the exercise and then sharing the results with others is that one quickly recognizes how many potentially useful questions there are. It becomes clear that classroom observation must be preceded by at least one lengthy conference in which the teacher can indicate what his or her intentions for the class are.

Our own first attempt to complete the exercise yielded the following questions. They are by no means exhaustive. We shall see subsequently that the kinds of questions we ask will emerge out of a variety of frames of reference about curriculum. But for the present let us consider the following questions for purposes of illustration.

1. *Methods and instructional effectiveness.* Are any of these five ways the most effective way to teach this? Is there another way that would be demonstrably the *most* effective way to teach that material? Suppose that the students might have had the opportunity to travel to a nearby government research lab doing interplanetary research on light signals? Or might the teacher have invited the director of the lab to come to the school to put on a demonstration lab, using all the latest sophisticated technology involved in spectroscopy?

Does the teacher always or usually use this method? If the teacher uses other methods, what are they? Are they related to specific curricular objectives, or are they used primarily to relieve boredom (which could also be a curriculum objective)?

2. *Instructional activity and curriculum-instructional objectives.* What is the teacher trying to do? Is the teacher trying to teach one thing or several things simultaneously?

What precisely is it that she or he wants to teach? Was that clear to you? Was it clear to the students? Why did the teacher choose this precise activity as the best or at least as a good means to bring the students into a learning encounter with the curricular material? In your judgment, was the means effective? How effective was it? Was it effective for all the students or only for some?

How does what the teacher is doing today flow out of what the class has been doing in previous classes? Is there a sequential order to the course, and if so, how does this part fit into the sequence? How much time does the teacher plan to spend on this matter of theories of light? To what level of mastery does the teacher wish to bring the students? Is the time being spent adequate for this purpose? Is that degree of mastery required to grasp the material coming later? Is there a balance between the time spent on this topic and the time spent on earlier and later topics? Who decides that? Who ought to decide that?

Is the teacher aware of the hidden, or informal, curricula involved in this approach?

3. *Curriculum-instructional units and departmental or school objectives.* How do this class and this course fit in with the departmental or school objectives? Is there a particular focus or emphasis to the objectives that each course is supposed to reinforce? If so, was there evidence of that reinforcement in this class? Why does the department or school support, or at least tolerate, such divergent methods of teaching? Are there specific objectives that are served by these differing approaches? Are these approaches the only methods encouraged in the department or school, or are there others?

4. *Methods and teacher-supervisor platforms.* How does this teaching method or approach fit with the teacher's platform? Are there obvious discrepancies between the observable behavior and the platform? If there are, are there legitimate reasons for the discrepancies? How does the teaching method fit with your (the supervisor's) platform? Are you aware of your comfort or discomfort, pleasure or displeasure over the fit or lack of it? Did these feelings, perhaps unacknowledged during the classroom observation, lead either to perceptions of only weak points of the class or perceptions of only strong points? Do you need to review your observations to weed out at least some of the bias that comes from your own platform?

If you knew nothing about the teacher's platform prior to the observation, could you infer what it was from the instructional activity you observed?

If you knew nothing of the teacher's class plan, could you infer what the primary instructional objectives of this class were?

If you knew nothing of what preceded this class, what could you infer that students already knew about the topic? What could you infer about their possession of skills and understandings necessary for learning the topic of the class?

By comparing your questions with these and those developed by others, you may begin to see some pattern or points of emphasis developing. But where do these questions come from, and why are they important? A little reflection will indicate that many of them come from our concepts or beliefs about the nature of learning, about what a curriculum is supposed to be, about the nature of the academic discipline, and so on. In order for the supervisor to know at least some of the important questions to ask, he or she ought to have some clear ideas about curriculum and how supervisors can affect its improvement or effectiveness in an instructional setting.

SUPERVISORS AND CURRICULUM DEVELOPMENT

Some commentators on supervisory practice complain that "supervision is like a honeycomb without the honey."[2] Supervisors tend to focus on the methods of teaching and not on the content of teaching. Supervision began primarily as inspection by administrators, and only later was it linked with curriculum development. While some curriculum specialists are involved with classroom observation and some supervisors are involved with curriculum development, the roles tend to be split. Curriculum developers tend to spend their time on the design and testing of curriculum materials.

[2]Daniel Tanner and Laurel N. Tanner, *Curriculum Development,* New York: Macmillan, 1975, p. 621.

Supervisors tend to spend their time on improving instructional methodology and organizational support services for improving instruction.

Because of increased specialization in both roles, especially in large school systems, it would be difficult in practice for the curriculum designer and instructional supervisor to merge their roles into one. There simply are not enough hours in the week to meet the demands of both roles, even if a single person possessed the knowledge and skills needed in each role. Nonetheless, we affirm that supervisors have an important role to play in curriculum development.

One can view curriculum development as taking place outside the classroom or inside the classroom. The curriculum specialist normally is freed from teaching responsibilities in order to engage in the research of available curriculum materials and to design units of curriculum for use by classroom teachers. From this perspective curriculum is designed and produced outside the classroom and is subsequently taught in the classroom. From another perspective, however, curriculum is developed inside the classroom as teachers adapt the prepared materials for classroom episodes of teaching. Teachers frequently alter, expand, rearrange, and reinterpret what the curriculum developer outside the classroom has prepared. Through trial and error, intuition, and responsiveness to the immediate circumstances of students, teachers are or can be involved in curriculum development in the classroom.[3]

In working with teachers in classrooms, supervisors can promote this kind of curriculum development. While curriculum development takes place at many levels (state, school system, school building, classroom), the actual curriculum ends up being what the teacher teaches. Taba and others have stressed the importance of teacher involvement in curriculum development.[4] Unfortunately, the information coming from the classroom back up through the levels outside the classroom does not get communicated or attended to that easily. Nonetheless, it is in the laboratory of the classroom that practical curriculum development occurs. By providing encouragement, supporting exploratory modifications of curriculum materials, and asking probing questions about the effects on students, the supervisor can play a part in this form of curriculum development. As we point out later in this chapter, the supervisor, because of his or her key position in the school organization, can also carry information and suggestions back to those responsible for curriculum design.

Even though supervisors frequently have not been trained in the complex technology of curriculum design, they should bring to their work some broad principles of curriculum theory and development as well as a sensitivity to the complementary educational objectives served by various curriculum-instructional systems. The remainder of this chapter highlights some of these broader understandings and principles of curriculum and their implications for supervisory practice.

---

[3]Numerous studies and reports highlight this phenomenon. Cf. Michael Fullen and Alan Pomfret, "Research on Curriculum and Instruction Implementation," *Review of Educational Research,* vol. 47, pp. 335–397, 1977; and F. Michael Connelly and Freema Elbaz, "Conceptual Bases for Curriculum Thought: A Teacher's Perspective," in Arthur W. Foshay (ed.), *Considered Action for Curriculum Improvement,* Alexandria, Va.: Association for Supervision and Curriculum Development, 1980.

[4]Hilda Taba, *Curriculum Development: Theory and Practice,* New York: Harcourt Brace Jovanovich, 1962, pp. 439–440.

DEVELOPING ALTERNATIVE CURRICULUM AND INSTRUCTIONAL STRATEGIES

One of the more refreshing innovations in teacher training appears in the work of Bruce Joyce and Marsha Weil dealing with models of teaching.[5] They have studied a variety of teaching styles, processes, and interaction schemes and have come up with over 20 alternative models of teaching. Each model has some theoretical underpinnings to it, has a recognizable sequence of activities and a major orientation or a set of educational objectives, requires a consistent type of classroom interaction and a type of support system, and has, finally, general applicability to either specific purposes or many purposes.

Each one of these models also presumes a curriculum. That is, the models of teaching are not concerned exclusively with methodology, but imply a curriculum, at least in a general sense. Frequently, a theory of learning is embedded in the model. In some of the models a theory of groups or of society is also implied. These models are touched upon here to provide the prospective or practicing supervisor with some mental maps or schemata for use with teachers or others involved in the instructional system, rather than to propose any particular model as the best model.

It is our belief that different models are applicable to the demands of different situations. In that sense, using one model or approach may be "better," not in an absolute sense, but in the sense of its being more appropriate to a given set of circumstances. If a teacher engages in instructional activity that remains always the same, there may be circumstances in which that activity is counterproductive for at least some, if not all, of the students. A teacher's repertory of instructional strategies may be larger, consisting of three or four, but even then the teacher may still lack the versatility to respond to given situations that arise in a classroom.

In like manner, a supervisor may be working with a limited number of models in mind. In a given situation where a teacher asks a supervisor for help in tackling a difficult instructional task, this lack of versatility will limit the instructional options that the two of them produce. Moreover, some familiarity with a wide diversity of possible curriculum-instructional approaches will render the supervisor better prepared for the unexpected. When the unexpected occurs, we usually react negatively, because it does not fit our categories, our mental maps. If, for example, we conceive of art education only as discrete encounters with discrete art forms, then we might be upset by an art teacher whose class is involved in "environmental" art projects in which several art forms and media are simultaneously employed. Familiarity with a broad range of curriculum-instructional options enables the supervisor to appreciate truly unique and creative approaches.

Joyce and Weil have grouped various models of teaching according to four basic families. These families represent different orientations toward the learner and reflect different educational objectives.

I. Information Processing Models
This family of models stresses the development of general intellectual abilities, logical

---

[5]Bruce Joyce and Marsha Weil, *Models of Teaching,* 2d ed., Englewood Cliffs, N.J.: Prentice-Hall, 1980.

reasoning, methodologies of academic disciplines, concept formation, problem solving, and methods of inquiry. Examples: scientific inquiry models, moral problem-solving models.

II. Personal Development Models

This family of models stresses the development of self- and interpersonal awareness, self-understanding and taking responsibility, affectivity, and creativity. Examples: awareness training, reality therapy, nondirective teaching.

III. Social Interaction Models

This family of models stresses the development of group dynamics skills; social, political, and legal problem solving; academic inquiry on social issues; and decision-making skills. Examples: role playing, group investigation, simulations of economic decision making.

IV. Changing Behavior Models

Based on principles of stimulus control and reinforcement, this family of models stresses changing of visible behaviors that include acquisition of academic skills, social skills, stress reduction, and self-control. Examples: programmed instruction, assertiveness training, operant conditioning and training.

Joyce and Weil point out that these families are not mutually exclusive. There is some natural overlapping among methods and objectives. Furthermore, activities based on some models can be used to promote or complement learnings targeted more specifically by other models. For example, the stress on developing logical reasoning and concept formation (information-processing family) could be used in group discussion of a social problem (social-interaction family).

Clearly, further study of alternative models would be called for in order for supervisors to be more fully acquainted with the power and the methods inherent in various models. Suffice it here to point out that supervisors can bring to their work with teachers a wealth of curriculum approaches, as suggested by the inventory of teaching models cataloged by Joyce and Weil. Depending on the objectives of any given class, supervisors can explore with the teacher the possibility of increasing his or her effectiveness by developing alternative instructional strategies. Moreover, the supervisor who is familiar with a wide range of curriculum instructional models will more readily recognize which of various approaches teachers are employing. The hypothetical case above of the supervisor visiting five classes that are all taking a different approach to the study of wave and particle theory should make that point sufficiently.[6]

ADVANTAGES AND DISADVANTAGES OF SELECTED MODELS

In this section we provide a more detailed comparison of five models of teaching typically found in elementary schools. The models, as proposed by Jane Stallings, are exploratory, group process, developmental-cognitive, programmed, and traditional-fundamental.[7] A comparison of the five models appears in Table 14-1. Each of the five models is discussed below.

---

[6]Cf. Susan S. Ellis, "Models of Teaching: A Solution to the Teaching Style/Learning Style Dilemma," *Educational Leadership*, vol. 36, no. 4, pp. 274–277, 1979, for a description of how a school system used Joyce and Weil's work for staff development.

[7]Jane A. Stallings, *Learning to Look: A Handbook on Classroom Observation and Teacher Models*, Belmont, Calif.: Wadsworth, 1977.

TABLE 14-1
GROWTH AND DEVELOPMENT OF CHILDREN IN THE FIVE MODELS

	Exploratory	Group Process	Develop- mental- Cognitive	Programmed	Traditional- Fundamental
Reading achievement		N+*		C+†	N+
Math achievement		N+		C+	N+
Nonverbal problem solving	C+		C+		
Questioning	C+				
Independence	C+		C+		
Cooperation with others	C+		C+		
Accepts responsi- bility for success	C+		C+		
Accepts responsi- bility for failure				C+	
Absence rate	C+		C+		

*N+ = better than national norms.
†C+ = better than control group in the Follow-through Study.
SOURCE: Jane A. Stallings and David Kaskowitz, *Follow-through Classroom Observation Evaluation* 1972–1973, SRI Project URU-7370, Menlo Park, Calif.: Stanford Research Institute, 1974. ERIC Accession no. ED 104 969, in Jane A. Stallings, *Learning to Look: A Handbook on Classroom Observation and Teaching Models,* Belmont, Calif.: Wadsworth, 1977, p. 237.

Exploratory Models

Exploratory models are relatively unstructured, informal, activity centered, and open. They are based on the belief that students are inherently curious and intrinsically motivated. Learning takes place as a result of explorations in a responsive environment. Learning centers, resource centers, and interest centers are important to this approach. Successful articulation of this model requires that teachers carefully evaluate the social, emotional, and academic development of each student, develop goals and objectives in each of these areas, and plan the environment so that growth is facilitated. According to Stallings:

> The expected outcome of this environmental approach is children who are self-motivated and who not only succeed in their efforts to solve problems but also recognize their own successes—that is, they are self-motivated, self-directing, and self-evaluating. They explore or play the game because it is self-rewarding, not because it pleases the teacher.
>
> Advocates also believe that children learn to solve cognition and social problems through the experience of solving cognitive and social problems.[8]

In this model, children are allowed to experience dissonance and conflict and are encouraged to search for alternative solutions. They are allowed to risk failure and

[8]Ibid., p. 61.

learn from the consequences of actions. Advocates of the exploratory model envisage a citizenry that is independent in judgment, creative in problem solving, and socially responsible.

Group-Process Models

Group-process models rely heavily on group-interaction methods whereby students participate to discuss and resolve issues proposed by the teacher and of importance to them. Coming to grips with one's perception of reality and building a sense of responsibility are typical concerns of educators who use this method. Students deal with such classroom issues as curriculum, discipline, and general governance as well as the more weighty issues that emerge from subject matter under study and from the broader community and societal context.

> Theoretically, children in the group process model could be expected to develop an ability to govern themselves and express their ideas and feelings. They would listen to the ideas of other people and judge the merit of the ideas. Members of the group would generate several solutions to problems, and through discussion foresee consequences of possible actions. Because they learn to listen to each other, the children would develop empathy for others (the ability to put themselves in another's shoes). Because they deal fairly with each other, they would feel self-worth and would gain experience in giving and receiving love.[9]

Group meetings are used on a regular basis as a means for teaching. Often role playing, simulation, and other group-process techniques are used. The group-process model is not sufficiently embedded in a set of curriculum ideas to establish it as an independent approach to teaching. Typically, the model is used as an adjunct to or within the broad framework of another model. The exploratory model and the developmental-cognitive model are natural companions for the group-process strategy, though presumably this approach could be incorporated into programmed and traditional-fundamental approaches as a formally distinct teaching option.

Developmental-Cognitive Models

The developmental-cognitive model of teaching, based on the theories of Jean Piaget,[10] assumes that a student's intellectual or logical thinking occurs in stages according to the student's age and experience. Students learn, according to the theory, through involvement in and manipulation of the environment. The teacher's role in developmental-cognitive teaching is to respond to each developmental level by providing appropriate materials and activities. The physical environment is rich with materials. Interest centers are used extensively.

> To implement this model it is essential that the room be arranged into several learning centers and that a wide variety of materials be made available to the children. The materials and equipment can be ordinary, routine items—they need not be purchased. For instance, a teacher might take the children on a scavenger hunt across the school yard. The children would fill their bags with items they found along the way: seeds, gum wrappers, sucker

[9]Ibid., p. 92.
[10]Jean Piaget, *The Origins of Intelligence in Children,* New York: International Universities Press, 1952.

sticks, paper clips, a leaf, a button, safety pins, stones. Back in the classroom, the children could arrange or classify their findings into categories according to color, shape, or whatever. Then they could play "What's My Set?" In this game, the children take turns guessing by what rules the others classified their objects.[11]

Programmed Models

Programmed models of teaching are based on the operant-conditioning theories of Skinner.[12] Basically, behavior is modified because desired behavior is reinforced. Carefully structured educational programs are developed in a manner that permits instructional materials to be sequenced in small steps. It is believed that students can progress through these steps if provided with consistent reinforcement. As they progress, they master the basic skills necessary to achieve grade-level reading and math scores on national tests. The basic skills in reading and math are stressed above all, with other subject-matter areas receiving considerably less attention. Advocates believe that once basic skill levels are up to normal, youngsters will develop better self concepts and be better able to engage in more complex learning. Essentially the teacher's job is to state beforehand desired goals and outcomes in a form that can be measured; evaluate the students' present level of functioning; provide sequenced learning materials; drill students, providing reinforcement as necessary; keep track of student progress; and repeat the cycle.

Traditional-Fundamental Models

The traditional-fundamental approach to teaching is perhaps best known. In this model it is believed that students learn best in quiet and orderly classrooms where teachers are in complete control and assume sole responsibility for administering a structured academic program. Most of the instructional time in this model is spent on basic skills. Curriculum is traditional and textbook-oriented. Drill and homework are common.

Table 14-1 compares each of the five models across several dimensions considered to be important to teaching. Based on the studies summarized in this table, programmed and traditional-fundamental approaches to teaching are superior in their ability to teach basic skills but inferior in obtaining other, equally desirable results such as responsibility, cooperation, independence, and problem-solving outcomes.

BLOOM'S TAXONOMY

Bloom's *Taxonomy* provides another useful interpretive map, or conceptual frame of reference, for the supervisor.[13] Within the cognitive domain especially, Bloom's analysis of levels of learning can illuminate the focus of the instructional activity. The six cognitive levels proposed by Bloom and widely used in educational circles are:

1. Knowledge—ability to recall information from memory; knowledge of specific facts, definitions, symbols, formulae, conventions, and steps in a process.

[11]Stallings, op. cit., p. 145.
[12]B. F. Skinner, *The Technology of Teaching*, New York: Appleton-Century-Crofts, 1968.
[13]Benjamin S. Bloom, *Taxonomy of Educational Objectives: The Classification of Educational Goals. Handbook I—Cognitive Domain*, New York: McKay, 1956.

2. Comprehension—understanding. Ability to translate, rephrase, interpret, recognize essentials, extrapolate or recognize implications and limitations.
3. Application—(some call this transfer). Ability to use knowledge and understanding in a novel situation to solve problems.
4. Analysis—breaking a whole into its elements. Analysis of relationships, organizational principles, multiple causation, etc.
5. Synthesis—putting together elements and parts to form a new whole.
6. Evaluation—making judgments in a field using internal evidence or external standards.

With these levels of learning in mind, one can read through a teacher's manual, or a lesson plan, or a curriculum guide and quickly perceive the objectives of learning units or parts of units. Likewise, by observing the questioning patterns of teachers in an instructional setting, one can quickly see whether the teacher is focusing on simple recall or memory of terms or whether he or she is asking for more. All too often, teachers test for memory only and seldom go beyond that to require students to think. On the other hand, supervisors need to caution the inexperienced teacher who expects third graders to handle an abstract analysis of energy transfers in electronics. The ideal instructional objective would be to gear the learning tasks to the levels of cognitive development that students at their age level should have achieved. Most of the learning exercises should allow the student to employ those cognitive structures that have developed at his or her age level with increasing facility, providing enough repetition to solidify the learning and ensure a feeling of competence and enjoyment. The supervisor, on the other hand, should encourage the teacher to stretch the abilities of the students from time to time, to place expectations on their performance that go just a little bit beyond what they can comfortably handle. Thus, in observing the instructional interaction, supervisors should look for clear evidence that teachers are stimulating the students' learning transactions to move to deeper or broader levels of understanding, application, and analysis.

A whole level of learning that is frequently neglected, even in the best of schools, has to do with *evaluation.* Evaluation can be considered to apply to two distinguishable levels of learning or learning experiences. One involves a type of analysis that leads to judgments of value. Such and such a poem is a "good" poem because it combines startling metaphors with appropriate rhythms to create a unified effect on the listener. Such and such a political decision by such and such a president was decidedly contrary to the Constitution, as Supreme Court decisions two generations later showed. In the above two instances, the learning experience culminates in a judgment of value (as opposed to a judgment of fact). Evaluation in this sense predominantly involves rational factors. Another learning experience one could label "evaluation" has more to do with *appreciation.* Whether the learning involved mastering a piece of music on the piano or completing a complex mathematics problem or reviewing the intricacies of the physical and psychological processes of sight, the learner dwells in, or simply experiences, the pleasure, harmony, mystery, and complexity of what he or she is doing or observing. The learner in this instance experiences the value intrinsic to the learning transaction itself and enjoys it for its own sake. Frequently students dislike the learning tasks of the school because they seldom move into the level or the experience of evaluation. Sometimes learning ought to culminate in genuine enjoyment.

As with earlier perspectives on curriculum, Bloom's levels of learning are not content specific. The supervisor could apply this analysis, however, to almost any curriculum content, whether it involves language arts, group counseling, or vocational education. The usefulness of Bloom's taxonomy is that it can help the supervisor and the teacher explore ways to lead students beyond simple memorization to a more mature grasp of the learning intended.

THE IMPORTANCE OF LEARNING STYLE

Recent research is uncovering important information about how students learn, what has been labeled *learning styles*. Some students learn best what they hear; others remember best what they see. Still others learn better by hands-on manipulation of materials, while others use a combination of senses for learning.[14] These findings have clear implications for curriculum materials design. Dunn and Dunn have identified several variables that affect learning and can be said to contribute to differences in learning style. These are grouped under four categories: environmental, emotional, sociological, and physical. Figure 14-1 represents 18 variables under these four categories.

Environmental variables suggest that the absence or presence of sounds, bright or

[14]Rita S. Dunn and Kenneth J. Dunn, "Learning Styles/Teaching Styles: Should They . . . Can They . . . Be Matched?" *Educational Leadership*, vol. 36, no. 4, pp. 238–244, 1979; and Dunn and Dunn, *Teaching Students Through Their Individual Learning Styles: A Practical Approach*, Reston, Va.: Reston Publishing Company, a division of Prentice-Hall, 1978.

Figure 14-1 Learning style variables. *Presented in R. S. Dunn and K. J. Dunn, "Learning Styles Teaching Styles: Should They . . . Can They . . . Be Matched?"* Educational Leadership, *Vol. 36, No. 4, p. 241, 1979)*

subdued light, cooler or warmer rooms, and formal or informal seating will either enhance or detract from learning.

Emotional factors involve the motivation to achieve, the ability to stay with a task, the ability to hold oneself responsible, and the ability to work in structured or unstructured lessons. In general, some students learn best when their independence is recognized, whereas less motivated students require more structure and extrinsic motivation.

Sociological factors cluster around how students respond to people in a learning situation. Some students work best alone, some better in a team, others prefer to work directly with an adult.

Physical factors concern elements such as the freedom to move around, the time of day when one's learning energy is high, food intake, and especially which senses are used most comfortably for receiving and processing information.

Fisher and Fisher[15] present a different array of variables on learning styles. Some of their variables coincide with those of Dunn and Dunn. Other variables include whether students normally proceed from the part to the whole or from the whole to the part.

Once again it is clear that the supervisor who is sensitive to curriculum alternatives targeted to differing learning styles will be able to recognize these alternatives in action and be able to encourage their use by teachers who are unfamiliar with them.

GENERAL PRINCIPLES OF CURRICULUM AND INSTRUCTION

We have looked at a diversity of curricular-instructional strategies with which supervisors should be familiar. Now, however, we raise the question of whether there are some general principles that should apply to all or almost all units of instructional activity. Research and experience answer affirmatively. We propose the following series of normative principles that should be evident in any instructional setting and that supervisors would do well, gently and persistently, to insist on.

1. Students must be given the opportunity to practice the kind of behavior implied by the learning-teaching objective. In the case of simple memorization of terminology, students should be called on rather often to repeat that terminology precisely and accurately. In the case of the learning objective of application, students must be given the opportunity to make several applications and to return from time to time to other applications to reinforce the learning desired. In all of this first principle, we stress the importance of the activity of the students. Unless they are actively involved in learning, they will not learn except in the most superficial way.

2. The learning experience must give students the opportunity to deal with the content implied by the objective. If the objective is to develop the skill of inductive scientific reasoning, then the learning experience must place students in a genuinely

[15]B. B. Fisher and L. Fisher, "Styles in Teaching and Learning," *Educational Leadership,* vol. 36, no. 4, pp. 245–254, 1979.

scientific setting where they encounter scientific data that can be analyzed by means of appropriate scientific instruments. Insofar as that learning experience lacks specifically scientific content, then the experience becomes diluted, or thinned out.

3. Students must obtain satisfaction from carrying out the behavior implied by the objective. This principle insists on some sense of successful closure in the learning episode. One of the major problems in nonindividualized instructional settings is that one-third of the class seldom catches up with the rest of the class; they only partially complete their assignments. Their grades usually reflect the penalties imposed and lead to further loss of sense of worth and interest in the learning tasks.

4. The desired learnings or level of performance must be within the range of possibility for the students involved. This principle calls for an awareness on the part of both teachers and supervisors of the development stages and levels of cognitive, moral, and psychosocial growth. Some teachers expect fourth and fifth graders to engage in democratic group decision making. They will severely punish the miscreant who destroys the phony harmony of a simulated town meeting by laughing at the "goody-goody" who is simply trying to imitate the teacher. This is not to say that teachers should not introduce simple concepts of democracy. This principle holds for appropriate expectations of pupils' performance—appropriate to their level of development.

5. There are many particular experiences that can be used to attain the same objectives. Frequently teachers settle on only one or two examples or one or two ways to look at the problem or concept. This principle encourages more concern for diversity of student learning styles, or cultural or ethnic backgrounds. It also encourages the teacher and supervisor constantly to be enlarging their repertory of teaching aids and resources, their bag of tricks, so to speak, in order to provide the student with a new approach to a learning task when another one has failed to bring about the desired results.

6. The same learning experience will usually bring about several outcomes. Not infrequently a student's response to a question will take the teacher completely by surprise. Instead of responding that that was the wrong answer, the teacher should ask the student to clarify how he or she came up with that response. Frequently students come to quite legitimate learning or insights that the teacher had not foreseen as flowing from the assignment. This principle also alludes to the hidden, or indirect, curriculum. Sometimes the teacher unwittingly communicates a value, an attitude, or a reward system that is quite contrary to the objectives of the instructional activity. Supervisors can be especially helpful in pointing this out to teachers.

7. Student learnings will be strengthened, deepened, and broadened if a skill, a concept, relationships, principles, etc., are encountered and used repeatedly in several disciplines or discrete frameworks of learning. This principle points to the importance of a teacher's knowing what other teachers are teaching and have taught to their students. In that way the teacher can draw many comparisons, contrasts, and examples from the student's own experience. Consistent repetition in the use of learning and expressive skills will not only lead to their habitual use but to their refinement and broader scope as well. Not enough attention has been given in the literature on teaching and learning to the importance of repetition and review. The rhetoric of the literature on learning and teaching leads the inexperienced teacher to believe that instructional activity must always move into new material after initial mastery has been achieved. This often results in a wide but shallow coverage of many topics rather than a solid and usable mastery of the learning task. This principle seeks quality, not quantity, in instructional activity.

THE SUPERVISOR AND THE EDUCATIONAL PROGRAM

Sometimes the function of supervision is completely separated from the function of curriculum development. Sometimes the same person is involved in both, such as a building principal or a department chairperson. In either event the supervisor, who normally would focus primarily on the instructional activity of teachers and the use of their instructional materials, of necessity must observe the effectiveness of the curriculum in action. Where one and the same person, such as a department chairperson, is involved with both supervision and curriculum development, the information about the effectiveness of the curriculum on classroom learning comes immediately through the observation of instructional activity.

The department chairperson, observing teachers use the new textbook that the department had chosen that year, not only observes the teachers' adaptation of the textbook but the influence of the textbook on the teachers, on the flow of learning tasks, and on the attention, interest, and attitudes of the students. Through such observation, the supervisor may discover a considerable gap between two major sections of the text, a gap that the students were having difficulty crossing. With this information, and from discussions with the teachers, the chairperson may design a transitional unit to help teachers and students bridge the gap. This would be a clear example of the activity of supervision involved not only with the instructional activity of the teacher but, in a real sense, with the educational program. From this perspective, then, it is appropriate to speak of supervising the curriculum or the educational program.

The distinction between supervision and curriculum development can still remain. The activities relating to both can be assigned to different roles in the school system, if that seems best. Nonetheless, the supervisor can act as one of the main sources of feedback to the curriculum developer. The supervisor observes both the instructional activity of the teacher and the learning activity of the student. From such a vantage point, the supervisor can make some valid inferences about the effectiveness of the curriculum design, its scope, its sequence, its pedagogical appeal, its pace, and its effective marshaling of available learning resources. The supervisor may not be in a position to suggest *another* way of designing the curriculum, but he or she can at least point out what works and what does not.

In some cases, such as that of the department chairperson, this feedback can immediately begin to generate modifications in the sequence, the pace, the clarity or dramatic appeal of the advanced organizers, and so on. A department usually is self-enclosed enough that programs can be modified quickly and easily.

In other instances, a supervisor may be working with an age or grade cluster of teachers and students, say grades 1 through 4. It may happen that the sequence of curriculum materials between grades 3 and 4 is causing considerable problems for the youngsters, and therefore problems for the teachers who have run out of alternative strategies to effect the learning encounter. The supervisor can huddle with teachers from all 4 years and try rearranging the learning units, with the end result that the second-grade teacher will now spend twice as much time teaching and reinforcing the learning of a specific spatial concept, the grasp of which is required for the third graders to handle related conceptual material. Or the supervisor and teachers may decide to remove those one or two learning units from the curriculum altogether and place them in the sixth-grade curriculum where the youngsters' cognitive structures will have developed adequately to handle such cognitively complex material.

In other instances, several supervisors from different grade or school levels or from different discipline areas may be in a position to address a curricular problem common to each of their areas of responsibility. By teaming up to attack the problem, they may come up with at least a clear identification of what the problem is (say, lack of software resources to support such a curriculum), where it primarily is (say, in the seventh grade when the inquiry method is introduced), and what needs to be done about it. By taking this kind of action, the supervisors, even though their primary responsibility is not in curriculum development, can effect beneficial changes in the curriculum.

THE CENTRAL ORGANIZATIONAL POSITION OF SUPERVISORS

In systems where different people are responsible for supervision and for curriculum development, such cooperation and mutual support are necessary for both the supervisor and the developer of the curriculum in order to maximize their common objectives—the best opportunities for the most appropriate growth of youngsters. From the human resources perspectives of supervision, which the authors advocate, the supervisor appears in a key position to bring complementary influences to bear on the instructional tasks of the school. The supervisor can be an advocate for the students vis-à-vis the teacher. The supervisor can be an advocate for the teacher vis-à-vis the administration (say, in urging a different class schedule). The supervisor can also be an advocate for the teacher vis-à-vis the curriculum developer *and vice versa*. In other words, the supervisor frequently stands between the instructional activity and the organizational resource staff and administration. The supervisor is, in a sense, the link. He or she sends messages in both directions. While within the organization chart the supervisor may not appear to, he or she occupies what is perhaps the key position in the school system. The supervisor is close enough to the instructional activity of the school and yet sits in on most of the important administrative meetings. Both by the relative prestige attached to various supervisory positions and by the range of contacts within the school system, the supervisor occupies a key position in the organizational network, from which it is possible to marshal and channel all the best resources the system possesses toward more effective instruction. In small systems where the supervisor is also the chief administrator, the concentration of this potential in one person (there being no need for numerous meetings with different bureaucratic layers of support staff) offers the possibility of rapid program change. And, as the literature on instructional leadership has urged for the past 50 years, that kind of administrator ought to spend much more of his or her time doing instructional supervision.

SUMMARY

This chapter has attempted to focus the supervisor's attention on how the curriculum influences the instructional activity under observation. Besides the more general platform of beliefs, theories, and attitudes upon which teachers habitually base their instructional activity, teachers also bring to the instructional setting their knowledge of the subject matter or discipline and their strategies for bringing the student into a genuine encounter with some aspect of it. In the examples cited, we saw how five different teachers approached the teaching of the nature of light. The group inquiry approach, the historical approach, the experimental approach, the conceptual approach through a lecture or film, the analogy approach—all provide access to the reality of light and to theories to explain the physical properties of light. The supervisor needs to be able to move freely into the frame of reference of the teacher and student in order to support the genuine learning and sound instruction that can and does take place within that perspective. Hopefully, the supervisor will be able to rummage about in his or her own repertory of curriculum-instructional strategies to come up with additional suggestions to enrich, enliven, and open up to even further possibilities the teaching and learning that could be occurring within that framework.

Joyce and Weil's inventory of curriculum-instructional models and Stallings's models of teaching can further enlarge the supervisor's repertory. They provide additional maps, or paradigms, to enable the supervisor to interpret the instructional activity being planned or under observation. Bloom's *Taxonomy* reminds the supervisor that any instructional activity can be pointed to various levels of learning. By examining the levels of learning possible within the curriculum-instructional models, the supervisor is equipped for a kind of two-dimensional analysis or interpretation of the teacher's instructional activity. Research on learning styles provides additional insight into the need for alternative instructional strategies.

Regardless of the type of its instructional activity, the following seven principles should apply to every instructional unit:

1. The student must be given the opportunity to practice the kind of behavior implied by the learning-teaching objective.

2. The learning experience must give the student the opportunity to deal with the content implied by the objective.

3. The student must obtain satisfaction from carrying out the behavior implied by the objective.

4. The desired learnings or levels of performance must be within the range of possibility for the students involved.

5. There are many particular experiences that can be used to obtain the same objectives.

6. The same learning experience will usually bring about several outcomes.

7. Student learnings should be reinforced by being used in different settings and disciplines, and by being used repeatedly.

Finally, the role of the supervisor, while remaining distinguished from that of the curriculum developer, was studied in terms of its potential for curriculum revision. It is legitimate to speak of supervising the curriculum. The supervisor, because of his or her central position in the organizational network of the school, can have considerable influence on curriculum reform.

STUDY GUIDE

Recall the concepts and meanings associated with each of the following phrases and terms included in this chapter. Can you discuss them with a colleague and apply them to the supervisory context of your school? If you cannot, review them in the text and record the page number for future reference.

1. Curriculum _____
2. Exploratory models _____
3. Four families of teaching models _____
4. Instructional activity _____
5. Learning styles _____
6. Normative instructional principles _____
7. Supervision and curriculum development _____
8. Taxonomy of educational objectives _____

EXERCISES

1. Observe a film of a teacher teaching a class. Does that teaching fit into one of the families of teaching models? Go back and see which of the levels of learning are getting most of the teacher's attention. Go back a third time and see whether the seven instructional principles are being followed.
2. What kinds of other questions are generated by viewing the film? Imagine that you would be meeting with that teacher within an hour for the post-observation conference. Divide up into teams of three and plan your strategy for the conference. Perhaps someone could role-play the teacher.
3. Consider all the classes you attend in your college or graduate program. How would you analyze and describe the instructional activity that goes on in them? Are they effective in the instructional strategies employed?
4. Ask someone who is involved in curriculum design and development where he or she receives most of the feedback on the curriculum's effectiveness. Ask a practicing supervisor how often she or he gets involved in curriculum revision.

CHAPTER 15

SUPERVISION AND PROGRAM EVALUATION

Evaluation is a growing concern in education. From the federal and state governments down to local taxpayer groups, one finds an increasing demand for evaluation. Much of this stress on evaluation arises from a desire to find out what is wrong with the schools, why test scores are declining, why schools seem ineffective in controlling violence and vandalism, teenage pregnancies, and drug abuse. Some would stress evaluation as a way of holding schools accountable to taxpayers and funding agencies for the money they spend. Others, such as university researchers, are seeking to increase information about effective programs or teaching strategies. A new wave of books and articles on evaluation is growing in volume as researchers, foundations, and government agencies seek not only to evaluate what goes on in schools but to develop the most effective evaluative tools and procedures for generating useful information.

The supervisory process, whether exercised by a superintendent or by a department chairperson, inescapably involves evaluation. In order to establish precisely what that means, however, several distinctions are needed. First, we should distinguish between evaluation that is exercised as part of a supervisory process and evaluation exercised by other agents or professionals. Second, we should distinguish between the object of evaluation, such as the evaluation of a school system, the evaluation of an individual school taken as a single social entity, the evaluation of a program, the evaluation of a process, the evaluation of a teacher, the evaluation of a student, and so on. Third, we should distinguish between the various audiences for which an evaluation is intended. Fourth, we should distinguish between various types of evaluation procedures and the assumptions behind the procedures employed in an evaluation. Fifth, we should distinguish between the purposes of evaluation. Basically, these distinctions involve the who, what, for whom, how, and why of evaluation. Once we have clarified these distinctions, we should be able to narrow our focus on the more important and essential tasks of program evaluation with which the supervisory process is involved.

THE QUESTION OF WHO EVALUATES

Evaluation is carried on by a number of professional agents in the educational universe. At the federal level, where special programs are funded, personnel within the agencies or, more commonly, outside evaluation experts are called upon to evaluate the impact of these programs on the target populations. Head Start, for example, has been evaluated several times in order to determine whether that program was accomplishing its objectives. Evaluation experts from universities, state departments of education, or consulting agencies are frequently called in to use their technical expertise to evaluate special or new programs. State and regional accrediting agencies employ teachers and administrators who visit schools for cyclical reevaluations in order for the schools to retain their accreditation. Research and development centers employ evaluators to assess the impact of new or experimental programs. Foundations usually require a thorough evaluation of programs they fund, either by outside or inside evaluators. Department chairpersons evaluate new teachers. Teachers evaluate students. Supervisors evaluate teachers and programs. Therefore, when discussing evaluation in education, who is doing the evaluation makes a considerable difference to the discussion.

THE QUESTION OF WHAT IS BEING EVALUATED

Many things or many people can be the object of an evaluation. The evaluation of a national program such as Head Start involves broad evaluation technologies and standardized testing of both product and process; a national evaluation of library expenditures involves the appraisal of different data; a local evaluation of a consumer education program would involve the measure of outcomes different from those in a state evaluation of fair hiring procedures for school personnel. A systemwide evaluation of a reading program would differ from teacher X giving a home-grown test to her third-grade pupils. A supervisor's evaluation of a department's testing procedures would differ from a supervisor's evaluation of a beginning teacher. To evaluate students' reading skills involves a search for specific behaviors; to evaluate students' practices of democratic citizenship behaviors would involve a search for quite different kinds of data.

THE QUESTION OF THE AUDIENCE OF THE EVALUATION

An evaluation report can be prepared for different audiences. The evaluation of an experimental program, when prepared for a research community, might be unintelligible to a citizens' oversight committee. A self-study report prepared by a schoolwide, faculty-parent committee would differ from a student's report card. A faculty report on new textbooks prepared for the school board would differ from a psychologist's evaluation of the match between students' stages of cognitive development and a new textbook prepared for a publishing house. Recent research on the politics of evaluation reporting indicates that not only what is evaluated but the way conclusions are drawn from the evaluation depends a lot on the audience for whom the evaluation is prepared.[1]

[1]See Ernest R. House (ed.), *School Evaluation: The Politics and Process,* Berkeley, Calif.: McCutchan, 1973; W. James Popham, "The Evaluators Curse," in Ronald S. Brandt (ed.), *Applied Strategies for Curriculum Evaluation,* Washington, D.C.:Association for Supervision and Curriculum Development, 1981; and Deborah G. Bonnet, "Five Phases of Purposeful Inquiry," ibid.

For the supervisor, it makes a difference whether an evaluation of a class is prepared for the superintendent or for the teacher who is seeking instructive information in order to test a new teaching strategy. Sometimes the audience for whom the evaluation is targeted, as well as the evaluators themselves, can seriously disrupt the very activity on which the evaluation is supposed to report.

THE QUESTION OF EVALUATION PROCEDURES AND TECHNOLOGY

Currently there is a debate over the use of "hard" or "soft" evaluation procedures and technologies.[2] The earlier and more widespread practice of evaluation appear to have employed the hard procedures and technologies, namely, the quantification of what was being evaluated. Such an approach, based upon an analogy with research in the natural sciences, is seen as more "scientific," or more "objective." By quantifying data through testing or through numerical checklists, evaluators have attempted to provide a basis for comparing their data with data reported by others, using the same or similar scientific procedures, and for measuring "input" and "output."

There has been a reaction against this emphasis on quantification, a reaction that has been growing steadily over the past 10 years. Using analogies with methodologies employed in anthropology, aesthetics, literary criticism, and political analysis, the proponents of the "soft" approaches to evaluation argue that they can capture more of the human variables through "naturalistic" or ethnographic or case-study methodologies. Their argument also refers to the scale of evaluation. They claim that the individual school site or an individual classroom ought to be the locus of evaluation rather than a national, statewide, or even systemwide sample. They maintain that the study of large populations tends to depress the unique features of smaller segments and settings. Evaluation studies that are more attentive to individual schools and individual classrooms do in fact point up significant differences between schools and between classrooms in the same school.[3]

The focus on the smaller unit of schooling, whether the individual school or the individual classroom, as the unit where evaluation produces the most sensitive and useful information, receives further substantiation from several studies of change.[4] They conclude that the individual school, with its unique mix of people, practices, and environment, is the unit most suited for and effective in managing successful change. It seems reasonable, then, to argue that evaluation on or within that scale, rather than on a larger scale, would produce the most accurate and useful information.

[2]For a good summary of this debate see E. G. Guba and Y. S. Lincoln, *Effective Evaluation,* San Francisco: Jossey-Bass, 1981. The essays in Brandt (ed.), op. cit., aptly illustrate various approaches to program evaluation.

[3]See Michael Rutter, Barbara Maughan, Peter Mortimer, and Jarret Ouston, *Fifteen Thousand Hours: Secondary Schools and Their Effects on Children,* Cambridge: Mass.: Harvard University Press, 1979; and George F. Madaus, Peter W. Airasian, and Thomas Kellaghan, *School Effectiveness,* New York: McGraw-Hill, 1980.

[4]See John L. Goodlad, *The Dynamics of Educational Change: Toward Responsive Schools,* New York: McGraw-Hill, 1975; Paul Berman and Wilbrey W. McLaughlin, *Federal Programs Supporting Educational Change, Vol. IV: The Findings in Review,* Santa Monica, Calif.: Rand Corporation, 1975; Daniel A. Neale, William J. Bailey, and Billy E. Ross, *Strategies for School Improvement: Cooperative Planning and Organizational Development,* Boston: Allyn and Bacon, 1981; and Gilbert R. Austen, "Exemplary Schools and the Search for Effectiveness," *Educational Leadership,* vol. 37, no. 1, pp. 10–14, 1979.

While supervisory personnel will make some use of quantitative data for evaluation, it appears that much of their involvement in evaluative activity will occur within the "responsive" or "naturalistic" mode and within the smaller scale of the individual school. As the scale of supervisory activity enlarges, the evaluative procedures will probably move toward the more impersonal and quantitative mode. Thus, a program director at the state Department of Education with responsibility to supervise, for example, the state-mandated program for educating sight-impaired children would probably require quantifiable information for annual reports on this program. This does not rule out using additional modes of evaluation, especially where improvements at particular sites are being sought.

THE PURPOSES OF EVALUATION

Finally, the purpose for which evaluation is undertaken will shape the form and process of evaluation. If the purpose of an evaluation is to provide information about the more effective of two or three approaches to the teaching of reading, then it is supposed to lead to the choosing of one over the other(s) for future implementation or continuation. If the purpose of an evaluation is to seek improvements in an existing reading program, then it is supposed to lead to improvements in that program. An evaluation of teaching effectiveness in a department will start out with the objectives of that department and seek to verify whether the students achieve those objectives. An evaluation of the stated objectives of a department will compare those objectives with the objectives of similar departments in other schools, or with objectives laid down by state or professional associations involved with that academic area in order to judge whether they fall within accepted standards and criteria. Some evaluations may involve comparison of two or more schools in order to see which schools produce the highest student scores on national achievement tests or do best according to some other standardized criteria.

PROGRAM EVALUATION AND THE SUPERVISORY PROCESS

The supervisory process can be exercised on any level, from the supervision of a federal or state program to a districtwide program. It can involve the total educational program of a single school or, within a school, a departmental curriculum or an individual course. Figure 15-1 highlights some of the many levels at which program evaluation takes place. At whatever level supervision is involved with program evaluation, we believe that it is exercised best when the supervisor monitors and participates in the evaluative efforts of those implementing the program. This is to say that the supervisory process ought to be separated from evaluation of the program by an evaluation expert. It is not to say that supervisors do not evaluate. Their evaluation, however, is not as an outsider but as an insider, working with those who are delivering the instruction or the program.

We believe that the principles that guide the supervisory process when it is engaged in program evaluation are best illustrated at the level of a specific program in a single school, working with teachers who are implementing the program through

Level	Example	Type of evaluation	Purpose
Federal	Head start	Statistical norm referenced test	Report to congress & federal officials
State	Vocational education	Statistical survey	Report to state legislature and state officials
Independent research and development center	Experimental reading programs	Highly sophisticated psychometrics; use of experimental and control groups	Isolation and measurement of program effects
Regional accrediting agency	Cyclical self-evaluation and assessment by visiting team	Self report, observation by visitors, naturalistic evaluation	To judge whether school meeting minimum standards
Local school system	K-12 Modern language program	Norm reference and criterion referenced testing	To judge effectiveness of their program compared to other school systems using different approaches
Single school	Volunteer community-service program	Supervisor reports, agency reports, teacher reports, student reports	To assess impact on improved citizenship attitudes
Single course	Geography	Criterion referenced tests, student inclass responses, supervisor's observation, student interviews, etc.	To improve over all course design, sequence, pacing, use of audio visuals, etc.

Figure 15-1 Evaluation of programs according to scale.

instructional activity. That could be a third-grade program, or a science program in a senior high school. As distinguished from other kinds of evaluation activity, the supervisor's evaluation activity is exercised with and for teachers, for the purpose of program and instructional improvement, and for enhanced student learnings; it is exercised more by soft technology than by hard technology. The who, for whom, how, and why distinctions were made above in order to clarify more precisely how supervision can involve program evaluation and to distinguish supervision from the more formal aspects of program evaluation by nonsupervisory personnel. Figures 15-1 and 15-2 map out those distinctions.

Furthermore, the point of view adopted in this chapter is that supervisory evaluation of program effectiveness is exercised with teachers as they seek practical ways to improve their instruction. That is, evaluation activity is not extrinsic to instruction but is intrinsically involved with instruction itself and with instructional

WHO	Administrators	Supervisors	Evaluation Experts
Does what	Decide whether to initiate, continue or terminate programs, based on information received by evaluators Decide whether to alter program, or commit more resources to program, based on information received by supervisors and program implementors	Work on program improvement with implementors (teachers) of the program. Examine effectiveness of small segments of the program implementation. Help program implementors assess multiple effects of program on recipients (students) Explore alternative forms of implementing the program Help program implementors and recipients review the overall impact of the program.	Gather data on a program Assess program effectiveness Compare this program with alternatives Report results to various publics Interpret results to various publics
How	Review reports	Responsive evaluation Participative observation Work with mediating variables Looking for unintended effects Clarifying objectives Posing alternative approaches	Clarifying goals, means, and products Measuring, testing, observing, charting, comparing Clarifying relationships between program design, implementation activities and results on tests and other hard and soft measures
Why	Responsibility and accountability to publics Seeking maximum effectiveness for enhanced student learning	Seeking best fit between program design, learning resource materials, teacher activities and student learning To improve program effectiveness, teacher effectiveness and student learning	To measure what the program accomplishes. To establish relationship between program and results To provide basis for making enlightened decisions about the program

Figure 15-2 Role of administrators, supervisors, and evaluation experts in program evaluation.

improvement. As will become clear in later parts of this chapter, there is a dynamic relationship between evaluating student learnings, evaluating teachers' activities in stimulating student learnings, and evaluating the effectiveness of the curriculum that the teachers use. Hence our primary focus in this chapter will be the supervisor's monitoring and assisting in teachers' evaluation of their own activities for improved student learnings, for improved instructional planning, and for improved program design. Much of the teacher's evaluation of the program will depend very much on how the teacher evaluates student learnings. The supervisor, by assisting the teacher to ask the right questions when evaluating student learning, will also help the teacher explore ways to improve the program in order to enhance student learnings.

THE ACTIVITY OF EVALUATION

Program and pupil evaluation formerly was thought of primarily as something that happened at the end of the term or the end of the year. At the conclusion of the course, students were evaluated on their progress in attaining the goals of the program by means of a test, a "final exam" of some kind or other. When the course was over, the teacher might have spent some time looking back over the curriculum and specific instructional strategies to see whether or not some units clearly were inappropriate and unsuccessful. In the case of a new course, the teacher and supervisor might compare student achievement with the earlier course. They also would probably ask teachers in whose classes their students subsequently enrolled whether there was any noticeable difference after the new course.

Michael Scriven, in writing about curriculum revision, calls this type of evaluation *summative evaluation*.[5] It sums up, so to speak, the cumulative impact of the curriculum on learning, or it makes a general assessment of the cumulative learning of the whole curriculum by the student. He distinguishes summative evaluation from *formative evaluation* by positing formative evaluation as an ongoing process within the curriculum—instructional activity sequence. Through formative evaluation of the instructional program the teacher, learner, and curriculum designer can receive rapid feedback on the effectiveness of short-term segments of the program, rather than having to wait until the conclusion of the program for the more summative type of evaluation. Formative evaluation, since it goes on so close in time to the instructional activity and the learning encounter, can have a formative influence on the instructional activity and the learning encounter. In a given situation the teacher can see that use of a particular advanced organizer or a demonstration simply is not getting the students' attention or, by questions from the students, that it is well over their heads. This kind of quick feedback will probably lead the teacher to discard that approach on the spot and to try a new tack. Or a student may discover that he has not yet mastered the rule on capital letters. He and the teacher can then set up some exercises to ensure a more adequate grasp of those rules.

Bloom and associates divide evaluation into three types: *diagnostic, formative,* and *summative*.[6] Diagnostic evaluation is closely related to both formative and summative evaluation, but it is distinguished by its purposes. Diagnostic evaluation is used to place a student properly in the level of instruction that best matches his or her entry behaviors and skills with learning objectives of the instructional unit. It is also used to determine the underlying causes or circumstances behind repeated deficiencies in a student's performance that have not responded to ordinary remedial measures.[7] Diagnostic evaluation usually employs some recognized standardized test or battery of tests that will highlight cognitive, affective, physical, psychological, and environmental factors in the student. With such information concerning how well the youngster is functioning in his or her stage of development, more appropriate resources can be

---

[5]Michael Scriven, "The Methodology of Evaluation," in Robert Stake (ed.), *AERA Monograph Series on Curriculum Evaluation,* no. 1, pp. 39–83, 1967.
[6]Benjamin S. Bloom, J. Thomas Hastings, and George F. Madaus, *Handbook on Formative and Summative Evaluation of Student Learning,* New York: McGraw-Hill, 1971, p. 87 et passim.
[7]Ibid., p. 87.

made available. Some of the similarities and differences between diagnostic, formative, and summative evaluation as listed by Bloom and associates appear in Figure 15-3.

FORMATIVE EVALUATION

For the moment, we will consider the activity of formative evaluation, for the supervision of evaluation activity would seem more involved in that form of evaluation. A brief overview of formative evaluation of the curriculum points to particular activities of students, other activities of the teacher, and the formative use of testing for both. Depending on the situation, supervisors may or may not participate in the evaluation activities, but they will certainly be expected to monitor in some fashion the effectiveness of these evaluation activities.

Student Evaluative Activity: Evaluation of the Curriculum-as-Learned

Let us consider an ordinary class setting, say a self-contained classroom with 1 teacher and 24 students. The class has just concluded a comparison of two poems. Previous classes have dealt with aspects of poetry, such as mood, figures of speech, rhythm, unity, image, and symbol. They have seen a variety of poems and have done some analysis using these critical concepts. The objective of today's class was to have them use these critical concepts to compare two poems and to argue why one poem was a "better" poem than the other. This objective fit into the larger goal of the course that aimed at the students' developing a discriminating taste for superior literary expression.

Toward the end of the class the teacher felt satisfied that most if not all of the students reflected a good grasp of the analytical concepts and had applied them well in arguing for the superiority of one poem over the other. In an attempt to further reinforce the learning and to test out her impressions that the class had pretty well achieved the instructional objectives she said, "Now let's all pause a minute and reflect what it is we learned today. What new thing struck us? What have we understood with greater clarity? How does what we've done today fit with what went on before? Of what practical use was this whole experience, anyway?"

The following answers came back:

"I learned that it makes a difference when you read a poem out loud. I could *hear* how much superior that first poem was to the other one."

"I learned that you can still like an inferior poem—I mean, yeah, the first poem is a better poem, by all the measures we apply to it, but I like the second poem because it expresses a feeling about being alone that I've had many times. Just because a poem is a mediocre poem doesn't mean it's no good at all."

"I learned that I had to read both poems at least four times before they made any sense to me. It seems that with poetry, kinda like music, you gotta acquire a kind of familiarity with it before it really says anything to you."

"I learned that all this art stuff isn't entirely a matter of feeling, you know, all from inside someone's fantasy. There's something to it, some kind of intelligence. And you can talk about poetry intelligently, instead of simply leaving it to subjective feelings of like or dislike."

"I learned that I have no poetic imagination. I never thought those kinds of

Type of Evaluation

	Diagnostic	Formative	Summative
Function	Placement: Determining the presence or absence of prerequisite skills Determining the student's prior level of mastery Classifying the student according to various characteristics known or thought to be related to alternative modes of instruction Determination of underlying causes of repeated learning difficulties	Feedback to student and teacher on student progress through a unit Location of errors in terms of the structure of a unit so that remedial alternative instruction techniques can be prescribed	Certification or grading of students at the end of a unit, semester, or course
Time	For placement at the outset of a unit, semester, or year's work During instruction when student evidences repeated inability to profit fully from ordinary instruction	During instruction	At the end of a unit, semester, or year's work
Emphasis in evaluation	Cognitive, affective, and psychomotor behaviors Physical, psychological, and environmental factors	Cognitive behaviors	Generally cognitive behaviors; depending on subject matter, sometimes psychomotor; occasionally affective behaviors
Type of instrumentation	Formative and summative instruments for pretests Standardized achievement tests Standardized diagnostic tests Teacher-made instruments Observation and checklists	Specially designed formative instruments	Final or summative examinations

Figure 15-3 Similarities and differences between diagnostic, formative, and summative evaluation.

thoughts. And I'm wondering how one gets to be a poet—are you born that way, or can you develop it?"

"I'm really having a hard time understanding what makes a poem 'unified.' It's a word that seems to me to mean perfect, or perfection. Like a perfect circle or something. So if a poem has unity, then it must mean that every word, every line is in perfect place. But who could ever decide that? Maybe I need to see examples of *really* unified poems and some that are a little off-center and maybe I'll catch on."

"I learned that it feels good to discover that a lot of people agree with my conclusions. Before the class started, I wasn't sure whether my picking the first poem as better was the right answer, you know. But when other people gave the same reasons as I had, I really felt good, because I figured—yeah, for the first time—that I'm understanding all the stuff we've been doing on poetry."

Suppose you were observing in that class. After the class you and the teacher sat down to review the class. What practical things would the two of you do as a result of those student responses?

The example illustrates a range of student learnings that reflected not only the achievement of the teacher's objectives, but also the many idiosyncratic, ancillary learnings that always occur. The example points to the importance of taking that kind of time to let students reflect on what they have learned. Obviously, the students in that honors poetry class had rather high levels of motivation and of verbal and abstractive abilities. Students in third or fourth grade will come up with simpler responses, to be sure. But getting them into the habit early of evaluating what they are learning will pay enormous dividends as it develops into ongoing reflective habits of mind and a genuine satisfaction over knowing that they are making progress.

Students' evaluation of their appropriation of the curriculum can lead to both cognitive and affective results. On the one hand, by reflecting on their grasp of the learning task, they can clarify what they know. Frequently, the simple recall of the class material or unit will reinforce the grasp of the material. When this reflection is done in a nonthreatening environment, students can also clarify and admit what they have not yet grasped or understood. They can trace back the instructional sequence until they get to the point where the teacher or the textbook lost them. This clarifying of what one does not know will often lead to a desire to learn that, to get at that the first thing in the next class.

On the affective level, students can also be encouraged to review what they learned, not so much for intellectual understanding but simply for enjoyment. The youngster who had to repeat the poems many times was discovering how poems are meant to be enjoyed. This kind of enjoyment is not limited to those subjects within the humanities. A sensitive biology teacher or a physical education teacher can lead students into a kind of repetitive appreciation of what they have learned. Sometimes that leads to genuine wonderment.

In either case, student evaluation of this learning can lead to ownership. Recognizing what they have learned, what it means, how it is related to what they have learned before, how they can use it, what a sense of excitement or enjoyment comes with that mastery of a skill or discovery of a surprising piece of information—all of this leads students to appropriate that learning as theirs. Once appropriated, the learning tends to be effective, which is to say the student owns it and can use it in many ways in the immediate future. Unfortunately, many teachers fail to take the time to encourage this sense of ownership. What they miss by omitting the encouragement of student self-evaluation is the genuine satisfaction of knowing how much actually gets absorbed and how fascinating it is to observe the individual coloring of the learning that was supposed to take place. Moreover, much of the formative evaluation the teacher engages in will not pick up the obvious clues that students put forth in their self-evaluation. A supervisor who helps a teacher to initiate student self-evaluation may have provided a stimulus for instructional and program improvement more effective than several semesters of in-service lectures on the topic.

The Teacher's Formative Evaluation Activity: Evaluation of the Curriculum-as-Taught

By means of student self-evaluation, brief quizzes, questions right in the middle of instructional activity, by checking homework assignments, and through informal out-of-class conversations, teachers can get an idea of the effectiveness of the curriculum unit as well as their teaching strategies. It will take a multiplicity of feedback mechanisms rather than the single mechanism of an occasional test to provide the formative information. Sometimes a test will be the real problem because it has been poorly constructed.

In any event, the teacher's formative evaluation activity will have several foci. The teacher must try to evaluate how well the student is encountering and mastering the learning task. There may be several reasons why the student is having difficulty. There may be emotionally upsetting conditions at home; a fight in the school yard that morning could have made concentration on schoolwork impossible. But it may be that the pace of the class was too fast, or that the examples used were too strange, or that the student was distracted briefly at the beginning of the class and missed one of the initial steps in the explanation.

If most or all of the class is showing disinterest or confusion, then the teacher has to evaluate what in his or her teaching is lacking. Or is it the learning-unit design in the textbook that is confusing or flat? Sometimes the only way to identify the cause is to ask the students. From time to time, however, the teacher is not all that aware of the deficiency in the textbook or in his or her teaching. Sometimes the problem does not surface for a week or two, when a test shows up a consistent gap in the class's grasp of an essential part of the sequence of learning.

And then there are the teachers who are perpetually unaware of how they smother any student initiative in learning. Low grades are simply their way of punishing what they perceive as the recalcitrance and general laziness of youth. Here, the formative evaluation of the teacher is almost totally ineffective because the source of the problem is ignored.

Supervisors can help teachers address the difficult task of formative evaluation primarily by communicating to the teacher a sense of respect for the teacher's competence to refashion his or her curriculum-instructional plan more effectively. Frequently, teachers think that a textbook is too sacred to be altered one iota. On the contrary, the teacher is in the best position to know what will work with his or her youngsters and should deviate from the textbook when that is called for. The supervisor can work alongside the teacher, exploring alternative strategies, testing out an idea on one or two students before trying it with the whole class, and looking for gaps and blind spots and filling them in so that students can move easily from one thing to another. Once the teacher gains the self-confidence, then he or she will be much more likely to carry on such self-corrective activities independently.

In cases where substantial program revision may be called for, the supervisor can enlist the assistance of someone more skilled in curriculum design to work with several teachers. The point is, however, that the teacher ought to be the central person in this kind of formative evaluation, not the supervisor. Frequently the most important activity of the supervisor is convincing the teacher that he or she can do it, and furthermore ought to, and finally, has to do it. Familiarity with a variety of evaluation techniques such as those presented by Bloom and associates[8] will equip the supervisor with a certain repertory of approaches, some of which may be useful to get the teacher started.

In this regard, a formative use of testing can be a key source of feedback data that will unlock the problems besetting both teachers and students. More often than not, quizzes and tests are not carefully reviewed. The grades are entered into the mark book, and the papers are handed back to the students, who look at the grade at the top of the page, give off a whine, a curse, or a gleeful expletive, crumple up the paper, and toss it in the basket.

A careful review of tests and quizzes, however, can be turned into very effective learning. First, there is usually a high level of interest because of the grade involved. By reviewing the quiz or the test, students have a chance to see where they made their mistake, thereby clearing up what could be a lingering problem if not corrected. It also provides the teacher some clues as to why some students failed to achieve the objective of the instruction. Such information often leads to more appropriate remedial exercises. In the exchange of information, the teacher can likewise score all kinds of other useful points, such as reinforcing the main point of the instruction, reviewing previous learnings leading up to the material under consideration, clarifying the level of exactitude or logic or basic English required in the course, pointing out the necessity to ask questions in class when points are unclear, etc.

Students, even the ones who put down most of the correct answers, have an opportunity to review the essentials of the previous class or learning unit. For students whose low performance was due to one key deficiency, the opportunity is there to see the principle or concept or formula or rule as such, that is, as a generalization that applies to many particulars; through the review of the mistake that is underlined before them in glowing red, they can now have the insight that they could not grasp before.

Such review also allows the rhetoricians in the class an opportunity to debate the precise meaning of a word or phrase in the question that they took to mean something other than what the teacher intended. Sometimes a student has a legitimate complaint when the wording of the question allows for two different readings and therefore for two different responses. The teacher's review of the test can help clear up such problems before some disgruntled younster goes home to enlist the support of his or

---

[8]Bloom, Hastings, and Madaus, op. cit.

her parents who in turn become disgruntled and demand an appointment with the principal.

Again, supervisors can help teachers get far more instructional mileage out of their tests and quizzes. Rather than being something extraneous to instruction, this kind of formative evaluation can become one of the regular tools of instruction. Only in this way can testing be restored to its proper place as an aid to instruction rather than being a specter dominating both instruction and student motivation.

The Supervisor in Formative Evaluation

As should be evident from the above, the role of the supervisor is that of monitoring the type and effectiveness of the formative evaluating activity that goes on in the classroom. By keeping uppermost in mind that this type of evaluation is intended to improve the learning of the student, as well as the instructional effectiveness of the teacher and the curriculum program, the supervisor can help the teacher and student stay on target in their evaluation efforts.

Furthermore, the supervisor should have enough distance from the evaluation activity itself to perceive the values that are brought into play by the type and style of the evaluation procedures employed by the teacher. That is to say, evaluation is a process of assigning value and significance to actions, things, answers, or questions. Behind any evaluation activity there is a whole host of assumptions that have value content. These assumptions usually go untested or unquestioned.

Some assumptions behind some forms of evaluation include the following: that knowing or understanding something means giving this response to that question; that this curriculum design or this text contains a legitimate approach (or the most legitimate, or the only legitimate approach) to this area of human knowledge (for example, modern Latin American history), and therefore a test of the student's knowledge of this approach indicates that he or she knows something true or objective or valid about that area of human knowledge; that using the language of public discourse in evaluation is the best means of measuring what the student has learned (rather than using poetry or music or graphics to measure it); or that teachers and other school officials have the authority and competency to decide the criteria for evaluating and ranking students.

Behind these assumptions, of course, are other assumptions: that learning primarily involves learning what others have discovered (and seldom the way they discovered it), and so evaluation monitors learning on that level; that there is always a causal connection between learning and instruction (rather than learning and the *students'* search, inquiry, practice, trial and error, or logical deduction), and hence evaluation of learning implies an evaluation of instruction; that the proper place for most learning is a classroom, and so evaluation never compares classroom learning (with all its constraints) with learnings in other settings. One could go on and on, describing assumptions behind assumptions. The point of listing these is to encourage supervisors occasionally to create enough distance from the evaluation activity for both the teacher and themselves so that they can perceive the value assumptions that are embedded in their evaluation procedures. If nothing else, such distancing can be a healthy antidote to dogmatism; at best it will encourage flexibility and more holistic approaches to evaluation.

Kunkel and Tucker propose five criteria by which supervisors and other evaluators might evaluate the quality of their evaluation activity.[9] These criteria were developed as part of their perception-based model of evaluation. Even without endorsing the theory of knowledge upon which the model is based, we believe these criteria can be applied to ensure quality evaluation in any evaluation scheme.

Quality 1. *Holism.* The evaluation should avoid distortion of the toal reality being evaluated by an undue emphasis on quantification or on only a few variables. Toward this end both statistical and existential forms of inference should be used.

Quality 2. *Helpfulness toward program improvement.* This is really the key to formative evaluation, and what distinguishes it from summative evaluation. The primary purpose of formative evaluation is to assist the one responsible for the curriculum program. It looks to growth, improvement, increased effectiveness, rather than to ranking, judging, categorizing, criticizing.

Quality 3. *Acceptance of hard and soft data.* In order to reduce distortion through methodological rigidity or theoretical bias (e.g., positivism or mechanistic reductionism), the reality being evaluated should be described by both empirical and intuitive methodologies. The qualites of the phenomena as well as the quantitative properties deserve attention.

Quality 4. *Evaluation vulnerability.* The process of evaluation requires dialogue between the evaluator and the evaluated in which the theory and methodology of the evaluator are open to question. Rather than assuming an elitist posture, the evaluator must enter a shared enterprise with the evaluated in which perceptions are discussed and conclusions negotiated. The evaluator has to be as vulnerable as the evaluated.

Quality 5. *Vision of the future.* Since the purpose of the evaluation is the improvement of the program or the behavior being evaluated, the evaluator ought to be able and willing to disclose his view of the future context in which such improved programs or behaviors will function better. In this way, evaluation is seen as dynamic, as creative, and as open to the future, as in fact that essential activity that keeps an action system in a process of self renewal.[10]

These criteria will also be evident in our later treatment of clinical supervision.[11] For the moment, however, we can appreciate the necessity of the supervisor's awareness of the values embedded in any evaluation scheme. In the ongoing process of formative evaluation, it is possible to achieve a more holistic appraisal of teacher, student learning, and program. When one moves into summative evaluation, however, supervisors will have a much more difficult time preventing the exterior imposition of the one exclusive set of values.

SUMMATIVE EVALUATION

In treating summative evaluation, we wish to distinguish between the *activity* of summative evaluation and the *reporting* of the results of summative evaluation.

[9]Richard C. Kunkel and Susan A. Tucker, "A Perception-based Model of Program Evaluation: A Values Oriented Theory," paper presented at AERA Annual Meeting, New York, 1977.
[10]Ibid., pp. 2–4.
[11]See Chap. 17.

Frequently summative evaluation is spoken of exclusively as the reporting of results. Supervisors ought to monitor not only the reporting of results, but also how the activity of summative evaluation itself is designed and carried out. For example, a teacher may have a very fine method of preparing her students for a final exam, but may have a very one-sided approach to reporting results. Beyond the individual teacher's reporting of results, the supervisor needs to look at the system's use of these reports and the system's reporting procedures to outside agencies.

When dealing with summative evaluation of students, then, supervisors can help teachers realize the significant instructional activity and learning that can take place through summative evaluation. Teachers, for example, can encourage students to engage in a summative-type self-evaluation, aiming for the students' review of what significant things *they* think they have learned in the course. Some teachers will assign a final project of this type. Even in a more structured class review of the course prior to a final exam, the students can deepen much of what they have learned. Frequently the review provides the opportunity for a whole new synthesis of learnings. What was said in the discussion of formative evaluation about going over test results would also apply here: it would be the teacher's last chance to get the point across before the students move on.

When considering the reporting of summative evaluation results, we may wish that the five criteria mentioned earlier could be applied. There are many reasons why summative evaluation usually is far less complete than what the five criteria would require. Summative evaluation has as its primary purpose the reporting of results at the conclusion of a program or of a time span. Among the people reading these reports of summative evaluation are guidance counselors, principals, parents, college admission officers, employers, state licensing officials, and so on. By and large, they are looking for brief reports using recognizable symbols of a quantifiable result. It would be impossible for this reporting system to work with substantially expanded reports that measured up to the five criteria. First, it would put an intolerable burden on teachers to prepare an extensive portfolio on each of their students. The agencies receiving these reports would have to hire additional personnel simply to read and code these reports. Given the political and legal climate surrounding information systems and their use, a more expansive summation of the pupil's achievements would open a Pandora's box of problems. While more holistic summative evaluation reports would be desirable for a variety of purposes, then, the practical difficulties involved would seem to prevent any useful developments in this arena.

When we move into the *reporting* of summative evaluation of the teacher's effectiveness and the effectiveness of the curriculum, we move into a process fraught with problems and misunderstandings. Because of the neoscientific-management influences in education[12] and political and economic issues surrounding schooling, summative evaluation of teachers, instructional strategies, curriculum design, and instructional materials has been used for purposes other than what might be called scientific objectivity.

Recently, schools are being held accountable by local, state, and federal agencies. Teachers, supervisors, building principals, and superintendents are under increasing

---

[12]To be taken up in more detail in Chap. 17.

pressure to give an account of themselves to the taxpayers and legislatures. There is the simplistic assumption that if youngsters are falling behind in scores on standardized tests, then the fault can be laid exclusively on the school's doorstep.

Even if the schools were largely to blame, a conclusion certainly without any clear evidence, the methodologies of reporting and evaluation used in most accountability schemes, and the theory of knowledge upon which they rest, are highly simplistic and value-biased. First, the issue of accountability has become a highly political issue. It is impossible to assume that the evaluation, interpretation, and reporting of school results would remain untainted by political motives. Any claim to scientific objectivity in accountability reports will involve at least as much rhetoric as truth.[13]

Second, the almost total reliance of accountability schemes on test scores or quantifiable aspects of learning rests upon a theory of knowing or learning that comes out of behavioristic psychology. The view of human beings reflected by behavioristic psychology would more than likely be rejected by most citizens as entirely too simplistic or reductionist. Yet measures of learning dictated by this model of humanity are used as the primary source of evidence that the schools are doing—or not doing—what these same citizens are paying taxes for. That the irony in this goes unnoticed or is ignored only points to the muddying of evaluation purposes by political concerns.[14]

Supervisors have recognized competence and expertise within the school system. They should use their authority and join forces with other supervisors and teachers to resist accountability schemes that take such a one-dimensional and biased view of learning and instruction. If supervisors and teachers allow accountability schemes to intrude more and more into the schools, the end result will be a program that leaves teachers and students little or no latitude in the classroom. Everything will already have been spelled out in a tightly systematic process leading to the achievement of preestablished behavioral objectives.[15]

Finally, supervisors and teachers (and, where possible, students) will engage in summative evaluation activities at the end of the course. Not only will they review what the final results were in student learnings, but they will review the results of their formative evaluations throughout the course. It is during the summative evaluation activity that one can see again the usefulness of the five criteria of good evaluation. The entire program should be reviewed as to the effectiveness of its scope and sequence. This comprehensive evaluation should also include an assessment of the adequacy of instructional materials such as films, slides, reference books, field trips, etc. Those involved in the evaluation should also question whether the use of time and space was helpful. Was the pace about right? Is there any way to revise the class schedule to allow for longer or shorter periods or for a more flexible schedule for large and small group sessions? Such a general overview should also include a look at the high and low points of the course and some guesses at the probable reasons for both. This comprehensive

[13]See Bonnet, op. cit.

[14]See House, op. cit.; Robert E. Stake, "Overview and Critique of Existing Evaluation Practices and Some New Leads for the Future," paper presented at AERA Annual Meeting, San Francisco, 1976; and Kunkel and Tucker, op. cit.

[15]Ernest R. House, "Beyond Accountability," in Thomas J. Sergiovanni (ed.), Professional Supervision for Professional Teachers, Washington, D.C.:Association for Supervisors and Curriculum Development, 1975.

summation of the course or program will enable the teacher to make those necessary decisions about changes in the program next time around. Here is where the supervisor can be an enormous resource as the two come up with a variety of program changes and test them out for logic and "fit" in the overall program. Such a program evaluation often becomes the starting point for the supervisor's agenda the following year.

SUMMARY

This chapter has taken up the supervisor's role in program evaluation. In order to clarify what that role is and to distinguish it from that of the evaluation expert, we presented an overview of program evaluation, of its different levels and technologies and audiences and purposes. Then the thesis was presented that a supervisor's role in program evaluation is primarily to work alongside the teachers as they engage in the ongoing task of evaluating the impact of the program and their implementation of it on students.

We established the distinctions between formative and summative evaluation. We saw that students can engage in their own self-evaluation process in both formative and summative evaluation. This is a central activity that reveals to the teacher how the student is personally appropriating the learning tasks. We saw how in the teacher's use of tests for both formative and summative purposes valuable learning could be taking place. In other words, we stressed that evaluation can be and ought to be viewed as an intrinsic element in both teaching and learning.

While the supervisor acts in a manner supportive to the teacher's evaluation activities and occasionally becomes involved with the teacher in planning and designing evaluation activities, we saw that one essential activity of the supervisor is to keep enough distance from the evaluation activity to perceive the values embedded in the process. Some value assumptions behind rather standard evaluation procedures were highlighted. The five criteria for good evaluation were presented as a means for both teacher and supervisor to check that their evaluation activities were on target.

It is apparent, then, that evaluation is a critical aspect of the supervisor's professional responsibility. Evaluation must be continuous and not simply an end-of-year or end-of-semester assessment. It involves much more than rating the teacher according to the test results of students, and much more than the grading and promotion of students. Rather, the comprehensive evaluation process provides a continuous and responsible basis for decision making throughout the curriculum-instructional program. Only by means of an ongoing evaluation process can the program be improved and adapted to the human needs of students and hence result in more effective student learnings. The neglect of continuous and thoroughgoing evaluation on the part of supervisors, teachers, and students can be cited as the single most pervasive cause of stale and irrelevant instructional programs. Continuous and honest appraisal of the quality and effectiveness of the instructional program, on the other hand, can be the necessary catalyst for imaginative curriculum development itself, as well as for improved teaching strategies.

STUDY GUIDE

Recall the concepts and meanings associated with each of the following phrases and terms included in this chapter. Can you discuss them with a colleague and apply them to the supervisory context of your school? If you cannot, review them in the text and record the page number for future reference.

1. Diagnostic evaluation _____
2. Evaluation activity _____
3. Evaluating evaluation _____
4. Evaluation expert _____
5. Evaluation reporting _____
6. Formative evaluation _____
7. Misuses of testing _____
8. Student self-evaluation _____
9. Summative evaluation _____

EXERCISES

1. Inquire at a school you are familiar with about current accountability reports that the state requires. Do you think the taxpayers are receiving adequate information about the effectiveness of that school? Discuss your reactions in class.
2. Write out your own assumptions behind a method of formative student evaluation that makes sense to you.
3. In your formal education, have you been asked to evaluate what you have learned? How might a student encourage that practice with his or her teachers?
4. Discuss the supervisor's role in program evaluation with two practicing supervisors. How do their views differ from those in this chapter?

CHAPTER 16

SUPERVISION FOR CLASSROOM EFFECTIVENESS

A primary focus of human resources supervision is on increasing the effectiveness of teaching. Teaching effectiveness is, by definition, to bring about the desired student learnings or the objectives of the units of instruction. If the objective of a particular classroom segment is to have every student spell 10 new words correctly, then the teacher who by his or her teaching activity brings all the students to that happy conclusion is said to be effective. Further, the more students learn, the more effective is the teaching. The supervisor's job is to help teachers increase their effectiveness in bringing about increased student learnings.

In this chapter we will review some recent research findings on teacher effectiveness and draw out some implications for supervisory practice. As with our earlier discussions on curriculum, we find that the conclusions from research on effective teaching are not all pointing in the same direction. Frequently the assumption and beliefs of the researchers lead them to focus more on certain aspects of teaching than on others. We will focus here on teaching methodologies and their impact on student learning rather than on the content of what is taught and the adaptation of instructional formats to various content and skill objectives of learning episodes.

There is a burgeoning literature of research on teaching effectiveness.[1] Some school systems have already begun staff development programs to help teachers

[1]C. W. Fisher, N. N. Filby, R. Marliave, L. S. Cahen, M. M. Dishaw, and D. C. Berliner, "Teacher Behaviors, Academic Learning Time and Student Achievement," final report of Phase III-B, *Beginning Teacher Evaluation Study Technical Report Series* (Tech. Rep. V-l), San Francisco: Far West Laboratory, 1978.

Cf. *Educational Leadership*, vol. 37, no. 1, 1979, in which 12 essays on teacher effectiveness appear. One of the better collections of research reports on teacher effectiveness is Penelope P. Peterson and Herbert J. Walberg (eds.), *Research on Teaching: Concepts, Findings, and Implications*, Berkeley, Calif.: McCutchan, 1979.

Cf. Tamar Levin with Ruth Long, *Effective Instruction*, Alexandria, Va.: Association for Supervision and Curriculum Development, 1981. The annotated bibliography at the end of this book is first-rate. Three other books that contain very useful information on effective teaching are Don M. Medley, *Teacher Competence and Teacher Effectiveness: A Review of Process-Product Research*, Washington, D.C.: American Association of Colleges for Teacher Education, 1977; N. L. Gage, *The Scientific Basis of the Art of Teaching*, New York: Teachers College Press, 1978; and Doug Russell and Madeline Hunter, *Planning for Effective Instruction*, Los Angeles: University Elementary School, 1980.

develop classroom skills that research studies have shown to be related to increased student achievement. Others are talking about supervisory evaluation of teachers according to prescribed effectiveness behaviors in their classroom teaching.[2] Although the last word on teaching effectiveness has not been spoken, supervisors will need to be familiar with the findings of teacher-effectiveness research and will need to explore ways to incorporate effectiveness strategies in their work with teachers.

SUMMARY OF RESEARCH FINDINGS ON TEACHER EFFECTIVENESS

While the findings may sound very familiar to an experienced teacher or supervisor and appear to the ordinary citizen as good common sense, the research has been able to document that certain teacher behaviors are related to student gains on both criterion and norm-referenced tests. Among those behaviors frequently cited by research studies we find the following.

- Establish classroom rules that allow pupils to attend to personal and procedural needs without having to check with the teacher.
- Communicate expectations of high achievement.
- Start off each class by reviewing homework and by reviewing material covered in the previous few classes.
- Make the objectives of the new instructional episode clear to the students.
- Directly teach the content or skill that will be measured on the test.
- After teaching the new material, assess student comprehension through questions and practice.
- Provide for uninterrupted successful practice that is now monitored by the teacher moving around the classroom.
- Maintain direct engagement by the student on the academic task. Engaged academic time is a critical variable for student achievement.
- Assign homework to increase student familiarity with material.
- Hold review sessions weekly and monthly.

Before jumping to conclusions about the implications of these research findings for supervisory practice we need to see them in perpsective. First of all, most of these studies were concentrating on the teaching of basic skills in reading and arithmetic in the earlier grades of elementary school. Whether these teaching behaviors are appropriate for higher-level learning in reading and mathematics or for learnings in other areas, such as geography or art, is an open question.

Furthermore, the research on effective teaching does not necessarily account for other variables that may affect student achievement. Research on home influences, for example, indicates that family stability, the prior education of parents, juvenile delinquency, alcoholic or drug-addicted parents, family income, and so on can enhance

---

[2]David A. Squires, William G. Huitt, and John K. Segars, "Improving Classrooms and Schools: What's Important," *Educational Leadership*, vol. 39, no. 3, pp. 174–179, 1981; and Shirley B. Stow, "Using Effectiveness Research in Teacher Evaluation," *Educational Leadership*, vol. 37, no. 1, pp. 55–58, 1979.

or limit classroom effects.[3] While a teacher, following the prescriptions of effective teaching, may increase the achievement levels of most of his or her students, he or she may be unable to reach some students whose home backgrounds are so chaotic as to cripple their ability to concentrate on academic tasks. Likewise, the success of some teachers in bringing about higher achievement of their students may be enhanced by the stable family backgrounds of their students, rich in educational resources. Would we rate one teacher as more effective than another whose students come from far less favorable home environments?

Research on effective schools reveals that there are schoolwide variables that can enhance or limit the impact of a given classroom teacher's efforts to move toward more effective teaching behaviors. While no one school variable of itself may account for school effectiveness, taken together a critical mass of positive school factors can support an individual teacher's effective teaching practices.[4] If all the teachers in the school have high expectations of students, a single teacher's effectiveness will be greater than if he or she is the only one in the school with high expectations. If no one else in the school assigns homework, then that teacher's effectiveness will be diminished when he or she initiates the effort to assign homework.

SUMMARY OF RESEARCH ON TEACHING

Recently, Herbert Walberg and his associates Diane Schiller and Geneva Haertel became interested in assessing the adequacy of educational research completed in recent years. They conducted a thorough review of research published between 1969 and 1979.[5] Of particular interest was research on teaching and instruction. They sought to demonstrate that during the decade in question the educational research community had accumulated highly useful findings addressed to policymakers and professional practitioners alike. A side benefit of this review was to demonstrate the effects of a variety of approaches to teaching and instruction. Some of the studies tabulated by Walberg and his associates are shown in Table 16-1.

The studies we select from Walberg's summary are grouped into three categories: those that support aspects of structured approaches to teaching, those that compare aspects of structured with unstructured approaches to teaching, and those that support the effects of climate on learning.

Most approaches to teaching characterized as structured are similar in their emphasis on cognitive learning, predetermined objectives, teacher direction, and

---

[3]See Ralph Scott and Herbert J. Walberg, "Schools Alone Are Insufficient," *Educational Leadership*, vol. 37, no. 1, pp. 24–27, 1979; James S. Coleman et al., *Equality of Educational Opportunity*, Washington, D.C.: U.S. Office of Education, National Center for Educational Statistics, 1966; and Christopher Jencks et al., *Inequality: A Reassessment of the Effects of Family and Schooling in America*, New York: Basic Books, 1972.
[4]See Gilbert R. Austin, "Exemplary Schools and the Search for Effectiveness," *Educational Leadership*, vol. 37, no. 1, pp. 10–14, 1979; and Michael Rutter, Barbara Maughan, Peter Mortimer, and Janet Ouston, *Fifteen Thousand Hours: Secondary Schools and Their Effects on Children*, Cambridge, Mass.: Harvard University Press, 1979.
[5]Herbert J. Walberg, Diane Schiller, and Geneva D. Haertel, "The Quiet Revolution in Educational Research," *Phi Delta Kappan*, vol. 61, no. 3, pp. 179–183, 1979.

TABLE 16-1
**SELECTED SUMMARY OF RESEARCH ON TEACHING AND LEARNING AS
TABULATED BY WALBERG, SCHILLER, AND HAERTEL**

I. SELECTED RESEARCH ON STRUCTURED APPROACHES TO TEACHING

Topics	No. of Results	Percent Positive
Behavioral instruction on learning	52	98.1
Personalized system of instruction (PSI) on learning	103	93.2
Mastery learning	30	96.7
Programmed instruction on learning	57	80.7
Advanced organizers on learning	32	37.5
Direct instruction on achievement	4	100.0

II. SELECTED RESEARCH COMPARING MORE AND LESS STRUCTURED APPROACHES

Topics	No. of Results	Percent Positive
Lecture favored over discussion on		
Achievement	16	68.8
Retention	7	100.0
Attitudes	8	86.0
Student-centered discussion favored over teacher-centered on		
Achievement	7	57.1
Understanding	6	83.0
Attitude	22	100.0
Factual questions favored over conceptual on achievement	4	100.0
Open or informal education favored over traditionally structured education on		
Achievement	26	54.8
Creativity	12	100.0
Self-concept	17	88.2
Attitude toward school	25	92.0
Curiosity	6	100.0
Self-determination	7	85.7
Independence	19	94.7
Freedom from anxiety	8	37.5
Cooperation	6	100.0

III. SELECTED RESEARCH ON CLIMATE AND TEACHING

Topics	No. of Results	Percent Positive
Motivation and learning	232	97.8
Sociopsychological climate and learning		
Cohesiveness	17	85.7
Satisfaction	17	100.0
Difficulty	16	86.7

TABLE 16-1 *(Continued)*

III. SELECTED RESEARCH ON CLIMATE AND TEACHING

Topics	No. of Results	Percent Positive
Formality	17	64.7
Goal direction	15	73.3
Democracy	14	84.6
Environment	15	85.7
Speed	14	53.8
Diversity	14	30.8
Competition	9	66.7
Friction	17	0.0
Cliqueness	13	8.3
Apathy	15	14.3
Disorganization	17	6.3
Favoritism	13	10.0

SOURCE: Herbert J. Walberg, Diane Schiller, and Geneva D. Haertel, "The Quiet Revolution in Educational Research," *Phi Delta Kappan,* vol. 61, no. 3, pp. 180–181, 1979.

carefully paced instruction. A personalized system of instruction (PSI), for example, relies on small units of written instruction, student self-pacing, mastery of subject matter at level A before proceeding to level B, and repeated testing. Mastery learning relies on diagnosis of entry-level skills and understandings, on clear objectives and specified learning procedures, on small units of learning, feedback, and on flexible learning time. Direct instruction refers to methods of instruction, under tight teacher control, that focus specifically on the content of tests. These are overwhelmingly effective techniques for teaching the basic skills in reading and math and for teaching subject matter where achievement is measured by recall.

Notice in the comparisons depicted in the second category of Table 16-1 that lecturing is favored over discussion in achievement and retention of subject matter but that student-centered discussion is favored over teacher-centered discussion for building understanding of subject matter and promoting positive attitudes toward learning. The lower the level of learning (facts, simple recall), the more appropriate are direct methods of instruction.

Informal or more open teaching strategies seem superior to structured approaches in promoting creativity, self-concept enhancement, positive attitudes toward school, curiosity, self-determination, independence, and cooperation.

Teaching approaches, therefore, seem less an issue of which is the best way than of which is the best way for what purpose. Good classrooms and gifted teachers exhibit a variety of teaching approaches, mixing both formal and informal methods as circumstances require.

Teacher-effectiveness researchers and consumers of this research are naturally excited about the discoveries, and in their commitment to improve practice, they often make unrealistic and misleading claims as to what constitutes effective teaching. Typically, teacher-effectiveness research attempts to link certain teacher behaviors and modes of instruction to student outcomes. When the link is established (as in the case of direct instruction being related to higher student achievement in the basic skills), the claim is often made by researchers, and interpreted as such by practitioners, that the instructional methods investigated are generally effective. Not specifying exactly what student outcomes are of issue or what relationships between teacher behaviors and outcomes are suggested can lead to confusion and misunderstanding of the facts.

Medley's comprehensive review of teacher-effectiveness research, which links teaching processes to student outcomes, is a case in point.[6] He is careful to point out that the research he reviews involves correlational studies; thus relationships observed do not prove that certain teacher behaviors *cause* particular student outcomes. These studies show only that a relationship exists. Further, the studies he reviews consist almost entirely of dependent variables, defined as pupil performance on reading and mathematics achievement tests in the primary grades. Despite Medley's care in pointing out these limitations, his findings are often assumed to refer to general concepts of teacher effectiveness that apply to all students, for all outcomes, in all settings.

SOME NECESSARY CONDITIONS TO EFFECTIVE SUPERVISION AND EVALUATION

Perhaps most fundamental to the process of supervision and evaluation is that the supervisor have a firm and informed knowledge of substantive aspects of educational programs and teaching. It is true that certain aspects of teaching are so obviously ascertained that even amateurs can successfully evaluate them. Picking up indicators of warmth, patterns of classroom interaction, differences between on- and off-task behaviors, describing classroom arrangements, and detecting teacher or student boredom do not require that one be well versed in pedagogy, principles of learning, or curriculum development. But discerning the appropriateness of a teaching strategy given a particular set of objectives, commenting on the adequacy of an advanced organizer, detecting whether an interest center is functioning properly, understanding how the inquiry method works, judging the adequacy of chosen curriculum materials, and commenting on the implications of a particular reinforcement pattern on student long-term motivation require a higher level of sophistication in things educational.

Teacher-effectiveness research can play a critical role in increasing our understanding of supervisory issues and in helping to develop supervisory strategies. But the relationships uncovered to date are too complex and too situational to become surrogates for educated judgments. Gage's suggestions that we view teaching as a practical art with a scientific basis may well be worth noting:

> Scientific method can contribute relationships between variables taken two at a time and even, in the form of interactions, three or perhaps four or more at a time. Beyond say, four, the usefulness of what science can give the teacher begins to weaken, because teachers cannot apply, at least not without help and not on the run, the more complex interactions. At this point, the teacher as artist must step in and make clinical, or artistic, judgments about the best ways to teach. In short, the scientific basis for the art of teaching will consist of two-variable relationships and lower-order interactions. The higher-order interactions between four and more variables must be handled by the teacher as artist.[7]

[6]Medley, op. cit.
[7]Gage, op. cit., p. 20.

Efforts to bring a scientific basis to teaching are important despite the fact that a one-to-one correspondence does not exist between scientific knowledge and practice. Instead, such knowledge can best serve and inform the decision-making process in supervision and enhance the art of teaching.

MATCHING TEACHING AND EVALUATION STRATEGIES

The following assumptions are essential to developing a balanced perspective in supervision and teacher evaluation.

1. No one teaching method is inherently better than another.

2. Supervisors and teachers need to be sensitive to the conditions under which various approaches to teaching are more and less effective.

3. Evaluation strategies need to take into account the characteristics of the teaching strategy under study in evaluating teaching.

4. Effective evaluation requires that the supervisor be well informed about such educational matters as curriculum, models of teaching, principles of learning, and classroom arrangements.

5. Asking the supervisor to develop a sense of purpose and a vision of future possibilities should not be confused with asking the supervisor to develop a narrow, rigid, dogmatic view of teaching.

6. A choice of a teaching approach is *contingent* upon a number of factors found in the teaching situation such as purposes, characteristics of students, availability of materials, space and time, and needs of teachers.

7. Adopting a variable approach to teaching does not obviate the necessity for *any* chosen approach to contain certain nurturing and human characteristics toward students.

In the following sections, we provide some guidelines in the form of questions that can help supervisors apply a contingency perspective, identify evaluation issues, and plan an evaluation strategy.

• What is the approach to teaching this teacher has in mind?

Let us assume that the teacher plans a role-playing exericse that engages students in a mock trial.

• Is this approach appropriate to the teaching purposes or outcomes sought? Is this approach appropriate to the teaching setting envisaged?

Role playing is a suitable teaching strategy for clarifying student values and addressing attitudinal issues. If the teacher envisions a lesson designed to help students learn the official names and duties of various roles common to jury trials, this method is less appropriate than direct instruction. Discussions with the teacher as to how students will be evaluated can provide clues to intended purposes. If the teacher has a matching test in mind, then probably role playing is a poor teaching choice. Perhaps the teacher is not sure of intended outcomes but feels that role playing is a good educational encounter anyway. In evaluating students the teacher might have in mind an open-ended essay as to how the student profited from the lesson. Then under these circumstances role playing might well be an excellent choice.

• Given what is known about the particular approach to teaching, how knowledgeable is the teacher about the theoretical aspects of this approach? How successful is the teacher in implementing this approach?

Evaluation strategies and methods need to take into account the purposes of the teacher and the proposed method of teaching. It would not be appropriate to criticize a teacher using direct instruction for too much teacher talk. Collecting materials used by students to assess their diversity or photographing students every 5 minutes to determine the extent to which they are engaged in a variety of learning settings does not fit this teaching method either. Certainly the evaluator can and should comment on whether direct instruction fits the purposes intended. But once teacher and evaluator agree that this method makes sense, the evaluation should do justice to the method. The same can be said for more informal or open methods of teaching. Asking all students to measure up to certain standard and predetermined criteria may well be an evaluation techinque inappropriate to informal methods of teaching.

• How does this approach fit into the teacher's overall frame of reference or philosophy of teaching? How does this approach fit into the school's overall frame of reference or philosophy of teaching?

One danger in adopting a contingency perspective is that it leads teachers and supervisors to conclude that anything goes. The supervisor need only ask the teacher what the intents are and evaluate accordingly. We do not accept this point of view. Schools and classrooms should operate from a set of principles and a vision of ideals. An educational platform should be developed from this broad view of the desirable and possible. This educational platform should serve as a basis for decision making and as a standard for evaluating the appropriateness of decisions about curriculum matters and broad teaching strategies. Particular teaching strategies selected by the teacher should be evaluated for goodness of fit against this standard.

• Given the array of approaches available to the teacher and acceptable to the school, does the selection of a given approach suggest a balanced repertoire of teaching strategies?

Though it is not reasonable for a school to permit teachers complete autonomy in the selection of teaching strategies, it is reasonable and indeed imperative to expect that teachers incorporate a variety of strategies to accommodate the diverse purposes of education and the array of unique learning styles of students.

CRITERIA FOR TEACHING EFFECTIVENESS

By raising questions about the findings of research on teaching effectiveness, have we destroyed any basis for evaluating effective teaching? On the contrary, we have attempted to broaden the base for recognizing and evaluating effectiveness. The statements below can be viewed as offering criteria for evaluating effectiveness.

1. *Explains Objectives of the Learning Unit.* The teacher explains what the class is going to do, why they are going to do it, what will be expected of the students as a result of the learning unit, and how that unit relates to what went before and what comes after. This is essential to provide clarity, a sense of purpose and intelligibility to their activities, and a sense of accountability for the results.

2. *Engaged Time.* Whether the objectives of the unit are focused on acquisition of lower-level, basic skills or on higher-level reasoning and imaginative expression, the teacher must provide ample opportunity for the student to practice the skill, apply it to similar material, and understand the meaning of the conceptual material in a way that is developmentally appropriate for students at that age or grade level. In other words, the instruction, the question and discussion period, the seat work exercises, the homework, and the periodic review bring the students into interaction with the material for a long enough time for them to grasp, understand, and apply what they are supposed to be learning.

3. *Attention to Diversity of Learning Objectives.* Since schools have a variety of goals and objectives, some academic, some social, individual classrooms should reflect the pursuit of those goals and objectives. Teachers should attend to these objectives by engaging students in a variety of activities that promote the objectives. For example, a school objective might be to encourage students to "learn how to learn." If students are taught by only one method, let us say through direct instruction, then they will tend to learn only through that method. This criteria proposes that students be encouraged to be active as well as passive; to employ convergent and divergent reasoning; to be exact in repeating some learnings and to interpret according to personal experience in other learnings; to learn impulse control and disciplined attention to tasks, as well as to learn how to use imagination, fantasy, and humor to accomplish other tasks; to learn how to disagree in group discussions as well as how to arrive at a consensus; to work individually as well as in a group on problem solving; and to reflect on value implications of what they are learning as well as to explore other points of view. While all of these objectives may not be attended to simultaneously, does the teacher vary the classroom activities so that during the course of a week or so many of the objectives are attended to?

4. *Variety of Instructional Techniques.* In order to prevent boredom and to reach students with diverse learning styles and diverse home backgrounds, teachers should present material in a variety of ways, now verbal, now visual, now through hands-on experiments, now through puzzles, simulations, or stories, and so forth, even for the same learning objective.

5. *Feedback.* To provide students with a sense of success or achievement as well as to discover which students are still experiencing difficulty, the teacher employs a variety of techniques to elicit responses from students and to respond to student expressions. This teaching behavior prevents some students from falling behind, provides encouragement and motivation, and keeps student on-task engagement at a high level. Both formative and summative evaluation techniques are required.

6. *Review and Recapitulation.* In order to solidify the learning gains and to place individual learning units into a larger perspective, teachers must regularly spend time reviewing what the class has learned in earlier lessons. This enables students to deepen their grasp on the material, prepares them for tests, helps them to see larger relationships, and corrects incomplete learnings. Except for the few students who enjoy the ability of instant and total recall, repetition, review, and recapitulation are absolutely essential for a more permanent grasp, retention, and application of learning.

7. *A Caring Relationship for Students.* Teachers manifest caring in a variety of ways. Some stern, demanding teachers convey a lot of caring. Some "democratic" teachers are actually highly manipulative and uncaring. No matter how the caring is expressed, students know, after a short while, whether the teacher cares for them. That relationship of caring is not only important for motivating students to work harder at their subjects, but is intrinsic to the essence of teaching. Caring does not guarantee by itself increased student achievement, but it is impossible to be effective without it.

8. *Holding Students Responsible for Results.* This is related to holding high expectations of students. It goes beyond simply expressing expectations, however, to demanding that students complete the tasks expected of them. In other words, if the objectives of a learning unit require the student to produce something, the teacher must insist that the student produce it. There will always be the exceptional case (death of a parent, sickness, etc.), but the rule is that students are expected to fulfill the requirements of the learning unit.

Perhaps other criteria can be added to these. None of these effectiveness criteria in isolation will guarantee effectiveness. Rather, it is through the complex influence of all of these behaviors on student learnings that teachers will find their work with students leading to enhanced student learning.

SUPERVISORY SKILLS AND TEACHER EVALUATION

It is useful to view the process of teacher evaluation as requiring three levels of skills from supervisors: technical, human, and conceptual.[8] The skills are actually quite interdependent but can be treated separately for purposes of analysis.

Technical skills assume ability to use knowledge, methods, and techniques to perform specific tasks. The mechanics associated with conducting an analysis of classroom interaction, in videotaping a teaching episode, in applying teacher-

[8]See Robert L. Kata, "Skills of an Effective Administrator," *Harvard Business Review,* vol. 33, no. 1, pp. 33–42, 1955.

effectiveness research to the construction of rating scales, in assembling a portfolio of classroom artifacts, in developing a narrative or a case description of life in a given classroom, in writing up an evaluation report, and in using criterion reference tests are examples of techincal skills in evaluation.

Human skills refer to one's ability and judgment in working with people. This skill requires self-understanding and acceptance as well as consideration for others. Its knowledge base includes an understanding of and facility for providing leadership, the helping relationship, adult motivation, attitudinal development, change intervention and behavior, and group dynamics. Establishing rapport, giving support and help, building trust, colleagueship, and other aspects of interpersonal relationships essential to effective supervision are examples of human skills in evaluation.

Conceptual skills refer to one's ability to view the process of supervision and evaluation more holistically. This skill includes the effective mapping of the interdependence between evaluation strategies and teaching strategies, evaluation strategies and curriculum designs, and evaluation strategies and the program and staff development aspirations for the school. Understanding the assumptions underlying a particular evaluation approach, its purposes, and methods and the circumstances under which this approach is more or less suitable are examples of conceptual skills in evaluation.

Various models of teaching differ on a number of key dimensions, including basic assumptions about learning theory, knowledge worth and usage, purposes and priorities, student and teacher roles, the use of materials, the amount of structure, and the formality and design of the learning setting. Developmental-cognitive approaches to teaching young children are quite different in all these respects from programmed approaches. This is the case as well at the high school level when comparing, for example, direct instruction with inquiry teaching. Conceptual differences in teaching models require conceptually different evaluation strategies.

Despite the fact that many approaches to teacher evaluation are conceptually distinct, it is possible to speak of certain universal evaluation skills that transcend the particular evaluation strategy under study. These skills would be as much a part of a clinical supervision cycle as they would be a goal-setting evaluation strategy. Conceptually distinct teacher-evaluation strategies differ less on which technical evaluation skills are used and more on the unique emphasis given to a particular pattern of skills as compared to other patterns.

Clearly the human skills required of supervisors involved in teacher evaluation transcend the particular approach or strategy chosen. All approaches require that teacher and supervisor be in communication with each other, trust each other, and believe in each other. All require a knowledge of the change process, some ability to give leadership and support, and a commitment to be responsive to teacher needs.

SUMMARY

This chapter attempted to alert those with supervisory responsibilities to the emergence of impressive research findings on teacher effectiveness. These findings can be very helpful in providing supervisors with useful information when working with teachers who are seeking to improve their effectiveness. We suggested, however, that supervisors beware of creating a new dogma on teaching methodology that would be applied exclusively and uniformly to all classroom situations at every level of schooling. We suggested that the type of teaching methods be adapted to the learning objectives being pursued, and that the learning objectives of schooling are multiple. They include student achievement in the basic skills of reading and mathematics, to be sure, but they also include a variety of problem-solving skills, analytical reasoning, metaphorical expression, group skills, creativity, citizenship skills, divergent thinking, and so on.

In raising larger questions about an exclusive focus on the findings of research on effective teaching, we do not want to discourage the use of those methods that can appropriately be used to enhance student achievement on measures of basic-skill development. Supervisors, especially those dealing with elementary school teachers, can find these approaches enormously helpful. We believe, however, that in their concern for the more total human growth of the student, supervisors should also promote other teaching methods that deal with other learning variables.

STUDY GUIDE

Recall the concepts, ideas, and meanings associated with each of the following phrases and terms included in this chapter. Can you discuss each of them with a colleague and apply them to the supervisory context of your school? If you cannot, review them in the text and record the page number for future reference.

1. Academic engaged time _____
2. Criteria for effectiveness _____
3. Direct instruction _____
4. Effective instruction _____
5. Matching teaching to objectives _____
6. Personalized system of instruction _____
7. Three levels of supervisory skills _____

EXERCISES

1. Assume a basic economics class is studying a unit on paying taxes. What would be some potential learning outcomes from teaching by direct instruction? What different outcomes would emerge from a class discussion on the fairness of tax loophole? Are the two methods opposed or complementary? Are they both necessary?
2. List least three different sets of learning outcomes you have focused on in your teaching. Do they require different teaching methods, styles of classroom management, and performance evaluations?
3. Has a school or school system you are familiar with used any of the research findings on teaching effectiveness? What are the results in terms of student achievement, teacher attitudes, and supervisory practices?
4. Visit a class and try to estimate how much time students are actually engaged in academic learning. Should there be more engaged academic time in that class? If so, what changes in the teacher's behavior would be necessary? Would anything valuable be lost by increasing students' engaged academic time in the classroom?
5. Show the eight criteria for teaching effectiveness to three veteran teachers. Ask the teachers to comment on the criteria, and ask the teachers whether they would wish to be evaluated according to them.

PART FOUR

A HUMAN RESOURCES APPROACH TO STAFF DEVELOPMENT, CLINICAL SUPERVISION, AND TEACHER EVALUATION

INTRODUCTION: GROWTH-ORIENTED CLASSROOM SUPERVISION

The state of the art of classroom supervision is perhaps best illustrated by examining prevailing teach-evaluation strategies. Teacher evaluation has typically meant the rating, grading, and classifying of teachers using some locally standardized instrument as a yardstick. The instrument generally lists certain traits of teachers assumed to be important, such as "the teacher has a pleasant voice," and certain tasks of teaching considered to be critical, such as "the teacher plans well." The evaluator usually writes in comments as, increasingly, does the teacher.

This evaluation instrument is filled out after a classroom observation of the teacher, often lasting from one-half to one hour. The observation visit is usually preceded by a conference, which varies from a brief encounter to a session where lesson plans, objectives, and teaching strategies are discussed. Sometimes a post-observation conference follows, wherein comments and ratings are discussed and negotiated. Usually, the teacher-evaluation procedure is concluded when both parties sign the instrument. The instrument is then forwarded to the district archives. This teacher-evaluation procedure may occur once or twice a year for the tenured teacher and two to four times a year for novices. Many teachers report having been observed in the classroom only a handful of times, and reports of almost never being observed after achieving tenure are common. Though exceptions exist and progress is being made, by and large neither teachers nor administrators and supervisors are satisfied with present procedures. More damaging, many supervisors privately view the procedures as lacking in credibility. What are the likely effects of participating in a system characterized by such doubts? The system takes on a certain artificial or mechanical quality, a routine functioning that becomes an end in itself.

The present state of classroom supervision can be attributed to *faulty ideology* and *faulty technology*. The dominant ideologies in supervision are those associated with human relations and scientific management. The effects of human relations have been to adopt laissez faire approaches that severely downgrade classroom supervision. Presumably, it is considered that teachers are professionals, and if treated nicely, but otherwise left alone, they will respond properly. The classroom is the castle of the teacher as a professional, and classroom supervision is viewed as threatening to, or usurping of, teacher authority. This argument is an attractive rationalism for many principals and supervisors who have good management skills and some interpersonal facility but are otherwise weak or uncomfortable in dealing with the educational side of the enterprise.

Increasingly, the emphasis in schools has shifted from classroom supervision to general supervision, and this is the scientific-management side of the ideology question. In the scientific-management view it is felt that if one can focus primarily on educational program administration and supervision through developing a materials-intensive curriculum, usually linked to a detailed curriculum syllabus or detailed predetermined objectives, then teachers can be supervised in classrooms by remote control. Teaching behavior becomes more predictable and reliable as teaching objectives and materials become more detailed, structured, and standardized. Thus we can control what teachers do by controlling the objectives they pursue, the materials they use, the curriculum they follow, the assignments and tests they give, and the schedule they follow. Granting that the existence of this kind of materials-intensive program is a means to control classroom practices, nagging questions born of the accountability movement remain. How can supervisors *be sure* that teachers are indeed performing prescribed duties up to standard? What evaluation technology can be used to answer this question? Technologies are associated with ideologies, and the language of scientific management (objectivity, rationality, reliability, precision) has been found by most Americans to be irresistible. The technology of classroom observation and evaluation, as most readers will attest, is shrouded in a sense of scientism not found even in the more legitimate sciences. This phenomenon is contrary to what most educators actually believe—*that teaching is far more an artistic enterprise than a scientific one*. Not willing to admit this publicly, we continue our deception by willy-nilly participation in a doubtful system of supervision and evaulation.

The pressure for accountability is, in our view, legitimate and cannot be ignored. Classroom supervision and evaluation is important and is needed and desired by teachers and the public alike. But the typical response to this pressure—tightening up a set of procedures with ideological and technical shortcomings, doing more of the same but now doing it with more intensity—needs to be reversed. These issues are discussed in Chapter 17, where more artistic approaches to supervision and evaluation more consistent with the values of human resources supervision and the nature of work in education are suggested. A caveat at this point is significant. Though we are strong advocates of more artistic approaches, we seek not to throw out the proverbial baby with the bath water. Present methods have value if viewed more modestly and intelligently, if applied in a more discriminating fashion, and if supplemented by more artistic approaches. (On this note, a theory of supervisory practice that brings together scientific and artistic views will be presented in Chapter 19. Chapter 16, concerned with classroom and teaching-effectiveness research and models of teaching, adopted a contingency perspective in search of useful insights into teaching. Key to this perspective is that a particular method of teaching or style of classroom organization should be judged in terms of what it can and cannot accomplish. This relative view is recommended over more dogmatic views that seek to establish true and false ideologies in teaching.)

GENERAL VERSUS CLINICAL SUPERVISION

Most of the literature on supervision and textbooks on supervision tend to emphasize either (or some combination of) the organizational and behavioral aspects of general supervision or the educational program administration aspects of general supervision. Most notable in recent years are books by Harris[1] (educational program administration emphasis), Alfonso, Firth, and Neville,[2] and Wiles and Lovell[3] (organizational and behavioral emphasis). Parts One and Two of this book are also concerned with general supervision. Part One, for example, is concerned with the organizational-leadership aspect of general supervision and Part Two with the educational-leadership aspects of general supervision. The strong emphasis one finds in the literature on general supervision is related in part to the decline of interest in classroom supervision by scholars and practitioners.

In the interest of focusing attention anew on classroom supervision, some have attempted to distinguish between the two by referring to classroom supervision as clinical and out-of-class supervision as general. Cogan, for example, cites two purposes of clinical supervision in his popular book entitled *Clinical Supervision:* "The first is to develop and explicate a system of in-class supervision that, in competent hands, will prove powerful enough to give supervisors a reasonable hope of accomplishing significant improvements in the teacher's classroom instruction. The second purpose is to help correct the neglect of in-class or clinical supervision and to establish it as a necessary complement to out-of-class ('general') supervision."[4]

In a similar vein Goldhammer refers to clinical supervision as follows:

> First of all, I mean to convey an image of face-to-face relationships between supervisors and teachers. History provides the principal reason for this emphasis, namely, that in many situations presently and during various periods in its development, supervision has been conducted as supervision from a distance, as, for example, supervision of curriculum development or of instructional policies framed by committees of teachers. "Clinical" supervision is meant to imply supervision up close.[5]

General and clinical supervision are, of course, interdependent. Meaningful classroom interventions are built upon healthy organizational climates, facilitated by

---

[1]Ben N. Harris, *Supervisory Behavior in Education*, 2d ed., Englewood Cliffs, N.J.: Prentice-Hall, 1975.
[2]Robert Alfonso, Gerald Firth, and Richard F. Neville, *Instructional Supervision: A Behavioral System*, Boston: Allyn and Bacon, 1975.
[3]Kimball Wiles and John Lovell, *Supervision for Better Schools*, Englewood Cliffs, N.J.: Prentice-Hall, 1975.
[4]Morris L. Cogan, *Clinical Supervision*, Boston: Houghton Mifflin, 1973, p. xi.
[5]Robert Goldhammer, *Clinical Supervision: Special Methods for the Supervision of Teachers*, New York: Holt, 1969, p. 54.

credible leadership and premised on a reasoned educational program. Though general supervision is an important and necessary component of effective supervision, without clinical supervision it is not sufficient.

THE FOCUS OF CLINICAL SUPERVISION

Clinical supervision refers to face-to-face contact with teachers with the intent of improving instruction and increasing professional growth. In many respects, a one-to-one correspondence exists between improving classroom instruction and increasing professional growth, and for this reason staff development and clinical supervision are inseparable concepts and activities. How does evaluation fit into this picture? Evaluation is a natural part of one's professional life and occurs continuously. Every decision that teachers, administrators, and supervisors make is preceded by evaluation (often latent) of some sort. Evaluation is valuing, and valuing is judging. These are natural events in the lives of educational professionals and, of course, are critical aspects of clinical supervision and staff development.

But evaluation can take a number of foci, some of which are more compatible with events, purposes, and characteristics of educational supervision than others. Evaluation experts, for example, make an important distinction between *formative* evaluation and *summative* evaluation.[6] Teacher-evaluation procedures typically found in school can be classified as summative. Evaluation that emphasizes ongoing growth and development would be considered formative. Consider the following distinctions:

1. Summative evaluation of teachers has a certain finality to it—it is terminal in the sense that it occurs at the conclusion of an educational activity. In evaluating a teacher's performance, summative evaluation suggests a statement of worth. A judgment is made about the quality of one's teaching.

2. Summative evaluation is a legitimate and important activity which if done carefully can play a constructive role in a school's total evaluation strategy.

3. Formative evaluation of teachers in intended to increase the effectiveness of on-going educational programs and activity. Evaluation information is collected and used to understand, correct and improve on-going activity.

4. With respect to teaching, formative evaluation is concerned less with judging and rating the teacher than with providing information which helps improve teacher performance.

5. In the strictest sense formative and summative evaluation cannot be separated, for each contains aspects of the other, but it is useful nevertheless to speak of a formative focus and a summative focus to evaluation.[7]

[6]Michael Scriven, "The Methodology of Evaluation," in Robert Stake (ed.), *AERA Monograph on Curriculum Evaluation,* no. 1, Chicago: Rand McNally, 1965. See also Benjamin Bloom, Thomas Hastings, and G. F. Madaus, *Handbook on Formative and Summative Evaluation of Student Learning,* New York: McGraw-Hill, 1971.
[7]Thomas J. Sergiovanni, *Handbook for Effective Department Leadership Concepts and Practices in Today's Secondary Schools,* Boston: Allyn and Bacon, 1977, p. 372.

The focus of clinical supervision should be on formative evaluation. The supervisor is first and foremost interested in improving instruction and increasing teachers' personal development. Does this emphasis conflict with demands that teachers be held accountable for their actions? We think not. A formative evaluation emphasis is entirely consistent with holding teachers accountable, but in a professional, not occupational, sense. Professional accountability is growth-oriented and implies a commitment to consistent improvement. Occupational accountability is not growth-oriented at all, but merely seeks to meet some predetermined standard. Presumably, once this standard is met—that is, once the teacher is judged to meet minimum standards of "satisfactory" teaching—the teacher's growth obligations cease.

From time to time supervisors will indeed be engaged in a more summatively focused evaluation. Though the supervisor's major commitment is to formative evaluation, occasional problems occur and incompetent teachers or teachers whose philosophy and orientation are disengaged from that of the school will be discovered. As a result, withholding tenure or dismissal of a tenured teacher may well be considered. Personnel actions of this sort are so intertwined with existing local administrative policies and state statutory restrictions and requirements that a totally different mind-set is needed. Such a procedure is best placed in the hands of a line administrative officer of the district. In the case of a principal who assumes both a supervisory and administrative role, the teacher should be informed of the focus and the tone of the evaluation procedure that is to follow. The school attorney would most likely be consulted regarding due process if administrative guidelines on this question are wanting. Many state education agencies and state school board associations publish pamphlets and other guidelines on this touchy and increasingly legalistic problem.[8] These issues are discussed in the latter part of Chapter 17.

Practically speaking, if we are interested in improving classroom instruction, we must start with the teacher. Sustained changes in teacher behavior and sustained improvements in classroom functioning occur as a result of teachers who are committed to these changes. That being the case, supervisors are forced to depend upon the willing cooperation of teachers. Indeed, the supervisor does not change teachers but helps them to change, a condition more suited to formative evaluation.

In addition to what is known about changing behavior, the supervisor needs to face up to the reality resulting from increased staff stability today and in the decade or so ahead. Good teaching jobs are increasingly difficult to find, and teachers are less likely to leave once they are employed. Low teacher turnover is often viewed initially as a blessing, particularly by those who just a few years ago experienced difficulty in finding and keeping teachers. But in reality, low turnover poses serious problems for schools. For example, dissatisfied teachers are now less likely to leave. Their reasons for staying in the job are too important.

With regard to change, in an expanding district one can impose changes on existing staff, and by the process of staff attrition and careful replacement, transfers, and careful new assignments, obtain commitment to these changes. But under present

[8]See, for example, Newell N. Jenkins, Terrence Barnicle, Gerald Dempsey, and J. Todd Franklin, *Formal Dismissal Procedures under Illinois Teacher Tenure Laws*, Springfield: Illinois Association of School Boards, 1975.

conditions of stability, changes in educational programs and teaching practices must be accompanied by parallel changes in identity and commitment of the present teaching staff. And finally, many schools are faced with the prospect of a relatively young teaching staff likely to grow old together over the next 2 or 3 decades. Age in itself has the potential to provide natural benefits that accrue from experience and maturity. But this potential can be lost unless marked by a commitment to continuous personal and professional development. The critical nature of staff-development needs in the decades ahead is a convincing argument for every school district to adopt a formatively oriented system of clinical supervision.

SUMMARY

In this introduction current practices relating to teacher evaluation were criticized. It was suggested that teachers and supervisors alike have doubts about the credibility and usefulness of current practices but seem nevertheless to participate in them. Doubtful participation results in the system being characterized by a certain mechanical, artificial, and routine quality, whereby the evaluation process becomes an end in itself. It was further suggested that defects in the system could be attributed to faulty ideology and faulty technology. The ideology of human relations seems to have resulted in a neglect of classroom supervision, though present accountability pressures are intent on correcting this neglect. The technology of scientific management has armed the supervisor with an array of teacher-evaluation weapons that may not be as suited to the basically artistic nature of teaching as might be first assumed. More artistic practices, better suited to the educational enterprise, will be offered in Chapter 17.

In the interest of focusing attention anew on classroom supervision, a distinction was made between clinical and general supervision. The former refers to face-to-face contact with teachers intended to improve both the quality of instruction and teacher professional growth (Part Four of this book). The latter refers to the organizational and behavioral aspects of supervisory life (Part One) on the one hand, and educational programs administration and supervision (Part Three) on the other. It was claimed that an emphasis on educational programs administration and supervision to the exclusion of more than token clinical supervision was akin to supervising teachers by remote control.

Formative and summative evaluations were then discussed. Though both emphases are inevitable in any system of supervision and evaluation, it was suggested that the proper and dominant focus of clinical supervision is formative. Formative evaluation is consistent with a growth-oriented approach to classroom supervision, and this approach is in turn consistent with a school district's commitment to professional rather than occupational accountability.

CHAPTER 17

CLINICAL SUPERVISION AND TEACHER EVALUATION

In the introduction to Part Four a distinction was made between general supervision and clinical supervision. General supervision referred to the attention and concern supervisory leaders give to organizational factors such as healthy climate and supportive relationships, on the one hand, and the broad educational leadership and statesmanship responsibilities of supervision, on the other. Clinical supervision, by contrast, refers to face-to-face encounters with teachers about teaching, usually in classrooms, with the double-barreled intent of professional development and improvement of instruction. In this chapter we refer directly to clinical supervision and teacher evaluation, describing and advocating approaches more consistent with the aspirations of the introduction to Part Four. This chapter complements the discussions of student and program evaluation that appear in Chapter 15.

This chapter is only part of the story, however, and should be read as an integral part of the staff development process (considered in the next chapter) and in light of the *theory of practice* in supervision and evaluation discussed in Chapter 19.

PUBLIC AND PRIVATE VIEWS OF TEACHER EVALUATION

Assume that you are at a workshop for supervisors and others with responsibility for teacher evaluation. The workshop leader asks you to write three statements, each of which expresses a personal feeling or belief you have about teacher evaluation. First write a *public* statement that you would be willing to share with teachers, board members, and parents; next a *confidential* statement that you would be willing to share only with trusted colleagues; and finally a *private* statement that you would not readily share with others. Chances are that doubt in the credibility of present practices characterizes your confidential and/or private statements. If this is the case, you join many others with responsibility for teacher evaluation who share your doubts. Indeed, these thoughts become major supervisory problems when one realizes that the same teacher-evaluation practices that raise doubts of credibility are today being implemented with more intensity and on a wider scale than ever before. Let us assume for a moment that our hypothesis that by and large supervisors and others responsible for teacher evaluation privately view the procedures as lacking in credibility is correct. What are the likely effects of participating in a system characterized by such doubts? We have noticed that the system takes on a certain artificial or mechanical quality, a routine function, that becomes an end in itself.

SCIENTIFIC AND ARTISTIC ASSUMPTIONS

This section reviews some of the assumptions basic to present teacher-evaluation practices and contrasts these with alternative assumptions and practices we believe hold promise for increasing meaning in the process of teacher evaluation and that seem more naturally compatible with the work of educational enterprises.

At present the dominant view of teacher evaluation is characterized by a commitment to technical-rational values. These values are expressed in the form of predetermination and the scientific method. Predetermination is evidenced, for example, by establishing before a teaching episode, outputs such as specific objectives and competency levels to be exhibited and by otherwise specifying the rules of the game, or the blueprint for evaluation, before the evaluation takes place.

The scientific method is evidenced, for example, by an emphasis on empirical design characteristics in the evaluation process and on a primary concern for precision in measurement. Rating scales are often emphasized as means to measure predetermined competencies displayed by teachers, and effectiveness in teaching is often defined as accomplishing predetermined intents, sticking to predetermined rules, or displaying predetermined behavior.

In recent years a number of prominent program-evaluation experts have developed and begun to test alternatives to this technical-rational approach that rely far less on the scientific method and far more on the intuitions, aspirations, and capabilities of those involved at both ends of the evaluation.[1] Theirs is an approach that sees value in discovering as opposed to determining and in describing as opposed to measuring. Though the primary focus of this pioneering work is on program evaluation, its underlying assumption, characteristics, and design features apply to teacher evaluation as well.[2]

In Table 17-1 key assumptions and practices associated with technical-rational

[1]See, for example, Robert E. Stake, *Program Evaluation, Particularly Responsive Evaluation*, paper 5 in Occasional Paper Series, Kalamazoo: Western Michigan University, Evaluation Center, November 1975; Robert E. Stake (ed.), *Evaluating the Arts in Education: A Responsive Approach*, Columbus, Ohio: Merrill, 1975; Elliot W. Eisner, "Emerging Models for Educational Evaluation," *School Review*, 80, no. 4, 1972; Decker Walker, "A Naturalistic Model for Curriculum Development," *School Review*, vol. 80, no. 1, 1971; Michael Scriven, "Goal-free Evaluation," in Ernest House (ed.), *School Evaluation: The Politics and Process*, Berkeley, Calif.: McCutchan, 1973; George Willis, "Curriculum Criticism and Literary Criticism," *Journal of Curriculum Studies*, vol. 7, no. 1, 1975; and John S. Mann, "Curriculum Criticism," *Teachers College Record*, vol. 71, no. 1, 1969.

[2]See, for example, Elliot Eisner, "The Perceptive Eye: Toward the Reformation of Educational Evaluation," Washington, D.C.: AREA, Division B, Curriculum and Objectives, 1975, invited address; Morris Cogan, *Clinical Supervision*, Boston: Houghton Mifflin, 1973; James Raths, "Teaching without Specific Objectives," *Educational Leadership*, vol. 18, no. 7, 1971; and T. J. Sergiovanni, "Toward a Theory of Clinical Supervision," *Handbook for Effective Department Leadership: Concepts and Practices in Today's Secondary Schools*, Boston: Allyn and Bacon, 1977.

TABLE 17-1
CONTRASTING TEACHER EVALUATION ASSUMPTIONS

Scientific	Artistic
1. Evaluation can be viewed as a process designed to determine the worth of something—a teacher, teaching episode, or performance.	1. But evaluation is also valuing something. Before one can begin to value something fully, one needs to understand it. Therefore, evaluation is seeking to understand something. What is going on in this classroom and why? What does it mean?
2. The emphasis is often on observing words and behavior and not on intuition and understanding. Indeed, intuition can be considered as something to be controlled because of its impressionistic rather than scientific nature, and understanding is often a luxury that may distract the evaluation process from its true course.	2. But words and behavior are only proxies for understandings and meanings and therefore much is missed by focusing only on the proxies. The evaluation is designed to inform the supervisor's intuition, not to replace it.
3. At times it is appropriate for the evaluator to follow a blueprint and evaluate the teacher according to the specifications called for in the blueprint.	3. But at times the evaluator should develop a representation of events that have taken place—a portrait of the teaching episode. Thus "specifications" not previously determined are included in the evaluation.
4. The blueprint characteristics of the evaluation specify what is of worth and define meanings and understandings. This is an exclusive process.	4. The portrait characteristics of the evaluation assume that multiple and sometimes contradicting understandings and meanings exist. The evaluator's job is to identify and describe them. Portraits of teaching episodes often reveal a hidden curriculum more potent than that intended and the achievement of unanticipated outcomes that may have more value than those intended by the teacher or specified in the lesson planned. This is an inclusive process.
5. Sometimes what is important to the evaluator are the stated intents of the teacher and the predetermined objectives held for the student.	5. Sometimes what is important to the evaluator are the implicit assumptions and guiding platform statements that teachers bring to the classroom, the manner in which these assumptions and platform statements are articulated into classroom activities and practices, and the implications and effects of these activities and practices.
6. When using scientific approaches, the evaluator is primarily concerned with methodology. He or she asks, How can I be sure that I can describe and measure without error the extent to which predetermined objectives are being met by the teacher and that this teacher exhibits predetermined competency levels in teaching?	6. When using artistic approaches, the evaluator is primarily concerned with discovering, describing, and measuring important things that occur. He or she is willing to choose methods suited to important things even though they may be weak or considered by others as subjective or impressionistic.

Table 17-1 (Continued)

Scientific	Artistic
7. The evaluator relies heavily on reading scales and other teacher-evaluation instruments. These help him or her to be objective, to treat all teachers the same, and to ensure that the focus of the evaluation is on important events.	7. The evaluator believes that rating scales and other teacher evaluation instruments often prevent him or her from fully understanding classroom events and prevent the evaluator and teacher from becoming personally involved in the evaluation process. The evaluator prefers to use data from the situation at hand to help define the parameters of the evaluation and to help understand crucial evaluation issues. He or she prefers to use videotape, teacher and student interviews, artifact collections, and evaluation portfolios and considers these as better methods of representation than instruments and rating scales.
8. The evaluator is primarily concerned with estimating the worth of a particular teaching performance and by inference the teacher. The teacher assumes a subordinate role in the process. The evaluator is the expert. Evaluation is something done to teachers by evaluators.	8. The evaluator is primarily interested in increasing understanding and stimulating thought and in extending the experiences of the teacher being evaluated. The teacher assumes a key role in the process. The evaluator and teacher share the expert role and evaluation is something done together.
9. Even when it makes sense to use more scientific approaches to evaluation, artistic aspects cannot be ignored.	9. Even when it makes sense to use more artistic approaches to evaluation, scientific aspects cannot be ignored.

SOURCE: Thomas J. Sergiovanni, "Reforming Teacher Evaluation: Naturalistic Alternatives," *Educational Leadership*, vol. 34, no. 8, 1977.

approaches to teacher evaluation are contrasted with those associated with more naturalistic approaches.

Why is it important to describe prevailing assumptions behind teacher-evaluation practices? Technologies are associated with ideologies, and the language and values of science (objectivity, rationality, reliability, and precision) have been found to be irresistible to educators. Present classroom observation and evaluation technology is shrouded with a sense of scientism often not even found in the more legitimate sciences. The irony in this is that most educators believe that teaching is far more of an artistic enterprise than a scientific one. That being the case, it may be that we have adopted a technology of teacher evaluation ill-suited to the nature of the educational enterprise.

In the sections that follow, several strategies for teacher evaluation more characteristic of naturalistic assumptions and more consistent with the artistic nature of the educational enterprise are described. Well-known traditional methods have a place in teacher evaluation, but they should play a minor role as compared with the alternatives we propose.

CLINICAL SUPERVISION

Earlier we referred to clinical supervision, which emphasizes working with teachers about teaching in classrooms, as an activity distinct from general supervision. There is, however, a special meaning associated with the phrase that refers to a cycle, or pattern, of supervision as pioneered by Anderson, Cogan, Goldhammer, and others and is perhaps best known through Cogan's book entitled *Clinical Supervision.*[3]

Born in the real world of professional practice, this technique evolved from a series of problems faced by supervisors as they worked with teachers and would-be teachers. As problems were faced, a set of practices emerged, at first sporadically, then incrementally, and finally becoming a systematic form now known as the cycle of clinical supervision. The essential ingredients of clinical supervision, as articulated by Cogan, include the establishment of a healthy general supervisory climate, a special supervisory mutual support system called "colleagueship," and a cycle of supervision comprising conferences, observation of teachers at work, and pattern analysis.

Clinical supervision is based on a number of assumptions different from those of traditional rating and evaluating and prescribes a pattern of action that departs substantially from present practice. In clinical supervision it is assumed, for example, that the school curriculum is, in reality, what teachers do day by day, that changes in curriculum and in teaching formats require changes in how teachers behave in classrooms, that supervisors are not teachers of teachers, that supervision is a process for which both supervisors and teachers are responsible, that the focus of supervision is on teacher strengths, that given the right conditions teachers are willing and able to improve, that teachers have large reservoirs of talent, often unused, and that teachers derive satisfaction from challenging work. These assumptions are consistent with those associated with McGregor's Theory Y as discussed in Chapter 5.

Following these assumptions, clinical supervision is an in-class support system designed to deliver assistance directly to the teacher. In practice, clinical supervision requires a more intense relationship between supervisor and teacher than that found in traditional evaluation, first in the establishment of colleagueship and then in the articulation of colleagueship through the cycle of supervision. The heart of clinical supervision is an intense, continuous, mature relationship between supervisor and teacher with the intent being the improvement of professional practice.

Since the second edition of this book appeared, interest in the development of clinical supervision has been substantial. Representative of this progress is the appearance of the second edition of Robert Goldhammer's classic book *Clinical Supervision: Special Methods for the Supervision of Teachers,* first published in 1969. The second edition was revised by Robert H. Anderson and Robert J. Krajewski.[4] The original version was pioneering, and the revised edition sets a new standard for the state of the art in clinical supervision. The good news, as reflected in this book and in

[3]Clinical supervision evolved from a series of techniques developed as a result of the pioneering work of Robert Anderson, Morris Cogan, and Robert Goldhammer in the Harvard MAT program of the late fifties and early sixties. Originally conceived as a component of preservice teacher education, the technique has since been developed for in-service use. Morris Cogan, *Clinical Supervision,* New York: Houghton Mifflin, 1973.
[4]Robert Goldhammer, Robert H. Anderson, and Robert J. Krajewski, *Clinical Supervision: Special Methods for the Supervision of Teachers,* 2d ed., New York: Holt, 1980.

developments of other scholars interested in clinical supervision,[5] is a decided shift from the steps of clinical supervision per se to its concepts, assumptions, and basic framework. Increasingly, clinical supervision is viewed as an overall pattern of working with teachers that operationally should take a number of forms and follow a number of paths. Consistency is needed, of course, at the strategy level, where assumptions and the overall framework come to play. But diversity is needed in developing operational tactics if clinical supervision is to accommodate itself to the array of needs of supervisors and teachers and to the particular characteristics of teaching situations. Clinical supervision is, therefore, basically a design for working with teachers within which a number of technologies, perspectives, and approaches can be used.

Some excellent "hands-on" books and articles are available that provide specific operational techniques for use within the clinical supervision framework. One we especially recommend is Keith A. Acheson and Meredith Damien Gall's *Techniques in the Clinical Supervision of Teaching.*[6] Many highly developed observational systems are also available for use in collecting information within the clinical supervision framework. The Galloway, Flanders, Blumberg, Kounin, and Morine systems are some examples. Respectively, they provide techniques and instruments for accurately recording nonverbal behavior in classroom interactions, student-teacher verbal interaction in classrooms, interaction of supervisors and teachers in conference, teacher-classroom management techniques, and a system for observing behaviors teachers find most important. As useful as these hands-on materials may be, as a *group* of techniques available to clinical supervision, they are still underdeveloped. Too much emphasis is given to objectives and systematic collection of *readily observable* data. They tend to emphasize "low-inference" tactics rather than "high-inference." High-inference tactics require that judgments be made and data be interpreted to assess unique meanings given actual persons in situations involved in teaching. Low-inference tactics, by contrast, more precisely define behaviors to be observed and the data-collection strategies to be used. All in all, not enough attention is given to artistic perspectives in clinical supervision, a topic to be pursued later in this chapter. This bias toward the scientific and neglect of the artistic may well reflect the present state of the field, with better balance between the two forthcoming as clinical supervision continues to mature.

THE CYCLE OF CLINICAL SUPERVISION

One cannot provide in a few pages all the techniques and know-how associated with clinical supervision. Competency will come with practice as supervisors team together in learning the skills of clinical supervision. The intent here is to describe the cycle of supervision, to provide some basic principles and concepts underlying clinical superviso-

---

[5]See, for example, Noreen Garman, "A Clinical Approach to Supervision," in Thomas J. Sergiovanni (ed.), *Supervision of Teaching*, 1982 Yearbook, Association for Supervision and Curriculum Development, Arlington, Va., 1982, pp. 35–52.
[6]Keith A. Acheson and Meredith Damien Gall, *Techniques in the Clinical Supervision of Teaching*, New York: Longmans, 1980.

ry practice, and to suggest some techniques and tools which supervisors might find useful as they begin to develop competencies as clinical supervisors.

Cogan identifies eight phases to the cycle of supervision.[7]

1. *Phase 1 requires establishing the teacher-supervisor relationship.* This first phase is of particular importance, for upon its success rests the whole concept of clinical supervision. Teachers are suspicious of evaluation in general, and the intense sort of supervision prescribed by Cogan can be even more alarming. Further, the success of clinical supervision requires that teachers share with supervisors responsibility for all steps and activities. The supervisor has two tasks in Phase 1: building a relationship based on mutual trust and support, and inducting the teacher into the role of co-supervisor. Cogan believes that both tasks should be well advanced before the supervisor enters the teacher's classroom to observe teaching. Phase 1 establishes the colleagueship relationships deemed critically important by Cogan. This relationship is in a large part the focus of Part One.

2. *Phase 2 requires intensive planning of lessons and units with the teacher.* In Phase 2 teacher and supervisor plan, together, a lesson, a series of lessons, or a unit. Planning includes estimates of objectives or outcomes, subject-matter concepts, teaching strategies, materials to be used, learning contexts, anticipated problems, and provisions for feedback and evaluation.

3. *Phase 3 requires planning of the classroom observation strategy by teacher and supervisor.* Together teacher and supervisor plan and discuss the kind and amount of information to be gathered during the observation period and the methods to be used to gather this information.

4. *Phase 4 requires the supervisor to observe in-class instruction.* Cogan emphasizes that only after careful establishment of the supervisory relationship and the subsequent planning of both the lesson or unit and the observation strategy does the observation take place.

5. *Phase 5 requires careful analysis of the teaching-learning process.* As co-supervisors, teachers, and supervisors analyze the events of the class. They may work separately at first or together from the beginning. Outcomes of the analysis are identification of patterns of teacher behavior that exist over time and critical incidents that occurred that seemed to affect classroom activity, and extensive descriptions of teacher behavior and evidence of that behavior. It is believed that teachers have established persistent patterns of teaching that are evidenced and can be identified as a pattern after several carefully documented observations and analysis.

6. *Phase 6 requires planning the conference strategy.* Supervisors prepare for the conference by setting tentative objectives and planning tentative processes, but in a manner that does not program the course of the conference too much. They plan also the physical settings and arrange for materials, tapes, or other aids. Preferably, the

[7]Cogan, op. cit.

conference should be unhurried and on school time. Cogan notes that it may well be necessary to arrange for coverage of a teacher's classroom responsibilities from time to time.

7. *Phase 7 is the conference.* The conference is an opportunity and setting for teacher and supervisor to exchange information about what was intended in a given lesson or unit and what actually happened. The success of the conference depends upon the extent to which the process of clinical supervision is viewed as formative, focused evaluation intended to help in understanding and improving professional practice.

8. *Phase 8 requires the resumption of planning.* A common outcome of the first seven phases of clinical supervision is agreement on the kinds of changes sought in the teacher's classroom behavior. As this agreement materializes, the eighth phase begins. Teacher and supervisor begin planning the next lesson or unit and the new targets, approaches, and techniques to be attempted.

As one reviews the cycle of clinical supervision, it appears as though it describes that which many supervisors have been doing all along. But a quick review of the assumptions basic to clinical supervision, particularly the concept of co-supervisor, suggests that the resemblance may be superficial. The supervisor works at two levels with teachers during the cycle: helping them to understand and improve their professional practice and helping them to learn more about the skills of classroom analysis needed in supervision. Further, while traditional classroom observation tends to be sporadic and requires little time investment, clinical supervision asks that supervisors give 2 to 3 hours a week to each teacher. Supervisors can better manage their time by involving only part of the faculty at a time—perhaps one-third for 3 months in rotation. As teachers themselves become competent in clinical supervision and assume increased responsibility for all phases, they will need supervisors less.

TOWARD A THEORY OF CLINICAL SUPERVISION

It is not necessary, in our view, for supervisors to follow a specific or single set of procedures or phases in implementing clinical supervision. Indeed, specific steps and procedures will depend upon the nature of classroom activity, the strengths of the teacher involved, and the inclinations of the supervisors. Underlying clinical supervision, however, are some basic ideas and concepts from which supervisors may develop suitable practices for their own unique situations.

Herbert Simon differentiates between natural and artificial sciences. "A natural science is a body of knowledge about some class of things—objects or phenomena—in the world: about the characteristics and properties that they have; about how they behave and interact with each other."[8] The artificial sciences, on the other hand, are created by human conventions.

In Simon's words, "The thesis is that certain phenomena are 'artificial' in a very special sense: They are as they are only because of a system's being molded, by goals or

---

[8]Herbert A. Simon, *The Sciences of the Artificial*, Cambridge: M.I.T., 1969, p. 1.

purposes, to the environment in which it lives." The study of human inventions such as formal organizations, the suburban family, and the professions (medicine, business, law, and education, for example) is the study of human creations rather than of natural phenomena. The design of these human inventions is artificial in the sense that they depend upon the goals that people seek and on their view of reality rather than on natural phenomena or natural laws.

On a smaller scale, the classroom can be seen as an artificial setting whose form and function are determined largely by the stated and implied assumptions, beliefs, and intents of individual teachers and by their attempts to adjust the classroom to their perception of a larger environment. This larger environment, equally artificial, is composed of the expectations and other conventions found in the school as an organization, in parents, in other professionals, and in the community and the society at large. Further, all the other people involved in the life of that classroom live in behavioral worlds of their own, artificial in the sense that it is influenced by their goals, needs, perceptions, and aspirations, and by their relationships with others.

We view clinical supervision as planned intervention in this world of the artificial. Its objective is to bring about changes in classroom operation and teacher behavior. The behavioral world of individual teachers is, in turn, shaped and influenced by their stated and implied assumptions, beliefs, and goals, and therefore successful changes in the former require changes in the latter.

This world of the artificial is further complicated by the incompleteness of knowledge that one has about oneself and the world in which one lives. "In actuality, the human being never has more than a fragmentary knowledge of the conditions surrounding his actions, nor more than a slight insight into the regularities and laws that would permit him to induce future consequences from a knowledge of present circumstances."[9] Clinical supervision therefore is not only concerned with teacher behavior and the antecedents of this behavior but with the incompleteness with which most of us view our assumptions, beliefs, objectives, and behavior.[10]

EDUCATIONAL PLATFORM

It is tempting to view the classroom enterprise as a rational set of activities, each generated in pursuit of clearly stated and understood objectives. Indeed, one is often led to believe that classroom activity is a logical process of determining objectives, stating them in acceptable form, developing learning experiences, and evaluating the outcomes of these experiences in relation to the predetermined objectives. This view assumes that the teaching arena is objective, and that teachers come to this arena with a clean slate, free of biases, willing and able to make rational choices.

In reality, however, most supervisors know that teaching is not nearly as antiseptic an enterprise as one might think. Indeed, teachers, supervisors, and others bring to the classroom a variety of agendas, some public, many hidden, and probably most unknown,

[9]Herbert A. Simon, *Administrative Behavior: A Study of Decision-making Processes in Administrative Organizations,* 2d ed., New York: Free Press, 1957, p. 81.
[10]This section follows T. J. Sergiovanni, "Toward a Theory of Clinical Supervision," *Journal of Research and Development in Education,* vol. 9., no. 2., pp. 20–29, 1976.

each of which has a telling effect on educational decision making. The agendas that one brings to teaching tend to fall into three major categories: what one believes is possible, what one believes is true, and what one believes is desirable. Together the three are the essential ingredients of one's *educational platform*.[11] A platform implies something that supports one's actions and by which one justifies or validates one's own actions. An approximate analogy would be that of a political platform. This platform states the basic values, critical policy statements, and key positions of an individual or group. Once known, the political platform can be used to predict responses that a politician or political party is likely to make to questions on various campaign issues. The concept of educational platform, particularly as it affects curriculum and educational program matters, is discussed at length in Chapter 13. Here our attention is on platform as it relates to clinical supervision.

Assumptions, Theories, and Beliefs

The components of one's educational platform are the assumptions, theories, and beliefs one holds for key aspects of effective teaching, such as the purpose of schooling, perceptions of students, what knowledge is of most worth, and the value of certain teaching techniques and pedagogical principles. For purposes of illustration, let us consider each component below, recognizing that operationally they are inseparable.

Assumptions that teachers hold help answer the question "What is possible?" Assumptions are composed of our beliefs, the concepts we take for granted, and the ideas we accept without question about schools, classrooms, students, teaching, learning, and knowledge. Assumptions help the teacher to define what classrooms are actually like and what is possible to accomplish within them. Assumptions are important to the decisions that teachers make, because they set the boundaries for what information will or will not be considered and for other possibilities and actions at the onset of instruction.

Theories we hold help answer the question, "What is true?" Theories are beliefs about relationships between and among assumptions we consider to be true. Theories form the basis for developing instructional strategies and patterns of classroom organization.

Beliefs about what is desirable in classrooms are derived from assumptions and theories that one holds regarding knowledge, learning, classrooms, and students. What is desirable is expressed in the form of intents, aims, objectives, or purposes.

Consider, for example, a teacher whose educational platform includes the assumptions that "little or no knowledge exists that is essential for everyone to learn" and that "youngsters can be trusted to make important decisions." The two assumptions might well lead to the theory that "students who are allowed to influence classroom decisions will make wise choices and will become more committed learners." That being the case, a corresponding aim for that teacher might be "to involve students in shared decision making," or perhaps "to have students interact with subject matter

---

[11]Decker Walker, "A Naturalistic Model for Curriculum Development," *The School Review,* vol. 80, no. 1, pp. 51–65, 1971.

in a manner that emphasizes its concepts and structure rather than just its information."

Contrast this with a teacher whose educational platform includes the assumption that "the only justifiable evidence of good teaching is student acquisition of subject matter as specified by the teacher" and the assumption that "motivation of students should reflect the realities of the world outside the school, where good behavior and performance are publicly rewarded and poor behavior and performance are publicly punished." The two assumptions might well lead to the theory that "students need to be motivated, on the one hand, and disciplined, on the other, by any means necessary to get the behavior and performance that leads to acquiring the most subject matter in the least amount of time." In this case a corresponding aim might be "to provide visible rewards and privileges to students who behave and perform to the teacher's expectations and visible punishment to those who do not."

Educational platforms are powerful determinants of the nature and quality of life in classrooms. For example, imagine the fate of students in the classrooms of people who consider themselves teachers of French or biology and not of students as compared with teachers who view instruction in a more holistic and integrated way. With the same example, consider the fate of the supervisor who wants the first sort of teacher to be more sensitive to individual differences of students and to emphasize more the joy of learning French or biology as well as mastery of subject matter, but does not take into account the educational platform of such teachers. Unless the supervisor is a master at behavior modification and the teachers witless enough to respond passively to stimuli from the supervisor, change in teaching behavior will require some altering of those persons' educational platforms.

Known and Unknown Platform Dimensions

In the world of the classroom the components of educational platforms are generally not well known. That is, teachers tend to be unaware of their assumptions, theories, or objectives. Sometimes they adopt components of a platform that seem right, that have the ring of fashionable rhetoric, or that coincide with the expectation of important others, such as teachers whom they admire, or of groups with which they wish to affiliate. Though teachers may overtly adopt aspects of educational platforms in this manner, covertly, or unknowingly, they are often likely to hang onto contradictory assumptions, beliefs, and theories. Publicly they may say (or espouse) one thing and assume that their classroom behavior is governed by this statement, but privately, or even unknowingly, they may believe something else that actually governs their classroom behavior. Indeed, teachers are not aware that often their classroom decisions and behavior contradict their espoused platform.

THEORIES GOVERNING TEACHER BEHAVIOR

It has been suggested that the classroom is an artificial setting where form and function are influenced largely by the stated and implied assumptions, theories, and aims of individual teachers. Together these beliefs form an educational platform that supports teachers' actions and by which they justify or validate their actions. As has also been suggested, many aspects of a teacher's platform are unknown or perhaps known but covert. When covert dimensions differ from espoused, the former are likely to constitute the *operational* platform for a given individual.

The clinical supervisor needs to be concerned with two theories that the teacher brings to the classroom—an *espoused theory* and a *theory in use.* As Argyris and Schön suggest:

> When someone is asked how he would behave under certain circumstances, the answer he usually gives is his espoused theory of action for that situation. This is the theory of action to which he gives allegiance, and which, upon request, he communicates to others. However, the theory that actually governs his action is his theory in use. This theory may or may not be compatible with his espoused theory; furthermore, the individual may or may not be aware of the incompatibility of the two theories.[12]

When one's espoused theory matches one's theory in use, they are considered congruent. Congruence exists, for example, for the teacher who espouses that self-image development in youngsters is desirable in its own right and is related to student achievement and whose teaching behavior and artifacts of that behavior confirm this espoused theory. Lack of congruence between a person's espoused theory and theory in use, *when known,* proposes a dilemma to that individual. A second teacher, for example, shares the same espoused theory regarding self-concept, but his pattern of questioning, his use of negative feedback, his making on the bell curve, and his insistence on standard requirements may reveal a theory in use incongruent with his espoused theory. The social studies teacher who believes in and teaches a course in American democracy in a totalitarian manner represents another example of incongruency between espoused theory and theory in use.

THE JOHARI WINDOW

A useful way of understanding how known and unknown platform dimensions of teachers fit into clinical supervision is by examining the *Johari Window* as it relates to espoused theories and theories in use.[13] This relationship is illustrated in Figure 17-1.

The Johari Window in this case depicts the relationship between two parties, teacher and clinical supervisor. The relationship revolves around aspects of the teacher's educational platform known to self and others, known to self but not others, not known to self but known to others, and not known to self or others. Four cells are depicted in the Johari Window, each representing a different combination of what the teacher knows or does not know about his or her teaching as contrasted with what the supervisor knows and does not know about that teacher's teaching.

In the first cell, *the public or open self,* the teacher's knowledge of his or her teaching behavior and other aspects of his or her professional practices corresponds

[12]Chris Argyris and David A. Schön, *Theory in Practice: Increasing Professional Effectiveness,* San Francisco: Jossey-Bass, 1974, p. 7.
[13]Joseph Luft, *Of Human Interaction,* New York: National Press Books, 1969. The Johari Window was developed by Joseph Luft and Harry Ingham and gets its name from the first names of its authors.

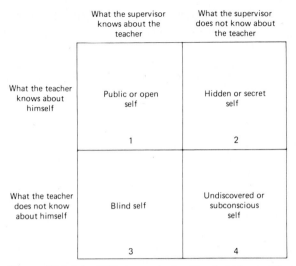

Figure 17-1 Johari Window and educational platform. *(From Thomas J. Sergiovanni,* Handbook for Department Leadership Concepts and Practices in Today's Secondary Schools, *Boston: Allyn and Bacon, 1977.)*

with the supervisor's knowledge. This is the area in which communication occurs most effectively and in which the need for the teacher to be defensive, to assume threat, is minimal. The clinical supervisor works to broaden, or enlarge, this cell with the teacher.

In the second cell, *the hidden or secret self,* the teacher knows about aspects of his or her teaching behavior and professional practice that the supervisor does not know. Often the teacher conceals these aspects from the supervisor for fear that the supervisor might use this knowledge to punish, hurt, or exploit the teacher. The second cell suggests how important a supervisory climate characterized by trust and credibility is to the success of clinical supervision. In clinical supervision the teacher is encouraged to reduce the size of this cell.

In the third cell, *the blind self,* the supervisor knows about aspects of the teacher's behavior and professional practice of which the teacher is unaware. This cell, though large initially, is reduced considerably as clinical supervision for a given teacher develops and matures. This is the cell most often neglected by traditional teacher-evaluation methods.

In the fourth cell, *the undiscovered self,* aspects of teacher behavior and professional practice not known to either teacher or supervisor are hidden.

HELPING TEACHERS CHANGE

Creating a condition for change greatly facilitates the change itself. If, for example, individual teachers are unaware of inconsistencies between their espoused theories and their theories in use, they are not likely to search for alternatives to their present teaching patterns. One way in which search behavior can be evoked in a teacher is by surfacing dilemmas. Dilemmas surface as a result of teachers learning that their theories in use are not consistent with their espoused theory.

Dilemmas promote an unsettled feeling in a person. Their espoused educational platforms mean a great deal to people, and what they stand for and believe in is linked to their concept of self and sense of well-being. Dilemmas born of inconsistencies between these images and the actual behavior of individuals are upsetting and need to be resolved. Indeed they are likely to lead to a search for changes either in one's espoused theory or in one's theory in use.[14]

Readiness for change is a critical point in the process of clinical supervision. It is at this point that an appropriate support system needs to be provided. Part of this support system will be psychological and will be geared toward accepting and encouraging the teacher. But part must also be technical and will be geared toward making available teaching and professional practice alternatives to the teacher.

Argyris and Schön point out that congruence is not a virtue in itself. Indeed a "bad" espoused theory matched to a theory in use may be far less desirable, from the supervisor's point of view, than a "good" espoused theory insufficiently matched.[15]

SOME EVIDENCE

To this point in our discussion of developing a theory of clinical supervision we have hypothesized that:

> A teachers' classroom behavior and the artifacts of that behavior are a function of assumptions, theories, and intents the teacher brings to the classroom. Together these compose the teacher's educational platform.

> Educational platforms exist at two levels: what teachers say they assume, believe, and intend (their espoused theory) and the assumptions, beliefs, and intents inferred from their behavior and artifacts of their behavior (their theory in use).

> Espoused theories are generally known to the teacher.

> Theories in use are generally now known to the teacher and must be constructed from observation of teacher behavior and artifacts of that behavior.

> Lack of congruence between a teacher's espoused theory and the teacher's theory in use proposes a dilemma to the teacher.

> Faced with a dilemma, a teacher becomes uncomfortable, and search behavior is evoked.

> Dilemmas are resolved by teachers modifying their theory in use to match their espoused theory. It is possible that espoused theory will be modified to match

[14]Leon Festinger, *Theory of Cognitive Dissonance*, Evanston, Ill.: Row, Peterson, 1975; and Milton Rokeach, "A Theory of Organizational Change Within Value-Attitude Systems," *Journal of Social Sciences*, vol. 24, no. 21, 1968.

[15]Argyris and Schön, op. cit.

theory in use, but because of the link between espoused theory and self-esteem, and self-esteem with the esteem received from others, the more common pattern will be the former.

Though a number of studies suggest that indeed teachers are likely to respond as suggested,[16] a number of caveats are in order. McGuire, for example, in reviewing the literature on consistency theory notes that search behavior is only one of several possible reactions to dissonance. Additional examples of dissonance reduction, he notes, are *avoidance*, whereby one represses the matter by putting the inconsistency out of mind; *bolstering*, whereby the inconsistency is submerged into a larger body of consistencies so as to seem relatively less important; *differentiation*, whereby one sees the situation causing dissonance to be different in a particular case ("I wasn't actually putting down the youngster but just giving her a taste of her own medicine"); *substitution*, whereby one changes the object about which he or she has an opinion rather than the opinion itself ("It is true that I said all school administrators are petty bureaucrats, and they are, but he is a statesman, not a bureaucrat"); and *devaluation*, whereby one downgrades the importance of the inconsistency in question, thus making it more tolerable.[17] The extent to which a teacher faces up to inconsistencies between espoused platform dimensions and those actually in use may well depend, as hypothesized earlier, upon the quality of climate and setting the supervisor provides— colleagueship, in Cogan's language.[18] In an extensive review of the literature Fuller and Manning conclude that self-confrontation and discrepancy analysis, though achieving uneven results, is by and large a powerful supervisory technique. In addition they note that "if the person is not too stressed, or closed, or anxious, or distracted, the self-confrontation experience 'takes,' i.e., the person notices some discrepancy. This is either a difference between what he thought he was doing and what he was actually doing (an incongruence discrepancy), or a difference between what he was doing and what he wanted to do (a deficiency discrepancy)."[19] This again highlights the importance of the climate that accompanies the process of clinical supervision. But as Fuller and Manning point out, a supportive climate is a necessary but not sufficient requirement for success: "Change is said not only to require the presence of facilitative conditions such as acceptance and empathy, but also 'confrontation.' . . .The teacher will not benefit from seeing her video tape alone since there is no confrontation. . . . Feedback that is not accompanied by some focus has been found to change behavior little, if at all.[20]

[16]Using Flanders's interaction-analysis techniques as a means of collecting information and as a basis for producing verbal feedback, Tuckman, McCall, and Hyman conclude that "behavior and self-perception of experienced, in-service teachers *can* be changed by involving a discrepancy between a teacher's observed behavior and his own self-perception of his behavior, and then making him aware of this discrepancy via verbal feedback." See Bruce W. Tuckman, Kendrick M. McCall, and Ronald T. Hyman, "The Modification of Teacher Behavior: Effects of Dissonance and Feedback," *American Educational Research Journal,* vol. 6, no. 4, pp. 607–619, 1969.

[17]William J. McGuire, "The Current Status of Cognitive Consistency Theories," in Shel Feldman (ed.), *Cognitive Consistency, Motivational Antecedents, and Behavioral Consequents,* New York: Academic, 1966, pp. 10–14.

[18]Cogan, op. cit., p. 67.

[19]Frances F. Fuller and Brad A. Manning, "Self-Confrontation Reviewed: A Conceptualization for Video Playback in Teacher Education," *Review of Educational Research,* vol. 43, no. 4, p. 487, 1973.

[20]Ibid., p. 493.

Alan Simon developed and field-tested a supervisory strategy that incorporates many of the features of clinical supervision described above.[21] Using videotaping techniques, Simon, as the supervisor, interviewed teachers, asking them to specify aspects of their espoused educational platform as it applies to education in general and to a particular lesson. He then videotaped the teachers actually teaching the lessons described. The videotape was then reviewed by the supervisor, sometimes with the help of outside experts not familiar with the teachers' espoused platform, and from this analysis a theory in use, as perceived by the supervisor, was constructed. This theory in use was also recorded on videotape. Together, the supervisor and teacher viewed the videotape now containing the teacher-espoused theory, an example of the teacher at work, and the supervisor's perception of the teachers' theory in use. The teacher was then interviewed to determine whether the videotaped espoused platform actually represented his or her thoughts before the lesson, whether the videotaped lesson represented his or her teaching, and whether the supervisor's videotaped rendering of the theory in use was fair and accurate. Overall the teachers verified the accuracy and fairness of the videotapes. Interviewing continued, to determine attitudes toward the process and to obtain perceptions of the effectiveness of the process from the teachers. Judges, listening to the audiotaped interviews, concluded that overall the teachers had positive attitudes toward the process and found it helpful. Further, by rating teacher responses into defensive and open categories, judges concluded that indeed dilemmas had surfaced and that search behavior had been evoked.

ARTISTIC EVALUATION

In Chapter 18 we refer to staff-development alternatives that emphasize formative evaluation and that involve teachers as partners in the process as being of first-, second-, or third-generation varieties. Target setting and self-evaluation are considered to be first-generation, clinical supervision to be second-generation, and emerging artistic approaches to evaluation to be third-generation.

Many forms of clinical supervision resemble artistic approaches. Such forms are artistic when they rely heavily on developing a complete representation of a teaching episode and when they use this representation as a basis for making inferences and building understanding of events. Videotaping is the most common method of representation associated with clinical supervision. Clinical supervision uses the data at hand (actually generated from the environment and activities being evaluated) rather than data that fit a preconceived rating form or a set of instrument specifications, and it places the teacher in a key role as generator, interpreter, and analyst of events described.

[21]Alan Simon, "Videotapes Illustrating Concepts of the Argyris and Schön Model in Instructional Supervisory Situations," doctoral dissertation, Urbana: University of Illinois, Educational Administration and Supervision, 1976. See also Alan Simon, "Analyzing Educational Platforms: A Supervisory Strategy," *Educational Leadership,* vol. 34, no. 8, pp. 580–585, 1977. For a further extension of this work and its application to high school teachers see Michael Hoffman, "Comparing Espoused Platforms and Platforms-in-Use in Clinical Supervision," doctoral dissertation, Urbana: University of Illinois, Educational Administration and Supervision, 1977; and Michael Hoffman and Thomas J. Sergiovanni, "Clinical Supervision: Theory in Practice," *Illinois School Research and Development,* vol. 14, no. 1, pp. 5–12, 1977.

Sometimes clinical supervisors take too seriously the need to "scientifically" and "objectively" document events. Sometimes they focus too intensely on the stepwise or work-flow aspects of clinical supervision. Sometimes they rely too heavily on predetermined objectives or on specifying detailed blueprints and plans that subsequently determine the direction of the evaluation. But clinical supervision can be geared to discovering and understanding rather than determining, and in that sense it has artistic potential. Additional artistic strategies that can be used either separate from clinical supervision or preferably, in our view, as a part of clinical supervision are described in the sections that follow. These techniques are powerful means for providing rich descriptions of classroom activity from which theories in use might be inferred.

CONNOISSEURSHIP AND CRITICISM

It is difficult to discuss artistic alternatives to present teacher-evaluation practices without reference to the work of Elliot Eisner.[22] Eisner is concerned with developing in supervisor and teacher the qualities and skills of appreciation, inference, disclosure, and description. He refers to these qualities as the cultivation of educational connoisseurship and criticism. It is through the art of connoisseurship that one is able to appreciate and internalize meanings in classrooms and through the skill of criticism that one is able to share or disclose this meaning to others. Eisner uses references to wine connoisseurship and art criticism as illustrations of these concepts. The art of appreciation is the tool of the connoisseur and the art of disclosure the tool of the critic. Cross uses the example of sports commentators and writers to illustrate the combined application of connoisseurship and criticism.

> Most of us are familiar with some of the techniques employed by commentators in describing and remarking on well-executed plays or potentially victorious strategies. Plays executed with finesse are often seen in stop action, instant replay, slow motion or are recounted in stirring detail on sports pages. One of the major contributions of these commentators is their great knowledge of sports, familiarizing them with possibilities so they know whether a flanker reverse, off tackle run, screen pass or drawplay was used or has potential for gaining yardage in a given situation, or when the bump and run, blitz, or single coverage was used or likely to prevent gain. Knowledge about educational potentials is also necessary. The potentially worthwhile tactics of teaching or those in use—the bump and runs or flanker reverses of schooling—need to be described and conveyed.[23]

[22]Elliot Eisner, "Applying Educational Connoisseurship and Criticism to Education Settings," Stanford, Calif.: Stanford University, Department of Education, undated, mimeo: see also his "Emerging Models for Educational Evaluation," op. cit., and "The Perceptive Eye: Toward the Reformation of Educational Evaluation," op. cit. Eisner notes that, unfortunately, to many the word "connoisseurship" has snobbish or elitist connotations, and criticism implies a hacking or negativistic attitude. In his words, "connoisseurship, as I use the term, relates to any form of expertise in any area of human endeavor and is as germane to the problem involved in purse snatching as it is to the appreciation of fine needle point." And "criticism is conceived of as a generic process aimed at revealing the characteristics and qualities that constitute any human product. Its major aim is to enable individuals to recognize qualities and characteristics of a work or event which might have gone unnoticed and therefore unappreciated." Quoted from "The Perceptive Eye: Toward the Performance of Educational Evaluation," footnote 2.

[23]James Cross, "Applying Educational Connoisseurship and Criticism to Supervisory Practices," doctoral dissertation, 1977, Urbana: University of Illinois, Educational Administration and Supervision.

The commentator's ability to render play-by-play action in a fashion that permits us to see and feel the game as he or she does depends upon a feel of intimacy with the phenomena under study not permitted by mere attention to game statistics and other objective information and upon a quality of disclosure more vivid than a box score. And in education, the evaluator's ability to describe classroom life in a fashion that permits us to see and feel this environment as he or she does depends upon a similar intimacy with classroom phenomena (educational connoisseurship) and a rendering of this intimacy (educational criticism) well beyond that provided by a brief observation or two accompanied by a series of ratings or a teacher-evaluation checklist. Eisner maintains that educational connoisseurship is to some degree practiced daily by teachers and supervisors:

> The teacher's ability, for example, to judge when children have had enough of art, math, reading or "free time" is a judgment made not by applying a theory of motivation or attention, but by recognizing the wide range of qualities that the children themselves display to those who have learned to see. Walk down any school corridor and peek through the window; an educational connoisseur can quickly discern important things about life in that classroom. Of course judgments, especially those made through windows from hallways, can be faulty. Yet the point remains. If one knows how to see what one looks at, a great deal of information . . . can be secured. The teacher who cannot distinguish between the noise of children working and just plain noise has not yet developed a basic level of educational connoisseurship.[24]

Eisner believes that the existing level of connoisseurship found in teachers and supervisors can and should be refined, that perception can be enhanced and sharpened, and that understanding can be increased. He further points out that

> . . . connoisseurship when developed to a high degree provides a level of consciousness that makes intellectual clarity possible. Many teachers are confronted daily with prescriptions and demands from individuals outside the teaching profession that are intended to improve the quality of education within the schools. Many of these demands the teachers feel in their gut to be misguided or wrong-headed; the demands somehow fly in the face of what they feel to be possible in a classroom or in the best interests of children.[25]

In this context he notes: "Many teachers, if you ask them, are unable to state why they feel uneasy. They have a difficult time articulating what the flaws are in the often glib prescriptions that issue from state capitols and from major universities. Yet, the uneasiness is not always, but often justified." And further: "Many teachers have developed sufficient connoisseurship to feel that something is awry but have insufficient connoisseurship to provide a more adequate conceptualization of just what it is."[26]

When applied to supervision, educational connoisseurship is a necessary but insufficient art. Classroom understanding needs to be described and communicated, and this aspect of the process, the art of disclosure, is what Eisner refers to as educational criticism. We have much to learn about cultivating the art of connoisseurship and the skills of disclosure. Much will depend upon our ability to regain confidence in ourselves,

[24]Eisner, "The Perceptive Eye," p. 9.
[25]Ibid., pp. 10–11.
[26]Ibid., p. 11.

in our ability to analyze and judge, in our willingness to rely on intuition and perception—all today often considered dubious skills, ones to be discounted in the face of objective and scientific demands for accountability.

MORE THAN DESCRIBING

Unique to artistic approaches to supervision and evaluation is the emphasis on identifying meanings in teaching activity and classroom life rather than only describing teaching and classroom events. Many advocates of clinical supervision, for example, recommend that the supervisor develop an accurate and objective record of teaching. Often videotapes of teaching, exact transcripts of teacher-student talk, or tally sheets of some sort that record data occurrences of interest to the teacher and the supervisor are recommended. Typically, the supervisor is expected to avoid interpretation, leaving the extraction of the meaning behind events to the teacher or, when a particularly good relationship exist between teacher and supervisory, to both parties during the conference phase of a clinical supervision cycle.

When using more artistic approaches to clinical supervision, supervisors are expected to go beyond description to the interpretation of teaching events. Following Ramsey,[27] John Mann distinguishes between *picturing* and *disclosure* models.[28] Picturing models of evaluation try to be much like the teaching activity and classroom life under study. Disclosure models, on the other hand, contain key characteristics of the teaching activity in classroom life under study but move beyond to interpreting meaning, raising issues, and testing propositions about this phenomenon. Some of these distinctions are suggested in Table 17-2. As you examine the disclosure side of the ledger in Table 17-2, notice the emphasis given to going beyond the data in the strictest sense to telling a story represented by the data. Consider, for example, the following excerpt from the "disclosure" of a classroom by Robert Donmoyer:

> All these forces combined to produce a profound effect upon the teacher and to profoundly influence her behavior in the classroom. She becomes, as she herself has said, an accountant. Most of her day is spent checking and recording what students have and haven't done. Math, spelling, and language assignments must be checked, and if there are mistakes (and there usually are) they must be rechecked and, sometimes, rechecked again. Then checked assignments must be checked off on each student's math, spelling, or language contract. When each contract is completed, each contract must be checked out. After this is done, the student must take home the work included on this contract and bring back a note signed by his parents indicating they saw the work. This note, of course, must be checked in.
>
> This checking and rechecking and checking out and checking in is all performed with mechanized precision. The teacher's face remains immobile except for an occasional upward turn at the corners of her mouth, the eyes never smile.
>
> The teacher exhibits great economy of movement and gesture. It's almost as if Ms. Hill were a marionette whose strings are too tight, hence her gestures must be tight and close to her body.[29]

[27]Ian Ramsey, *Models and Mystery*, London: Oxford University Press, 1964.

[28]John S. Mann, "Curriculum Criticism," *The Teachers College Record*, vol. 71, no. 1, pp. 27–40, 1967.

[29]Robert Donmoyer, "School and Society Revisited: An Educational Criticism of Ms. Hall's fourth-grade classroom," as quoted in Eisner, *The Educated Imagination*, op. cit., p. 231.

TABLE 17-2
COMPARING PICTURING AND DISCLOSURE MODELS OF TEACHER EVALUATION

Picturing	Disclosure
1. Intent	
To describe the teaching phenomenon under study as exactly as possible. To develop a replica, photo image, or a carbon copy of reality. Agendas and issues are those embedded in the data.	To interpret the teaching phenomenon understudy. To illuminate issues, disclose meetings, and raise hypotheses or propositions. Agendas and issues are those which emerge from the data.
2. Analogies	
Legal transcript, video-tape, photo-replica, interaction-analysis, electronic portrait, music or dance score, playscript, historical chronology.	Impressionistic painting, collage, book review, interpretive photo, music, dance or play performance, story.
3. Key Questions	
What exactly happened in this class? How can I describe events objectively?	What issues emerge from the study of this class? How can I represent or illuminate these issues in a meaningful way?
4. Validity Check	
Are events described accurately?	When actual events are observed, do they reasonably lead to the inferences and interpretations?

Notice that Donmoyer does not provide a detailed description of the number of times the teacher checks this or that, but offers instead the word "accountant" not only to suggest the actual checking of student work but to communicate a meaning that transcends the particular issues of checking and rechecking and instead comments on an important dimension of the climate and quality of life in this particular classroom.

The concepts of picturing and disclosure might be viewed as range parameters within which a supervior can work. At times picturing events as accurately as possible might make sense and at other times moving toward the disclosure end of the range might be more appropriate. One can catalog approaches to supervision and evaluation used by a particular school or a particular supervisor on such a range scale as a way of identifying the array of possibilities that exist in the school. It should be noted, however, that the more a supervisory and evaluation strategy approaches the disclosure end of this range, the more important is the quality of the relationship between teacher and supervisor to the success in this approach. Disclosure strategies of supervision and evaluation require a particularly strong climate of trust and understanding among those involved in the process of supervision and evaluation. The relatively safer picturing end of this continuum may be appropriate initially, and as the supervisory relationship matures, movement could then progress toward the disclosure end.

SUMMARY OF CONCEPTS BASIC TO ARTISTIC EVALUATION

In summarizing concepts basic to artistic approaches to supervision and evaluation Elliot Eisner identifies the characteristics he considers important;

1. Artistic approaches to supervision require attention to the muted or expressive character of events, not simply to their incidence or literal meaning.
2. Artistic approaches to supervision require high levels of educational connoisseurship, the ability to see what is significant yet subtle.
3. Artistic approaches to supervision appreciate the unique contributions of the teacher to the educational development of the young, as well as those contributions a teacher may have in common with others.
4. Artistic approaches to supervision demand that attention be paid to the process of classroom life and that this process be observed over extended periods of time so that the significance of events can be placed in a temporal context.
5. Artistic approaches to supervision require that rapport be established between supervisor and those supervised so that a dialogue and a sense of trust can be established between the two.
6. Artistic approaches to supervision require an ability to use language in a way that exploits its potential to make public the expressive character of what has been seen.
7. Artistic approaches to supervision require the ability to interpret the meaning of the events occurring to those who experience them and to be able to appreciate their educational import.
8. Artistic approaches to supervision accept the fact that the individual supervisor with his or her strengths, sensitivities, and experience is the major "instrument" through which the educational situation is perceived and its meaning construed.[30]

CRITICISMS OF ARTISTIC APPROACHES

Artistic approaches to supervision and evaluation are often criticized for lacking precision and for being subjective. These criticisms are undeniable, but the alternative, which is to limit analysis of teaching and supervisor practice to only what is precise and objective, is unacceptable. As we suggest in the next chapter, a helpful and effective system of supervision must give prime attention to data that make sense to teachers. Such data are, of course, based on "brute" data but become sensible as they are interpreted and as meanings are established. But can such a subjective system of supervision be fair? How can we have confidence that the meanings have validity? The key to solving these problems rests in the person who assumes responsibility for establishing meanings. Some protections are offered, for example, if proposed meanings are offered as hypotheses and if accepted meanings are arrived at cooperatively by teacher and supervisor.

The precision issue remains important. Some argue that only data that can be accurately and precisely observed and recorded should be part of the evaluation process. Unfortunately, evaluation issues that can meet this rigorous standard are often less important than those that cannot. Limiting the evaluation to issues that lend themselves to precision can lead to a serious measurement error, often referred to as an "error of the third type." In this type of error, statistical confidence limits are correctly set and precise measurements standards are applied but the *wrong problem* is addressed. This misplaced cogency might best be summed by Tukey's admonition: "Far better an approximate answer to the right question, which is often vague, than an exact

[30]Elliot W. Eisner, "An Artistic Approach to Supervision," in Thomas J. Sergiovanni (ed.), *Supervision of Teaching,* 1982 Yearbook, Association for Supervision and Curriculum Development, Alexandria, Va., 1982, p. 66.

answer to the wrong question, which can always be made precise."[31] A more helpful approach in sorting out the extent to which artistic approaches to clinical supervision are useful and the circumstances under which they are useful is to understand their limitations as well as their strengths.

THE EVALUATION PORTFOLIO

Videotaping is a common technique associated with clinical supervision and with the arts of educational connoisseurship and criticism. Indeed, videotaping can provide a useful and readily accessible representation of teaching episodes and classroom activities. But because of the selective nature of lens and screen, this technique can also frame perception and evoke slanted meanings. Further, what the screen shows always represents a choice between possibilities and therefore provides an incomplete picture. And finally, some aspects of classroom life do not lend themselves very well to lens and screen and could be neglected.[32]

Artifacts analysis and/or portfolio development, when used in conjunction with videotaping, can help provide a more complete representation of classroom life and therefore can increase meaning.[33] These approaches, however, can stand apart from videotaping and indeed can stand apart from each other.

Imagine a classroom or school deserted suddenly 20 years ago by its teacher and students and immediately being sealed. Everything there remains exactly as it was at the moment of desertion—desks, chairs, interest centers, work materials, test files, homework assignments, reading center sign-up lists, star reward charts and other "motivational devices," bulletin boards, workbooks, student notebooks, grade books, plan books, library displays, teacher workroom arrangements, student lounge-area arrangements, and so on.

Twenty years later you arrive on the scene as an amateur anthropologist intent on learning about the culture, way of life, and meaning of this class (its goals, values, beliefs, activities, norms, etc.). As you dig through the classroom, what artifacts might you collect and how might you use them to help you learn about life in this school? Suppose, for example, you were interested in discovering what was important to teachers, how teachers viewed their roles in contrast to that of students, what youngsters seemed to be learning and/or enjoying, and how time was spent. In each case what might you collect? What inferences might you make, for example, if you were to find most of the work of students to be in the form of short-answer responses in workbooks or on ditto sheets, no student work displayed in the class, all student desks containing identical materials, and a teacher test file with most questions geared to the knowledge level of the taxonomy of educational objectives?

Portfolio development represents a teacher-evaluation strategy similar to that of

---

[31]Quoted by R. Rose, "Disciplined Research and Undisciplined Problems," in C. Carol H. Weiss (ed.), *Using Social Research and Public Policy Making,* Lexington, Mass.: Heath, 1977, p. 23.
[32]This discussion follows Sergiovanni, "Reforming Teacher Evaluation," op. cit.
[33]See Patricia Scheyer and Robert Stake, "A Program's Self-Evaluation Portfolio," Urbana: University of Illinois at Urbana-Champaign, Center for Instructional Research and Curriculum Evaluation, undated mimeo, for a discussion and application of this concept for program evaluation.

artifacts analysis but with some important differences. The intent of portfolio development is to establish a file or collection of artifacts, records, photo essays, cassettes, and other materials designed to represent some aspect of the classroom program and teaching activities. Though the materials in the portfolio should be loosely collected and therefore suitable for rearrangement from time to time to reflect different aspects of the class, the portfolio should be designed with a sense of purpose. The teacher or teaching team being evaluated is responsible for assembling the portfolio and should do it in a fashion that highlights their perception of key issues and important concerns they wish to represent.

Like the artist who prepares a portfolio of his or her work to reflect a point of view, the teacher prepares a similar representation of his or her work. Together supervisor and teacher use the collected artifacts to identify key issues, to identify the dimensions of the teacher's educational platform, as evidence that targets have been met, and to identify serendipitous but worthwhile outcomes. A portfolio collection could be used, for example, to examine such issues as:

Are classroom activites compatible with the teacher's espoused educational platform and/or that of the school?

Do supervisor and teacher have compatible goals?

Are youngsters engaging in activities that require advanced cognitive thinking or is the emphasis on lower-level learning?

Do youngsters have an opportunity to influence classroom decisions?

Is the classroom program challenging all the students regardless of academic potential or are some youngsters taught too little and others too much?

Are the youngsters assuming passive or active roles in the classroom?

Is the teacher working hard? That is, is there evidence of planning, care in preparation of materials, and reflective and conscientious feedback on students' work, or are shortcuts evident?

Does the teacher understand the subject matter?

What is the nature and character of the hidden currciulum in this class?

Though portfolio development and artifacts analysis share common features, the most notable of which is the collection of artifacts, portfolio development is the responsibility of the teacher. The teacher decides what will be represented by the portfolio and the items to be included in its collection. Together the teacher and supervisor use this representation to identify issues for discussion and analysis.

In this chapter we have suggested that classroom supervision and teacher evaluation are shrouded with a false sense of scientism. Though present approaches have a place and can be helpful as an exclusive or even primary strategy, they have not been effective, and, indeed, teacher evaluation is characterized by widespread doubt among teachers and supervisors.

The proposed solution is to tighten up existing procedures, to get serious, to increase objectivity—or to otherwise emphasize even more our present technical-rational procedures. What we may not realize, however, is that the defects of technical-rational views are not just in the procedures, but are inherent in underlying assumptions. The practices we suggest, those based on artistic assumptions, are emerging and are yet to be refined. Much more work needs to be done by *practicing supervisors* and their university counterparts in developing these ideas. One cannot promise that practices based on artistic assumptions will be more effective, but if our original hypothesis is true, the assumptions suggest alternatives worth trying.

The primary emphasis in this chapter is on formative evaluation. But typically individuals with supervisory responsibilities must also concern themselves with summative evaluation. This problem is considered in the next section.

SUMMATIVE EVALUATION OF TEACHERS' PERFORMANCE

Suppose it is part of your job to evaluate teachers' performance and to recommend or decide, based on that evaluation, whether to retain, promote, or grant them tenure. As a person with supervisory responsibilities you have two basic questions to answer:

1. How can I evaluate a teacher responsibly and professionally?

2. How can I evaluate a teacher's performance (with the assumption that it will inevitably result in some critical judgments) and at the same time retain my role as facilitator of teacher growth?

For many supervisors, the second question poses the real dilemma. If one assumes that the purpose of supervision is to help teachers grow and improve their classroom effectiveness, an objective that requires trust and a collegial relationship, then to evaluate a teacher's performance will undermine that trust and cancel one's ability to facilitate teacher growth. This may be the primary reason why supervisors typically avoid evaluation. This part of a supervisor's job seems to place him or her in an adversarial, judgmental relationship with a teacher. The teacher will feel threatened and thus will not trust the supervisor, and he or she will tend to be defensive, closed, and legalistic in their relationship.

The first question poses serious difficulty as well. Anyone who has experienced the pain of telling a teacher that his or her performance does not measure up and that it would be best to seek employment elsewhere knows how difficult it is to document in a clear and unambiguous analysis the reasons why an unfavorable decision was rendered.

A review of the literature on supervision reveals that this aspect of teacher evaluation receives rather thin treatment. It is more important to talk about the formative aspects of teacher evaluation than the summative aspects. Exploring ways to generate teacher improvement through a shared quest with the teacher ought to be the emphasis for supervisors. We agree wholeheartedly with that emphasis. The uncomfortable reality of performance evaluation, however, will not disappear simply because theoreticians wish it would. Nor will the professional responsibility for someone in the school or school district to evaluate teacher performance disappear simply because it is done badly, or sporadically, or not at all.

Teacher Attitudes toward Evaluation

Having one's performance evaluated is distasteful and is especially so for a professional. Being a professional somehow connotes that one has already passed through a rigorous training and education that has equipped a person with the necessary skills and knowledge to handle the job requirements of the profession. Unskilled workers, on the other hand, require supervision for quality control, for task accomplishment, and for the prevention of abuses such as reporting for work late, leaving early, extended coffee breaks, and so on. One assumes that professionals are motivated and competent.

Probably the majority of teachers, even those who have never experienced human resources styles of supervision, would view summative evaluation of their performance as threatening. It can be perceived as a gathering of evidence *against* a teacher's chances for tenure and promotion. Some might view it as the administration "checking up" on them. It automatically tends to create an adversarial and legalistic relationship. Nonetheless, most would agree that someone has to evaluate performance. Often teachers will complain about irresponsible colleagues who can't keep discipline in their classes, who never get their marks in on time, who show up late and leave early, whose students are rarely taught what the syllabus calls for, and so forth. Evaluation of performance is necessary, most would agree, but for other people.

Summative evaluation of teacher performance is a Pandora's box of ambiguities, questionable assumptions, and psychological and legal complexities. Simply put, it is difficult to do well, and easy to do badly. Yet there is a folklore among educators that one can easily recognize superior teaching and poor teaching. When asked what makes the difference between a good teacher and a poor teacher, almost any educator can forward some commonsense opinons. When asked whether a specific person is a good teacher, however, some colleagues would pause and say, "Well, it depends. . . ." Others might immediately say yes. When asked to give reasons, some would respond, "Well . . . I just know, right off, after being in their class for five minutes. You can sense it right away. . . . The excitement, the student responses, the way she carries herself in the classroom. It's hard to describe. When you've been in schools awhile, you instinctively recognize the good ones and the bad ones." Elliot Eisner refers to this ability as connoisseurship.[34] There is no doubt that this informed intuition has significant validity. However, someone evaluating teacher performance has to articulate that intuition in a more specific analysis.

Some Problems with Teacher Evaluation

When faced with responsibilities to evaluate the performance of teachers, supervisors should beware of the land mines waiting to be stepped on as one ventures into this field for the first time. Many of these land mines concern facile and unsupportable assumptions that can explode if not carefully examined and avoided.

Assumption 1. There is a clear set of criteria or standards understood and accepted by all with which a teacher's performance can be evaluated.

[34]Eisner, *The Educational Imagination*, op. cit.

Assumption 2. Sporadic, unannounced classroom visits, with no prior conversation and no subsequent discussion, are a legitimate and an acceptable way to assess teacher performance.

Assumption 3. Student achievement of course objectives is the only way to evaluate teacher performance.

Assumption 4. Evaluation of teacher performance should only deal with observable classroom behaviors.

Assumption 5. One or two class visits are all that is required to make judgments about the quality of a teacher's performance and to make decisions about retention, tenure, and promotion.

These five assumptions will not measure up to rigorous cross-examination. If a supervisor, acting on these assumptions, were to render a recommendation or a decision not to rehire a teacher or not to grant tenure, the supervisor would encounter legal and professional difficulty. Courts have established very clearly that teachers, even beginning teachers, must be given due process. The essence of due process is that teachers know beforehand the criteria or standards as well as the procedures by which they will be evaluated, and that these procedures and standards have in fact been followed. Beyond due-process concerns, the very criteria and standards and procedures that a school or school system establishes for such evaluation can be challenged, as well as the evidence used to arrive at the unfavorable judgment.

Furthermore, a supervisor cannot employ haphazard procedures in visiting classes. Visits have to be preceded and succeeded by discussions with the teacher in which the purposes of the visit are established, an analysis of the class activity developed, and specific improvement efforts agreed upon. Some predictable and clearly understood procedures, acted upon over a period of time, have to be followed.

Even when a more detailed process is followed, there are questions both teacher and supervisor must clarify.

1. Is the evaluation seeking to determine whether certain specific teacher skills are practiced at all, are practiced with a certain mastery, or are practiced to a superior degree? In other words, is the evaluation seeking to establish evidence of rock-bottom, minimum competency of the teacher for decisions about retention, or is the evaluation to establish evidence of superior teaching qualities for merit or promotion?

2. What is the time frame of the evaluation? Suppose the first few evaluation sessions reveal several basic deficiencies. Will the teacher have an opportunity to correct those deficiencies before judgment is passed? If so, how much time will the teacher have before a decision will be made?

3. Are there serious differences between the educational platform of the supervisor and that of the teacher? Is the platform of either clearly out of phase with the educational platform of the school? If such differences exist, must they be reconciled? If so, who will arbitrate the reconciliation? If not, on whose platform will the teacher be evaluated?

4. Is the evaluation intended to be exercised in an exclusively summative way, or does it take place in a larger framework of formative evaluation and staff development? In other words, does the evaluation assume a static state, or is teacher growth primarily what is being assessed?

5. What evidence from student achievement and effective response to the teacher will enter into the evaluation?

6. Will observation and evaluation by a third party be used to establish the validity of the conclusions reached by the supervisor? If so, will the teacher being evaluated have any say about who that third party is?

7. If the evaluation is particularly rigorous, can the teacher cite examples of other teachers who received a far less rigorous evaluation? In other words, are there grounds for claiming that one is being singled out, or harassed, perhaps for extraneous reasons (race, age, sex, religion, ethnicity)?

Other equally important questions could be raised about aspects of summative evaluation of teacher performance. The above questions simply point to the general conclusion that a supervisor must think through the process he or she will use very carefully. More than likely, the school or school system will already have developed a plan and a procedure for carrying out performance evaluation. This plan should be reviewed with other supervisors and improved as circumstances may call for. Representatives from faculty groups should also participate in the formation and modification of evaluation policies and procedures.

Dealing with Extremes

Let us consider three situations where evaluation of teacher performance might lead to nonretention of the teacher.

1. Probably the easiest situation to deal with is a teacher who is so ineffective that it would be obvious to almost anyone that he or she should not be in a classroom. As a supervisor, your first visit to the class of this beginning teacher reveals that the teacher physically and verbally bullies the children in class, that children are intimidated, frightened, and angry, that the teacher responds to questions by personal insults and ridicule of the students, and that for most of the class time the teacher sits at the desk saying nothing while the children are simply required to read the textbook and do the exercises at the end of the chapter. Further discussions and visits reveal that this pattern continues, with the teacher refusing to alter his behavior.

By documenting this behavior of the teacher, having another teacher, supervisor, or administrator visit the class to corroborate your reports, and by putting in writing your recommendations for improvement, with the clear statement that his present behavior is unacceptable and must be changed, you can show that you have no alternative but to remove this teacher as soon as possible.

2. As a supervisor your visits to this teacher's classroom reveal a technically competent teacher. This teacher shows some of the behaviors called for in the research on effectiveness for achievement in basic learning skills. But you also find that the teacher holds to very narrow but strong religious convictions, and that she preaches these views to a religiously pluralistic class of students at every opportunity and unambiguously proposes her views as the only acceptable way to salvation. In this instance, you have on your hands a teacher who possesses certain technical teaching skills but whose educational platform is infused with religious values that aggressively deny any validity to other interpretations of ethical behavior. After several conversations with this teacher, you have evidence that she refuses to change her behavior. This involves the delicate issue of religious freedom, but you are convinced that the teacher is violating accepted professional practice in public education and is doing serious harm to some of the students in her class.

In this case, the supervisor should consult with school district officials, and perhaps with legal counsel, about ways to proceed. By following due process, however, and using extreme tactfulness, the supervisor can succeed in having that teacher removed.

3. A more difficult situation for supervisors involves a teacher with tenure whose performance occasionally rises to a level of mediocrity, but whose classes are normally dull and oppressive. Repeated efforts to get him to improve meet with verbal agreement but no improvement in practice. While his colleagues agree that he is an inferior teacher, and parents and students complain, the teacher union will not support efforts to remove him. In this instance, should you spend a lot of time and energy trying to get him to improve or spend even more time and energy trying to get him fired, or should you recommend administrative action whereby he will be transferred out of the classroom into some noninstructional job? A lot will depend on individual circumstances. Most experienced supervisors know of one or more cases like this, and they are a constant source of aggravation. In large public organizations, sometimes there is little one can do to change an incompetent veteran. The mistake was made years ago when he could have been weeded out.

Beyond the Extreme Case

There is an ancient adage in organizations that administrators and supervisors spend 80 percent of their time on 10 percent of the people in the organization. And that 10 percent are the problem people. Educational supervisors can easily fall into that trap. As proponents of a human resource theory of supervision, we would like to believe that every teacher has the potential to grow into an effective teacher and that a human resource style of supervision can promote that growth. The reality of the teaching profession reveals that, for a variety of reasons, some people in the profession do not respond to invitations to professional growth. A theory of practice therefore suggests that supervisors invest their priority time and energies in the large majority of teachers who are open to growth. The extreme cases will probably always be with us and need to be dealt with. But the extreme cases cannot and should not occupy center stage in considerations about teacher performance evaluation. The failures are the exception to the positive results of human resource supervision. We wish to turn our attention now to the more normal situations involving teacher performance evaluation.

Human Resource Development and Judgments about Performance

Let us assume we are beyond the stage of evaluating performance for job retention decisions. The question facing a human resource development supervisor is nonetheless quite real: How can I make an evaluative judgment on teachers' performance without destroying the trust and collegial relationship by which I exercise my human resources style of supervision? Even though teachers may feel secure in their job, will not critical judgments of their performance lead to resentment, defensiveness, and distance?

The reactions of teachers to negative assessment of their performance will depend on a variety of factors. Some of these factors will be personality variables, such as how teachers and supervisors deal with authority and the tact and sensitivity with which supervisors express themselves. Some of these factors will be process variables, such as whether there is a shared sense of purpose, an agreed-upon focus to evaluation episodes, a use of self-evaluation, a thorough discussion of the impressions of the supervisor after the class visit, the setting of clear growth targets, and so on. Other factors may relate to the overall climate in the school system, such as the feelings of an adversarial relationship between teachers and school board and superintendent, how teacher cutbacks are handled, levels of teacher dissatisfaction with conditions of their workplace, and so on. These latter factors are normally beyond the control of the supervisor.

Much of the resentment and defensiveness of teachers toward being evaluated will be diffused if the evaluation takes place in a clearly understood, mutually agreed-upon plan. Teachers want to know and deserve to know what the ground rules are. They also want to feel that those rules reflect their own thinking about how teachers should be evaluated. They will feel even more comfortable (or less uncomfortable) with performance evaluation if it is placed in a larger framework of formative evaluation and staff development. Hence we propose that the concerns of this chapter be situated within the larger perspectives developed in the next chapter.

One key to successful summative evaluation of teacher performance is the encouragement of self-evaluation. The evaluation by the supervisor should probably follow an initial attempt by the teacher to assess strengths and weaknesses. Furthermore, the teacher should be encouraged to use this self-evaluation to generate some needed growth targets. The evaluation of the supervisor can then support the teacher's own conclusions and the two of them can work on ways to build on strengths and improve on some weak areas. Self-assessment allows the teacher to set the initial agenda, to retain a sense of dignity because the judgment has been made initially by himself or herself. The supervisor may have some additional points to raise, but all things being equal, should hold off on them initially to work with the teacher on those points that seem significant to him or her.

Facing the Music

Some supervisors have high affiliation needs and hence are very reluctant to deal with anything potentially damaging to their relationships with teachers. Other supervisors have low affiliation needs and are insensitive to the feelings of teachers when expressing their evaluations. Both kinds of supervisors need to recognize that making judgments about the performance of others can be painful, but that it is a necessary part of the enterprise of maintaining and improving the learning environment for students. It is better to get those feelings out in the open, to deal with them in an adult and professional manner, and to get on with the task. Tiptoeing around the sensitivities involved will not make them go away. Making believe that no one is responsible for assessing the quality of instruction is irresponsible. Pointing only to the growth and development side of evaluation and not admitting that teachers also receive grades or performance ratings every year is not facing the realities of the school setting.

These realities can be faced honestly and rationally and can even be the source of improved performance and growth. Summative evaluation of teachers' performance, then, is not intrinsically contrary to human resource development supervision. In fact, the summative and the formative stages of the larger evaluation process can complement each other. If the supervisor and teacher work more and more as a team, then the summative evaluation that emerges can be more and more a team assessment. The following chapter highlights constructive approaches to staff development that can create a positive environment for the difficult task of performance evaluation.

SUMMARY

In this chapter it was hypothesized that by and large supervisors and others responsible for teacher evaluation privately view the procedures as lacking in credibility. The technology of present practices was characterized as scientific management and underlying assumptions as technical-rational. The internal integrity of these approaches was accepted, but their application to educational settings was described as ill-suited and inappropriate. The center of this mismatch is the willy-nilly application of the values of science to the art of teaching. Artistic assumptions and practices were suggested as alternatives more befitting the nature of work in education and the spirit of professional, as opposed to occupational, accountability in education.

Clinical supervision, in the specific sense of a supervisory cycle associated with Cogan, and adaptations of this process were presented as fairly well-developed techniques with artistic potential. It was argued that clinical supervision can and should take many forms, and that more experimentation with different forms is needed. A theoretical framework was offered as a means to conceptualize the process of clinical supervision. Basic to the framework was the assumption that teacher behavior is governed by the interplay of two theories: an espoused theory, which represents the teacher's public educational platform, and a theory in use, which represents the teacher's actual educational platform. Sometimes the actual platform is unknown to the teacher. Theory in use is inferred from classroom observations, analysis of videotapes, collected artifacts and portfolios, and other techniques. Confronting an individual with a theory in use inconsistent with that individual's espoused theory results in the surfacing of dilemmas that he or she seeks to resolve. This process acts as a stimulus to change and as a means to generate substantial change issues.

More emerging naturalistic techniques were then presented either as methods by which theories in use might be constructed or as techniques to be used independently of clinical supervision notions. These included concepts of educational connoisseurship and criticism and practices of artifact collecting and portfolio development. These ideas were not offered as tried and true practices but as alternatives worth trying. Universities have a role to play in developing and refining artistic approaches, but major headway is likely to depend upon the developmental efforts made by practicing supervisors.

Though the primary emphasis of this chapter was on formative evaluation, the realities of supervision today are that summative evaluation typically remains part of one's responsibilities. The chapter concluded with a discussion of this issue.

STUDY GUIDE

Recall the concepts, ideas, and meanings associated with each of the following phrases and terms included in this chapter. Can you discuss each of them with a colleague and apply them to the supervisory context of your school? If you cannot, review them in the text and record the page number for future reference.

1. Artifacts analysis _____
2. Artistic evaluation _____
3. Clinical supervision _____
4. Cogan's cycle of supervision _____
5. Connoisseurship in education _____
6. Criticism in education _____
7. Disclosure model _____
8. Educational platform _____
9. Espoused theory _____
10. Johari Window in supervision _____
11. Picturing model _____
12. Portfolio development _____
13. Private views of evaluation _____
14. Public views of evaluation _____
15. Technical-rational assumptions _____
16. Theory in use _____
17. Surfacing dilemmas _____

EXERCISES

1. Our contrast of technical-rational assumptions and practices and artistic assumptions and practices deliberately separates the views in an opposing fashion and indeed sets up the technical-rational assumptions as "straw men." Rewrite this section, showing the contrast between technical-rational and artistic assumptions as complementary and supplementary rather than competing, with each set adding power and meaning to the other.
2. Refer to Figure 17-1. Assuming the role of supervisor, identify three teachers in your school. For each, prepare a list of "public or open self" traits of his or her teaching. Compare the lists. Do the same sorts of characteristics appear in the "public self" for all three teachers? Repeat this procedure for the "blind self" quadrant. If you are a teacher, what sorts of characteristics would you write about your teaching in the "hidden or secret self" quadrant?
3. How would you describe concepts of educational connoisseurship and criticism to your superintendent?
4. Ask one or two teachers to prepare a portfolio collection over a span of 2 weeks of artifacts that highlight a particular issue, such as individualized instruction or whether youngsters are assuming more active roles in the classroom. How might the collection of artifacts and portfolio development be used to supplement more traditional "rating scale" approaches to teacher evaluation?

CHAPTER 18

SUPERVISION AS STAFF DEVELOPMENT

We are in a period of unprecedented interest in staff-development programs for teachers. This interest is fueled by the stark realization that a serious consequence of declining student enrollments and teacher surpluses has been an increase in staff stability. Simply put, when teachers land a decent job, they are likely to stay. Combine this phenomenon with a relatively young teaching force and many districts are faced with large numbers of teachers who are likely to stay employed in the same school or system for the next 2 or 3 decades. One side of the staff-development coin then is keeping a staff growing in competence and excitement about their work. The other side is a realization that most newly graduated teachers are not yet fully developed and functioning professionals.

Rubin speaks to these issues as follows:

> A teacher prepares to teach by spending four or five years at a training institution. There, in the existing order of things, he or she learns a sampling of all accumulated information, something about the theory of education, and a few prescriptions regarding the art and science of teaching. Even if this preparation were adequate, and it clearly is not, the training can become outdated in a very short time. Indeed, the moment teachers leave the training institution they embark upon a rapid journey to obsolescence. The eye of research may soon detect cracks in the foundation of old theory, lighten what were once dark voids, and illuminate new educational requirements. The social sciences are only now beginning to probe deeply into the dimensions of human interaction. And we have recently come to realize, with incredible lateness, that schools can teach children to be failures as well as successes. Beyond affective considerations, the continuous modernization of substantive knowledge is an accepted fact. It has often been noted, and with good reason, that the teacher who has not studied, say biology, during the last five years no longer knows the subject. The odds are therefore good that such a teacher will fill students with misconceptions. Preservice training alone, then, cannot produce great teaching.[1]

Staff development in education has come of age. Its importance is undisputed. But

[1]Louis J. Rubin, "The Case for Staff Development," in Thomas J. Sergiovanni (ed.), *Professional Supervision for Professional Teachers.* Washington, D.C.: Association for Supervision and Curriculum Development, 1975, p. 34.

what is the relationship between staff development and human resources supervision? In the sections that follow, we suggest that the relationship is intimate.

Special books have been written on the topic of staff development and a vast and usable literature exists.[2] In this chapter our intentions are primarily limited to providing supervisors with a theoretical map of this field designed to help organize their thinking and to assist in planning effective programs and evaluating existing ones.

STAFF DEVELOPMENT AND IN-SERVICE EDUCATION

Though in-service education of teachers has a long history, present practices have many shortcomings and have not been met with enthusiasm by teachers.[3] Reasons often given for such reactions are that in-service programs are often too formal and bureaucratic, are viewed as administrative responsibilities and teacher duties, and are too centralized, having a high degree of dysfunctional administrative planning and scheduling.

One effect of formal in-service programs that reflects a high degree of administrative responsibility is that the emphasis shifts from education to program. A successful program becomes one that meets legal requirements and one that is executed smoothly, efficiently, and according to schedule. Further, such programs are often characterized by activities that are selected and developed for uniform dissemination without serious consideration of the purposes of such activities and of the needs of individual teachers. We are not proposing that typical in-service education programs be abandoned, for they have their place, as limited as it may be. We are proposing, however, that they be drastically curtailed, and that they be supplemented by staff-development approaches, programs, and activities.

What is the difference between a staff-development orientation and in-service-education orientation? *Conceptually, staff development is not something the school does to the teacher but something the teacher does for himself or herself.* While staff development is basically growth-oriented, in-service education typically assumes a deficiency in the teacher and presupposes a set of appropriate ideas, skills, and methods that need developing. By focusing on these ideas, skills, and methods, in-service education works to reduce the teacher's range of alternatives—indeed, to bring about conformity. Staff development does not assume a deficiency in the teacher, but rather assumes a need for people at work to grow and develop on the job. Rather than reduce the range of alternatives, staff development works to increase this range.

Teacher growth is less a function of polishing existing teaching skills or of keeping up with the latest teaching developments and more a function of a teacher's changing as a person—of seeing himself or herself, the school, the curriculum, and students

[2]In addition to the sources cited in the footnotes throughout this chapter readers might be interested in the Winter 1981 issue of the *Journal of Research and Development in Education* (vol. 14, no. 2), the theme of which is "staff development: state of the scene and possibilities"; and two recent Association for Supervision and Curriculum Development publications, the 1981 yearbook, *Staff Development/Organizational Development*, Betty Dillon-Peterson (ed.), and the 1979 booklet, *Moving Toward Self-Directed Learning*, Delmo Della-Dora and Lois Jerry Blanchard (eds.).

[3]Ben Harris and Wailand Bessent, *In-Service Education: A Guide to Better Practice*, Englewood Cliffs, N.J.: Prentice-Hall, 1969, pp. 1–10; Henry J. Hermanowicz, "The Pluralistic World of Beginning Teachers," in *The World of Beginning Teachers*, Washington, D.C.: National Education Association, National Commission on Teacher Education and Professional Standards, 1966, pp. 16–25; and Rubin, op. cit., pp. 35–38.

differently. One should not have to make a choice between the two, for both are important. But it is the latter sort of change that is the essence of the staff-development orientation. The former emphasizes keeping teachers up to standard, the latter the continual raising of quality.

The distinctions we make between an in-service education and staff-development orientation is a *conceptual* one designed to help supervisors gauge their own thinking and monitor their own activities with better balance in the hope that we might be more responsive to teacher needs. The in-service orientation is necessary at times and seems best matched to formal intervention strategies. The staff-development orientation should receive major focus and seems best matched to informal intervention strategies. Though the emphasis of each may differ, both are concerned with remediation and growth.

A DESIGN FOR STAFF DEVELOPMENT

In the section that follows, a design for staff development in education is presented. This design is composed of five critical components. The components are *intents, substance, competency areas, approach,* and *responsibility.* The design requires staff-development planners to be concerned about program intents and substance and, in turn, to match these with appropriate approaches, competency levels, and responsibility designations. Let us consider each of the components separately.

Intents

Staff-development programs and activities are typically designed around such themes as presenting information of one kind or another, helping teachers understand this information, helping teachers apply this understanding in their teaching, and helping teachers to accept, and be committed to, these new approaches. Presenting information is a *knowledge*-level intent. A program, for example, might be designed to introduce a group of science teachers to the concept and nomenclature of inquiry teaching. Promoting understanding is a *comprehension*-level intent. The intent here might be to help teachers to understand how inquiry teaching might affect the way they presently plan and organize instruction. Using inquiry methods effectively in teaching a particular biology unit is an example of an *applications*-level intent. Though each of these levels is necessary, none is sufficient to gain sustained use of inquiry methods by teachers. Teachers may be able to demonstrate such methods on demand but are not likely to use them once out of the spotlight unless they believe in, and are committed to, such methods. Becoming committed to inquiry methods as a useful approach to science teaching is a *value-* and *attitude-integration*-level intent.

Often only knowledge and comprehension levels are legitimately appropriate focuses for staff-development programs. But programs specifically designed to meet intents at these levels are not likely to be sufficient for such higher levels as value and attitude integration. By the same token programs designed for higher-level intents, when only knowledge-level intents are necessary, may well be too elaborate, wasteful, and exhausting for both supervisors and teachers.

Substance

Rubin has identified four critical factors in good teaching, each of which he believes can be improved through appropriate staff-development activities:

> The teacher's sense of purpose
> The teacher's perception of students
> The teacher's knowledge of subject matter
> The teacher's mastery of technique[4]

Sense of purpose and perception of students are akin to a teacher's *educational platform* and as such represent values, beliefs, assumptions, and action theories a teacher holds about the nature of knowledge, how students learn appropriate relationships between students and teachers, and other factors.[5] One's educational platform becomes the basis for decisions one makes about classroom organization and teaching, and, indeed, once a platform is known, key decisions the teacher will make can be predicted with reliability.

A teacher, for example, who considers his or her purpose to be imparting information is likely to rely heavily on teacher talk and formal classroom arrangements. Likewise, a teacher who perceives youngsters as being basically trustworthy and responsible is likely to share responsibilities for decisions about learning with the class. If a supervisor were interested in reducing teacher talk and/or increasing student responsibility, he or she would have to contend with the critical factor of purpose and perception of teachers. His or her target is the restructuring of educational platforms of teachers.

In describing the importance of knowledge of subject matter, Rubin notes:

> There is a considerable difference between the kind of teaching that goes on when teachers have an intimate acquaintance with the content of the lesson and when the acquaintance is only peripheral. When teachers are genuinely knowledgeable, when they know their subject well enough to discriminate between the seminal ideas and the secondary matter, when they can go beyond what is in the textbook, the quality of the pedagogy becomes extraordinarily impressive. For it is only when a teacher has a consummate grasp of, say, arithmetic, physics, or history that their meaning can be turned outward and brought to bear upon the learner's personal experience. Relevancy lies less in the inherent nature of a subject than in its relationship to the child's frame of reference. In the hands of a skilled teacher, poetry can be taught with success and profit to ghetto children.[6]

Though content versus process arguments continue from time to time, both aspects of instruction are necessary for effective teaching. Our observation is that the less a teacher knows about a particular subject the more trivial the teaching and the more defensive the pedagogy. By defensive pedagogy we mean dominance by the teacher and strict adherence to curriculum materials. But one can have a great

---

[5]The concept of educational platform and how its variants, teacher-espoused platform and teacher platform in use, might be used as part of a clinical supervision strategy are described in the next chapter.
[6]Rubin, op. cit., p. 47.
[7]William B. Castetter, *The Personnel Function in Educational Administration*, New York: Macmillan, 1971, p.

appreciation for a particular field of study and still not be able to disclose its wonder and excitement effectively. Mastery of technique, classroom organization and management, and other pedagogical skills make up the fourth critical dimension of effective teaching.

These dimensions are the basis for deciding the substance of staff-development programs. Comprehensive programs are concerned with all four—the teacher's conception of purpose, sensitivity to students, intimacy with subject matter, and basic repertory of teaching techniques.

Competency Areas

What are the major competency areas for which teachers should be accountable? It is reasonable to expect that teachers, as is the case with other professionals, *know how* to do their jobs and to keep up with major developments. The areas of knowledge for professional teaching are suggested above—knowledge about purposes, students, subject matter, and techniques. But knowing and understanding are not enough. Teachers are expected to put their knowledge to work—to demonstrate that they *can do* the job. Demonstrating knowledge, however, is a fairly low-level competency. Most teachers are competent enough and clever enough to come up with the right teaching performance when the supervisor is around. The proof of the pudding is whether they *will do* the job of their own free will and on a sustained basis. Finally, professionals are expected to engage in a lifelong commitment to self-improvement. Self-improvement is the *will-grow* competency area. Self-employed professionals (doctors, accountants, etc.) are forced by competition and by visible product evaluation to give major attention to the will-grow dimension. Teachers, as organizational professionals whose "products" are difficult to measure, have not felt this external pressure for continuing professional growth. Increasingly, however, school districts are making the will-grow dimension a contractual obligation, and indeed teachers who are perfectly satisfactory in the know-how, can-do, and will-do competency areas face sanctions (including dismissal) for less than satisfactory commitment to continuing professional growth.

The relationships between competency areas, intents, and substance are shown in Figure 18-1. Let us begin explaining this figure with the know-how competency area. Knowledge- and comprehension-level intents are associated with this competency area,

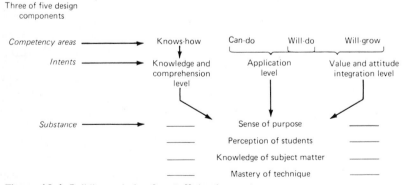

Figure 18-1 Building a design for staff development.

and the teacher is expected to know and understand purposes, students, subject matter, and techniques. In the can-do area, teachers apply this knowledge of substance to their classrooms. The will-do area, however, requires not only ability to apply this knowledge but also an identity and commitment to the application. Staff-development programs aimed at the will-do dimension must have value and attitude integration as well as application intents. Will-grow is equally dependent upon value- and attitude-integration intents. It follows, then, that supervisors who are interested in working with teachers in the will-do and will-grow competency areas and who choose programs and strategies suited only to knowledge and comprehension (they invite an expert from the state university to speak to teachers about inquiry teaching) are not likely to be successful.

Approach and Responsibility

We have now discussed three of five design components for staff development: intents, substance, and competency areas. Two more remain: the strategy, or *approach,* to staff development and the locus of major *responsibility.* Approaches can be grouped into three general categories: traditional, informal, and intermediate. Traditional approaches are generally more formal and structured and are designed to meet specific and uniform objectives. Informal approaches, on the other hand, are very low in structure and rely on discovery and exploration techniques. Often objectives are not predetermined but are discovered or assessed after the fact. Intermediate approaches are moderately structured with a predetermined agenda that permits a great deal of flexibility. Let us consider each approach briefly.

Traditional approaches and administrative responsibility Traditional approaches to staff development are well known to supervisors and administrators and need little elaboration. They seem best suited when a staff-development problem can be defined as a deficit in knowledge of some kind. Traditional approaches are typically accompanied by clear objectives and rely on conventional, though well-executed, instruction. Teachers generally assume passive roles and are exposed to logically structured programs or activities. Techniques most often used are lecture, illustrated lecture, demonstration, and observation, often followed by guided discussion activities.

Traditional approaches seem well suited to routine information updating of the latest books, techniques, principles, and ideas relating to one's work. It is assumed not that a particular group is considering adopting something new, but that the group is only learning more about it. As intents change from learning to understanding, to applying, to integrating new things into one's repertoire of behavior, approaches will need to change if staff development is to be effective. If one were to generalize about intents of staff development programs typically found in schools, the widespread use of traditional approaches to the virtual exclusion of other approaches would lead one to conclude that educators have an insatiable appetite for knowledge but are not interested in doing very much with this knowledge.

The locus of responsibility for traditional approaches to staff development is with the administration as it executes its personnel administration functions. In describing such functions Castetter notes that *"development* refers to provisions made by the school system for improving the performance of school personnel from initial employment to retirement. . . . Although it is recognized that personnel can and should improve their effectiveness without formal involvement of the system, attention here will be focused on those activities specifically planned and administered by school officials to facilitate staff development."[7] Though traditional approaches have a place and should remain administrative responsibilities, alone they represent a minimum commitment to staff development.

Informal approaches and teacher responsibility Perhaps the most innovative and provocative approaches to staff development are those that rely on exploration and discovery by teachers. It is assumed that by providing teachers with a rich environment loaded with teaching materials, media, books, and devices, and that with generous encouragement and support from principals and supervisors, teachers will interact with this environment and with each other through exploration and discovery. Exploration and discovery can help many teachers to find themselves, to unleash their creativity, to learn more about their own capabilities as people and teachers, and at the same time to pick up new teaching ideas, activities, and methods.

Thelen notes that in the most useful staff-development programs "one finds intensity of personal involvement, immediate consequences for classroom practice, stimulation and ego support by meaningful associates in the situation and initiating by teacher rather than outsider."[8] Informal approaches seem best able to meet these criteria, and because of their enormous potential, such approaches should play an important role in school district staff-development planning.

Major responsibility for informal approaches rests with teachers. Such efforts can take a variety of forms. Two teachers sharing ideas, a team or family of teachers working and planning together, teacher involvement in an in-building resource center, and participation in district or area teacher centers are examples. Informal staff-development approaches should be encouraged and supported. Indeed, the benefits derived from such approaches are a good reason for supervisors and administrators to advocate patterns of instruction that encourage teachers to plan and work together. Team teaching, schools within the school, and family grouping are examples of arrangements that naturally stimulate informal staff-development activities.

Teacher centers deserve special attention in that they represent fledgling, but promising, attempts to elevate and legitimize the role of teacher in accepting some of the responsibility for staff development. In describing such centers Kathleen Devaney notes:

> There is a notion of *teachers centers* which is essentially an image of a place—small, welcoming, hand-built—where teachers come voluntarily to make things for classrooms, to exchange ideas, and to learn in a format of one-shot or short-series workshops rather than semester-long courses based on lectures and texts. Because this place is non-institutional neutral ground, teachers can let down their hair, drop competitiveness and defensiveness, and thus find starting points for self-improvement and professional growth.[9]

[8]Herbert Thelen, "A Cultural Approach to In-Service Education," in Louis Rubin (ed.), *Improving In-Service Education,* Boston: Allyn and Bacon, 1971, pp. 72–73.
[9]Kathleen Devaney, "What's a Teacher Center For?" *Educational Leadership,* vol. 33, no. 6, p. 413, 1976. This issue of *Educational Leadership* was guest-edited by Vincent Rogers, and its theme is teacher centers.

Some centers indeed fit the "non-institutional neutral ground" pattern, but no hard and fast rules regarding location exist. A teacher center can be developed and operated in a surplus classroom or perhaps in an overlooked or poorly used basement location of a particular school. The center could be limited to only teachers of that school or perhaps expanded to serve district or area teachers. The closing of schools in many districts throughout the country lends itself to the establishment of a district or area teacher center in abandoned school buildings. Indeed, some centers are located in storefronts and warehouses. Regardless of scale or location, some common aspects exist, the most notable being that the locus of responsibility for planning and operation is with teachers. Further commonalities are suggested by Devaney:

> The common purpose which stands out as a bond linking widely dissimilar teachers centers is the aim to help teachers enliven, individualize, personalize, enrich, elaborate, reorganize, or re-conceptualize the curriculum within their own classrooms. Study of scores of teachers center program offerings and calendars demonstrates center leaders' belief that help to teachers in the area of curriculum is the most teacher-responsive service they can offer. These centers teach teachers how to use manipulative, real-world, exploratory, frequently individualized curriculum materials and how to gradually reorganize classroom space and time to accommodate greater student activity and interaction. They engage teachers in adapting packaged curriculum materials, making their own materials, or building classroom apparatus, and often they involve teachers in some new study—often math or science—or craft so as to reacquaint them with the experience of being active, problem-solving learners themselves.[10]

Changes of lasting quality in schools depend heavily on grass-roots processes. Further, it seems clear that teachers look to other teachers as important models for change. In two separate studies with similar themes both Haller and Keenan[11] asked teachers to identify to whom they go for help when they run into curriculum problems and to whom they could go for ideas and insights about teaching and learning. The Canadian and American teachers who responded to these questions were further asked which sources of new ideas were most creditable. Choosing from such categories as principal, supervisor, central office staff, professor, research journals, and so on, the overwhelming choice in response to each question was *other teachers*. Teachers go to other teachers for help and for sources of new ideas, and they believe in each other—potent reasons why supervisors need to provide support for informal staff-development approaches.

Intermediate approaches and supervisory responsibility The cornerstone of a comprehensive staff-development program for any school or district is a *supervisory* system of staff development. Traditional approaches with administrative responsibility and informal approaches with teacher responsibility should be viewed as supplements to this primary thrust.[12] Informal approaches are low-keyed, classroom-focused,

---

[10]Ibid., p. 414.

[11]Emil J. Haller, *Strategies for Change*, Toronto: Ontario Institute for Studies in Education, Department of Educational Administration, 1968; and Charles Keenan, "Channels for Change: A Survey of Teachers in Chicago Elementary Schools," doctoral dissertation, Urbana: University of Illinois, Department of Educational Administration, 1974.

[12]As education becomes professionally mature, the cornerstone position will likely shift to informal approaches with administrative and supervisory approaches as supplements.

teacher-oriented, and particularistic. Traditional approaches, on the other hand, are high-keyed, more formal, system- or school-oriented, and universal.

A supervisory system of staff development assumes an intermediate position whereby the supervisor enters into a relationship with teachers on an equal footing and assumes an active role along with teachers. The teachers' capacities, needs, and interests are paramount, but sufficient planning and structure is introduced to bridge the gap between these interests and school program and instruction needs.

Intermediate staff-development approaches usually have the following characteristics:

1. The teacher is actively involved in contributing data, information, or feelings, solving a problem, or conducting an analysis.

2. The supervisor shares in the contributing, solving, and conducting activities above as a colleague of the teacher.

3. In colleagueship the supervisor and teachers work together as professional associates bound together by a common purpose. The common purpose is improvement of instruction through the professional development of teacher and supervisor.[18] Neither the teacher's autonomy as a professional nor the supervisor's responsibilities as a professional are compromised in the process since the relationship is based not on authority but on a commitment to professional improvement.

4. Staff-development activities generally require study of an actual situation or a real problem and use live data, either from self-analysis or from observations of others.

5. Feedback is provided, by the supervisor, by other teachers, or as a result of joint analysis, which permits teachers to compare observations with intents and beliefs, and personal reactions with those of others.

6. The emphasis is on direct improvement of teaching and learning in the classroom.

For the remainder of this chapter and in Chapter 19 the focus will be on this intermediate approach to staff development in which supervisors play such an important part.

CHARACTERISTICS OF EFFECTIVE STAFF-DEVELOPMENT PROGRAMS

By way of summary, excerpts from a study of staff-development programs conducted under the auspices of the Florida State Department of Education are provided. The

---

[18]Our definition of colleagueship follows Morris Cogan, *Clinical Supervision*, Boston: Houghton Mifflin, 1973, Chap. 5. By contrast, the relationship between supervisor and teacher in traditional approaches is more clearly superordinate-subordinate, and in informal approaches the supervisor is more of a helper, facilitator, or passive supporter. In the intermediate approach the supervisor is neither dominating nor passive but is involved, side by side, with the teacher as a colleague.

study suggests a number of clear patterns of effectiveness consistent with the recommendations provided above:

> School-based programs in which *teachers participate as helpers to each other and planners of in-service activities* tend to have greater success . . . than do programs . . . conducted by college or other outside personnel without the assistance of teachers.
> In-service education programs that have *differentiated training experiences for different teachers* (that is, "individualized") are more likely to accomplish their objectives than are programs that have common activities for all participants.
> In-service education programs that *place the teacher in an active role (constructing and generating materials, ideas, and behavior)* are more likely to accomplish their objectives than are programs that place the teacher in a receptive role. . . .
> In-service education programs in which *teachers share and provide mutual assistance* to each other are more likely to accomplish their objectives than are programs in which each teacher does separate work.
> Teachers are more likely to benefit from in-service programs in which they can *choose goals and activities for themselves,* as contrasted with programs in which the goals and activities are preplanned.[Italics added][14]

Notice the importance given to teacher involvement in planning, differentiated experiences for different teachers, active roles, using ideas, materials, and behavior found in the actual teaching situation, teachers working with and helping other teachers, and teacher goals.

MAPPING STAFF-DEVELOPMENT STRATEGIES

We have now discussed the five critical components of staff development. In this section we arrange the components into a conceptual map, or design, to assist in understanding how the various components interact and to help in planning and decision making. This design for staff development is illustrated in Figure 18-2.

Before we begin to discuss this design, refer back to Figure 18-1 and note the relationship between three of the five design components. Here we suggested that staff-development intents at the knowledge and comprehension levels were suited to increasing teachers' knowledge; intents at the applications level, their can-do and to a lesser extent their will-do competence; and intents at the value and integration level, their will-grow competence. The content, substance, or "subject matter" of intents could be concerned with one or a combination of four aspects of effectiveness in teaching: purposes, perceptions of students, knowledge of subject matter, and technique. In Figure 18-2, two additional critical components, approach and responsibility, are included, and all five are illustrated in a fashion to help monitor existing staff-development programs or make decisions about new programs.

Let us consider the box in Figure 18-2 first. Notice that the box consists of four layers, each corresponding to aspects of teacher effectiveness. For illustrative purposes let us refer only to the bottom layer, mastery of technique, and specifically to the

[14]Roy A. Edelfelt and Margo Johnson, *Rethinking In-Service Education,* Washington, D.C.: National Education Association, 1975, pp. 18–19, as quoted in Devaney, op. cit., p. 416, The original report is Gordon Lawrence, *Patterns of Effective In-Service Education,* Tallahassee, Fla.: State Department of Education, 1974.

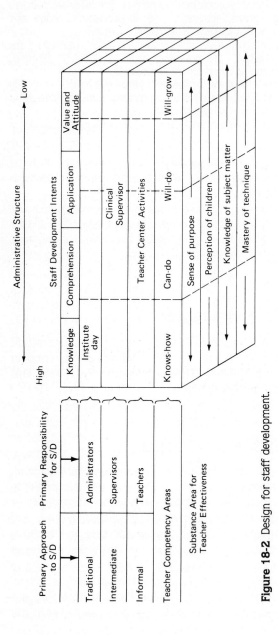

Figure 18-2 Design for staff development.

technique of inquiry teaching. Staff-development intents are shown across the top of the box and teacher-competency areas across the bottom of the box. If we are interested only in knowing about inquiry teaching, then we are concerned with knowledge-level intents and the know-how competency area. If we are interested in committed adoption and use of inquiry teaching, then we are concerned with value- and attitude-integration intents and will-do—will-grow competency areas.

The programs we develop for the latter intents should be different than those for the former. To the left of the box appear the approach and responsibility components of staff development. Traditional, intermediate, and informal approaches correspond to administrator, supervisor, and teacher responsibilities. The shaded box area directly to the right of each approach-responsibility designation suggests which intents and competency areas are likely to be effectively served by that approach. Traditional approaches seem best suited to knowledge-comprehension intents. Intermediate approaches seem best suited to comprehension, application, and value- and attitude-integration intents. Similarly, informal approaches point toward applications intents though these seem most potent for value- and attitude-integration intents.

What approaches to staff development should be used for our inquiry-method example? Who should assume major responsibility for this approach? The answer depends on the kind of purposes or intents sought. If one were interested only in knowledge and comprehension, then an administrator-directed-institute day might be best. Clinical supervision might be a strategy if inquiry teaching were seen as important to the school and the intent were committed implementation of this technique by teachers. Though informal approaches are typically more potent than others, staff-development agendas in this approach belong to teachers, and they may not choose to pursue inquiry teaching. If they did, then the approach might well be the most effective for achieving committed implementation of this technique by teachers. An additional drawback of informal approaches is that they are often not effective at the knowledge level. It seems best therefore to view staff development in a more comprehensive fashion.

LEADERSHIP STYLES AND SUPERVISORY ROLES

Supervisors assume a number of different roles in working with teachers to improve teaching. Sometimes they assume the role of "teacher" and actually plan programs and activities designed to help teachers learn about new ideas and practices. They might, for example, design programs aimed at informing teachers about new developments and insights revealed by teacher-effectiveness research or they might demonstrate how a learning resource center might be developed and used within the classroom to support more direct instruction. When assuming this role, they practice a more directive style of leadership, taking the major responsibility for developments.

Sometimes supervisors assume the role of colleague, and together with teachers work on teaching problems and issues. The format here is problem solving and the style is collaborative, with teachers assuming fairly equal responsibility for what is happening. Clinical supervision is an example of a teacher improvement strategy in this mode.

The supervisor-as-colleague role is best expressed by the team leadership style, where task and relationship emphases are brought together.

Sometimes supervisors assume the role of facilitator to the efforts of teachers. Here it is the responsibility of teachers to arrange the professional development activities they desire. As facilitators, supervisors provide support, encouragement, and council when asked. They attempt to remove obstacles that hinder teacher growth and development. They engage in target setting, provide for administrative arrangements, and otherwise support the initiatives of teachers. They give encouragement and provide rewards to teacher efforts. Responsibility for task, however, rests primarily with teachers, and supervisors, when in this role, practice the relationship-oriented leadership style.

These relationships are illustrated in Figure 18-3. Notice that as supervisors assume roles as teachers, teachers are in turn placed in the role of *consumer* of knowledge. As supervisors move toward the facilitative end, teachers increasingly become *sources* of knowledge. Deciding which role and accompanying leadership style is most appropriate to a given situation depends upon the ability of teachers (their motivation, talent, interests, etc.) to operate at a particular level on the continuum between consumer and source of knowledge.

SUPERVISION AS STAFF DEVELOPMENT

Supervisors are involved in the more administrative aspects of district and school staff-development programs and are facilitators and supporters of more informal thrusts. However, they assume active roles in, and major responsibility for, intermedi-

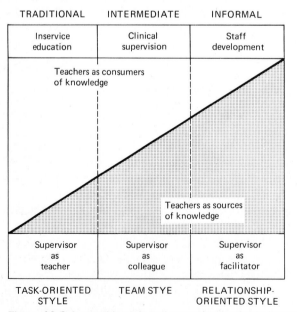

Figure 18-3 Leadership style and supervisory roles in improving teaching.

ate approaches that rely heavily on face-to-face interaction with teachers at work in classrooms. In this effort, they rely heavily on materials and observations generated from the work itself in an attempt to promote professional growth and to directly improve classroom instruction.

As indicated in the introduction to Part Four, traditional involvement of supervisors in the classroom has generally boiled down to summative teacher evaluation characterized by a technology associated with the ideology of scientific management. Reliance on rating scales, "scientific" measurements of one sort or another, and evaluation based on behavioral objectives-oriented evaluation are examples. We suggested further that though administrators and supervisors publicly participate in this system of supervision, privately most have doubts about its effectiveness. The irony in using such methods of supervision and evaluation is that the methods tend not to match the nature of work in education. The heart of the mismatch is using quasi-scientific methods to evaluate activities that are basically artistic.

A number of alternatives, each with a more formative emphasis targeted to professional development and improvement, were suggested in the introduction. It is useful to group these alternatives into generations in an attempt to understand their evolution. First-generation alternatives rely heavily on involving teachers in target setting. Second-generation alternatives are associated with the cycle of clinical supervision popularized by Anderson, Cogan, Goldhammer, and others. Third-generation alternatives are the more artistic approaches to supervision. The use of educational connoisseurship based on the analogy of aesthetic criticism, as suggested by Eisner, as well as portfolio development and analysis and the collection of artifacts stand out as examples of more naturalistic approaches. Second- and third-generation alternatives are considered in the next chapter. Here we give brief attention to the use of target setting in supervision.

TARGET SETTING AND EVALUATION

One way in which a target-setting procedure might be arranged is as follows:

Step 1 *Target setting.* Based on last year's observations, conferences, and summary reports, on clinical supervision episodes, and/or on self-evaluation, teachers develop targets or goals they would like to reach in improving their teaching. Targets should be few in number and within reach—rarely exceeding 8 or 10, preferably 3 to 6. Estimated time frames are provided for each target. Targets are then shared with the supervisor.

Step 2 *Target-setting review.* The supervisor reviews each target and estimated time frame and provides the teacher with a written reaction. A copy of both may be forwarded to the principal for his or her review and comments. A conference appointment is made with the teacher.

Step 3 *Target-setting conference.* The teacher and supervisor meet together to discuss targets, time frames, and reactions, and to revise them if appropriate. A written summary of the conference is prepared.

Step 4 *The appraisal process.* This begins at the conclusion of the target-setting conference and continues in accordance with the agreed-upon time frame. The specific nature of the appraisal process depends upon each of the agreed-upon targets and could include formal and informal classroom observations, an analysis of classroom artifacts, videotaping, student evaluation, and/or interaction analysis. The teacher participates in this step by suggesting appraisal methods and by periodically conferring with the supervisor.

Step 5A *Summary appraisal.* The supervisor prepares a summary appraisal commenting on each of the targets and confers with the teacher.

Step 5B *Summary of appraisal procedures.* In addition to the summary appraisal the supervisor prepares a summary of appraisal procedures that details dates and frequency of contacts with the teacher, a general review of targets and progress noted, a summary of help given to the teacher, an indication of the comprehensiveness of the appraisal, and recommendations. This statement is also discussed in conference with the teacher, step 5A.[15]

The setting of targets, or supervision by objectives as some call it, is becoming a popular alternative to evaluation strategies that rely heavily on checklist rating scales in many schools. Target setting should not be confused with using student-oriented behavior objectives and evaluating teachers on the amount of pupil gain demonstrated for each objective. Widespread as this particular practice may be, it is regarded with suspicion by leading evaluation experts and is totally unacceptable as a primary or exclusive evaluation strategy.

Some school districts link the entire teacher-evaluation system to the target-setting strategy and others see target setting as a critically important component of a more comprehensive evaluation strategy. Either alone or in combination with other approaches, target setting can be a powerful means for linking teacher evaluation and supervision to continuous staff development.

Target setting is subject to abuses and has shortcomings that, if ignored, can seriously undermine the development of an effective evaluation strategy. The most serious problems arise from supervisors' rigid adherence to prespecified targets and autocratic imposition of targets on teachers. Rigidly applying the system unduly focuses the evaluation and blinds individuals to many important events and activities not originally anticipated or stated. Teachers may focus all their concerns and energy on the targets at issue and neglect other areas not targeted at the time. Target setting is meant to help and facilitate, but rigid application can actually hinder teacher growth.

Target setting should not be seen as a system of management control (although for weak teachers who show little or no capability for self-improvement, it might legitimately be used as a management system of close supervision) but as a cooperative system of self-improvement. Supervisors and teachers together should discuss events and participate in the development of targets, with the teacher assuming the primary role and the supervisor an influential but supporting role.

[15]This section on target setting follows Thomas J. Sergiovanni, *Handbook for Effective Department Leadership Concepts and Practices in Today's Secondary Schools,* Boston: Allyn and Bacon, 1977, pp. 394–396.

SUMMARY

This chapter was concerned with the supervisor's role in staff development. It was noted that current declines in student enrollments and shortages in teaching jobs have combined to increase the stability of teaching staffs. A relatively young and stable teacher force is requiring policymakers to focus anew on the necessity for staff-development programs in education.

Though no operational distinction was intended, a conceptual distinction was made between an in-service education orientation and a staff-development orientation. The former tends to focus on deficiencies in teachers and on bringing them up to standard. The latter tends to focus on professional growth and on raising the quality of performance.

A design for staff development consisting of five critical components was presented. The components were intents, substance, competency areas, approach, and responsibility. The relationships and interdependencies between and among intents were discussed. With respect to approach and responsibility three approaches to staff development with corresponding responsibility designations were described. Traditional approaches were seen as administrative responsibilities, intermediate approaches as supervisory responsibilities, and informal approaches as teacher responsibilities. Corresponding staff-development-program examples might be institute days, engaging teachers in clinical supervision, and developing a teacher center.

The chapter concluded with a discussion of more formative alternatives to traditional teacher evaluation that could be considered as intermediate staff-development approaches. Target setting was cited as a first-generation alternative, strategies associated with the cycle of clinical supervision as second-generation alternatives, and artistic approaches such as connoisseurship and criticism, and portfolio development, as third-generation alternatives. A chart depicting appropriate leadership styles given certain supervisory roles was provided. Key to this formulation is the need for supervisors to assume teaching rolls, colleague roles, and facilitator roles at appropriate times.

STUDY GUIDE

Recall the concepts and meanings associated with each of the following phrases and terms included in this chapter. Can you discuss each of them with a colleague and apply them to the supervisory context of your school? If you cannot, review them in the text and record the page number for future reference.

1. Administrative approaches to staff development _____
2. Colleagueship _____
3. Competency areas _____
4. Critical factors in teaching _____
5. Design for staff development _____
6. First-generation alternatives _____
7. Ideology of scientific management _____
8. In-service-education orientation _____
9. Intermediate approaches to staff development _____

10. Second-generation alternatives _____
11. Staff-development orientation _____
12. Staff stability _____
13. Target setting _____
14. Teacher center _____
15. Third-generation alternatives _____
16. Value and attitude integration _____

EXERCISES

1. Though the distinction between staff-development and in-service organization is conceptual and not operational, try to classify activities and programs in your school into each of the two categories.
2. Develop a 10-item attitude questionnaire assessing teacher feelings about staff development in your school. Use the questionnaire to collect teacher impressions and views and to prepare a "state of the art" report on staff development in your school.
3. Prepare a short talk (10 minutes) to be given before a citizen's advisory committee or school board entitled "Staff Development: Important in the Seventies—Critical in the Eighties."
4. Using the design summarized in Figure 18-2, select another topic for staff development, perhaps one from a teacher-effectiveness area other than mastery of technique. Work this new topic through the design, reaching staff-development decisions about approach—responsibility, types of intents, and competency areas.
5. Refer to Figure 18-3. Give specific examples of supervisory incidents and staff-development occasions where teachers in your school were consumers of knowledge and sources of knowledge.

CHAPTER 19

THEORY OF PRACTICE IN THE SUPERVISION AND EVALUATION OF TEACHING

What are the requirements for a theory of supervision and evaluation of teaching able to capture the complexities of this undertaking and to inform practice? Goldhammer, Anderson, and Krajewski provide some answers to this question by setting forth an agenda for the further development of supervision:

> We require a supervision that is basically analytical and whose principle mode of analysis comprises highly detailed examination of teaching behavior. We require a supervision whose precepts and methods are basically rational and unmysterious and in which teachers may participate with all of their intellectual offense. We need a supervision whose effect is to enhance and to actualize and to fulfill, in degrees that are appreciable and sensible in the teacher's own experimental frameworks. Teachers (like anyone) must be able to understand what they are doing and the goals and processes that govern their behaviors and supervision must provide adequate illumination for such understanding. We require a supervision that is basically teacher-initiated and consistent with independent, self-sufficient action. Our supervision must result, regularly and systematically, in palpable technical advancement; it must have methological and conceptual rigor and it must produce real and measurable accomplishments.[1]

In dealing specifically with clinical supervision, we argued for better balance between scientific and artistic perspectives. In this chapter we continue this theme by pointing out the importance of interpretation and meaning in evaluation and by specifying some dimensions we feel are needed in developing a theory of practice in the supervision and evaluation of teaching.[2]

---

[1]Robert Goldhammer, Robert H. Anderson, and Robert J. Krajewski, *Clinical Supervision: Special Methods for the Supervision of Teachers,* 2d ed., New York: Holt, 1980.

[2]This chapter is based on T. J. Sergiovanni, "Interpretation and Meaning in the Evaluation of Teaching," presented at the Annual Meeting of the National Council of Measurement in Education and the American Education Research Association, Los Angeles: April 1981; and T. J. Sergiovanni, "Toward a Theory of Supervisory Practice: Integrating Scientific Clinical and Artistic Views," in T. J. Sergiovanni (ed.), *Supervision of Teaching,* 1982 Yearbook, Association for Supervision and Curriculum Development, Alexandria, Va., 1982, pp. 67–78.

THEORY OF PRACTICE

Consider the following allegory. Suppose there is a windowless classroom with three doors A, B, and C. Next to each door is a switch. The switch by door A puts on a green light, the switch by door B a red light, and the switch by door C a blue light. Suppose that students, a teacher, and a supervisor enter the room often, each always using the same door, but never the door of the others. Students use door A, the teacher uses door B, and the supervisor door C. Each of the parties will firmly believe, and have evidence that substantiates his or her belief, that the room is a specific color. Is it the task of the supervisor in this case to establish the facts as he or she sees them? What is truth and what facts exist in this instance? No matter how carefully the supervisor builds a case, truth and fact can not be separate from the meanings and realities of each of the participants involved in this allegory, and such is the case as well in the real world of supervision.

A useful and realistic conception of evaluation in teaching cannot be developed separate from a concern for purpose and for beneficiaries. If the purpose of evaluation is to inform and improve teaching practice and the beneficiaries are teachers, students, and supervisors, then we should distinguish between theories of measurement and evaluation and theories of practice. Theories of measurement and evaluation are concerned with the discovery of truth, the establishment of fact, and the accurate recording of the world as it is. Frequently such theories seek to advance the science and art of measurement and evaluation, and the prime beneficiaries of such efforts are theorists and analysts.

Theories of practice, on the other hand, are designed to improve things, to bring about higher standards, to cause individuals to strive for a better life. They have, in other words, purposive and practical qualities. When applied to such fields as supervision and teaching, theories of practice must account as well for the particularistic and phenomenological qualities of human activity.

Teaching and supervision might well be characterized as human sciences. Unlike the study of natural phenomena, as might be the case in chemistry or physics, the human sciences are distinctly more artificial. As Herbert A. Simon suggests, "A natural science is a body of knowledge about some class of things—objects or phenomena—in the world: about the characteristics and properties that they have; about how they behave and interact with each other."[3] The sciences of the artificial, on the other hand, are created by human conventions. The natural sciences are more concerned with how things are; the sciences of the artificial with how things ought to be and with designs that help to attain goals. "The thesis is that certain phenomena are 'artificial' in a very special sense: they are as they are only because of a system's being molded, *by goals or purposes,* to the environment in which it lives. . . . Artificial phenomena have an air of 'contingency' in their malleability by environment."[4] It is this malleability, this air of contingency that is determined by persons according to their perceptions of reality and according to their known and unknown goals or purposes, that raises for Simon this interesting question about the sciences of the artificial: "The genuine problem is to

---

[3]Herbert A. Simon, *The Sciences of the Artificial,* Cambridge: Massachusetts Institute of Technology, 1969.
[4]Ibid., p. ix.

show how empirical propositions can be made at all about the systems that, given different circumstances, might be quite other than they are."[5]

In sum, theories of measurement and evaluation are helpful but are not sufficiently comprehensive or sensitive to account for the purposive, practical, and artificial qualities that characterize supervision and teaching.

INTERPRETATION AND MEANING

We arrive at these conclusions by recognizing that there are at least two dimensions in describing a classroom event or action: a *configuration* dimension and a *meaning* dimension. In its configuration sense, the emphasis in evaluation is on describing an element's features and factual basis. In the jargon of social science, this emphasis can be referred to as establishing "social facts." What are the social facts of teaching and its observed or otherwise documented effects in a given classroom? A carefully delineated objective, criterion-referenced test questions, and student response data; an accurate record of teacher "moves" on a classroom map; a chart depicting how students spend time; a transcript of the teacher's lecture designed to assess uses of advanced organizers; and a recording of student winks, smiles, nods, and frequency of hand waving are examples of social facts. Evaluation that seeks to determine social facts relies heavily on "brute" data.[6]

In its meaning sense the emphasis in evaluation is on establishing the meanings of an element to an individual or a group. In the jargon of social science this emphasis has been referred to as establishing "social meanings." What are the meanings of a particular classroom element or of several in combination to an individual or group? The extent to which behavior modification techniques of classroom management are being used, and their subsequent effect on student attention spans, can be accurately recorded in a brute-data sense. But the meanings to students and teachers that result from using this technique can escape undetected.

In contrast to emphasizing exclusively brute data, the supervisor should be interested in "sense" data as well. Social facts, as determined by brute data, are typically the starting point in an evaluation, but brute data cannot stand alone and still have sense in a particular context any more than a word can stand separate from its context or a color from its field. The word "spirit," for example, defies understanding separate from its use in context (is it whisky, ghost, élan, or soul?). And even such basic words as "eat" take on different meanings in use and different meanings in different cultural contexts. As a further example, yellow is a color quite different against a field of white than black. And so it is with brute data recorded from classroom activity. Observation A when combined with B may have quite different meanings and significance than when combined with C.

At a simple level, supervision and evaluation of teaching does emphasize meaning when it seeks to determine teacher intents or to understand what are the intended outcomes of a particular curriculum format and related teaching sequence. But

[5]Ibid., p. x.
[6]Charles Taylor, "Interpretation and the Sciences of Man," *The Review of Metaphysics*, vol. 25, no. 1, pp. 3–51, 1971.

classroom meanings can be understood at three levels: intended, common, and intersubjective.[7] Common meanings, for example, are the shared sentiments and beliefs of those having a common social identity. Though symbolic interactionists might view this description of common meanings as too simple,[8] for our purposes common meanings might be thought of as the shared meanings derived from membership in or identity with a particular school culture such as that of teacher, student, or supervisor. Intersubjective meanings are those derived individually from interaction with or experiencing of a particular classroom element or event. Basic to intersubjective meanings is that the same element or event has different meanings for different people and takes on different meanings when combined with other elements.

THE DOMAINS OF INQUIRY

Classrooms are social systems and, like other social systems, can be viewed as possessing three interdependent components; a theory, a structure, and a technology.[9] Theory refers to the rules, beliefs, and standards that help to define and promote understanding of reality; structure refers to the set of roles and relationships that exist among system members; and technology refers to the actual procedures and practices by which things get done. With respect to classrooms, the interdependent components might be thought of as educational platforms, social structures, and educational activities.

In seeking the domains of inquiry in teacher evaluation one can look to the social system components on the one hand and the actions and activities that take place and

[7]Ibid.
[8]Herbert Blumer, "Society as Symbolic Interaction," in A. M. Rose (ed.), *Human Behavior and Social Processes,* Boston: Houghton Mifflin, 1962.
[9]Donald A. Schon, *Beyond the Stable State,* New York: Random House, 1971.

	Intended meanings	Observed events	Common meanings	Interobjective meanings
Educational platform	Stated intents	Intents observed	Culturally interpreted intents	Subjectively interpreted intents
Social structure	Relationships desired	Actual relationships	Culturally interpreted relationships	Subjectively interpreted relationships
Educational activity	Developed plans	Activity observed	Culturally interpreted activity	Subjectively interpreted activity
	What ought to be? (espoused theories)	What is? (brute data)	What do "is" and "ought" mean? (Sense data)	

Figure 19-1 The domains in inquiry in the supervision and evaluation of teaching.

their multiple meanings on the other. The domains as depicted in Figure 19-1 suggest that the task of teacher evaluation is more complex than is normally assumed and that a variety of techniques might be appropriate given the particular domain of interest at the moment.

Brute-data-collection strategies, therefore, have a role to play along with sense-data strategies if a complete picture is sought. Further, since the social system features of classroom life are interdependent, evaluation needs to be viewed as dynamic. A change in classroom practices or in organization of instruction, for example, influences the existing social structure and the shape and texture of the educational program. As these social system dimensions change, so do the meanings to be inferred from the brute facts of what is.

MODES OF INQUIRY

Within a theory of practice a variety of modes exists by which the domains might be analyzed and understood. As Garman suggests, modes of inquiry should be viewed as alternate ways of knowing, with no one mode designed to rival others. Instead, modes give attention to and highlight different issues of interest in supervision and evaluation.[10] She proposes five modes as follows:

> *Discovery* has as a goal the inductive search for well-articulated phenomena and appropriate questions inherent in the classroom scenario. Both qualitative and quantitative data are appropriate here. The analysis often begins by identifying the teacher's stated intent of the lesson and the signs of consistency or inconsistency as a result of subsequent actions.
>
> *Verification* is a deductive mode that provides for a degree of objectivity, (which suggests that others using the same method with the same data can arrive at similar conclusions). When the salient features of the lesson have been discovered, it is imperative that the supervisor verify, usually with quantitative methodology, the extent to which the discovery was justified. Objectivity is also regarded as a general frame of mind that helps the supervisor assume a detached and neutral posture. Hypothesis testing is a feature of the verification mode.
>
> *Explanation* is both inductive and deductive. Its purpose is to explain the verified phenomena through inference derived from the content analysis of stable data. The supervisor and teacher bring their subjective "best estimates" of what is happening from their own reality base. Concept formation is a vital part of the process since this becomes the means for the two to share their construed realities from both worlds. Understanding through language is the basis for explanation.
>
> *Interpretation* is the search for meaning in the events under study. The interpretive mode often provides a way to get to what really matters, to derive mature interpretations from that which has been verified and explained. Through appropriate methodology one has the sanction to go beyond the literal, encouraged to look for deeper meanings than the inferences derived through explanation. The supervisor understands internally by intuitively refering to his/her experience and externally by searching for symbolic acts which reveal insights about the myths and predispositions of those involved. Through the interpretive mode the supervisor and teacher are able to seek deeper significance beneath the surface content that may appear trivial.
>
> *Evaluation* is a normative mode which addresses values and judgments about the

[10]Noreen Garman, "A Clinical Approach to Supervision," in T. J. Sergiovanni (ed.), *Supervision of Teaching,* op. cit.

events under consideration. Evaluative methods are used to determine the effectiveness of a particular action or the worthiness of the meaning. They help the teacher answer such questions as, "How well have I performed?" or "Am I doing what I should be doing?" By valuing, the supervisor and teacher come to know the internal and external criteria for setting priorities and making judgments in the evaluation mode.[11]

THE BASIC QUESTIONS

In the remaining sections we wish to emphasize the interpretive aspects of the pursuit of meaning in supervision. This emphasis is taken with the recognition that the pursuit of meaning is an exercise of little value without having established as well what is and what ought to be in the evaluation of teaching. We conclude by suggesting some modes of inquiry that need to be developed if a theory of practice in supervision and evaluation of teaching is to emerge.

Three major avenues of inquiry are suggested as being important in a theory of supervisory practice. Interpretation is an art that is enhanced by multiple perspectives on reality, and meanings are sufficiently idiosyncratic to require that avenues of inquiry be pursued in partnership by teachers and supervisors. The avenues of inquiry are suggested by three questions.

1. *What is going on in this classroom?* How does this work? Can it be explained and predicted? What laws and rules govern behavior in this context? How can I accurately and vividly describe classroom events?

Thin descriptions of reality are important in presenting an overall map of classroom events. Such a map gives a general orientation of the classroom's breadth and scope, much like that a road map provides for a particular region. Thick descriptions of reality are important in identifying and recording aspects of the hidden curriculum, estimates of quality, and indicators of cultural imperatives that provide a more vivid portrayal of classroom life. The maps in a travel atlas, for example, present a general descriptive orientation of a particular region, but the accompanying text and photographs describe the mind and pulse of this region. Each is useful to the traveler.

2. *What ought to be going on in this classroom?* What cultural imperatives should determine action? What values should be expressed? What qualities of life should be in evidence? What standards should be pursued?

"Ought" dimensions of classroom life can be obtained and verified from empirically established standards (i.e., teacher effectiveness research) on the one hand and from cultural preferences, values, and beliefs (i.e., conservative or humanistic ideology) on the other. Admittedly, the two sources are more easily separated in word than in action. Symbolic interactionists, for example, would suggest that values are products of interaction among people and are qualities of mind that arise through such interaction on the one hand and through symbolic meanings on the other.

[11]Ibid., pp. 50–51.

Establishing that a particular level of student achievement can be obtained if teachers follow closely a given set of teaching procedures suggests a standard of fact. Such relationships ought to be rigorously pursued and empirically established as *teaching facts.* Deciding that the particular level of student achievement that might be obtained is valuable and that the trade-offs of what is lost to students and others by obtaining this gain in achievement or by adopting this method of teaching are acceptable, however, does not necessarily follow from teaching facts. Making decisions among alternatives is the establishment of *teaching values.* Strong teaching facts scientifically determined are important prerequisites for establishing teaching values but are not substitutes for these values. The establishment of both teaching facts and teaching values is important in the development of the theory of supervisory practice.

3. *What do events and activities that constitute the "is" and "ought" dimension of classroom life mean to teachers, students, supervisors, and significant others?* What is the cultural content of the classroom? What implicit educational platforms exist? What values are suggested by actual behavior and events? What are the meanings implicit in discrepancies between the espoused and in-use theories?

The discovery of meaning and the creation of meaning await the further development of the art of interpretation in the supervision and evaluation of teaching. The work of Eisner in an important step in this direction.[12]

It may be helpful in illustrating the importance of social facts and social meanings in the evaluation of teaching to distinguish between *picturing* and *disclosure.*[13] Picturing models of evaluation try to be as much like the teaching activity and classroom life under study as possible. In contrast disclosure models contain key characteristics of the teaching activity and classroom life under study but move beyond picturing per se to the interpretation of meaning by raising issues and testing propositions about the phenomenon. Picturing and disclosing models were contrasted in Chapter 17. In examining the disclosure side of the ledger emphasis was given to going beyond the data in the strictest sense to telling a story represented by the data. The data are enriched in disclosure as a means of communicating more vividly and fully. But disclosure is not invention, and the story developed is based on the social facts present in teaching. Meaningful disclosure requires accurate picturing.

THE DIMENSIONS IN ACTION

We have suggested that the problems of supervision and evaluation of teaching need to be addressed in a fashion that emphasizes interpretation and meaning. Developing accurate and objective records of the real world of teaching as defined by the canons of objectivity would be only part of the process. Of no less importance would be the subjective world of teaching. The phenomenological life of the classroom and teaching as an expression of cultural and hermeneutical inquiry are the areas that should now receive our attention. Looking to hermeneutics, for example, as a method of analysis,

---

[12]Elliot W. Eisner, *The Educational Imagination,* New York: Macmillan, 1979.
[13]Ian Ramsey, *Models and Mystery,* London: Oxford University Press, 1964.

supervision and evaluation of teaching would require that one give attention to normative and descriptive knowledge and theoretical and practical perspectives at the same time.[14]

Of interest in using a hermeneutical frame of reference would be the accurate recording of concrete facts that describe in practice classroom events. Important as well is sensitivity to what the best of educational research says are the predictable relationships between and among these classroom events. For example, what does educational research say about the relationship between academic engaged time of students and subsequent results on mathematics achievement tests? And to what extent are youngsters in a particular classroom academically engaged?

Also of interest would be the teacher's stated and unstated intents, stated and unstated assumptions, and stated and unstated beliefs that constitute his or her educational platform. Important as well would be the teacher's sensitivity to the broader social and cultural imperatives that delineate and define a value system from which standards of quality and excellence are born. For example, what does this teacher say are his or her intents and what intents can be inferred from the teacher's actual behavior and from other factors found in the classroom? These dimensions are illustrated in Figure 19-2 in the form of a grid containing four quadrants. The quadrants compare descriptive knowledge and normative knowledge with practical and theoretical perspectives. One quadrant, for example, is concerned with descriptive

[14]Taylor, op. cit.

The Pursuit of Descriptive Knowledge

1. PRACTICAL — DESCRIPTIVE	2. THEORETICAL — DESCRIPTIVE
Supervisor and teacher seek to record the facts which exist in a particular classroom. Scientific strategies yield "thin" descriptions over an array of concerns and artistic strategies "thick" descriptions of selected concerns. The intent is to establish "what is".	Supervisor and teacher review social science and educational research as well as the humanities disciplines (culture, ethics, values) in an effort to determine "what is" good practice. Scientific perspectives favor searching the wisdom of empirical research and theoretically establish facts and artistic the humanistic disciplines. Both provide insights into "what ought" but as establish facts rather than individual preferences.
The supervisor seeks to understand and help the teacher understand his or her stated and implied goals and objectives. Scientific strategies favor the analysis of stated goals and objectives and artistic, the implied. The "ought" dimension is of concern in both manifest and latent forms. Ought refers to stated and implied individual preferences of the teacher.	The supervisor seeds to understand the teacher's stated and implied educational platform and the stated and implied cultural value system which serve as determinants of classroom life. The emphasis is on interpretation and meaning which in turn fuels further inqury into the other three quandrants. Aristic strategies are better able to provide interpretation and meaning.
3. PRACTICAL — NORMATIVE	4. THEORETICAL — NORMATIVE

The Pursuit of Normative Knowledge.

Figure 19-2 Avenues of inquiry in the supervision and evaluation of teaching.

knowledge of a practical nature, a second with descriptive knowledge of a theoretical nature, a third with normative knowledge of a practical nature, and a fourth with normative knowledge of a theoretical nature.

The quadrants of Figure 19-2 depict the avenues of inquiry that we believe should be considered in a practical theory of supervision and evaluation of teaching. The task is more complex than rating teachers' effectiveness against a standard of validated teacher competencies or conducting a discrepancy analysis between stated intents and actual student achievement. Inquiry, for example, would require that one move from quadrant to quadrant repeatedly in the analysis of classroom events in search of meaning. Of interest is not only teacher behavior and other descriptions of what is, but the quality of life that exists in the classroom and the cultural imperatives defining that quality. Meaning, it is assumed, is the vehicle for increasing one's vision about classroom happenings and for informing one's intuition. These in turn are keys to understanding and improving teaching.

To what end is a theory of practice perspective advocated? Is the purpose of such inquiry to advance the science and art of evaluation? Are the prime beneficiaries theorists and analysts? We think not. Of concern is improving the practice of teachers and the quality of classroom life. Thus a key fourth question must be considered. Given what is (as established by theories of measurement and evaluation), what ought to be (normative theories), and what events mean (interpretive science), what should supervisors and teachers "do" (supervisory practice)? If we are concerned with "doing," then we should accept the reality that the evaluation data of prime interest are sense, not brute. Sense data are embedded in the cultural nuances that exist in a particular situation and become meaningful to an evaluation as events and actions are interpreted.

SUMMARY

In this chapter the need for a theory of practice in the supervision and evaluation of teaching was argued. Further, some criteria for developing such a theory were proposed. Such a theory would, for example, be concerned with describing classroom and teaching events as accurately and objectively as possible, with struggling to determine what ought to be good teaching and what is quality in classroom life, with seeking to determine what events and activities observed and noted in the evaluation process mean to particular individuals involved and in different circumstances, and with determining what actions supervisors should take given this integrated analysis. Both scientific and artistic views of teaching and evaluation would be brought together in such a theory. Some examples of how such a theory might work in use were suggested as were needed avenues of inquiry in the evaluation of teaching. Throughout this chapter it was pointed out that theories of measurement and evaluation serve principally to advance measurement and evaluation knowledge and *not* to improve teaching or to promote changes in teachers. Measurement and evaluation theories are important to but cannot replace a theory concerned with supervisory practice.

STUDY GUIDE

Recall the concepts and the meanings associated with each of the following phrases and terms included in this chapter. Can you discuss them with a colleague and apply them to the supervisory context of your school? If you cannot, review them in the text and record the page number for future reference.

1. Brute data _____
2. Descriptive knowledge _____
3. Domains of inquiry _____
4. Interpretation and meaning _____
5. Measurement and evaluation theories _____
6. Modes of inquiry _____
7. Normative knowledge _____
8. Picturing models _____
9. Sciences of the artificial _____
10. Sense data _____
11. Teaching facts _____
12. Teaching values _____
13. Theory of practice _____

EXERCISES

1. Refer to Chapter 17, "Clinical Supervision and Teacher Evaluation." Make a list of strategies and techniques discussed in Chapter 17 that can best help answer each of the following questions of concern in the evaluation of teaching: What is going on in this classroom? What ought to be going on in this classroom? What do events and activities mean? What should the supervisor do given this analysis?
2. Given the point of view described in this chapter, prepare a one-page evaluation of the teacher evaluation processes now used in your school.
3. Give an example of evaluation artifacts, material, and data that might be considered "brute" data. Indicate how this brute data can become sensible to teachers involved in the evaluation process. How is it possible that sense data might differ given different people involved in the evaluation or as circumstances change? Provide examples.

CHAPTER 20

HUMAN RESOURCES SUPERVISION: WHAT LIES AHEAD?

The decades ahead can be viewed as the best of times or the worst of times for educational supervision. Uncertain economic and political, demographic, and professional conditions point toward numerous difficulties supervisors must face. Yet research, theory, and practice point toward some promising developments for enhancing the influence of supervision on the schooling enterprise.

The more discouraging news includes declining financial support for public education due to taxpayers' revolts and federal cutbacks, declining student enrollments and their impact on teacher layoffs and school closings and the attendant effects of teacher demoralization and community protests, the apparently discouraging results from massive research and development efforts at school improvement over the past 20 years, and the increased politicization of the environment and administration of schooling. Working for improved educational practice in the face of these discouraging variables places supervisors in a matrix of forces that not only hinder progress but also threaten their job security itself.

The more encouraging news includes a greater awareness that change and improvement can take place, but on a human scale and at the local school level rather than at the massive, impersonal bureaucratic scale of large systems; growing awareness of the limitations of any one theory or technology of education to solve educational problems and a concomitantly increasing respect for the informed intuition of practitioners; an increasing openness to incremental development in which those immediately involved have a greater say in developing appropriate educational responses to their situation; and a growing appreciation within the educational research community that multiple factors, in a dynamic and organic mix within the school setting, contribute to student growth and learning, rather than a single factor in a classroom, such as a curriculum unit, or an instructional activity, or certain instructional resources. In other words, the encouraging news is that the educational community is learning from the unproductive results of unrealistic attempts to improve the schooling enterprise and turning toward more realistic and pragmatic efforts. From this perspective, human resources supervision has an encouraging future, since greater emphasis on local initiatives and a clear view of effectiveness variables should highlight the importance of teacher and supervisor teamwork.

As the awareness grows that the most critical decisions and educational activities take place in the classrooms, where the primary effects of the schooling enterprise take place, more and more people in the educational profession are becoming convinced of the importance of a strong role for the supervisor. It will be the supervisor, working in an informed support role with teachers and directly involved in promoting internal staff development, who will be the practical, day-to-day driving force in school improvement. In order to exercise that influence, those in supervisory roles (as well as supervisor trainers and administrators who place supervisors in positions of influence) should develop a larger, more comprehensive role of supervision.

A LARGER VIEW OF SUPERVISION

One of the disadvantages of supervisory specialization is that it is easy to lose a unified perspective on supervision as a comprehensive process. Some supervisors deal with discrete areas of the curriculum such as science or language arts across the whole school district. Other supervisors occupy positions within individual schools, such as assistant principal for instruction or department chairperson. Some are in charge of beginning teachers, others are in charge of recommending teachers for promotion. Such divisions of supervisory tasks can fragment the view of supervision as one process that touches multiple facets of the schooling enterprise.

Supervision as a process involves multiple activities. It begins with the decision to hire a teacher and proceeds with support efforts for beginning teachers wherein individual strengths are identified and growth targets set. The process complements the supervision of individual teachers with both departmental concerns and schoolwide staff-development concerns. Finally, the supervisory process can marshall all these individual and group efforts toward larger program and schoolwide improvements.

FOCUS ON DEVELOPMENT

Human resource supervision assumes a dynamic environment. Unlike supervisory practices, which focus on control and fitting people into prepackaged job specifications, human resources supervision is aimed at the human and professional growth of the people in the school. Hence the relationship between supervisor and staff is primarily proactive, seeking improvement, development, and increased effectiveness based on a shared perception of individual strengths, talents, and interests. In this process supervisors deal with the human and professional needs of the staff from three perspectives. One perspective involves the individual, his or her unique personality and talents, and the seeking of ways to promote a fuller expression of personal strengths in the individual's work. A second perspective involves the supervisor with groups of the staff, where common staff-development concerns are addressed. A third perspective involves program improvement, where supervisor and staff seek ways to increase the school's overall effectiveness.

Frequently these three aspects of the supervisory process are in dynamic

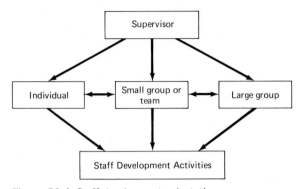

Figure 20-1 Staff-development orientation.

interdependence. Figures 20-1, 20-2, and 20-3 illustrate how the three perspectives can function in isolation or in dynamic interaction. Work with individual teachers on increasing their effectiveness in the classroom often relates to achieving program goals more effectively. As individual teachers improve, the program improves and student learning improves. Likewise, a teaching team or department's efforts to improve their program by the use of new resources, such as more sophistocated audiovisual materials, computers, or simulation games, inevitably involves teachers in learning new skills and mastering new methods of teaching. What began as program development merges into staff development. So, too, staff-development workshops that begin by focusing on skill development often lead to program considerations whereby the program gets modified to better accommodate the exercise of these new skills. Thus staff development frequently leads to program development.

From this outlook, therefore, we can see that supervision takes place in a dynamic environment. Work with individuals flows frequently into and out of work with groups; work on staff development flows frequently into and out of work on program development. The size of the group keeps shifting from a subgroup in a department to the whole department and then back again to work with individuals. The focus likewise shifts dynamically, moving from clarification of program goals to concentration on

Figure 20-2 Program-development orientation.

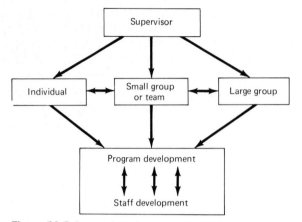

Figure 20-3 Interaction of program and staff development.

specific classroom skills and activities that will promote those goals and then back to program modifications for increased program effectiveness.

A SENSE OF DIRECTION

The supervisor, therefore, must have a larger perspective than improving individual performance. Ultimately the improvement and growth of individual teachers must contribute to and in some way be directed by overall program goals. Supervisors need to keep those larger program goals in mind when working on staff development with individuals, small groups, and departments. Sometimes staff-development activities will involve more general skills such as communication or conflict-resolution skills. At other times staff-development activities will be directly related to acquiring skills needed for increased program effectiveness, such as learning how to manage computer assisted simulation games or how to introduce students into role-playing exercises. Sometimes a supervisor will be working on an overall staff-development program for the whole faculty and simultaneously be working with individual teachers on more basic growth targets. Through all of these multifaceted activities, the supervisor should have a sense of the larger direction to the activities, namely, that the whole department or whole school faculty is moving toward greater program or schoolwide effectiveness. This movement will take place slowly, perhaps over a 3- to 5-year time frame. But it is within this larger sense of direction that most or all of the individual efforts of the supervisor take on significance.

HEURISTIC DEVELOPMENT

The focus on staff and program development toward some long-range goals is essential to provide the supervisory process with a larger meaning. However, while long-range

planning is essential, the process cannot be forced into the straightjacket of a rigid plan with an inflexible timetable. More often than not, long-range plans are altered by unpredictable developments and by new insights that emerge out of the staff- and program-development experience itself. The plan therefore has to be flexible, open to pursuing new avenues as their promise becomes evident from the group's experience. Such a heuristic process is self-educating and self-correcting. Heuristic staff and program development keeps the planning responsive to needs as they emerge, yet the plan keeps the heuristic process from an aimless meandering through a smorgasboard of unrelated exercises.[1]

COORDINATION OF SUPERVISORY PRACTICE

A supervisory process that assumes and promotes this dynamic interaction between staff and program development requires coordination on a school- or districtwide level. A language arts supervisor may be working on program and staff developments that will cause organizational problems with the social studies teachers. For example, language arts teachers may be using media software that requires a certain television system, whereas the social studies teachers may be exploring media software that requires a different television system. If the school district's finances are limited, only one television system can be afforded. Hence both groups should have known ahead of time what the others were doing, in order to forestall a needless conflict. In another instance, a supervisor may invite a consultant to work with her teachers. That same consultant could have been used to work with another supervisor and his teachers on the same topic, had the supervisors been sharing their plans with each other.

When several supervisors are working in the same school or in the same school district, their efforts need to be coordinated. Such coordination can prevent unforeseen conflicts and needless duplication of efforts. More importantly, supervisors and policymakers can establish some long-range plans. Within such plans the efforts of individual supervisors can be arranged to complement one another and work in a more unified way toward schoolwide or districtwide development. Again, the schoolwide or districtwide long-range plan must be flexible enough to allow supervisors to respond to unforeseen needs and opportunities. Nevertheless, such a long-range plan for staff and program development on a school- or districtwide level will enable supervisors to work with a larger sense of direction.

This kind of coordination requires the development of long-range goals and long-range plans to achieve those goals. When the long-range plans are spelled out, supervisors will need to further refine these into intermediate plans for 1 year or 6 months. Given the dynamic environment assumed above, such planning will obviously include discussions with teachers.

Supervisors should subsequently meet to reflect on how their plans are working out in practice, to pick up creative ideas from one another, and to continue to coordinate their efforts in the immediate future. As a result of these regular meetings,

[1]For a stimulating discussion of a research foundation for this approach to supervision, see Donald P. Sanders, "Education Inquiry as Developmental Research," *Educational Researcher*, vol. 10, no. 3, pp. 8–13, 1981.

supervisors will be able to advise the top administrators of the school or school district about common organizational dysfunctions, program resource needs, and staff needs that require their attention. This coordination effort will also enable supervisors to work more closely with curriculum specialists in the district whose job it is to facilitate curriculum development.

HUMAN RESOURCES SUPERVISION: SUMMING UP

We have tried to show how human resources supervision differs from, and goes beyond, other forms of supervision. We believe that there is sufficient—not extensive enough yet, but still sufficient—evidence from the field of organization and management research to validate this claim.

We believe that when human resources supervision is self-consciously exercised within an organizational setting, it can simultaneously increase the effectiveness of the people involved and their job satisfaction and human growth. The application of this form of supervision to schools leads to some obvious conclusions, which we have touched upon.

At the same time that we developed the rationale for this style of supervision, we were attempting to expose the reader to the dynamics of organizational life. The supervisor functions within that matrix of organizational and bureaucratic activity. If the supervisor knows how the organization works, then he or she can use the potential of the organization for educational purposes, rather than be victimized by unintended, perhaps, but actually dysfunctional aspects of the organization.

Because they are so often at a middle level in the organization, supervisors have access to top-level decision makers as well as to the instructional scene. Because supervisors can interpret the different levels to one another, serve as advocates of now one level, now the other, and tap and coordinate the very considerable resources of the organization as well, they can actually keep the organization on course.

The organization—the school or the school system—was set up to serve a purpose, to provide for the formal education of children. Those at the top are frequently distracted by financial or political concerns from that primary goal. Those individual teachers in the classroom are so close to their own activities that it is difficult for them to see other aspects of the school organization as deserving of equal attention. The supervisor is usually in the best position, then, to help the organization function the way it was intended to. And therefore it is essential, absolutely essential, that supervisors understand how organizations in general and schools in particular function. Without such understanding, they, and all the participants in the school organization will end up floundering their way through crisis after crisis without knowing why things are always turning out so badly.

Every bureaucracy began, as Weber noted,[2] with a charismatic vision or an inspiration. The resulting organization or bureaucracy was a way of enfleshing that vision, making it operative, functional. Organization or bureaucracy ensured an orderly

[2]S. N. Eisenstadt, *Max Weber: On Charisma and Institution Building*, Chicago: University of Chicago Press, 1968.

continuation of the vision and intentions of its founders throughout following generations.

Public schools as well as private schools were founded on such visions and inspirations. Some would call these inspirations myths, not in the sense of wild fancies or improbable superstitions, but rather in the sense of beliefs in a possibility that could not be empirically verified at the time, perhaps could never be empirically verified. We have argued that, besides understanding how organizations function and utilizing those managerial skills that will make the organization responsive to human beings, supervisors need to reestablish or clarify what that myth or that vision is for themselves. We have called it a platform because it is a term that is more manageable for our more empirical sensibilities.

Whatever one wants to call it, the organization does not function well when its participants lose sight of the basic purpose of the organization. One of the essential tasks of a human resources supervisor will be to encourage the formulation and/or review of these basic purposes as they are personally appropriated by the staff. In that way, many arguments over ancillary purposes can be put in their proper perspective and the major focus of people's energies can be kept on the educational purposes of the school.

Finally, human resources supervision acts on very basic beliefs about human nature. We think that these beliefs about human beings are most consistent with our most cherished political and religious beliefs as well as with the expressed purposes of the schools. We know from our own experience as well as from research findings that acting on those beliefs more often than not enables men and women to work together effectively.

These three characteristics of human resources supervision should be highlighted: it is founded on beliefs about human nature that center on human beings as active, responsible, and growing persons; it is exercised with a conscious understanding of organizational dynamics; and its logic and intelligibility are rooted in an educational vision and platform that is both personal and yet legitimated within educational tradition. These three characteristics of human resources supervision give it a power and a direction that we believe enable it to accomplish the upgrading of the quality of education in a local school or school system. And no matter at what higher level of government, plans, laws, projects, and policies are made for the improvement of education, the proof of the pudding will always be found at the local level. If it does not happen there, it does not happen.

Hence, those concerned with the formulation and enactment of public policy should recognize the need for qualified and committed educators at the local level. The local-level educators, moreover, need to appreciate the issues at stake in the deliberations of state and federal legislators. They will need to be more active in making their voices heard, as well as to listen carefully to the points of view being argued before the legislatures.

We close with this word. Supervision, in our opinion, is entering a phase bright with promise but also one in which supervisors will have to stay alert to the political arena as never before. It can be the best of times or the worst of times—but it will be an exciting time, a time for making history.

A FINAL SALUTE

In closing, we salute those exercising supervisory responsibility in schools. Theirs is a difficult profession, demanding skill, sensitivity, intelligence, and leadership. Upon their shoulders, and the shoulders of their teacher colleagues, rest the brightest hopes of our romance with wisdom through education. This book is a modest attempt to inform their practice. It is an easy thing to write a book, however. It is a great thing to contribute to the development of human beings and human intelligence. Despite the difficulties besetting education today and the work of supervisors in particular, that is a work worth giving one's life to.

INDEX